MYTH,
FAITH AND
HERMENEUTICS

yasyāmatam tasya matam
matam yasya na veda saḥ /
avijñātaṁ vijānatām
vijñātam avijānatām

By whom it is unthought, by him it is thought;
By whom it is thought, he does not see.
Not understood by whom it is known;
Understood by whom it is not known.

KenU II, 3 (+)

+ Cf. RV I, 164, 32.

MYTH, FAITH AND HERMENEUTICS

CROSS-CULTURAL STUDIES

R. PANIKKAR

PAULIST PRESS
New York/Ramsey/Toronto

Library of Congress
Catalog Card Number: 77-99306

ISBN: 0-8091-0232-3

Published by Paulist Press
Editorial Office: 1865 Broadway, New York, N.Y. 10023
Business Office: 545 Island Road, Ramsey, N.J. 07446

Printed and bound in the
United States of America

Acknowledgments

Grateful acknowledgment is made to the editors and publishers of the following books and journals for granting permission to use material that appeared there in earlier versions:

II. 'Tolérance, idéologie et mythe', *Démythisation et idéologie*, edited by E. Castelli (Paris: Aubier, 1973).

III. 'Morale du mythe et mythe de la morale. Mythologie et logomythie', *Démythisation et morale*, edited by E. Castelli (Paris: Aubier, 1965).

IV. 'La faute originante ou l'immolation créatrice; le mythe de Prajāpati', *Le mythe de la peine*, edited by E. Castelli (Paris: Aubier, 1967).

V. 'Le mythe comme histoire sacrée: Shunaḥshepa, un mythe de la condition humaine', *Le Sacré*, edited by E. Castelli (Paris: Aubier, 1974).

VI. 'La foi dimension constitutive de l'homme', *Mythe et foi*, edited by E. Castelli (Paris: Aubier, 1966); also published as: *L'Homme qui devient Dieu. La foi dimension constitutive de l'homme* (Paris: Aubier, 1969). English version: 'Faith: a Constitutive Dimension of Man', *Journal of Ecumenical Studies* (Temple University Press), Vol. VIII, No. 2 (Spring 1971).

VII. 'Témoignage et dialogue', *Le témoignage*, edited by E. Castelli (Paris: Aubier, 1972).

VIII. 'Le silence et la parole. Le sourire du Buddha', *L'analyse du langage théologique. Le nom de Dieu*, edited by E. Castelli (Paris: Aubier, 1969). Spanish translation: 'La sonrisa de Buda', *La Revista de Occidente* (Madrid), No. 76 (July 1969). A revised version appeared as: 'Nirvāṇa and the Awareness of the Absolute', *The God Experience. Essays in Hope* (The Cardinal Bea Lectures), edited by J.P. Whelan (New York & Toronto: Newman Press, 1971).

IX. 'Advaita and Bhakti. A Letter from Vrindaban', *Bhagawan Das Commemoration Volume* (Varanasi: Kashi-Vidyapeeth University, 1969); 'Advaita and Bhakti. Love and Identity in a Hindu-Christian Dialogue', *Journal of Ecumenical Studies* (Temple University Press), Vol. VII, No. 2 (Spring 1970).

X. 'The Ultimate Experience', *Indian Ecclesiastical Studies* (Bangalore), No. 1 (January, 1971); 'The Ways of West and East', *New Dimensions in Religious Experience*, edited by G. Devine (New York: Alba House, 1970).

XI. 'Metatheology or Diacritical Theology as Fundamental Theology', *Concilium* (Nijmegen), Vol. 6, No. 5 (June 1969).

XII. 'Die Philosophie in der geistigen Situation der Zeit', *Akten des XIV. Internationalen Kongresses für Philosophie* (Wien, 2-9 September 1968) (Wien: Herder, 1971).

XIII. 'The God of Being and the "Being" of God', *Harvard Divinity Bulletin* (Spring 1968); a modified version in: 'The God of Silence', *Indian Journal of Theology*, Vol. XXI, Nos. 1 & 2 (January and June 1972).

XIV. 'La loi du karma et la dimension historique de l'homme', *La théologie de l'histoire. Herméneutique et eschatologie*, edited by E. Castelli (Paris: Aubier, 1971). A modified English version appeared as: 'The Law of *Karman* and the Historical Dimension of Man', *Philosophy East and West*, Vol. 22, No. 1 (January 1972).

XV. 'Le sujet de l'infaillibilité. Solipsisme et vérification', *L'infaillibilité, son aspect philosophique et théologique*, edited by E. Castelli (Paris: Aubier, 1970). A Spanish translation appeared as: 'El sujeto de la infalibilidad', *Revista de Occidente* (Madrid), No. 108 (March 1972).

XVI. 'Herméneutique de la liberté de la religion. La religion comme liberté', *L'herméneutique de la liberté religieuse*, edited by E. Castelli (Paris: Aubier, 1968).

Unless otherwise noted, all quoted texts are the author's own translations.

Table of Contents

III. MORALITY AND MYTH. THE 'MORAL' OF
     MYTH AND THE MYTH OF MORALS

IV. THE MYTH OF PRAJĀPATI.
    THE ORIGINATING FAULT OR CREATIVE
    IMMOLATION

V. ŚUNAḤŚEPA.
A MYTH OF THE HUMAN CONDITION

PART II: FAITH

VI. FAITH AS A CONSTITUTIVE HUMAN DIMENSION

VIII. SILENCE AND THE WORD.
      THE SMILE OF THE BUDDHA

1. Introduction: The Spirit, the Word
   and the Name of God 258

2. The Double Silence of the Buddha 261

   a. First Degree Silence:
      The Silence of the Answer 261

   b. Second Degree Silence:
      The Silence of the Question 264

3. The Dialectical Game 265

   a. The Dialectic of the Name of God 266

      i. Single God, One Name 266

      ii. Many Gods, Many Names 266

      iii. Many Names, One God 266

      iv. The Hidden (Revealed) Name of God 267

      v. Who? The Interrogative Name of God 267

      vi. Is 'God' a Euphemism for Man? 267

      vii. Silence as Answer 268

      viii. Silence as Question 268

      ix. The New Innocence 268

PART III: HERMENEUTICS

XI. METATHEOLOGY AS FUNDAMENTAL
     THEOLOGY

XII. THE PHILOSOPHICAL TRADITION

XV. THE SUBJECT OF INFALLIBILITY. SOLIPSISM AND VERIFICATION

XVIII. INDEXES

Abbreviations

Texts

AB	Aitareya Brāhmaṇa
ASS	Āśvalāyana Śrauta Sūtra
AV	Atharva Veda
BG	Bhagavad Gītā
BhagP	Bhāgavata Purāṇa
BS	Brahma Sūtra
BU	Bṛhadāraṇyaka Upaniṣad
CU	Chāndogya Upaniṣad
GopB	Gopatha Brāhmaṇa
IsU	Īśa Upaniṣad
JabU	Jābāla Upaniṣad
JaimB	Jaiminīya Brāhmaṇa
KaivU	Kaivalya Upaniṣad
KathU	Kaṭha Upaniṣad
KausB	Kauṣītaki Brāhmaṇa
KausU	Kauṣītaki Upaniṣad
KenU	Kena Upaniṣad
MB	Mahābhārata
MaitS	Maitrāyāṇi Saṃhitā
MaitU	Maitrī Upaniṣad
MandU	Māṇḍūkya Upaniṣad
Manu	Mānava Dharmaśāstra
MarkP	Markaṇḍeya Purāṇa
MundU	Muṇḍaka Upaniṣad
PancB	Pañcaviṃsa Brāhmaṇa (same text as TMB)
Ram	Rāmāyaṇa
RV	Ṛg Veda
SB	Śatapatha Brāhmaṇa
SSS	Śāṅkhāyana Śrauta Sūtra
SU	Śvetāśvatara Upaniṣad

TB	Taittirīya Brāhmaṇa
TMB	Tāṇḍya Mahā Brāhmaṇa (same text as PancB)
TS	Taittirīya Saṁhitā
TU	Taittirīya Upaniṣad
VisnP	Viṣṇu Purāṇa
VSS	Vaitāna Śrauta Sūtra
YSB	Yoga Sūtra Bhāṣya
YV	Yajur Veda (Vājasaneyi)

Bible

The usual abbreviations are employed.

AV	Authorized Version
NEB	New English Bible
OAB	Oxford Annotated Bible
RSV	Revised Standard Version
RV	Revised Version

Other abbreviations

ABAW   Abhandlungen der Berliner Akademie der Wissenschaften.

Denz. Schön. Denziger, H., *Enchiridion symbolorum, definitionum, et declarationum de rebus fidei et morum*, newly edited by A. Schönmetzer (Barcinone: Herder, 1973).

ERE   *Encyclopaedia of Religion and Ethics*, edited by J. Hastings (New York: Scribners Sons, 1928). Reprint (Edinburgh: T. & T. Clark, 1969-1971).

IS   Indische Studien.

JAS   Journal of the Asiatic Society (of Bengal).

JRAS   Journal of the Royal Asiatic Society.

P.G.   Migne, J.P., *Patrologiae Cursus Completus, Series Graeca* (Paris: Migne, 1857-1866).

P.L.   Migne, J.P., *Patrologiae Cursus Completus, Series Latina* (Paris: Migne, 1844-1855).

RGG   *Die Religion in Geschichte und Gegenwart*, third edition, edited by K. Galling (Tübingen: J.C.B. Mohr [P. Siebeck], 1961).

SBAW	Sitzungsberichte der Berliner Akademie der Wissenschaften.
SBE	Sacred Books of the East.
ZDMG	Zeitschrift der deutschen morgenländischen Gesellschaft.

Ad Enrico Castelli
    in testimonianza di trent'anni
    d'amicizia
    e di comunione nel mito . . . della non-ermeneutica
    della fede

        con un legame che non si disfa
        ormai più
        perchè sigillato
        dalla morte

I.
Introduction

athāto brahma jijñāsā

And now it is the proper moment to tend
with our entire being
toward the sapiential experience
of the all-embracing Mystery.
BS I, 1, 1.

1. THE VOLUME

Is it just and proper to stop looking ahead or rather to slow down what the ancients called *epektasis* (the forward tension of Man towards his goal—the infinite Mystery) and busy oneself by revising old thoughts written during the last decade? Or again, what is the value and justification of such a compilation when people are dying of malnutrition, are victims of war and oppression and suffer injustices of all sorts? I feel that these questions cannot in any way be dismissed as unscholarly or nonpertinent. If intellectual activity divorces itself from life, it becomes not only barren and alienating, but also harmful and perhaps eventually criminal. The *urgency* of these issues cannot be minimized, but it should not obscure the *importance* of the problems we deal with here in this volume. I am convinced that we live in a state of human emergency that does not allow us to entertain ourselves with bagatelles of no relevance whatsoever. But I am equally convinced that, precisely because of the seriousness of the human situation, mere short-term solutions and technical stopgaps will not do. We need the respite given by contemplation, the perspective offered by *asakti*, detachment—which does not mean indifference (*pace* the *Gītā*); we need an insight into the deeper strata of reality that might permit us to go to the roots of the problems. The roots may not be too conspicuous, but they sustain and give life to the tree. In these collected studies I would like to contribute to this radical conversion, this turn of spirit, which I feel is necessary for the survival of humanness. They are not on the level of practical or technical solutions, but on that radical level at the basis of questions vital for humanity today. They are not about what is happening, but are part and parcel of the total human event itself. If I restrain myself now from making connections with action, or from proposing practical programs, it is because the nature of radical reflections is that they do not impose just one line of conduct. They leave room for tensions and polarities; they nurture branches and leaves, even fruit and flowers, without reducing everything to a single manifestation. An authentic idea inspires, but does not dictate. Commitment, responsibility and active involvement are not logical conclusions of syllogisms, nor do they abolish the constitutive polarities of the human condition. Moreover, when combined with contemplation, reflection and loving serenity, these polarities do not degenerate into irreconcilable—or only dialectical—oppositions. Wisdom does not mean a monochromatic world view, nor an amorphous multitudinous atomization, but a combination of the many colors into one universe full of polarities because it is full of life. The Western traditions at one time interpreted the biblical χιτῶνα ποικίλου, 'polymitam tunica, circumdata varietate' of Joseph, the son of Jacob, precisely in this sense of tension and diversity within a higher—mythical—nonmanipulable unity.

It is not for me, and probably not for anybody, to elaborate all the conditions and exigencies of this radical *metanoia*. I may only point out that overcoming the subject-object dichotomy, as well as the almost schizophrenic split between *mythos* and *logos*, heart and mind, action and contemplation, belong to it, along with an undivided vision of reality in which the cosmic, divine and human dimensions are reintegrated in a cosmotheandric experience. The studies in this volume would like to contribute, from several angles, to this turning of heart and mind. The volume itself is an expression of the urge felt in our times for a serene symbiosis between the *nova et vetera*; or, in other words, between tradition and modernity.

Perhaps the injunction of James, the brother of the Lord, could express our intention:

γίγεσθε δὲ ποιηταὶ λόγου . . . 'become doers of word [artists of the word, poets of the *logos*] and not hearers only, deceiving yourselves [παραλογιζόμενοι, miscarrying, misleading, misplacing the *logos*]. . . .'

Bring back the unity of word and work, become also a ποιητὴς ἔργου, a doer of work, a poet of action, a 'prophet in word and deed' so as to make the words mighty and the works transparent, so as to be word incarnate or 'lamps unto yourselves', as Lord Buddha said.

The threefold trait that links together these papers is manifest in the title of the volume.

2. THE TITLE

The first part of the volume centers on *myth* but does not attempt to offer a treatise on that fundamental area of human experience. This field demands a peculiar attitude: You cannot look directly at the source of light; you turn your back to it so that you may see—not the light, but the illuminated things. Light is invisible. So too with the myth—myth here is not the object of discourse, but the expression of a *sui generis* form of consciousness. Myth and wisdom go together, as Aristotle had already seen when he affirmed, at the beginning of his *Metaphysics*, that the lover of myth is a sort of philosopher, a lover of wisdom: ὁ φιλόμυθος φιλόσοφος πώς ἐστιν. Is this not also the central experience of Taoism, which invites us to regain the uncarved block, or of Shinto, which emphasizes an unthought communion, an ontic solidarity with the whole of reality?

A living myth does not allow for interpretation because it needs no intermediary. The hermeneutic of a myth is no longer the myth, but its *logos*. Myth is precisely the horizon over against which any hermeneutic is possible. Myth is that which we take for granted, that which we do not question; and it is unquestioned because, de facto, it is not seen as questionable. The myth is transparent like the light, and the mythical story—*mythologumenon*— is only the form, the garment in which the myth happens to be expressed, enwrapped, illumined.

Myth is not the object of thought, nor does it give food for thought. Rather it purifies thought, it bypasses thought, so that the unthought may emerge and the intermediary disappear. Myth is the salutary fasting of thinking; it liberates us from the burden of having to think out and think through everything and thus it opens up the realm of freedom: not the mere liberty of choice, but the freedom of being. When the thinking has not yet landed on the thought so that it cannot yet know what is being thought in the thinking, we are still in the domain of the myth.

This does not at all mean that we should neglect, let alone despise, the value of thought and ignore the realm and the inviolable rights of the *logos*. It only means that Man cannot be reduced to *logos*, nor awareness to reflexive consciousness. But we reserve our theories about myth for another occasion.

The second part of the volume deals with different problems regarding faith.

Faith is understood as that dimension in Man that corresponds to myth. Man is open to an ever-growing horizon of awareness, a horizon provided in the myth. Belief is taken to be the vehicle by which human consciousness passes from *mythos* to *logos*. Belief articulates the myth in which we believe without 'believing' that we believe in it. To believe is not to hold a belief as one holds an object of knowledge; it is simply the act of believing—which may express itself in different formulations but which does not believe in them: the *fides qua* of the scholastics. Human reflection on belief can fall either on the fact that we believe, or on the contents of our belief. The former case makes discourse about belief possible and gives us an awareness of the results of believing. The latter one either destroys itself as thinking reflection, because it does not understand its contents, or if it does, it destroys belief, for it converts belief into knowledge. This is what the Latin Middle Ages called the incompatibility between the *cognitum* and the *creditum*, that which is known and that which is believed. We know *that* we believe (former case) but we do not know *what* we believe (latter case), which is why we believe and do not know. In other words, faith that expresses itself in belief has no object, it is not an *ob-jectum* of our mind. Thomas Aquinas, in the second part of his *Summa*, formulating a common Christian conviction, could say:

actus autem credentis non terminatur ad enuntiabile sed ad rem 'the act of the believer does not end at the formulation, but in the thing itself.'

—in the reality itself. Reality is here the ever-inexhaustible mystery, beyond the reach of objective knowledge.

'I believe in God', for instance, is a cognitive statement when it stands for the expression of the act of believing (former case) and is a real belief only when I do not know *what* God is, i.e., when I do not *know* God as the object of my belief (latter case). If you ask me if I believe in God I cannot properly respond, except when giving a rhetorical answer to a rhetorical question. Otherwise, I simply do not know what you are asking: I do not know what you mean by 'God' and so cannot answer whether I believe in this 'God'. The question about God either destroys itself because it does not know *what* it is asking for or dissolves the God we are asking about into something that is no longer God, but a sheer idol. The God of belief is a symbol but not a concept. In a way we believe only (what we 'believe' to be) the unquestionable.

The fact that the believed is not the known does not subordinate the one to the other, but it relates knowledge and belief as different forms of consciousness without allowing the reduction of awareness to mere knowing (of objects) or to sheer believing (in myths). This fact opens up an image of Man irreducible to mere *logos* or to sheer *mythos*.

What expresses belief, what carries the dynamism of belief—the conscious passage from *mythos* to *logos* —is not the concept but the symbol. Symbol here does not mean an epistemic sign, but an *ontomythical* reality that *is* precisely in the symbolizing. A symbol is not a symbol of another ('thing'), but of itself, in the sense of the subjective genitive. A symbol is the symbol of that which *is* precisely (symbolized) in the symbol, and which, thus, does not exist without its symbol. A symbol *is* nothing but the symbol of that which appears in and as the symbol. Yet we must beware of identifying the symbol with the symbolized. To overlook the *symbolic difference*, i.e., to mistake the symbol for the symbolized, is precisely *avidyā*, ignorance, confusing the appearance with the reality. But reality is reality precisely because it 'appears' real.

By reality I mean not only the *res* over against the ἰδέα, but all that there *is*, in one way or another, i.e., the entire realm of being, according to another nomenclature. Now all-that-there-is, is 'there' precisely because it appears 'there' (as what-there-is). This real appearance is the symbol. Or, in other terms, the symbol is that appearance of the real which also includes the subject to whom it appears. Appearance is always for somebody, some consciousness.

Error is not the appearance as such, but the forgetfulness that the appearance is appearance. And this applies to every being, even to Being itself: Being is also the appearance of Being. This appearance is precisely the Truth of Being. Truth and Being are not the subjective and the objective sides of the 'real'. The 'real' as such is *satya*, i.e., truth and being all in one ('ideality' as well as 'reality'). The Real is also the trusty, trusted, truthful, faithful, loyal. The Truth is also the realization, real, thing, matter. Yet several Upaniṣads will remind us that

hiraṇmayena pātreṇa satyasya apihitam mukham
'the face of the truth (the nature of being)
is hidden with (concealed by)
a golden jar'

And it is the function of the sacrifice to break the vessel with which the light is covered. Revelation is this uncovering of the symbol.

The symbol is neither a merely objective entity in the world (the thing 'over there'), nor is it a purely subjective entity in the mind (in us 'over here'). There is no symbol that is not in and for a subject, and there is equally no symbol without a specific content claiming objectivity. The symbol encompasses and constitutively links the two poles of the real: the object and the subject. *Pātra*, the word for jar, vessel, recipient, also means *persona*, πρόσωπον and person:

'The symbol of the truth is concealed by a shining person.'

This is why a symbol that requires interpretation is no longer a living symbol. It has become a mere sign. That with the aid of which we would ultimately interpret the alleged 'symbol', that would be the real symbol.

To say it in the words of that genial master and monk of the 12th century Alanus de Insulis, in his *De Incarnatione Christi*:

> *omnis mundi creatura quasi liber et pictura nobis est et speculum.* 'Every creature of the world is for us book, picture and mirror'.

The crisis begins when people forget how to read, look and understand.

And yet there are many things that demand interpretation. Man does not live by symbols alone. Thus, the third part of this book. Hermeneutics is the art and science of interpretation, of bringing forth significance, of conveying meaning, of restoring symbols to life and eventually of letting new symbols emerge. Hermeneutics is the method of overcoming the distance between a knowing subject and an object to be known, once the two have been estranged. Hermes is the messenger of the Gods but only outside of Olympus.

Now one could distinguish a threefold hermeneutics, or rather three kairological moments in the hermeneutical enterprise, three intertwined ways of overcoming the epistemological distance and thus the human estrangement. *Morphological* hermeneutics entails the explanation or deciphering done by, say, parents, teachers, elders, the more intelligent, etc., for those who have not yet had full access to the treasure house of meaning in a particular culture. It is the reading of the text. Morphological hermeneutics is the homogeneous unfolding of implicit or de facto unknown elements. Here logic is the great method. It moves from past (which was once present in the elders) to present. It proceeds by way of com-par-ison—and all the other rules of correct thinking.

Diachronical hermeneutics refers to the knowledge of the context necessary in order to understand a text, because the temporal gap between the understander and that which is to be understood has obscured or even changed the meaning of the original datum. Diachronical hermeneutics also implies the problems of ideology and time. It takes the temporal factor as an intrinsic element in the process of understanding. Its method is fundamentally historical. Action and involvement are its basic constituents. It implies going out from my own 'stand' in order to under-stand another world view. This is the proper place for dialectics: The movement here is from present to past in order to incorporate, subsume or delete it. Diachronical hermeneutics is not the youngster learning about the past from contemporaries. It is the adult firmly based in his present degree of awareness trying to enrich himself by understanding the past.

There is however a third moment in any complete hermeneutical process and the fact that it has often been neglected or overlooked has been a major cause of misunderstandings among the different cultures of the world. I call it *diatopical* hermeneutics because the distance to be overcome is not merely temporal, within one broad tradition, but the gap existing between two human *topoi*, 'places' of understanding and self-understanding, between two—or more—cultures that have not developed their patterns of intelligibility or their basic assumptions out of a common historical tradition or through mutual influence. To cross the boundaries of one's own culture without realizing that another culture may have a radically different approach to reality is today no longer admissible. If still consciously done, it would be philosophically naive, politically outrageous and religiously sinful. Diatopical hermeneutics stands for the thematic consideration of understanding the other without assuming that the other has the same basic self-understanding and understanding as I have. The ultimate human horizon, and not only differing contexts, is at stake here. The method in this third moment is a peculiar *dialogical dialogue*, the διά-λόγος piercing the *logos* in order to reach that dialogical, translogical realm of the heart (according to most traditions), allowing for the emergence of a myth in which we may commune, and which will ultimately allow under-standing (standing under the same horizon of intelligibility).

Diatopical hermeneutics is not objectifiable, because it considers the other an equally original source of understanding. In other words, Man's self-understanding belongs not only to what Man thinks of himself, but to what Man is. In order to understand what Man is we need a fundamentally different method than a 'scientific' approach, because what Man understands himself to be is also part of his being. Indeed, how to understand Man's different self-understandings is a central problem of diatopical hermeneutics. Here we shall put diatopical hermeneutics to work without a systematic study of its theory, which I reserve for another occasion.

I have already indicated the importance and also the limits of hermeneutics. Neither by bread alone nor by word alone does Man live. Myth and faith defy hermeneutics, but without hermeneutics myth and faith would perish the moment that the innocence of the ecstatic attitude passes away. Yet it remains true not only that Man alone can interpret, but also that interpretation is inbuilt in Man's very nature. Not only does Man's self-interpretation belong to what Man is, but Man's interpretation of the world also belongs, in a way, to what the world is. This is why our search here is constitutively open, unachieved, not finished, not finite, infinite.

The title has still two more signs: a comma and a conjunction. These two signs would like to express what we said earlier concerning the urgent and important need to bring together heart and mind, myth and *logos*, personal involvement and critical reflection. This cosmotheandric insight, as we have called it, realizes that myth, faith and hermeneutics belong to the cosmic, divine and human dimensions of reality, respectively. But we ought to stress again that these three are one, like 'the spirit and the water and the blood', in Christian Scripture and many others as well.

Myth, *Faith* and *Hermeneutics* then might represent the threefold—cosmotheandric—unity of the universe, that unity which neither destroys diversity nor forgets that the world is inhabited, that God is not alone and that knowledge is based on love.

So much for the title. I should perhaps add that I have been working for many years on a more elaborated theory concerning these three topics; the purport of these essays is only introductory. And although an introduction into new lands is an important venture, I cannot help feeling that this compilation is only a timid invitation to what it wants to say. In this sense the book is a challenge and a prayer. I am convinced of its precariousness and I can only ask you the reader to translate my words into your own. It is the reader who redeems the writer. And, in point of fact, if I publish all these insights *in statu nascendi* it is because I have been asked from very many sides to do it.

3. THE STYLE

A word on style may be appropriate at this point. The articles collected here were originally not only written, but also thought, in four languages. And yet in a way I have no language of my own, because a language is more than a tool; it is a body, a part of oneself, a part that in a way stands for the whole, a *pars pro toto*. A language is a way of looking at and, ultimately, of being in the world. This is precisely the characteristic feature of the word: to be the image, the *eikon*, the expression and manifestation of the totality, the First-born of God, following Hindu, Christian and other sacred Scriptures. But here the singular is essential. The many words do not substitute for the word. Certainly, descending from the ontocosmological to the personal field, a plurality of languages can be enriching, but it is also debilitating. A Man of many original languages has no word of his own, no image to reflect him, no *eikon* to manifest him. His only salvation lies not in what he says but in the mystical realm, in his entire life, in his silent incarnation—in becoming Word. But, making a virtue of these factual conditions, this deficit might well suggest the very symbiosis needed for our time. We have to speak a language and in a sense this language even has to be the regional dialect of the concrete community to which we belong. Only a dialect is vital, vivid, and able to express what no contrived idiom, however basic, can ever express. The poets know this. Nonetheless, our present-day forms of dialect can no longer afford to be the slang of a closed group or the mere repetition of clichés. Our dialect must integrate in itself the experience of other world views. Yet we cannot pour all of human experience into language, not because the poet lacks the skill, but because the enterprise defeats itself. If a language could say all that it wants to say, this would be the end of the world: Nothing would remain to be said and without language the world would perish. The poverty of my language may perhaps spur the reader to accelerate not the end of the world, but certainly the end of the divisive times in which we live.

As an aside, I am reminded how irritated my theological 'Gemüt' was when I read an English translation of Saint John's Prologue: "In the beginning of time was the Word." If the Word belongs only to Time we have Arius at hand: Christ is only the 'First-born' of all creatures, but not the 'Only Begotten' of the Father. Now, when I have lived most of my life and probably written most of the things I am ever going to *write*—I don't say '*wanted* to write'; now, when the inflation of books and mass media has put every sublime thought within the reach of everybody, even at the risk of cheapening it; now, when the tempiternal side of existence not only overwhelms me—as ever—but overpowers me in that it takes from me the urge to speak and especially to write; now, I begin to discover the grain of truth in the idea that Word and Time go together and that it was at the beginning of Time that the *Logos* was—*cum tempore* and not *ex tempore*.

A second note on semantics may be still needed. I have strained English grammar enough to be allowed to raise my voice regarding a delicate and touchy point. It is the question of sex and gender. When using the word Man I mean *Mensch, homo,* ἀνφφῶπος, *manu*, i.e., that word which distinguishes the human beings from the Gods on the one hand and the animals on the other. I do not mean male, *vir,* ἀνήρ, *manuṣya*, and I have too much respect for 'women' to call them just 'wo-man'. The ambivalence of the word deteriorates when the third person pronouns are used. In point of fact, only the third person, that is, the reified reference outside a living dialogue, is either masculine or feminine. The 'I' and the 'thou' are androgynous, complete human beings. When I call you 'you' I call upon your entire humanness, not disregarding but including your sex. I discriminate only when I no longer treat you as a person, as a you, when I no longer speak to or with you, but about you with or to a third party, or when I make you the subject of an objectifying sentence (e.g., when I affirm that you are this or that—which may require a gender in many languages). The trouble then is with 'pro-nouns' and '*ad*-tributes'; they discriminate. And the neuter is not a solution. What we need is not a neuter (*ne-utrum*, neither of both), but an *utrum* gender, an *utrumque*, a gender that embraces the two without reducing them to a neuter 'thing', even if we call it 'personhood'. Provisionally I solve the difficulty by stating that Man for me stands for the human being and man for the male, and 'he' for the entire personal pronoun 'he-she' (except where the context makes it clear that it is male). I do not think women should use another word for their humanness. What we should do is to break the male monopoly on Man.

It is the work and the merit of two students of mine, Christine Hopper and Scott Eastham, to have transformed these varied perspectives into a coherent and we hope readable book. Uma M. Vesci has given valuable suggestions. With the inflation of thanks-giving and the recession of gratitude in our contemporary world, to express heartfelt thanks here is only a pallid expression of the χάρις of having found such collaborators.

Many other people in the past have spurred my thinking, criticized my views and stimulated my responses. To mention them only by name would not be enough to express my deep indebtedness. I can only assure them here that in no way can I forget that wonderful net of friendships that sustains my life and contributes to authentic human existence.

The book is dedicated to my good friend Enrico Castelli, with whom I had the privilege seventeen years ago to begin the by now well-known annual Colloquium at the University of Rome under the auspices of the 'Istituto di studi filosofici'. It has been Castelli's merit to gather year after year a number of thinkers who otherwise could not have come together. I say 'could' and not just a factual 'would', because only under the primacy of the myth could people of such different tendencies come together. Two-thirds of the chapters of this volume were papers for those occasions.

But my dedication is to him, the Man. Again another example that what bears fruit is not a powerful organization, but a living person. I would like to assure him that I apply to myself the many-faceted sentence of that 'gentile' of the Old Covenant who dared to stand by his conscience not only against Men but also contesting God:

> *semitam per quam non revertar ambulo*
> 'I walk a path on which there is no return, I live a life from which I do not come back.'

When these lines were written and this book was going to press, just three months after our last meeting at the University of Rome in January 1977 for the XVII Colloquium, Enrico Castelli finished his earthly pilgrimage. He wrote to me when he knew of my intention of dedicating this volume to him:

> Grazie prima di tutto per la dedica in testimonianza di trent'anni di amicizia. L'amicizia è un'intesa, la vera intesa. L'altra, quella che si riferisce alla presunta evidenza cartesiana (2 + 2 = 4) non è un'intesa, anche se si dice: 'Siamo intesi che 2 + 2 = 4, proprio perché estranea alla possibilità del contrario, quindi alla libertà. Ecco per me un modo di ripensare l'amicizia'.

I told him that I don't have a family of my own, but that I live because of the family of friends, the *mitrabandhu* that sustains Man. Friendship is for me the highest form of love: If Genesis says "let us make Man in our image and likeness", St. John's Gospel adds: "I have called you friends."

4. THE CHAPTERS

It would be somewhat artificial now to stitch these essays together with a single logical thread. I have already indicated their existential connection. The only real thread is the personal life, but life is lived and not written, although writing may be part of one's life. Now human life lives, first of all, out of myth. The mythical context is always the first given. But human life is not only awareness of the given. It is also awareness of itself on all possible—and sometimes impossible—levels. Faith stands at both ends of the line of awareness: the *archai* and the *eschata*, the origins and the 'terminals'. There is no human life without faith. Yet this very faith longs to overcome itself, it searches for understanding and when the intuition does not dawn, the quest for interpretation begins: Hermeneutics make their appearance. Myth, Faith and Hermeneutics are here the sigla.

Five other chapters, originally built into this same book, have been set apart to make another volume dealing with the more concrete problem of the intrareligious dialogue within this same dynamism of a human life searching its place in the multireligious and multicultural world of our times. This second volume complements this one.

The first part of this book is dedicated to myth. It is not a study on myth, but it tries to unravel a little the mystery of myth by a double approach. On the one hand, the first two chapters relate myth to some fundamental human attitudes like tolerance, ideology (chapter II) and morality (chapter III). On the other hand, the *mythologumena* studied in the following two chapters (IV and V) offer some insights on the nature and power of myths.

The second part focuses on faith, and again from a double angle. Chapter VI relates directly to the nature of faith and tries to break the monopolizing of faith by a certain restricted understanding of it. Only the symbolic character of words and the mythical use of them can overcome the tendency of our reason to claim a monopoly on the meaning of words. We offer here a concrete example without indulging in a general theory about names (as I plan to do in a forthcoming publication). Chapter VII is the bridge between the foregoing and the following. It still reflects on faith, but it leads already to the second group of essays in which faith is not thematically reflected upon, but so to speak put into action in order to illuminate some other concrete cross-cultural issues involving a plurality of human traditions. Chapter VIII touches the

very limits of the human experience, drawing from a fundamental
Buddhist insight, while chapter IX explores the possibility of finding harmony between one of the most basic tensions of the human
spirit at hand of the wisdom drawn from the Hindu and Christian
traditions. Chapter X attempts to enter that religious or rather
mystical core common and accessible to the human experience. It
finishes offering a typology of this ultimate experience.

The third part of this volume tries to make hermeneutics
function in such a way as to interpret some of the problems in
today's encounter of religions and the meeting of world views. My
attempt here is to integrate the understandings that arise from the
contemporary situation, first of the so-called fundamental theology (chapter XI) and then of philosophy (chapter XII), ending with
a study on the nature of atheism in the light of the world religions
(chapter XIII). From this hermeneutical perspective two examples
are discussed, one coming mainly from Eastern religions (chapter
XIV) and the other from Christianity (chapter XV), opening both
of them to reciprocal dialogal interactions. The last chapter (XVI)
analyzes an important aspect of every religion, which seems often
to have been unduly neglected. Secularization and religion certainly meet in stressing not only liberation, but freedom.

Perhaps what we need today is not so much intellectuals
saying what has to be done, or scholars writing what is the case, or,
for that matter, preachers proclaiming the truth, but people living
it, people writing with their blood and speaking with their lives.
Fortunately we still have more of these living people than entries in
the various editions of *Who's Who*.

So now, after the excruciating experience of trying to put
these studies together by revising them, I shall revert to where I
began: to being coauthor of my life.

Santa Barbara, California
Pentecost, 1975 & Dîpâvali 1977
R. P.

Part I

MYTH

ὅσω αὐτίτης καὶ μονώτης
εἰμί, φιλομυθότερος γέγονα

The more myself and solitary
I am, the more a lover of the myth
I become.

Aristotle
ad Antipater (1582 b 14)

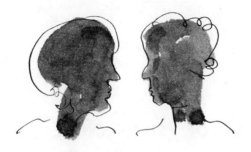

II.
Tolerance,
Ideology and Myth

Ἐν τῇ ὑπομονῇ ὑμῶν κτήσεσθε
τὰς ψυχὰς ὑμῶν.

In your tolerance you will win your lives.
Lk. 21:19

1. THE LAW OF TOLERANCE

I intend to discuss the contemporary connections between ideology and demythicization by focusing on the concrete issue of tolerance, which will enable us to bring to light several of its characteristics that would remain invisible from a more abstract or a more direct perspective. Myth—like the divine—is unseen except from behind, when it has already passed, and then only in the vestiges it leaves in the *logos*.

I would like to state a law that has an anthropological foundation, but that shows itself more clearly in the sociological realm. I might call it the law of tolerance ('things happen as if . . . *et hypothesis non fingo*') and formulate it thus: *The tolerance you have is directly proportional to the myth you live and inversely proportional to the ideology you follow.*

2. TERMINOLOGICAL CLARIFICATION

Let us first clarify our terms, and then try to explicate the meaning of this law.

The myth you live is comprised of the ensemble of contexts you take for granted. Myth gives us a reference point that orients us in reality. The myth you live is never lived or seen as one lives or sees somebody else's myth; it is always the accepted horizon within which we place our experience of truth. I am immersed in my myth like others are in their own. I am not critically aware of my own myth, just as others are not aware of their own. It is always the other who, to my ear, speaks with an accent. It is always the other whom I surprise speaking from unexamined presuppositions.

And it is the other who discloses the myth I live, since for me it is invisible as myth. My myth is what makes me unique and, hence, irreplaceable; it is at the base of my own history and at the foundation of my language. It is expressed and manifested through my being without my being aware of it; it is what the other sees when he establishes a fully personal relationship with me, which transcends the purely dialectical level. Only beyond dialectics, on the level of the *dialogical dialogue*, do I open myself to the other as I am, allowing myself to be discovered by him—and reciprocally, without either of us taking refuge in a neutral objectivity.[1]

The ideology you follow is the demythicized part of the view you have of the world; it is the result of the passage from *mythos* to *logos* in life and personal reflexion; it is the more or less coherent ensemble of ideas that make up critical awareness, i.e., the doctrinal system that enables you to locate yourself rationally—ideologically—in the world at a particular time, in a particular place. Ideology always implies a spatio-temporal system constructed by the *logos* as a function of its concrete historical moment. An ideology is a system of ideas formulated by a *logos* incapable of transcending its own temporality. The problem of ideology arises once the human *logos* is assumed to have lost its trans- and/or in-temporal character.

The ideology I follow stems from this conscious part of myself that allows me to integrate my ideas more or less systematically into a doctrinal framework (even if that system declares itself 'open'). In contrast to myth, I can recognize both my own ideology and those of others; this allows a dialectical rapport with them.

The word ideology, like the word myth, has an almost bewildering multiplicity of meanings, which we cannot examine here. I shall discuss only one of the usages most common today: ideology as an intrinsically temporal system of ideas governing our social life, especially at the level of the *res publica*.[2]

The tolerance you have is difficult to define because it depends on the particular ideology that defines it. We must, then, seek some phenomenological traits of the notion of tolerance, which, like symptoms, will help us to discover the ideological coefficient of a given culture.

3. THE FOUR MOMENTS OF TOLERANCE

We can readily agree that tolerance does not necessarily imply either the relativism of truth or indifference to it.[3] You are scarcely tolerant when you disavow any defense of truth whatsoever simply because you are skeptical or indifferent. The radical *relativity* of human values is not the same thing as a more or less agnostic *relativism*. You can be truly tolerant only if you do not compromise, having realized that truth itself is tolerant.[4] Tolerance does not come from an indifference to truth but from a deeper realization of truth itself.[5] We cannot deny, however, that skepticism and indifference of every sort have contributed to the practice of tolerance and encouraged reflexion upon it.

Tolerance is characterized by four traits that, in one form or another, are present in those cultures where tolerance still means something.

a. Political

You tolerate what you cannot pigeon-hole. You put up with a burden, you tolerate a lesser evil. You tolerate what you cannot completely assimilate, approve, or agree upon. You are tolerant in order to avoid the greater evil of intolerance which would wipe out many other 'goods'. At bottom, tolerance has to do with prudence and political prudence in particular, at least in the Aristotelian sense. Most civil codes recognize that this kind of tolerance cannot serve as a source of law.

b. Theological

Tolerance is a practical necessity. Here it is a positive attitude, it places existence before essence, practice before theory, common sense before logical reasoning and, in the final analysis, goodness before truth. But at the same time it is provisional, since it is only justified in the *status deviationis*, in the itinerant condition, the still-imperfect society, etc. Tolerance bears with it a secret hope of becoming obsolete. Genuine tolerance would rather *not* be necessary, it would like to become superfluous, it lives in the hope of disappearing. And this is understandable, for we could not accept a definitive rupture between goodness and truth. This tolerance then is always the index of the provisionality of existence.

c. Philosophical

Tolerance is also a theoretical necessity that derives from a reflexive awareness of our limits and limitations. It rests on the respect due to what I do not understand, because I understand that I do not understand everything. It is respectful tolerance. It leads us to respect someone else even though we do not agree with his ideas and/or actions.

If the first form of tolerance can be labeled *political tolerance*, the second might be called *theological tolerance* since it follows from the awareness of what different theologies call Man's unnatural, exceptional, fallen or unachieved situation. This third form of tolerance bears the name *philosophical tolerance*, since it is grounded in recognizing our limits and the necessarily limited perspective of all human knowledge.

d. Mystical

But we can discover still a fourth type of tolerance.

The experience, and so the practice, of tolerance reveals a dimension that is not apprehended by theoretical reflexion alone. This experience leads us to something more positive that we could call *mystical tolerance*. It presupposes that you may be capable of assuming what you tolerate.[6] You redeem, you raise up what you tolerate; you transform it, and this transformation purifies the active agent as well as the passive agent of the tolerance. Tolerance here is experienced as the sublimation of a state of affairs by the power of tolerance itself. Mystical tolerance represents a nonobjectifiable vision of the world and implies the conviction that every human act has a value that is not purely objective. This notion of tolerance implies that all reality is redeemable because it is never immutable. It also supposes the existential character of truth and the radical relativity of personal being. Tolerance, then, is the way one being exists in another and expresses the radical interdependence of all that exists. The strength of many traditional cultures is not only their resistance to suffering or misfortune, but their ability to tolerate, and by so doing to integrate more thoroughly what in other circumstances would exasperate or even destroy ordinary people.

This may be clearer if we describe a concrete instance. We will use a Christian example: What ought the Christian to tolerate? Evil! The parable of the wheat and the tares leaves us in no doubt of this. But this is not all. Man should tolerate not only the tares but also the wheat. I would say quite simply: Man has to tolerate the world. Beginning with himself, the Christian must tolerate the world. Man must tolerate that he is not yet what he can become, what he wants to be, what he will be. In short, the Christian has to tolerate that he has not reached his goal, the perfection of his being. He has, further, to tolerate that here he cannot be holy in twenty-four hours, that he is a sinner. He ought to tolerate himself in his entirety—as unfinished, moving on, *viator*. And just so, he ought to tolerate this unfinished cosmos, this fragile, broken temporality, as well as his fellow pilgrims. Whoever is self-satisfied, no longer receptive, no longer able to learn; whoever no longer feels and suffers as a pilgrim—he cannot share this mystical tolerance.

But here the Christian does not simply suffer error and disbelief, he bears them. And this is possible because Man is not alone; the Son of Man is with Man. The Christian bears all human situations in and with Christ, the bearer, creator and redeemer of the world. The Christian neither judges the world nor stands to one side and observes, secure in his right opinion. He has something to *do* on earth, a task takes shape in him, a liturgical, sacred and therefore priestly task. He is a co-worker, a concelebrant, a co-redeemer with Christ. The Christian enacts a cosmic role in shaping the new heaven and the new earth. And this role is precisely tolerance, which we might translate here as 'patience'.[7]

Tolerance is that patience by which we save our souls, our very lives.[8] Tolerance also means expectation and hope, not just the perseverance and steadfastness by which this Christian and biblical notion is often rendered (a stoic translation, it seems to me).[9]

Seen in the light of tolerance, then, the Christian task is to bear and endure the burden of the other in hope and thereby, following Paul, fulfill Christ's law.[10] The kingdom of God is in a certain sense already God's kingdom, i.e., the whole of creation. To participate in its fulfillment does not mean raising up an edifice—a mundane, powerful, triumphant Christendom—but it means beginning now, on earth, through all things great and small, to collaborate with matter, which is itself called upon to arise, and so already on the way to resurrection. In this way is the Christian the light and leaven of the world.[11]

But rather than pursue these considerations further with examples of other traditions, we would like to go back to our thesis.

4. BETWEEN IDEOLOGY AND MYTH: TOLERANCE

a. The Limits of Tolerance

The more perfect an ideology, the less tolerant it is, but also the less it needs to tolerate tolerance. In an ideological system, tolerance is the exception; it is always tolerance of the exceptional. But the more ideologically perfect a society, the more these exceptions are reduced to a minimum.

There is no room for tolerance in a perfect ideology. Insofar as it is not yet perfected, ideology must put up with tolerance. To the extent that an ideology reaches its perfection, it must be intolerant.[12]

Tolerance is only fully justified outside the limits of an ideology (this is why partial ideologies become partially 'tolerable'); but when an ideology becomes totalitarian—when it wants to encompass the totality of human experience—it becomes absolutely intolerant and hence also intolerable if you do not submit to it.[13]

Ideology can at most tolerate the practice of tolerance, but it can neither approve nor justify it theoretically. Tolerance is the very index of a particular ideology's weakness. An ideology is forced to tolerate what it cannot yet extirpate.[14]

Some examples will clarify this.

When we (ideologically) label certain people 'criminal' or 'sick', we agree not to tolerate the freedom of those whose free movements pose a danger to society and we imprison them or confine them to hospitals.[15]

The example of the mentally ill may be especially enlightening. The ideology of each culture fixes what we might call the index of tolerability of 'abnormals'. For example, in countries where hysteria and certain types of schizophrenia still have a mythic dimension and have not yet been ideologically diagnosed as illnesses, no one would dream of confining or isolating these people; the threshold of the tolerable is fixed as a function of ideology, not of myth.

When a particular communist ideology is convinced that religion is wrong, the opium of the people, it feels obligated to uproot this evil lest it poison the whole of society. It can tolerate religion only when a complete or premature elimination of it would provoke even greater ills.

When a certain Christian ideology is convinced that heresy is wrong or apostasy criminal, it will tolerate them only to avoid major upheavals. But where these scourges can be eliminated without creating other problems, this will be done at once. We obviously try to integrate the other dialectically, which means I tolerate another as long as he acquiesces to the rules of the game that enable me to triumph over him. Here the Inquisition may serve as an example: The prisoner is freed if he confesses, because admitting his guilt implies he accepts the rules of the game. The culprit even accepts punishment since it has for him a purifying value.

In a democratic ideology, to broaden the spectrum of our examples, the other will be tolerated insofar as he does not represent a menace to the system. He can speak, write or act as long as he does not endanger the system that allows these freedoms.

As an ideology (insofar as it is not a myth), democracy has produced a social system based on the rights of the individual as expressed by universal suffrage. Here we do not eliminate the law of the jungle or the law of the strongest, but we mellow it, 'civilize' it, by voluntarily accepting majority rule. If someone does not accept the fundamental rules of democracy, democracy cannot tolerate him.

We measure the perfection of a democratic ideology by its level of unmanifest intolerance, i.e., insofar as it does not need to have recourse to blatant intolerance. When an ideology feels threatened in its existence or its very essence, it neither is nor *can* be tolerant any longer. You tolerate only what you can bear without being crushed.

Can we consciously accept our own destruction? Can we voluntarily abdicate our rights? Can we resign in the face of the evidence? If in my system 2 and 2 make 4, can I tolerate them making 5? I can tolerate the error of another who affirms, for example, that 2 and 2 make 5 as long as his affirmation does not interfere with my calculations and I can continue to work from the supposition that 2 and 2 make 4.

Can I tolerate someone who does not accept my interval of the tolerable? Can I tolerate somebody who says he would wipe me out if he could? Or someone who would make use of my tolerance to seize power, enabling him to be intolerant?

For an ideology, tolerance becomes a prudent political strategy. 'Since we are a minority, we demand our rights'. But the moment we are in power, 'we can no longer tolerate error'. It would contradict our own standing and even render 'aid and comfort' to our opponents. The history of every age supplies us, alas, with plenty of examples. After Constantine came Theodosius; after the 'revolution', the dictatorship; after the myth of a free world, an ideology of freedom that does not hesitate to wage war in order to impose a democratic regime.

In short, you can tolerate only what you believe you can tolerate, but outside or beyond these limits, no tolerance is possible.

Some would say we should be intolerant only of the intolerable.[16] Of course, but the problem is the threshold and the consciousness of the intolerable. To tolerate the intolerable is a contradiction. All intolerance can justify itself to itself and to others only because it believes it has already reached the limits of the tolerable. But where are these limits?[17] Could we not define law as that which regulates the limits of the tolerable?

b. Ideology and Tolerance

The fundamental difference between a philosophy that would also like to be practical and an ideology is that you reverse the classical relation of *theoria* and *praxis*.[18] The traditional attitude of any philosophy is that practice follows from theory, implying the primacy of thought. Ideology, on the contrary, derives theory from practice; action takes primacy. But we must be more precise: For any ideology, truth and beauty and being—essence and existence—are exclusively what is given in practice, what happens in the world. There is no other reference point, no ulterior instance. Real transcendence is ideologically unthinkable. We could cite here the radical atheism of certain totalitarian ideologies; there is no other reality than the given. When 'revelation' becomes a given and is no longer a mystery, religion is on the way to becoming ideology. When transcendence becomes an idea, a concept, and is no longer a myth, it shows its internal contradiction. The concept of absolute transcendence denies what it supposedly affirms: that there is something 'beyond' the very idea of this beyond.

If the problem is whether action or practice takes primacy over thought, the difficulty is philosophical. Some philosophical systems willingly accept the primacy of practice. We think only within given parameters, we exist only within a given existence; and although Man may say he shapes his own destiny, he does so within a given world, a situation, a horizon, which does not enter the process itself, etc. A practical philosophy or a philosophy of action, like any ideology, recognizes the primacy of the given over thought. But unlike all ideology, philosophy does not turn the given into thought; it does not identify them; it conserves the raw, irreducible character of the action, the existence, in short, of the given. Ideology, on the other hand, identifies them; it wants to dominate the given, the existence, the action.[19] Here also, action certainly has the primacy, but a primacy mastered and domesticated by thought. This action, this given reality becomes thought—even thinkable—and not only the source of thought.

Ideology is integral monism seen from an idealist perspective that embraces all that is real. Here action is the deployment of the given without any other possible interference from an order that is not already given or manipulable. Ideology destroys any transcendence and certainly the transcendence of thought in relation to action.

In other words: Action, *praxis* itself, becomes *theoria* — ideology. The 'factual' situation is here no longer the source of thought, but thought itself. It is easy to see the idealist climate of all modern ideology.

The limits of the tolerable, then, are simply what you de facto tolerate. Beyond there is the intolerable. Each era, each human power has its inbuilt criteria for what it will tolerate and for what it will not tolerate, and there is no possibility of appeal to any superior instance.

If, on the contrary, *praxis* is not identified with *theoria*, the limits of the tolerable stem from an order of thought that is independent of action. Hence tolerance is a function of thought and can therefore be delimited within each cultural or philosophical universe. The transcendence of thought with respect to *praxis* is the basis of tolerance. When ideology identifies them, the intolerable is exactly what does not adapt to or is not included in the field of thought, i.e., of ideology.

You can only tolerate the tolerable, but ideology says that the tolerable is what *it* tolerates. On the other hand, for anyone who does not want to identify with an ideology, the limits of the tolerable do not derive from *praxis*, but arise from an intellectual *consensus* open to evolution and/or change, and thus to the possibility of discussion and appeal. Now in any ideology, as long as you do not make explicit room for the tolerable, you cannot tolerate it. To make room for the tolerable amounts to fitting it into the system, albeit in a particular way, i.e., as a factor still to be assimilated, an evil to be borne with for a while in order to integrate or destroy it later, without destroying other values at the same time. A scholastic ideology, for example, could tolerate human error or ignorance as long as it was confident that someday truth would win out. God would be the guarantor; he would fill in the margins of human ignorance. But at bottom this means we have already left the ideological terrain. It represents our entry into myth, into what we find self-evident, what we believe without believing that we believe it.

c. Tolerance and Myth

Now the other part of our law: the direct proportionality between the myth you live and the tolerance you have.

Myth represents the invisible horizon on which we project our notions of the real. I tolerate the other as long as I find him tolerable. Now on the conceptual level, I find intolerable all that I cannot integrate into my system of thought in one way or another. But to tolerate positively what is outside my system, I must discover another mode of communing in spite of dialectical incompatibility. This mode is myth. Myth offers us an interval of the tolerable.

Perhaps an example will help us here. You hold political opinion *A* while I am persuaded that *B* is the system adequate and just for the same situation. As long as we remain within the party system, i.e., within a whole comprised of several parts, we can tolerate each other because we consider the other practically indispensable for maintaining the creative polarity necessary for us to complete one another and achieve a more equitable way of life. We disagree about means and perhaps about particular issues, but we agree about ends and about the prevailing ideals that enable us to dialogue and contend. The problem looms large when I no longer consider you as a 'part' of the whole and completely reject you as an entity incompatible with my ideas. I can tolerate you provided that I find some ground where there is sufficient room for both of us. This place is not your ideas nor, in this second case, the role you might play in a healthy balance of power. I may still tolerate you, on a third level, as a human being since I am still convinced your human value supersedes that of your ideas. I tolerate you in this case because we both believe in the human myth. We still commune in the myth that tolerance is good for both of us. I respect your person. But then I tolerate you as long as you accept being tolerated by me, that is, as long as you do not hinder my being from developing and realizing itself. It is a sort of implicit pact: You tolerate the other in order to be tolerated in your turn. We are both aware of the precarious nature of such a tolerance. As soon as you lose power or cease to be a threat, I shall no longer tolerate you. A glance at the global political scene is enough to convince anyone that we are not idly speculating.

The extent to which we tolerate one another outside a dialectical framework of contending powers depends precisely on the myth in which we believe. I tolerate you, for example, because I believe human nature is good, or because I think there is a Providence that guides us, or because I still believe in Man, in humanity, in the possibility of your 'conversion', etc.; in a word, I tolerate you because there is yet a common mythical 'surround' that embraces us, that unites us.

To give an example, the average American citizen is convinced that if his nation possesses unchallenged military supremacy, there will be worldwide peace since he has no direct intention of attacking any country in order to dominate it.[20] But he thinks it possible, even probable, that a communist power with such superiority could very well annihilate millions of Americans. This is why the ordinary American supports a military budget counted in the billions of dollars. What is dangerous here is the double standard; You judge yourself differently from the way you judge the others. You are not living the same myth. 'We' do not tolerate 'them'. We live in a state of tension and cold war— 'détente' notwithstanding. We only begin to tolerate the other when we believe in his good intentions without sharing his ideas. But this is only possible if the ideal (the myth) is not identified with the idea (my *logos*).

In any case, I do not tolerate you because of the ideas we share, i.e., because of the *logos* contents of our relationship, but through the myth that unites me to you. When the myth disappears or where the myth does not cover you, I become intolerant, I no longer tolerate you. Where there is intellectual dissension, I can tolerate you only if I manage to commune with you mythically. Demythicization of myth, inevitable as it is, breeds intolerance, since an idea cannot bear, cannot tolerate, a contradictory one.

I tolerate inasmuch as I share with another something that is outside the intellectual domain, insofar as we commune without needing to know it explicitly. I tolerate you as long as I trust you, as long as I do not judge you. As long as we live in the same myth, tolerance is possible. But the moment I demythicize you or you demythicize me, I can no longer fully agree with you since my concept is my 'conception', hence mine and not yours. The relationship of reason is dialectical; that of myth, dialogical. We fully agree only in what we do not consider reflexively, in what we accept as beyond any analysis, in what neither of us considers his own idea, his own discovery.

We should add immediately that communion in a myth does not automatically bring peace or eliminate dissension and struggle. On the contrary, fratricidal vendettas and civil wars seem even more violent than cross-cultural conflicts, for they are cases of two or more ideologies wrangling for hegemony.

d. Myth and Ideology

We can now summarize our thesis. You can tolerate in a positive and total way only what you accept. Now you can accept only what you either understand with the *logos* or embrace in myth. In the first case, i.e., if and insofar as you understand, there is no need to tolerate. On the other hand, positive tolerance has to do with what you accept fully without understanding it. Here is the place and the role of myth. Communion in the same myth is what makes tolerance possible. Love that loves without understanding could be an example.

But human reality is complex because it is one: You cannot completely cut the *logos* from myth. You can distinguish but not separate them, since the one nourishes the other, and all human culture is a texture of myth and *logos*. They are like two aspects of one and the same Reality, or rather, they are like two constitutive threads that intertwine to fabricate Reality.

On the other hand, the myth-*logos* relation is so deeply anchored in human reality that even so-called developed countries have built formidable ideologies only on one front, exposing their flank, as it were, to infiltration by other myths. It is thus that even ideologies end by turning into myth. And so they become tolerable.

Now the ideological coefficient of a culture is what determines that culture's degree of tolerance. A contradiction has no place in ideology and a contrary will be found there only when it is integrated into an actual or possible synthesis. The more a civilization is ideologically organized, the bigger is its ideological coefficient, thus the less it needs to be tolerant and, in fact, the less it is tolerant. It has had the opportunity to broaden the field of its comprehension, but at the same time it has reduced the field of its tolerance. Obviously, once a culture achieves a higher degree of civilization, people accept its criteria willingly, so that it has less need to be tolerant. Since exceptions are rare and minor in a more 'evolved' or 'perfect' society, it is even less tolerant of them.

The extent of tolerance an average citizen in a technological society enjoys is of another order altogether than the extent of tolerance in a situation where a different relation between myth and *logos* exists. Possibly the average citizen does not always notice this, above all if he is already accustomed to the *status quo* and has nothing with which to compare his lot, if he is already 'integrated' into society and has become a cog in the huge, complex technocratic megamachine we call modern civilization. So it does not disturb many 'civilized' people that their civilization does not tolerate anyone who is not useful or does not work. Technologically 'evolved' societies can hardly tolerate anyone who arranges his or her own life. The 'modern' mentality is unawakened to any other alternative.

Today's pan-economic civilization is radically intolerant of any human activity (contemplation for example) that is not at least indirectly profitable. It leaves room for antieconomic factors only insofar as it cannot eliminate or co-opt them.

We can give yet another example. The more a marriage ceases to be a myth and becomes ideology, the more conjugal tolerance diminishes.

Yet to demythicize is always equally to remythicize, and this change of myths is a genuine reentry into myth. Tolerance is the inherent mythical dynamic that allows remythicizing. And here a further path invites our inquiry—the human adventure of reconquering myth and even, perhaps, conquering a new innocence. Might we not envision a *metanoia* instead of an ideological *paranoia* in the *nous* of contemporary culture?[21]

Notes

1. So much has been said and written about myth, and today the bibliography is so huge that I need not develop this theme at greater length here. Cf. however, the volumes of the Colloquia organized by the Istituto di studi filosofici (Roma), edited by E. Castelli (Paris: Aubier, 1961-1978).

2. "Bestimmte begriffliche Systeme von praktischer Bedeutung nennen wir Ideologien", notes H. Kuhn at the beginning of his essay 'Ideologie als hermeneutischer Begriff', *Hermeneutik und Dialektik*, edited by R. Bubner, K. Cramer, and R. Wiehl (Tübingen: J.C.B. Mohr [P. Siebeck], 1970), vol. 1, p. 343. Cf. also: "Ideology, a system of views and ideas: political, legal, ethical, aesthetical, religious, philosophical. I. is part of the superstructure . . . and as such ultimately reflects economic relations." *A Dictionary of Philosophy*, edited by M. Rosenthal and P. Yudin (Moscow: Progress Publishers, 1967), *sub hac voce*. Again, "Die I. ist ein System des gesellschaftlichen Denkens, worin die ausserempirischen Kategorien und die Auswahl des empirischen Materials durch die gesellschaftlichen Interessen und Affekte des Betrachtenden beeinflusst, wenn nicht gänzlich bestimmt werden", N. Birnbaum, *RGG* (1959), *sub hac voce*. Or also Karl Rahner affirming that Ideology's "Wesen darin besteht, eine bestimmte, einzelne Wirklichkeit der pluralistischen Welt der Erfahrung als absoluten Fixpunkt zu setzen." *Schriften zur Theologie* (Einsiedeln, Benziger, 1965), VI, 82.

3. Cf. A. de Waelhens, 'Sur les fondements possibles de la tolérance', in E. Castelli (ed.) *L'herméneutique de la liberté religieuse* (Paris: Aubier, 1968): "C'est parce que la vérité est non une possession qu'il faudrait défendre ou imposer, mais une maniere de s'ouvrir à . . ., [sic] voire cette ouverture elle-même" (p. 394).

4. This makes no sense at all if we consider truth exclusively as logical truth; but the truth that frees us is not this sort of truth (i.e., logical). Cf. my study, 'Die existentielle Phänomenologie der Wahrheit', *Philosophisches Jahrbuch der Görresgesellschaft*, Nr. 64 (1956), pp. 27-54 and in *Māyā e Apocalisse* (Roma: Abete, 1966), pp. 241-89.

5. Cf. Div. Thom. in *De malo* II, 2 saying that there is a kernel of truth in every viewpoint.

6. It is interesting to note that many Sanskrit, Greek and Latin words used to express the idea of tolerance are derived from roots that also mean victory, conquest, power, force and hence the capacity to

resist, maintain, wait patiently, assume, i.e., tolerate. Cf. this same notion in the three groups of Japanese words that express the notion of tolerance in W.M. Fridell, 'Notes on Japanese Tolerance', *Monumenta Nipponica, 27*(3), 1972, 254-56.

7. This translation, incidentally, is not original. At least once in the Vulgata ὑπομονή is translated not by 'patience' (*patientia*) but by *tolerantia* (2 Cor. 1:6).

8. Cf. Lk. 21:19.

9. Following Thomas (*Sum. theol.* II-II, q. 136, a. 4), patience is 'pars fortitudinis'. Yet Hellenistic courage is not the same as Christian patience, not even in a passive sense. Patience, 'the perfect value' (Jas. 1:4) is not only, nor even primarily, mere steadfastness and persistence in the face of evil; but rather bearing the destiny of Man and of the entire world. Τλάω (from the root ταλ from which comes tolerance, cf. the Latin *tolo*) means to bear, suffer, endure, persevere, hold out; hardly ever in a physical sense, but rather in a spiritual sense of redeeming. From the double sense of τέλλω (raise and fulfill), we might say that by tolerating, by 'loading' something onto himself (in the first sense), the Christian tolerates this as the object of his tolerance and therefore realizes it (the second sense). From this it is clear that there can be no Christian tolerance—as generally no Christian value—without love that alone transforms simple endurance into hopeful bearing.

10. Cf. Gal. 6:2.

11. Cf. my study on Christian tolerance: 'Pluralismus, Toleranz und Christenheit', *Pluralismus, Toleranz und Christenheit* (Nürnberg: Abendländische Akademie, 1961), pp. 117-42, and in *Los Dioses y el Señor* (Buenos Aires: Columba, 1967), pp. 116-46.

12. In all scholasticisms making distinctions is the dialectical procedure by which one can be doctrinally tolerant. You are tolerated if you succeed in fitting your opinion into the mainstream of orthodox opinion by making the appropriate distinctions.

13. Cf. the principle *de internis non judicat Ecclesia* and, on the other hand, the totalitarian principle of certain communist and religious ideologies that demand the submission of private convictions. Cf. the problem of religious obedience and how, once demythicized, it becomes intolerable.

14. An analysis of arguments for or against tolerating pornography these last years, especially in the United States, offers an interesting example favoring our law. The more one lives in one or another myth (that of morality or of democracy), the more one tolerates one side or the other. The more one follows one or another ideology (that of the common good or freedom), the more one is intolerant of one cause or another. Those mainly concerned with morality and the common good will espouse stringent antipornography laws. Those mainly concerned with democracy and freedom will defend a 'liberal' attitude.

15. Cf. as an example: "Now quite a few people are beginning to understand that jail increases both the quality and the quantity of criminals, that, in fact, it often creates them out of mere nonconformists. Far fewer people, however, seem to understand that mental hospitals, nursing homes, and orphan asylums do much the same thing." I. Illich, 'The Institutional Spectrum', *Cross Currents, 21*(1) (Winter, 1971), 89.

16. Cf. the final sentence in the article of H.-W. Bartsch, 'L'idée de tolérance chez Paul', in the volume cited, *L'herméneutique de la liberté religieuse*, p. 205: "L'intolérance de Paul ne se dresse que contre l'intolérance." Obviously, intolerance is that which one does not tolerate.

17. "La tolérance ne saurait donc consister à accepter n'importe quoi de n'importe qui, au sens où nous disons accepter les pensées et les actes de quelqu'un. Elle devra consister à laisser chacun exercer les possibilités, de dévoilement ou de découverte, théorique ou pratique, qui lui sont dévolues de par sa 'situation' dans la totalité de l'étant." A. de Waelhens, *loc. cit.*, p. 394. Certainly, but where are the criteria? Who tells us what these possibilities are? Perhaps we could go so far as to permit suicide, but murder?

18. "Ideologie = Aktion, in Theorie umgesetzt; praktische Philosophie = Theorie, aus der eine Aktion folgt." Cf. H. Kuhn, *op. cit.*, p. 348.

19. ". . . für die Ideologie ist der Sachbezug, so wenig er fehlen kann, *nicht* das Entscheidende. Sie *will* etwas, und im Licht des von ihr Gewollten liest sie die Chriffren der Wirklichkeit. . . . die Theorie und der Theoretiker (als wollendes Subjekt) bilden für sie eine untrennbare Einheit. Die Doktrin ist hier zugleich Aktionsprojekt." H. Kuhn, *op. cit.*, p. 348.

20. Cf. the casual remark of former President Richard Nixon to a group of Congressmen (quoted in an Editorial of *The Progressive*, *38*[2], February, 1974:6): "I can go into my office and make a telephone call and within twenty-five minutes seventy million people would be dead." No average American, believing in the myth of the Founding Fathers, would entertain such a thought. Watergate was only an anecdote of such an attitude of supreme might.

21. Cf. the bibliographical appendix on religious freedom and tolerance.

III.
Morality and Myth.
The 'Moral' of Myth and
the Myth of Morals

Only when the great Tao declines
Humanness and morality arise.
Tao Tē Ching 18 (+)

+ Humanness: *jēn*, human kindness, humaneness. Morality: *yi*, righteousness. When Kung-fu-tse (Confucius) was asked about the meaning of *jēn* he said: "don't do to others what you don't want others to do to you", *Analects* XII, 2; or again more simply: "love Men!" *ibid.* XII, 22.

1. MORALITY

It is characteristic, even symptomatic, that contemporary Man, having tried to demythicize dogma, now tries to demythicize morals. Previous centuries tended to moralize religion and so attempted to moralize myth, i.e., to reduce myth to its 'moral' by making it carry a moral message. The point was to salvage myth, or at least what was considered the essence of myth. The present-day tendency mainly wants to salvage morals, which otherwise seem so threatened.

And so we touch on a crucial problem that could easily be the starting point for an entire phenomenology of our times. I shall limit myself to some reflections that are more concentrated than systematic.[1]

Perhaps I should state—as tribute to Cartesian clarity?—the scheme of this study:

> The 'moral' of myth is the myth itself, and not its 'content' moralized. To moralize myth is to destroy it.

> The myth of morals is morality itself, and when morals cease to be a myth, they also cease to be moral. To demythicize morals is tantamount to murdering them.

> To remythicize morals does not mean consciously, artificially demythicizing them. Morals, insofar as they survive, remythicize themselves, like a serpent sheds its skin. They are not based on reason or on myth, but flow from faith. From faith—? *ad calendas graecas!*

a. The 'Moral' of Myth

The so-called Renaissance neither introduced nor rein-troduced myth to the European world; it only provoked a more or less rational reflection on myth.[2] Thus that hybrid and even self-contradictory science called *mythology* was born. In fact, by vir-tue of their very natures, as soon as one approaches *mythos* with the instrument of the *logos,* myth can only disappear, just as darkness is no longer darkness after light penetrates. The analogy is appropriate, since in this case the illuminating 'light' of reason indeed destroys the 'obscurity' of myth. To be sure, it has been said that God loves to dwell in 'thick darkness'[3] but it has also been said that the darkness did not receive the light.[4] Moreover, dark-ness cannot receive the light and remain darkness: the only way for the darkness to encounter the light is not to receive it. If darkness were not dark, it would need no light; but it cannot coexist with light. Can the creature, which is darkness insofar as it is not God,[5] truly receive the Creator and remain creature? If the Creator were really to descend into or unite himself with the creature, what would remain of it?[6] There is a deeper dialectic here than currently suspected. On God's side, redemption is free, but from the side of the created, it is the only way out of the existential impasse: Shadows have their *raison d'être* and so their justification, as a function of light.[7]

However this may be, mythology is the death of myth. Myth is not an 'object', but an instrument of knowing, a fundamental human attitude, if you like, beside, not in front of, the *logos.*[8] It cannot become the object of the *logos* without degenerating. Here already we have the whole problematic: When you make myth into an 'object' of knowledge, when you make it the subject-matter of analysis, you destroy it as myth. You can retrieve bits and pieces perhaps, but the myth is dead. Myth does not resist the objectifying light of reason, it demands the innocence of igno-rance. We shall see that this is also the case with morals.

There is however another, and in this case acceptable, way of understanding 'mythology'. Here it indicates not the invasion of the *mythos* by the *logos,* reducing the former to the latter, but rather *mythos-legein*: telling the myth, saying it, the integral word that is both *mythos* and *logos*. Myths can be told and told properly, when they are believed; they cannot be investigated by means of another organ just as sound cannot be perceived by the naked eye. Only recently has mythology renounced its pretension to being *science* and rediscovered that its role is once again to 'recount' the myth: μῦθον λέγειν. This is mytho-*logy* demytho-*logized*.[9]

In addition to these inherent contradictions, mythology as the science of myths is confronted with a practically insurmountable difficulty when it tries to save myth. Even today words like miraculous, marvelous, legendary, unreal, mythical, etc. are almost synonymous in common language. Seen in the light of the *logos*, myth is not only false, it also proves to be immoral. So a certain affable and apologetic mythology attempted to moralize it. How to moralize myth? By demythicizing it.

The subsequent reversal—demythicization of morals—now asserts itself with a vengeance. And we arrive at our problem. How to demythicize morals? By 'demoralizing' them. We are going to show this schematically.

b. Demythicizing Myth

A demythicized myth is by definition no longer myth. If it remains a myth, this means it has been imperfectly demythicized. A demythicized myth is a eunuch, a human face without a nose, without eyes, without ears. A demythicized myth is a cadaver. Some would demythicize to attain 'truth', pure truth, just as pure metal is obtained by physico-chemical experiments. This process kills myth just as vivisection kills a living being in order to extract its vital fluids. Advocates of this method consider truth a concept and thereby sever its umbilical cord with the very 'conception' that conceived it! Demythicization, then, means extracting the concept from the unformed, undiscriminated magma of myth. It goes without saying that this process of demythicization, though ultimately related, should not be confused with Bultmannian de-mythologization or with the 'personal decision' flowing from an 'existential interpretation' of a mythical text.

To take an example: Adam, it is said, could have not existed (note: historically, as an individual—as if existence could only be

an individualistically historical category); the apple could have
not been real (another note: biologically and materially—as if
reality could be exhausted by these dimensions); the snake could
have not had the power of speech (emphasis: phonetically and
with human words—as if all communication had to be in words),
etc., etc. But the core of the myth, so we are told, brings to mind
notions of obedience, humility, temptation, responsibility for suffering, and so forth.[10] Demythicization would then supply the
truth of the myth. The myth may not be 'true', i.e., 'historically'
true, but it will contain truths.[11]

The problem does not end here. After extracting its truth, we
'rehabilitate' the myth in moral terms. Adam 'knew' his wife,
who was in a certain sense his daughter. As for Cain and Abel,
Genesis does not tell us who their wives, the mothers of their
children, were.[12] Given the biblical context, we must assume
their wives were their sisters. The myth of incest begins; it will
develop throughout the Western world.[13] Greek myths on this
subject are well known. We also know analogies in India.[14] Once
again, we are not content to discover the truth-content of these
myths, we also want to interpret their message of goodness, to
discover their moral.[15] And although a parable is not a myth, we
have done the same with the Gospel parables: we want them to
give a moral lesson.[16]

In the case of Jacob's tricking Esau and Isaac,[17] so difficult
to moralize, Saint Augustine candidly admits: "non est mendacium, sed mysterium."[18] By so doing he refuses to demythicize,
because he understands very well that if he moralizes too much,
the entire myth will founder and with it whatever truth or goodness it might contain. The vehicle of the *mysterium* is the myth
itself. Without myth, the mystery is doomed and, vice versa,
without this sense of mystery, myth dies.[19] Augustine invites us
to open ourselves to the mystery and spurn the invasion of reason
into a realm that is not its own. But not everybody stops at this
threshold.[20] We demand explanations, we want to penetrate
everywhere with reason, we profane the cloister of being, we
violate the virginity of myth.[21] Strictly speaking it is re-flection,
my-self-consciousness, that kills myth. When knowledge loses its
ecstasy, when it no longer illumines, when it turns itself in,

glances backward,[22] it becomes knowledge of good and evil but it also loses its innocence and the myth vanishes. So to 'save' myth you demythicize it, you try at least to salvage its moral, which is not always easy. Then you demythicize further.

Let us take, as an example of moralizing demythicization, the Hindu myth of incest.[23] Here we find two different myths, or more precisely two dynamic moments of the same primordial myth of unity and multiplicity, of the absolute and the relative.[24] The first moment refers to the union between the Father of the Gods, Prajāpati, and his daughter, Uṣas. Prajāpati discovers himself alone and is bored. He desires a second.[25] He who is already complete, the primordial *ātman* identical to the Person[26] who could not be afraid of anyone because there is no one other than he,[27] the androgynous being, splits himself in two.[28] Then he (already a masculine priority) unites with Uṣas and mankind is begotten. One could say this myth represents the love of God for his creature and his descent to her in order to divinize her, to have her with him once again. Incest represents the ἀποκατάστασις πάντων and the ἀνακεφαλαίωσις of all things.[29] God grants his creature his own life. He is not content to love her 'platonically', he fertilizes her, makes her his wife.[30] 'God so loved the world'[31] that he 'descended' and 'entered' his creature and made his own creation fertile.[32] To the dereliction of the creation corresponds the embrace of God's descent, fecundation, incarnation, whose fruit is the creature's own divinization.[33] We are said to be far from incest at this point and someone is bound to tell us that the myth is only a particularly crude manner of speaking, and that the essence of the myth is really what we have just said.[34] So we make a cosmic hermeneutic.[35]

The second moment of this myth, already present to some extent in the first version, represents the historical dimension and the anthropological vision of the same problem. It is no longer a question of the union of God with his creature in an atemporal setting, but of the reintegration of Man. Since this is impossible in a single human exemplar, it ought to be accomplished by perpetuating the species.[36] Yama, the first man, must unite with his twin sister because the ancestors desire progeny from the only ones on earth.[37] The first human couple must overcome their repugnance at doing what is 'unheard-of and horrible' in order to reintegrate human being at the price of multiplicity. So it will be the whole of humanity that arrives at the fullness of reintegration. Yamī, the 'Eve of the Ṛg Veda' 'tempts' her brother Yama:[38]

> 'I offer my bed as a woman to her man;
> Let us roll like cart-wheels!'[39]

He refuses:

> 'Never will I unite my body with yours;
> Sin it is called to approach a sister.
> Go from me—take your delight elsewhere.
> Your brother, fair one, wants none of it.'[40]

Later Yama, the first mortal, dies and becomes king and God of the dead, the Yama of mythology.[41] In order to ease Yamī's grief, the Gods create night.[42] The heterogeneity of time is made for— and through—Man.[43] The modern West would no doubt try to interpret the myth by means of depth psychology.[44] But the process is the same in both cases: We have moralized the myth. We have 'saved' it, meanwhile condemning incest to the merely human level. The analogy however remains, as also the clear, unambiguous language of the myth.

Why then do we still talk about incest? Have we the right to cut the world in two—into the human realm of morals and the amoral cosmic order? Do morals have such ontological weight that they can divide beings into those addressed by moral law and those whom it does not concern? Is there not a continuum here, beginning with the divinization of the creature and leading to the incest?[45] What, then, are these morals that can demythicize myths with the same rights as reason? Which comes first—myth or morals? Is myth just a fable like those of Aesop or the Pañcatantra, valuable only for its 'moral'? Are we in this 'humanist' epoch so smitten with our little concepts that we are no longer aware that we have reduced them to explaining only the most superficial level of a much richer reality? Does 'incest'—to return to our example—only mean 'sexual relations within a certain range of consanguinity'? Or again, do 'sexual relations' mean exclusively the 'marriage act'? Is there no other 'marriage act' than this? We could multiply examples: We say 'matter' and understand 'physical mass'; 'physics' seems to stem only from the so-called natural 'sciences', and 'nature' only from the material world. Why have we reduced Man to an individual, truth to a concept, goodness to a legality and the flower to its utility? We cannot reduce the truth of myth to its conceptual truth. On the same note, we cannot but impoverish the meaning of goodness if we reduce it to moral goodness. Was Judith moral?

Somebody will object: What does myth want to say then, if it is more than the truth and the moral lesson we squeeze from it? I would answer first that neither truth nor morality will allow themselves to be imprisoned by concepts or 'morals'; secondly and above all, that myth means to say what it *says*. When we ask a myth what it means to say, it says it. The problem, rather, is that we have a much too limited idea of *saying*, a much too myopic conception of *speaking*, a much too narrow notion of the *word* that the myth says and speaks. The *fides ex auditu*[46] must be completed by the μῦθος ἐξ τοῦ λόγου. Faith born of knowing and hearing needs the complement of the myth that comes with the word. Perhaps through the intermediary of the image our era will be able to recover the meaning of myth.[47]

What remains of myth once we have demythicized it? Nothing. We have perhaps extracted some truth or moral lesson, but of the myth itself nothing remains. Now Man cannot live without myths. When the primordial myths are demythicized—and they are not yet, neither throughout the world nor even completely where they are most under attack—Man seeks others. These new myths begin as simple substitutes for the old ones, but slowly enrich themselves and absorb once again, little by little, all that had initially been rejected.[48] To the catabolism of ancient myths corresponds the anabolism of the new, which are built from the debris of the earlier ones. There is in humanity a mythical metabolism worth studying.

The necessity of myth appears in a striking and even tragic fashion in the problem of morals.

2. MYTH

a. The Myth of Morals

Here our modern era wields its pitiless critique with all the subtlety of a bludgeon. We wanted to moralize myth. What have we done? We have killed the myth. Now we shall demythicize morals. After all, aren't morals just another myth?

The 'primitive' follows his myth without question. The day he begins to ask why, he attains knowledge of good and evil[49] and immediately becomes aware of the unreasonable, irrational character of myth. By this very fact he loses his 'primitive' innocence; the myth of paradise is no longer valid for him, but he also finds himself expelled from the paradise of myth. An angel armed with a flaming sword guards the entrance to this paradise and forbids entry, lest he eat of the tree of life and understand the mystery of existence.[50]

Isn't it the same for 'civilized' people with respect to morals? They live according to their moral standards without asking for reasons. The moment they do, morals are plunged into crisis, and the day they find their reasons, morals cease to be moral. Morality becomes logic or dialectic; or science. Converted into *logos*, morals cease to be *ethos*. So we obey a syllogism. We are good by virtue of a logical conclusion. We accept the rules of this game of life because we have examined and judged their rationale. From here on the good is correct knowledge, and evil merely an error. This can be verified from the individual, as well as the sociological, perspective: Morals retreat as 'knowledge' advances.[51]

It is not by chance that Socrates has been called the first Western Man, the first 'civilized' Man, the first of a civilization that even today has not yet succeeded in destroying the mythical, a-rational and often irrational power of morals.

We act morally as long as we do not ask why. The moment we feel obliged to justify morals by reason (and how else could we do it?), they begin to crumble. What arguments do we not enlist today for or against birth control, abortion or euthanasia, for example? How many 'theories' do we construct pro or contra war, violence and deceit? We ignore the plea of believers who do not want to listen to reasons, but want to know what they ought to do. Obviously the blade is double-edged: The 'penitent' is within his rights in not wanting to hear 'reasons' in the confessional, but he is not if he asks for a simple 'recipe' that would spare him the responsibility of a free and personal stance.[52]

By this we do not intend to propose any theory whatsoever. We are simply setting forth the mythical character of morals, not only as they appear but in their deepest patterns. When morals are no longer self-sustaining, self-evident, when they are no longer accepted without discussion, when they are no longer self-asserting, then, like myths, they must appeal to reason to save and somehow justify themselves. But morality thereby sells its birthright;[53] it ceases to be autonomous and able to elicit a moral duty; it becomes probability (or 'probabiliority') and logic. It is the conclusion of an argument, the coining of a rationalization, the regularizing of propriety, the result of a syllogism, and not the expression of an Order,[54] the manifestation of a Will, the other face of Truth.

But then, he who finds other reasons, draws different conclusions, discovers a better rule (like a more perfect—because more practical—traffic system) is no longer really bound to the moral injunction, which by its very nature claims a far more universal validity than do the principles of reason. Morality is supposed to be valid (binding) even where reason is not too 'developed'. In short, morals cease to be moral; they become a pragmatic regulation of coexistence.

Faced with the advance of European culture, Western Man once (with Kant) believed that morality would be more universal, and so more valid, if based on reason rather than grounded in *ends*. We must note right away, however, that by then these ends had already become *aims*, that is, subjective intentions. In fact, conscious consciousness had already invaded the objective and cosmic order, the realm of ends. Kant's critique was then inevitable.

Both the heteronomous and the autonomous efforts have failed. In order to save morals we seem to have no other alternative than to demythicize them radically. Kant himself wanted to find the limits of reason *um zum Glauben Platz zu bekommen.*[55]

b. Demythicizing Morals

What then is left of morality? Even if we manage to preserve its truth-content, how are we to safeguard and justify its irreducible ultimacy, its authority, the full thrust of its command, its *ought*? At the very most, reason can prescribe what should be, as a function of certain presuppositions and given certain aims. But reason is absolutely unable to command what *ought to be*. It can give neither reasons nor grounds for the keystone of morals, namely that one *ought* to do that which should be. In short, you kill human conscience if you reduce it to tidy rational intellection. Morals would then be nothing else than the conclusion of a rationalization put in the form of injunctions so as to 'convince' those who are not smart enough to see the 'reasons'.

Let us consider, for example, the duty to obey. Why must Adam obey God rather than listen to Eve and the Serpent, or yield to the attraction of the forbidden fruit? Adam can obey or not, he has the choice. He is free to go either way. But once he is conscious of his freedom he is bound to ask why—why obey? And once he asks the reason for his obedience he thereby admits the possibility of disobedience if his question finds no satisfactory answer. In other words, once he begins to demythicize, he both loses innocence and eschews obedience. By asking himself 'why' he obeys, he no longer trusts the commandment on its own; he wants to justify it. His obedience is no longer spontaneous, it no longer presents itself immediately to his conscience, and so he must appeal to a third party, to the *reasons* that underlie his question and upon which he will rationally base his obedience.

Then he finds himself destitute; he discovers his nakedness.[56] And, since all dis-covery is an un-covering, he has in fact stripped himself naked. He was not naked before, he was covered by God, covered too by the myth until the dis-covery of his dis-obedience, the dis-closure of his co-gnition.[57] If I am prepared to trust these underlying reasons my questioning claims to discover, I no longer trust God but myself, who discovers the basic rationale for my obedience. If I am not prepared to follow—to obey—the findings of my reason, or if it is only a rhetorical question, hoping that the conflict will not arise, then I am no longer in good faith. For a time the Western post-Medieval Christian made God the rational basis he sought, which lead necessarily to the 'death of God' last century. If God is the 'reason' why I should obey, any other reason can supplant him. Authentic obedience tries to discover the *whom*, not to scrutinize the reason, the *what*. It does not confound a decision made *by* me with the foundation of this decision which is not *in* me. If I am the ultimate criterion, I become the rival of God—and there is no room for two on the ultimate level.

The traditional explanation of Adam's fall is simple: He fell into the devil's snare, he succumbed to temptation. Sin is alienation, letting oneself be led astray by another. Man has two *yeser*, Judaism at the time of Christ used to say, and this doctrine of two spirits, two ways, two inclinations and even two ends of Man, remains common throughout early Christianity.[58] One of these inclinations is the propensity to sin. This *yeser*, residing in the heart, is called διαβούλιον; later it will be replaced by λογισμός, a word of stoic origin.[59] What I wish to emphasize here is the universal belief in a δαιμόνιον as the immediate cause of temptation and sin. This belief, so ridiculed in modern times—doubtless because of the abuses it occasioned—sustained morals: As long as you do not look for a rational explanation, everything stands firm. There is not a *why* but a *who*, a demon or a spirit inciting Man to evil or to good. When the δαιμόνιον and the πνεῦμα disappear, we must explain sin by natural, even rational, causes and this amounts to explaining it away. Sin thereby becomes rational, even reasonable; at most it is an error.

But the problem does not stop here. In fact it begins with the question 'why?' It is facile to say that as long as you ask for an ulterior reason, you have not yet reached bedrock. The problem arises when we realize that once the question is posed, once the doubt appears, it is impossible *not* to ask the question; and afterwards it is impossible to ask it in any other way. The moment I ask why, I cannot ask otherwise. Either I do not ask at all and this is the myth and the state of innocence; or I ask and the question itself starts to demythicize and destroy morals. The tragedy of the *status deviationis* is that I cannot *not* ask why: reflective consciousness kills moral conscience, destroys not only its spontaneity, but also its irreducibility. In this case, moral consciousness is no longer ultimate, no longer a final instance. It merely manipulates the reasons that my rational mind supplies. Adam might not have been in this state, but we are. Nostalgia for a lost paradise is neither paradise nor redemption.

Today this dilemma is felt in all its acuity. If we do not demythicize, obedience—to stay with the example already given— becomes blind, the corresponding human attitude becomes fanatical and the resulting situation uncritical and untenable. Who tells me if it is God or Satan speaking? Yahweh or the Serpent? If I must decide, then I am the final court of appeal, the definitive judge between God and the devil. If we do not demythicize, anyone could command anything, and provided the appearances, at least, do not arouse suspicion, I will obey indiscriminately. We must not forget that the first question, therefore the first doubt, in the Bible is really the Serpent's.[60] Yet if we do not ask questions, we are not human. Man is a being who questions, and questions himself. And it is precisely here that most of the human traditions affirm that the existential condition of humanity is the *status deviationis* or *naturae lapsae,* understood not as a mere superficial blemish but as a wound that pierces to the deepest level of our being. The most primordial question—who am I?—is conditioned not only in its answer, but already in the very question, by the fallen existential situation of Man, by the *I* who questions himself.

We may not feel the need to demythicize, but the moment that somebody asks us, like the Serpent asked Adam, why we obey, we are no longer free to brush aside the question and must, instead, try to justify our decision—nay, our very freedom. On the other hand, if we demythicize obedience, we destroy it completely; obedience as such disappears. In demythicizing, we either discover the reason, the underlying why, or we do not. But in either instance we no longer obey.

In the first case, either this *why* we find is convincing or it is not. (Convincing means that I find a reason to obey.) If it convinces, I no longer *obey* a command, rather I follow my reason, my own criterion. I 'obey' because I have discovered, beyond the commandment itself, that I must do what is commanded: If there were no one commanding it, I *would obey*, i.e., I would do it anyway. This attitude typifies the 19th century. Religion—identified with morals—was considered good for people, particularly for the illiterates, who needed an authority to direct them. As for the *illuminati*, the *Aufgeklärter*, they needed neither religion nor morals outside of themselves.[61] This is also the most common Vedāntic attitude: he who has 'realized' the *ātman*, the αὐτός, is beyond every commandment and all morals.[62] He who has had the intuition of Reality is (has become) this Reality and there is no higher instance whom or which he must obey.[63] Authority is necessary only for those who have not yet come into their own. *Ipsi sibi sunt lex*.[64] The extremes meet!

If, on the contrary, the reason you have found is not convincing, then *a fortiori*, you do not obey. You discover at once the motive for the commandment and its weakness. We may suppose that Adam had found the reason God had forbidden eating the fruit in the motive suggested by the Serpent: divine jealousy, fear of rivals, the desire to keep for himself alone the privilege of knowing good and evil.[65] So Adam could have thought he was not obliged to obey; instead he might have felt a 'moral' obligation to risk the threat of death[66] and to challenge the right of God.

We could no doubt admit the possibility of 'obedience' in spite of everything, but then we either act contrary to our own conscience, which would be more immoral than flat disobedience (since we go along with the commandment out of calculation, fear, sloth, pragmatism, etc.—but we can no longer call this obedience); or despite all we remain tied to a myth superior to all 'reasons', which means we have not seriously demythicized it.

If we do not successfully demythicize, i.e., if we cannot disengage the *why*, the foundation grounding a commandment, we can indeed continue to believe 'mythically' that there is a hidden foundation that cannot be unveiled. By giving credence to this unknown factor, we only seem to obey when in reality we have already decided in its favor and trust blindly in its existence and power. Is this not perhaps the most common 'obedience'? Or we can believe that there is no *why*, no reason behind the commandment, and then we no longer obey, since the very fact of trying to demythicize means we have deemed this demythicization necessary in order to justify our obedience. But in this case you cannot obey; even if you want to, you cannot regain lost innocence, you cannot retrace your path and begin again as if you had not already taken a step (which faltered) in order to find reasons for obeying. Here is the real place for the current problem of serious atheism.

The dilemma is agonizing. If we do not demythicize morals, they become cancerous, invading everywhere, paralyzing everything with regulations, taboos and irrationality. Most moral laws no longer 'speak' to us, they are no longer self-asserting for us. Today we cannot dispense with finding—or rather searching for—a foundation for morals. If we demythicize morals, they can only disappear as morals, as the definitive criterion of conduct: There remains only a static rationality, which lacks any authority in which a dynamic duty might take root.

c. Remythicizing Morals

Is there a way out of this impasse? It is impossible to give here a solution that is thoroughly adequate to the problem. I shall limit myself to emphasizing the mythical morphology of morality, and to suggesting that the only way to provisionally sustain morals is through their possible remythicization.

This cannot be an artificial, or even a conscious and pragmatic, remythicizing. My only concern is simply to state the existence of a law and explain its importance.

I have spoken elsewhere of *Ummythologisierung*.[67] Remythicizing morals would be a case in point: It is clearly not a salvage job with more or less conscious, deliberate and artificial grappling hooks, but a spontaneous and natural process that unfolds before our very eyes.[68] Morals, like icebergs, are not only unconscious and hidden for nine-tenths of their 'substance', but they also sail and travel about, they move towards seas still untouched by reflection, by reflective consciousness. Is moral conscience just an ersatz for consciousness, so that when knowledge appears, morals disappear altogether? Are the two incompatible so that the one takes the other's place?

There is a kind of indeterminancy here, like the relation Heisenberg proposed between two conjugated variables in physics, between these two types of awareness, the reflexive and the moral. When knowledge waxes, morals wane, and vice versa. But just as in physics, the two orders are linked, conjugated; no dimension of pure knowledge exists, nor one of blind morality. Morals without knowledge amount to fanaticism and slavery, just as knowledge that tries to penetrate everywhere and everything kills Man and destroys life. Consequently an idealism that identifies being with knowledge is bound to eliminate morals, and any moral organization (any church for example) is always inclined to view the growth of 'reflexivity' with suspicion.

We have already noted that a morality that questions itself ceases to be moral. When I ask myself why I must love my parents or what reason obliges me always to be truthful, my filial love and sincerity begin to waver.

We do not question the moral values we accept. And this is 'why' we accept them, because we find them ultimate and thus without any further 'why'. Just so, in today's world there are certain social values we do not discuss: justice, democracy, communal well-being, loyalty to one's own country and even national integrity, particularly in the case of young nations. These values are rooted in humanity's *collective consciousness*.[69] India, for example, simply will not discuss the problem of Kashmir on neutral grounds without a preconceived solution. England will hardly acknowledge that a referendum could resolve the status of the monarchy. Spain flatly refuses to admit that its religious unity can be questioned. Similarly, the United States would scarcely accept a discussion of its right to be 'the most powerful nation'. Even the speculative sciences admit some principles—postulates—that one neither proves nor disputes. Should the need arise, one has recourse to another science, or to philosophy, or to the evidence, or to pragmatism, to justify the hypothesis upon which a science is founded. The example of mathematics is classic.

The traditional answer stands if we accept all its presuppositions: The moral order is founded on the will of God or nature of things, disclosed through Revelation or Reason, transmitted by the Church or culture, etc. Nevertheless, between the commandment, which is an absolute, general order—'you shall not kill', for example—and my concrete situation, there is enough distance for any particular instance to be 'picked off' by all the 'sharp-shooters' imaginable, from 'philosophical' reason or from any of the human 'sciences', psychology in particular. So the problem remains.

Significantly, when we lived morals as we live myth, that is, submerged in it without 'critical' distance; when we lived on the level of 'mythical' morality (modern Man would say), we would consider the gravity of a sin as a function of the amount of will involved in it, and thus with regards to reason as well. An act of passion was not traditionally as reprehensible as one executed with premeditation in cold blood. The seriousness of a sin was directly proportional to the reason and will involved in it. Today it is almost the opposite. If you can succeed in proving the rationality and intentional character of acts otherwise considered to be 'contrary' to accepted morality, society will probably excuse them. We are thinking here not only of the Vanderput case, nor only of abortion or conscientious objection to war, but also of so-called 'immoral' sexual relations between consenting adults, of lies uttered 'for the good of the cause', etc. It seems that if one can explain one's own actions and especially justify them rationally, the evil is eliminated. Rational explanation amounts to moral justification. But for what can we *not* find some explanation, especially when it is a question of justifying ourselves?

Where does this process lead? Is it a stage in evolution?[70] Is it the *kali yuga*, the age of original sin?[71] Or is it the entire human *kalpa*?[72] But is Man himself not just a strand in the web of space and time that unites and diversifies all creation? These are questions we can only mention here, keeping in mind how far they are from 'morals' and how close to myth.

The famous, albeit noncanonical, text of Saint Luke,[73] which precedes the liberating formula of Christ—that the Son of Man is also the master of the Sabbath[74]—seems to approve this line of thinking. Moreover it is corroborated by Saint Paul's audacious words: "Blessed is he who does not discern himself in what he experiences;"[75] blessed the Man who acts with a direct and non-reflexive attitude, so that there is no doubt about what he ought to do.[76] Luke's text reads: "On the same day, seeing one working on the sabbath, he said unto him: Man, if indeed thou knowst what thou doest, thou art blessed: but if thou knowst not, thou art cursed, and a transgressor of the law."[77] Christ then cited the example of David eating the shewbread, which only the priests were allowed to eat.[78] Must we conclude that provided you know what you are doing, you are free to do anything? I think not. The text cannot be interpreted in such a purely anarchist fashion. First of all, you must really know what you are doing.[79] Did this same Christ not ask his Father to forgive his executioners, "for they know not what they do"?[80] The text means that if you *know,* you are conditioned by that knowing. But true knowledge is always liberating.[81] Only if you know and do not act do you sin. You cannot *know* an error, but you can ignore a truth or esteem an action good when in fact it is not, if you know neither the Father nor the Christ.[82] What is this liberating knowledge?[83] According to Saint Paul, who based himself on the Gospel,[84] this knowledge is faith.[85] It is not rational knowledge, without however being unreasonable.[86]

Might we hazard a paraphrase of the first beatitude, the first and dominant note of the entire Sermon on the Mount?[87] "Blessed are the poor in Spirit!" —those who have a real, and thus spiritual, poverty; who do not possess their spirit; who do not own themselves; who are unconscious of their value and grandeur (which is no sooner known than lost). Blessed are those who are un-self-conscious, those born to Life, but who do not know how to handle that very life other than by living it. Blessed are those who have reached the *docta ignorantia*, those who pray and do not know it, those who do good and even on judgment day will avow they never knew it,[88] because their right hand was unaware of what their left hand was doing.[89] Blessed those who have this faith that moves mountains[90] and that saves.[91] Blessed those who have lost their life.[92] Blessed those who sing to the Lord a song[93] so new that it excludes all reflexion, for were attention given to it, the praise would no longer be virginal and would slide into flattery or even superstition. Our hours of psalmody do not 'touch' God or bring him anything except when prayed in the Spirit to the Father through the Son, when the Man of prayer is borne up and carried away by it—by prayer that gives God himself to God. Now the authentic awareness of this act cannot be self-conscious, since the αὐτός is no longer our *ego* but the Spirit;[94] our ego can only disrupt the intra-trinitarian symphony to which we are called and in which we share, provided we remain *ontically* silent.[95] True apophatism is never reflexive; the same holds for every pure affirmation.[96] "Blessed are those who have reached infinite ignorance."[97]

And now the question: How can we have this faith that frees us even from the Law?[98] How can we have this awareness of faith that does not destroy morals, that is neither blind knowledge nor fanatical adherence, nor simply a logical conclusion or a rational conviction, which would kill both the freedom and the 'voluntarity' of the act of faith?

Here again we refer to the case of obedience. If obedience is sheer rationality, it is not obedience. If obedience is sheer irrationality, it is also not obedience. I obey not because I see the rationale of the commandment, nor because I do not see it (following the line of irrationality), but because I *see* I must obey. Faith is this *vision*. It is ultimate and irreducible, without either ulterior motives or extrinsic reasons for believing (credibility and 'credendity' are very different things).

Here we are at the antipodes of fideism, which amounts to a real assault on the rights of reason. But we are equally far from all so-called naturalism, which claims to base morals on reason or on nature.[99] "Whatever does not proceed from faith is sin."[100]

Perhaps somebody will object that my argument only shifts the problem. It could be that I have unloaded it on the question of faith, but I am convinced that I have contributed to centering the problem. Must we remythicize or demythicize faith? Is there perhaps a third awareness, the awareness of faith? Has faith something to do with myth? Following chapters will take up that problem again.

Notes

1. Cf. as an introduction to this problematic the volumes: *Il Problema della Demitizzazione* (1961). *Demitizzazione e imagine* (1962), *Ermeneutica e tradizione* (1963), *Tecnica e casistica* (1964), the Proceedings of the Colloquia organized by the Istituto di studi filosofici (Roma) under the direction of E. Castelli (Padova: Cedam); and the collection, *Kerygma und Mythos* (Hamburg: Reich, 1963, 1964, 1967), Vol. VI, 1, 2, and 3.

2. Cf. merely as a reminder: M.D. Chenu, *La théologie au douzième siècle* (Paris: Vrin, 1966); H. de Lubac, *Exégèse médiévale; les quatre sens de l'Ecriture* (Paris: Aubier, 1959 sq.), 4 vols.

3. Cf. 1 Kg. 8:12; Ps. 17:12 (18:11), 97:2; Sir. 24:4; etc. Cf. *etiam,* Dionys. Aerop.. *Epist.,* 3; Maximus Conf., *Ambigua* (P. G., 91, 1048) and SU I, 3. Cf. SB VI, 1, 1, 2: "The Gods love the obscure, the mysterious [lit. the invisible, the unmanifest: *paroksa*]", or Heraclitus: φύσις κρύπτεσθαι φιλεῖ—"nature loves to hide itself" (περὶ φύσεως, *Fragm.* 42).

4. Cf. Jn. 1:5.

5. "Creatura est tenebra in quantum est ex nihilo." D. Thom., *De veritate,* q. 18, a. 2 ad 5.

6. Cf. the beautiful and suggestive expression of the RV I, 164, 47: *kṛṣṇam niyānam*, "the Path is dark" (cf. Kṛṣṇa, the God) (V. S. Agrawala): "Dark is the descent" (Griffith). Agrawala also translates it: "Dark is the Source", *Vision in Long Darkness* (Varanasi: Bhargava Bhusan Press, 1963), p. 185. According to the so-called hymn of creation, the *nāsadīya sūkta*, in the beginning there were two kinds of darkness: "Darkness was there, all wrapped around by darkness" (RV X, 129, 3). The first darkness is the Creator himself (*svayambhū*, the primordial principle, masculine) which envelops (the theme of incest appears) creation (*parameṣthi*, the feminine principle, emanation from the Creator).

7. Cf. Gen. 1:2-5, etc. Each era has had its own theology of light; even today we have begun slowly to elaborate our own.

8. Cf. R. Panikkar, *Le Mystère du culte dans l'hindouisme et le christianisme* (Paris: Cerf, 1970), pp. 177-182.

9. Cf. the works of O. W. Otto, K. Kerényi and M. Eliade, etc. on this subject.

10. Apropos of this, we could cite a good number of manuals of Theology and Scripture. The still-current discussion on the 'nature' of Adam's sin (pride, covetousness, disobedience, etc.) shows that we are far from having gone beyond the moralistic stage.

11. Even up to our own times, people still assert that Jesus Christ spoke in parables in order to 'adapt' himself to the 'uncouth and primitive' character of his listeners. Obviously, he ought to have spoken in scholastic or Marxist categories!

12. Gen. 4:17: "Cain cognovit uxorem suam".

13. We know that the strictest endogamy (marriage between brother and sister) in an ancient civilization such as Iran was encouraged by religion, not only for the royal families (as in Ptolemaic Egypt), but for everyone. "La théologie justifie, bien plus encourage cette pratique par toute une argumentation de caractère mythologique: Ahura Mazdah a pour épouse sa fille Spenta Aramati; Gayomart, le premier homme, issue de la terre, féconde sa mère, et le couple qui naît d'eux réalise le premier mariage entre frère et soeur, qui donne naissance à l'humanité tout entière." J.P. de Menasce, 'Le monde moral iranien', *Les morales non-chrétiennes*, Journées 'Ethnologie et Chrétienté' (Paris: Monde, 1954), p. 49.

14. We find a brief reference to incest in RV X, 162, 5. Incest between a brother and sister (Yama and Yamī) with the names of Yima and Yimak (Yimeh) is also found in the Avesta: the myth is rooted in a very ancient Indo-Iranian tradition (without doubt anterior to Manu, considered to be the first man). For the second kind of myth, cf. note 23. Cf. chapter 4 for the further problematic.

15. Cf. the recent work on this subject, written to defend Hinduism against the accusation of an 'absence of ethical sense': U.C. Pandey, 'Prajāpati and his Daughter', *Bhāratī,* Bulletin of the College of Indology—B.H.U., VIII, 1 (Varanasi, 1964/1965), 95-102. The young author sees here "a myth directly concerned with ritual performance or the natural phenomena of sun and dawn" (p. 102).

16. Cf. the traditional efforts to show that the 'wise virgins' were not selfish, that the owner of the vineyard was not unjust, that the servant who buried the talent acted improperly, that the man who lacked a marriage garment was wrong, etc.

17. Gen. 27:1 sq.

18. The text reads: "Jacob autem quod matre fecit auctore, ut patrem fallere videretur, si diligenter et fideliter attendatur, non est mendacium, sed mysterium. Quae si mendacia dixerimus, omnes etiam parabolae ac figurae significandarum quarumcumque rerum, quae non ad proprietatem accipiende sunt, sed in eis aliud ex alio est intelligendum, dicentur esse mendacia: quod absit omnino." (*Contra mendacium*, X, 24).

19. It is this that R. Garrigou-Lagrange seeks—albeit only in a single direction—in his fine book, *Le sens du mystère et le clair-obscur intellectuel* (Paris: Desclée, 1934).

20. His famous sentence concerning time: "What then is time? If nobody asks me, I know; if I want to explain it to someone who asks, I don't know" (*Conf.* XI, 14). Cf. KenU II, 2-3, chosen as the motto of this book.

21. We can compare reason's 'thirst' to decipher everything with the sobriety characteristic of canonical writings (so much so that this very

sobriety is almost a decisive criterion for distinguishing canonical from apocryphal texts). Myth is more hidden and implied than manifest and expressed. Wanting to describe the 'hidden life' of Jesus Christ, for example, or regretting it was never written amounts to destroying it.

22. Cf. Lk. 9:62.

23. For incest between God (Prajāpati, etc.) and his daughter (Uṣas—dawn, sky—etc.), cf. RV I, 71, 5; I, 164, 33; III, 31, 1; VI, 17, 3 (ambiguous); VI, 12, 4; X, 61, 5 sq.; AV VIII, 6, 7; TMB VIII, 2, 10; AB III, 33; SB I, 7, 4, 1 sq.; II, 1, 2, 8-10; JaimB III, 2, 61 sq.; TB II, 3, 10 sq.; BU I, 4, 3-4. Cf. also chapter 4. In the Purāṇas as well we find the same motif with more graphic and very often cruder details (cf. U.C. Pandey, op. cit.), vgr. Matsya Purāṇa III, 32 sq. (Brahmā and Śatarūpā, Sāvitrī, Sarasvatī, Gāyatrī, Brāhmaṇī); BhagP III, 12, 28 sq. (Prajāpati and Vāc, the Word!); ViṣṇuP I, 7, 6 sq. (Manu and Śatarūpā); Garuḍa Purāṇa V, 19; Vāyu Purāṇa III, 168; MarkP L, 13; Padma Purāṇa; etc.

24. Here we can only sum up briefly that we consider per longum et latum in a forthcoming book on the problem of creation.

25. "He desired a second" (sa dvitīyam aicchat), BU I, 4, 3. He, the "One without second" (ekam evādvitīyam, CU VI, 2, 1). Before the original sin of the creature, there was an originating sin on the part of the Creator, creation being this projection of a not-(yet)-being-(God), hence at one remove from God. God's sin is creation. And, in creating, he could only create the not-God, a distance, a deformation, a degradation, i.e., commit a sin. In God this sin is not real, since he has not created, but he creates in an eternal act by which the distance is (already) surpassed because creation is (already) 'achieved', that is, it is no longer simple 'creature'. This sin becomes 'visible' only in time and, further, it becomes real only when the creature stops midway, when it never becomes God (cf. chapter 4 and its note 43). Cf. the felix culpa mentioned in the Christian liturgy of Easter night. Cf. the famous etiam peccata of Saint Augustine and the two controversial articles of Saint Thomas, Sum. Theol. III, q. 1, aa. 1 and 2.

26. Cf. BU I, 4, 1 (puruṣa).

27. Cf. BU I, 4, 2.

28. This is not the place to establish comparisons, but we might recall that this myth is universal and Christian as well. Maximus the Confessor says, for example, that the resurrected Christ is no longer male or female since in his paradigmatic reintegration he unified the sexes (De divisionibus naturae, II, 4; II, 8, 12, 14). Cf. vgr. M. Eliade, Méphistophélès et l'androgyne (Paris: Gallimard, 1962), pp. 128 sq.

29. Cf. Act. 3:21 and Eph. 1:10.

30. This theme constitutes the leitmotif of the relationship between Yahweh and Israel. Cf. L. Bouyer, La Bible et l'Evangile (Paris: Cerf, 1953).

31. Jn. 3:16.

32. Cf.: "The Holy Spirit will come upon you (ἐπελεύσεται ἐπὶ σέ) and the power of the Most High will over shadow you" (καὶ δύναμις ὑψίστου ἐπισκιάσει σοι) Lk. 1:35. To avoid any possible misunderstanding (docetic, allegorical), the angel had previously announced: "ecce concipies in utero et paries filium." Cf. *etiam* Prov. 8:31.

33. Cf. the central idea of Christianity: "Factus est Deus homo, ut homo fieret Deus." "God became Man in order that Man might become God", Augustine, *Sermo* 128 (P. L., 39, 1997) and also *Sermo de nativitate*, 4 and 12 (P.L., 38, 999 and 1016); or again: "Verbum Dei . . . qui propter immensam suam dilectionem factus est quod sumus nos, uti nos perficeret esse quod est ipse", Irenaeus, *Adv. haeres.*, V, praef. (P.G., 7, 1120) *aut etiam*, III, 18, 1 (P.G., 7, 932): "Ostendimus enim, quia non tunc coepit Filius Dei, existens semper apud Patrem; sed quando incarnatus est, et homo factus, longam hominum expositionem in seipso recapitulavit, in compendio nobis salutem praestans, ut quod perdideramus in Adam, id est secundum imaginem et similitudinem esse Dei, hoc in Christo Jesu reciperemus" (. . . So that what we had lost in Adam, that is, to be according to the image and likeness of God, that, we would recover in Christ Jesus); again: III, 18, 7 (P.G., 7, 937): "Oportuerat enim mediatorem Dei et hominum, per suam ad utrosque domesticitatem, in amicitiam et concordiam utrosque reducere, ut facere, ut et Deus assumeret hominem, et homo so dederet Deo. Qua enim participatione filiorum adoptionis ejus participes esse possemus, nisi per Filium eam, quae est ad ipsum, recepissemus ab eo communionem; nisi Verbum ejus communicasset nobis, caro factum?"; cf. other texts *apud* J. Lemarié, *La manifestation du Seigneur* (Paris: Cerf, 1957), pp. 145-160.

34. Cf. another typical example, illustrating both an ancient and a modern attitude: "When Kumārila is hard pressed by his opponents about the immoralities of his gods, he answers with all the freedom of a comparative mythologist: It is fabled that Prajāpati, the Lord of Creation, did violence to his daughter. But what does it mean? Prajāpati, the Lord of Creation, is a name of the sun; and he is called so, because he protects all creatures. [Nevertheless we might note that the sun has never been called the father of the dawn (Uṣas), even though often identified with Agni (SB VI, 2, 1, 23; VI, 5, 3, 7 and 9; VI, 8, 1, 4) and Savitr (SB XII, 3, 5, 1; PañcB XVI, 5, 17); cf. U. C. Pandey, *op. cit.*, p. 98.] His daughter Uṣas is the dawn. And when it is said that he was in love with her, this only means that, at sunrise, the sun runs after the dawn, the dawn being at the same time called the daughter of the sun, because she rises when he approaches", F. Max Müller, *History of Ancient Sanskrit Literature* (London: Williams and Norgate, 1859), pp. 529-530. It is symptomatic that this entire passage is quoted in the English translation of the Ṛg Veda by R.T.H. Griffith, *The Hymns of the*

Rig Veda (Varanasi: The Chowkhamba Sanskrit Series Office, 1926), vol. II, 611.

35. Despite the human moral doubts so clearly expressed in the magnificent dialogue between Yama and Yamī (cf. verses 4-5 and 12).

36. 'Le secret de l'être humain est lié au secret de l'androgyne'. N. Berdiaev, *Le sens de la création* (Paris: Desclée, 1955), p. 261.

37. According to the translation of L. Renou, *Hymnes spéculatifs du Véda* (Paris: Gallimard, 1956), pp. 55 sq., Yama resists and there is no 'fall'. According to L. von Schröder, *Mysterium und Mimus im Rig Veda* (Leipzig: H. Haessel, 1908), pp. 275-303, incest was perpetrated, and he supports this thesis with parallel myths in the R̥g Veda itself. "Das Dialoglied von Yama and Yamī ist nur der erste Akt eines grösseren kultlichen Dramas, das nach Analogie des Agastyadramas auf einen Generationsritus, resp. phallischen Fruchtbarkeitszauber in grossem Stil hinauslief. Das erste Menschenpaar vereignigte sich zu einer rituellen Zeugung, und unermessliche Fruchbarkeit musste die Folge sien" (291). A.A. Macdonell, *The Vedic Mythology* (Varanasi: Indological Book House, 1963), p. 173 (reprint of the original, Strassburg: Trübner, 1897), also favors this interpretation.

38. Cf. J. Muir, *Original Sanskrit Texts* (Amsterdam: Oriental Press, 1967), vol. V, 288 sq.

39. RV X, 10.7.

40. RV X, 10, 12.

41. Cf. RV X, 14, 1 sq., etc.

42. Night, desired in the dialogue of Yama and Yamī in order to commit incest (RV X, 10, 9) and likewise in MaitS I, 5, 1 sq. (which presents a somewhat 'romanticized' version of the myth) is considered the creation of the Gods.

43. It is worthwhile to quote the entire passage in the fine translation of Schröder (Leipzig, 1881-86, p. 81 and *Mysterium*, pp. 277-278): "Yama starb. Die Götter suchten der Yamī den Yama auszureden. Wenn sie sie fragten, dann sagte sie: 'Heute ist er gestorben!'—Da sprachen sie: 'Fühwahr, so vergisst diese ihn nicht. Lasst uns die Nacht schaffen!' Es gab nämlich damals nur den Tag, (noch) nicht die Nacht. Die Götter schufen die Nacht. Da wurde ein morgender Tag. Darauf vergass sie ihn. Darum sagt man: Tag und Nacht lassen das Leid vergessen!" (MaitS I, 5, 12). Cf. the same idea in the Christian liturgy:

Aeterne rerum Conditor,
Noctem diemque qui regis,
Et temporum das tempora,
Ut alleves fastidium.
     Hym. dom. ad Laudes (Brev. Rom.)

44. For example, it is well known that for C.G. Jung, the archetype of incest represents the desire to unite with our true, hidden self, our authentic essence, and provides the path toward 'individuation'. The fact

that Yama and Yamī are twins (RV X, 10, 5) might lead one to consider Yamī as the true soul of man, his *alter ego*. Cf. vgr. from last century, H.E. Meyer, *Indogermanische Mythen,* I, 299, 232 (apud Macdonnell, *op. cit.*, p. 173).

45. No need to recall that all Christian scholasticism without exception maintains there is an imitation of God in any action. "Vestigium trinitatis invenitur in unaquaque creature . . .", says Augustine, *De Trinitate*, VI, 10, fin., and D. Thomas specifies: "in creaturis omnibus . . . per modum vestigii", *Sum. Theol.* I, q. 45, a. 7; "assimilare ad Deum est ultimus omnium finis", *C. Gentes*, III, 20 (2009). Cf. for a more systematic study, R. Panikkar, *El concepto de naturaleza* (Madrid: C.S.I.C., 1972, 2nd edition), pp. 238 sq.

46. ἡ πίστις ἐξ ἀκοῆς: Rom. 10:17.

47. Cf. R. Panikkar, 'Una meditazione teologica sulle tecniche di communicazione', *Studi cattolici,* VII, 37 (1963), 3-7. Christ is ἐικὼν as well as λόγος.

48. Cf. vgr. M. Eliade, *Mythes, rêves et mystères* (Paris: Gallimard, 1957). (English translation: *Myths, Dreams and Mysteries*. New York: Harper and Row, 1960).

49. Cf. Gen. 2:17.

50. Cf. Gen. 3:22-24.

51. The old thesis that original sin marks "the emergence of man into full consciousness" has been brilliantly revived in our time by the late R.C. Zaehner, inspired by Teilhard de Chardin. Cf. *The Convergent Spirit* (London: Routledge & Kegan Paul, 1963), pp. 44 sq. (p. 61 for the quotation).

52. The two, opposite reactions to the encyclical of Paul VI, *Humanae vitae* (June 29, 1968) provide a striking example of this. Those who moralize the myth will discuss the right of the Pope to such pronouncements; those who demythicize morals will focus on the validity of the arguments (used in the encyclical).

53. Gen. 25:29 sq.

54. It is rather significant that this word simultaneously expresses the ultimate structure of a process or a reality and the command of authority.

55. *Kritik der reinen Vernunft*, prologue to the second edition (1787) (edition Leipzig: Reclam, 1924), p. 32.

56. Gen. 3:7.

57. Gen. 3:10-11.

58. Cf. J. Daniélou, *Théologie de judéo-christianisme* (Tournai: Desclée, 1958), p. 413 sq. Cf. also, of course, the Platonic myth of the two horses (*Phaedrus*, 246b sq.), and the similar parable in KathU III, 3 sq.

59. Cf. the abundant documentation in J. Daniélou, *loc. cit.*

60. Gen. 3:1: "Now the serpent was more subtle than any other wild creature that the Lord God had made. He said to the woman, 'Did God

say, "You shall not eat of any tree of the garden?" ' " (NEB).

61. Cf. the well-known verse:
Wer Wissenschaft und Kunst besitzt, hat auch Religion,
wer jene beiden nicht besitzt, der habe Religion.
                    Goethe, *Zahmen Xenien*, 9.

62. Cf. vgr. TU II, 9, 2 quoted in note 81.

63. Cf. MundU III, 2, 9: "He, verily, who knows the Supreme Brahman becomes Brahman himself" *(sa yo ha vai tat paramam brahma veda brahmaiva bhavati)*.

64. Rom. 2:14.

65. Gen. 3:4-5.

66. Gen. 2:17.

67. Cf. R. Panikkar, 'Die Ummythologisierung in der Begegnung des Christentums mit dem Hinduismus', *Kerygma und Mythos* (Hamburg: Reich, 1963), vol. VI, no. 1, 211-235.

68. Cf. R. Panikkar, 'La demitologizzazione nell'incontro tra Christianesimo e Induismo', in *Il problema della Demitizzazione* cited above (note 1).

69. Cf. R. Panikkar, *Patriotismo y Cristiandad* (Madrid: Rialp, 1961), p. 37 sq.

70. Cf. the remarkable passage of Teilhard de Chardin: "Les éléments du Monde refusant de servir le Monde parce qu'ils pensent. Plus exactement encore, le Monde se refusant lui-même en s'apercevant par Réflexion. Voilà le danger. Ce qui, sous l'inquiétude moderne, se forme et grossit, ce n'est rien moins qu'une crise organique de l'Evolution." *Le phénomene humain* (Paris: Ed. du Seuil, 1955), p. 255.

71. The *kali yuga*, the fourth age of the world that supposedly began in 3102 B.C. and lasts 432,000 years, is the epoch of the cosmic decline and collapse.

72. Strictly speaking, a *kalpa* is only one day of Brahma, lasting 4,300 million years.

73. Lk. 6:4 add. according to code D (Cambridge).

74. Lk. 6:5.

75. Rom. 14:22: μακάριος ὁ μὴ κρίνων ἑαυτὸν ἐν ᾧ δοκιμάζει. A difficult text to translate, which the Vulgate renders: "Beatus qui non judicat semetipsum in eo quod probat"; the Bible de Jérusalem: "Heureux qui ne se juge pas coupable au moment même où il se décide"; the RSV: "Happy is he who has no reason to judge himself for what he approves", and the NEB: "Happy is the man who can make his decision with a clear conscience!"

76. We must remember that the context is that of an extremely serious problem, especially for the first Christians: participation in the rites and culture of the surrounding religions. In the same verse, moreover, Saint Paul adds: "The faith that you have, keep between yourself and God."

77. Even if, as most exegetes think, the text is not authentic, it is ancient. It could well express—in an ambivalent way perhaps—a profound lesson in the freedom of the spirit, a lesson that moreover follows from the whole attitude of Jesus (cf. *etiam* 2 Cor. 3:17).

78. Cf. 1 Sam. 21:1-6; Lev. 24:9.

79. Cf. Jas. 4:17: "Whoever knows what is right to do and fails to do it, for him it is sin" (OAB).

80. Lk. 23:34. Curiously enough this text is omitted in a good number of manuscripts: οὐ γὰρ οἴδασιν τί ποιοῦσιν.

81. Cf. the Upaniṣadic text:

Whence words recoil, together with the mind,
unable to reach it—whoso knows
that bliss of Brahman has no fear.

TU II, 4, 1 (cf. *etiam* II, 9, 1)

Or again: "He is not tormented at the thought: Have I done good, have I committed a sin? for he who knows is himself released from both. This is the teaching (*ity upaniṣat*)." TU II, 9, 2.

82. Jn. 16:2, 3.

83. Jn. 8:32: "Et veritas liberavit vos."

84. Cf. Jn. 17:3.

85. Cf. Rom. 3:22 sq.; etc.

86. The entire Gospel relates this 'super-understanding' of faith. An example at random: Having heard the parable of the pharisee and the publican (Lk. 18:9-14), what must we do? It destroys our innocence. If we abase ourselves *in order* to be raised, if we sit in the last place *in order* that our host might request us to go up higher (Lk. 14:10), if, knowing the last shall be first and the first last (Mt. 20:16; Lk. 13:30; Mk. 10:31), we consciously *choose* to be last, surely we will remain there, or at the very least we will not be justified. If one *considers* oneself first, if one believes himself justified, then the parable applies; likewise if one recognizes he is a sinner and deserves the lowest place. Reflexive consciousness hinders a moral existence. We must know, but unhappy the one who knows he knows. Cf. the same thrust in the Hindu, Buddhist, Confucian and Taoist traditions. Simplicity of heart, purity of eye (Mt. 6:22-23; Lk. 11:34-35) is an important, traditional Christian theme related to this topic. It is rather characteristic that the quoted ἁπλοῦς, translated in the Vulgate by 'simplex', in the modern translations is rendered (and indeed, not incorrectly) by 'sain' (Bible de Jerusalem), 'sano' (Nardoni), 'puro' (Instituto Biblico), 'sound' (NEB, OAB), 'clear' (Knox), 'gesund' (Tillmann, Rösch), etc. Cf. ἁπλότης as opposed to διψυχία in the early Christian tradition (cf. C. Edlund, *Das Auge der Einfalt*, Upsala, 1952), as synonymous with τέλειος (cf. J. Daniélou, *op. cit.*, pp. 418 sq.), and related to ἀκακία, innocence. Cf. the prayer without reflexive repetition, the προσευχή μονολόγιστος of the Patristics (vgr. I. Hausherr, *Noms du Christ et voies d'oraison*, Roma: Pont. Inst. Orient. Stud., 1960, pp. 250

sq.), etc. Cf. also: "Lucifer, because he looked upon himself and saw his own beauty, leapt into pride and from being an angel he became a loathsome devil. Of Eve, . . . the very beginning of her sin, its entry was through her eyes. And the woman *saw* that the tree was good to eat. . . ." [Gen. 3:6] *The Ancrene Riwle,* II, translated by M.B. Salu (Notre Dame, Ind.: University of Notre Dame Press, 1956), pp. 22-23.

87. Mt. 5:3.

88. Mt. 25:37-39.

89. Cf. Mt. 6:3.

90. Cf. Mt. 17:20; 21:21; etc.

91. Cf. Lk. 7:50; 17:19; 18:42; etc.

92. Cf. Mk. 8:35; Lk. 9:24; 17:33; Mt. 10:39; 16:25; Jn. 12:25; etc.

93. Cf. Ps. 40:3: "He [the Lord] put a new song in my mouth, a song of praise to our God." Also Ps. 144:9; 149:1; Is. 42:10; Rev. 5:9; 14:3; etc.

94. Cf. Rom. 8:15, 26-27; Gal. 4:6; etc.

95. A scriptural text of Hinduism which, in order to remain faithful to its message can only be lost, says "the *ātman* is silence", Śaṅkara, *Bhāṣya* III, 2, 17. Cf. as a counterpart Ignatius Antioq., *Epist. ad Magn.,* VIII, 2 (P.G., 5, 669): ὅς ἐστιν αὐτοῦ Λόγος ἀπὸ σιγῆς προελθών. . .("qui est Verbum eius a silentio progrediens . . .") The reading αἴδιος οὐκ i.e., ". . . Verbum eius aeternum non post silentium . . .", seems to be a mistake. Cf. M. J. Rouët de Journal, *Enchiridion patristicum* (Barcinone: Herder, 1969, 45) and G.W.H. Lampe, *A Patristic Greek Lexicon* (Oxford: Clarendon, 1961) sub σιγή both opt for the version I have given. God is Silence; his Word, his Son, his Expression and Image is no longer he but the *logos*. "Tibi silet laus", translates Saint Jerome, *Ps.* 65:2 (P.L., 28 1174) ("date gloriam laudi eius", silence is truly the creature's praise of the Creator, *Ps.* 66:2 (P.L., 28, 1175)). Augustine writes: "Sileant . . . et ipsa sibi anima sileat", *Confes.,* IX, 10, 25. Mary, "religiosum silentium Virginis . . . circa secretum Dei" (Rupert., *In Cantica,* I [P.L., 168, 844]), is the "Verbi silentis muta mater", Santeuil, *Hymne pour la Purification, apud* H. de Lubac, *Méditation sur l'Eglise* (Paris: Aubier, 3rd edition, 1954), p. 298.

96. Cf. several references that demand careful elaboration: Is. 45:15; Wis. 18:14-15; Col. 3:3; BG II, 25 ("Unmanifest, unthinkable, immutable is it called . . ." Zaehner trans.); XIII, 12; BU II, 3, 6; KenU I, 4; TU II, 9; MandU 7; etc.

97. Evagrius Ponticus, III *Centuria,* 88. Cf. KenU II, 2-3.

98. Cf. practically the entire Epistle to the Romans.

99. The Christian commandment is not to live *secundum rationem* or *secundum naturam,* but *secundum te.* Cf. the prayer of the Eighth Sunday after Pentecost: ". . . ut qui sine te esse non possumus, secundum te vivere valeamus."

100. Rom. 14:23.

IV.
The Myth of Prajāpati.
The Originating Fault or
Creative Immolation

Ἀρκετὸν τῇ ἡμέρᾳ ἡ κακία αὐτῆς

Sufficient for the day is the
evil thereof.
Mt. 6:34

1. THE PROBLEM

a. The Universal Fact of Pain

There is in the world an incontestable element of suffering. There is also evil; we can more or less affect indifference to it, call it real or imaginary, but we can scarcely deny it exists.

Let us straightaway state the traditional setting: The problem of pain stems from evil and suffering.[1] Pain seems to be always the consequence of evil and, at the same time, the first step in overcoming it. An evil without pain would remain hopelessly ever evil. Pain (ποινή, *poena*) is the ransom destined to redeem a murder. Starting from here it comes to mean: compensation, reparation and vengeance on the one hand; punishment, chastisement, penalty on the other.[2]

The word 'pain' originally presented this significant ambivalence; from the one side it meant suffering, sorrow, and from the other, chastisement, punishment.[3] In English this second sense has somewhat eroded over the years, but its roots are clear. In Sanskrit, for example, *śikṣaṇam* means educate, form, elevate, and also punish, make suffer, whip.

The bond uniting these two meanings is the notion that by the inflicted pain (punishment), one eliminates the pain (suffering) one has merited, that *by accepting the penalty, one effaces the pain*. The (accepted) penalty effaces the (merited) pain, because pain itself is a penalty.

Vicarious atonement, traditional penal laws, pardon obtained by repentance, perfection attained by asceticism, the suffering of Christ, etc., offer us some examples of the same problematic (although of very different value): Pain is redemptive; suffering has a positive, purifying function in human life.[4]

Since there is no pain without suffering, the implication is grave: Suffering seems to be the ultimate structure of the world, because it is through this suffering that the afflicted order seems to be restored.

This is *the myth of pain*. We suffer and we find in this suffering a value that transcends anything that a physical and psychic causality might propose. Each sin deserves its pain; the bond between sin and punishment is moral as well as ontological. The sin carries with it remorse, and at the same time a penalty, since an objective order of human or divine law has been broken. Such is the traditional position in most cultures and religions.[5] The traditional justification of hell, for example, is rooted in a similar rationale: A 'grievous' or 'mortal' sin merits an 'eternal' punishment. It would be divine injustice not to punish such a sin with a pain of the same order.

The ultimate issue in this problematic is this: There seems to be a defect, a sin, a taint in the cosmic order, in creation.[6] There must be something cutting very deep into Man and the World if perfection, destiny, joy, plenitude, divinization (small matter what name we prefer) can be attained solely on a path of suffering, by a way of the cross.[7]

b. The Awareness of Pain as Pain

We live the myth of pain fully when we do not question the fragile double sense of the word 'pain', that is, when we consider as self-evident the fact that pain-suffering and pain-punishment go together, with the effect of restoring order. It is a universal belief that misfortune is a consequence of sin and thus that pain-suffering is always pain-punishment and, so, pain-purification. This equation can still be found in Western countries in the popular conscience, education, penal laws, etc. We punish a child like we punish a criminal, or like the ascetic punishes himself: to repair a disorder, to pay a debt, to purify or correct oneself, to be worthy of pardon, to reconquer or acquire interior liberty, etc. It all rests on the myth of pain. We speak of appeasing a violated justice in order that a just vengeance may be obtained (we even speak of vindictive justice!). The guilty, we say, must pay their debt—but to whom? Further, we chastise them, so everyone affirms, in order to cure them, to correct them, restore them to new dignity in society, make them repudiate their affront to the established order, or so that their punishment might serve as example. A whole theology of redemption, of spiritual life and social order has been based on these presuppositions.

The essential question is not to know who has the right to inflict pain, but to understand *why* punishment exists at all. The first response, already a demythicized answer, speaks of the medicinal character of pain,[8] but clearly this is not satisfying. Experience alone shows, and psychology confirms, that pain has today largely lost its purifying value. Even if punishment still retained its medicinal character the question would not be resolved: One could yet ask *why* it is necessary to make someone suffer in order to purify him.

The problem looms large as soon as one begins to demythicize. The moment you ask why you must 'suffer' (for your neighbor, or due to a moral fault, or even without apparent reason), you no longer accept pain on its own; the purifying efficacy of pain shrinks in direct proportion to its demythicization. In short: *Pain without the myth loses its raison d'être* and becomes intolerable. The myth ceases to be effective as soon as you question pain as a purifying process. Without 'faith', no salvation; that is to say that once you cease to believe in the purifying function of pain, it loses its saving function.[9]

Here we are facing a universal problem: What is the meaning of suffering? Why do we suffer? The myth of the fall seeks only to explicate this cosmic scandal and at the same time safeguard the prestige of God. In the Indian tradition, the law of *karma* asserts the normality of suffering, since here pain is always 'consequence' and never 'original'; Buddhism likewise begins with the central fact of sorrow; the 'original sin' of the Bible claims only to explicate suffering and evil without blasphemy.

Until now the myth of pain has presented diverse modalities and provoked different reactions, but we have always respected the myth insofar as it is myth. Regarding suffering, for example, we seek to eliminate it (Buddhism) or deny it (Hinduism) or explain it (Judaism, Islam) or transfigure it (Christianity)—and we succeed to the extent that people believe the myth and live up to it. But now we demythicize even the myth of pain. What will come of this?

The majority of cosmogonic myths have, one way or another, tried to find a plausible answer to this anguishing human question. I do not wish to undertake such research here. I only want to present a myth of pain different from those current in cultures and religions that have grown up in the Mediterranean world. This may bring to light an important consideration for contemporary theology: namely, that faith is not necessarily bound to a particular religion. Faith is not *a* religion, but stands at the basis of *all* religion.[10]

I do not want here to Hinduize Christianity or to Christianize Hinduism. We are concerned with a human problem, felt and expressed by almost every religious tradition. I am convinced, in the first place, that this is preeminently a human problem that cannot be monopolized by any religion or philosophy, and in the second place, that a mutual fecundation between Hinduism and Christianity in the depths of myth is not only possible but imperative in our *kairos*. It will not do merely to compare doctrines, we must also reconcile myths. I should add further that in going beyond the classical Hindu interpretation, our hermeneutic is already a conscious attempt at symbiosis. But there is no need to burn our bridges and give as a synthesis what we offer only as a working hypothesis.

c. The Christian Answer, Original Sin

The answer that passes for the Christian response to the question of the origin of suffering, and that underlies the social order of the Western world, says that in the beginning God created the world, that the creation was good, and more particularly that God created Man in his own image and likeness.[11] Later, by at least a sin of disobedience, the first Man lost original innocence, became a sinner, was cut off from intercourse with God and punished, he and the entire human race that springs from

him.[12] This is the myth of the fall, the dogma of original sin. Man
falls, not God. We shall return to this point. It is hardly necessary
to recall that the myth of original sin is not originally Christian.
Yet the Christian fact, the fact of the Cross, is grafted into the
myth of original sin.

The myth of original sin exhibits two weak points. One concerns the origin of evil, which remains unexplained: How can
Man commit evil if he has been created 'good'? The other (our
focus here) is the problem of a God who must yield to the exigencies of justice: Man has sinned and God *must* punish him. God
can forgive Man's sin, but he cannot, apparently, spare Man's
pain. The myth of pain therefore seems superior to God.

Theology's response is familiar: God can avoid inflicting pain
but he does not want to, because pain is not malevolent but heal-
ing, medicinal.[13] Yet this same theology recognizes that God
could have 'invented' less bitter medicine. The myth of pain becomes the mystery of pain. The difficulty is patent: If God can
pardon sin and spare the pain, and he does not do so, his bounty
remains rather compromised.

2. THE MYTH OF PRAJĀPATI

The texts of Hindu Scripture are of dazzling richness and
extraordinary diversity; one can however discover a fundamental
intuition regarding the cosmogonic myth. But this root intuition
cannot be properly expressed in words, because it does not translate into *eidos*, into idea, except inadequately: 'Beyond' being
and nonbeing 'there is' a *this*, a *tad*, the *One*, *ekam*, which
'stands' at the source of everything.[14] It is here that we find the
myth of Prajāpati, the God par excellence,[15] the Father of creatures,[16] of all who are born (*jāta*).[17] He is the one who has procreative energy.[18] In the celebrated hymn to Hiraṇyagarbha, the
'golden germ' of Book X of the Ṛg Veda, Prajāpati is hailed as
Creator of heaven and earth, of the waters and of all that lives, the
one whose ordinance all the Gods recognize.[19] He is the Father of
the Gods,[20] the Unique One here from the beginning.[21] He is the
first to sacrifice.[22]

In all that follows we call 'God' the Supreme Principle,

brahman, Being considered as the Absolute, etc. These concepts doubtless have very different connotations, but since we cannot deal with everything at once, we call this Ultimate Reality God. For this study, it does not matter from which point of view we see it, or by what name we call it.

In the hymn mentioned, this Reality is designated by the interrogative pronoun *kah*, 'who?'[23] God is the *Who* underlying everything, and towards whom everything directs itself: action, thought, being, etc.

To better understand this myth, we might consider separately three moments: (a) solitude, (b) sacrifice and (c) integration.

a. Solitude

In the beginning there was nothing, not even nothingness; there was absolute vacuity.[24] "Neither being nor Non-being. There was not air nor yet sky beyond",[25] "there was no death then, nor yet deathlessness. Of night or day there was not any sign. The One breathed without breath, by its own impulse.[26] Other than that was nothing else at all."[27] "Darkness was there, all wrapped around by darkness."[28] Radical solitude is the primary symbol of the unity and transcendence of the Indescribable, its perfection as well as its simplicity, its original, primordial character.[29]

In a second moment, so to speak (clearly there can be no question of temporal or even ontological priority, which at this level would make no sense), "that which was hidden by the void, that One, emerging, stirring, through the power of Ardor, came to be".[30] The nonbeing wanted to be and there it was,[31] Prajāpati. It said: "That I may be!" and there it was, the Self (*ātman*) in the shape of a person (*puruṣavidhaḥ*).[32] The Self looks around and obviously can see nothing but itself. It thus becomes aware of itself, saying: "I am" (*so 'ham*).[33]

The One begins to be with itself and, discovering its own company, its shadow so to speak, breaks its total solitude. Solitude turns to isolation. The Self, conscious of this isolation, dreads.[34] Anxiety, the most pure anxiety of being, of being alone in the face of nothing, appears. It sees its own image and takes fright.[35] It has no joy in being alone, but is bored and disgusted.[36] It is on the way to losing innocence.[37]

Then reason overcomes dread: If there is nothing, there is nothing to fear, the Self thinks.[38] The irrationality of fear becomes plain. Self-reflection appears and innocence disappears. The Self, reflecting upon itself, loses its simple solitude. Finding itself naked so to speak, realizing it is alone, it desired a second.[39] The longing for a second became unbearable. It wanted to be many, it longed for procreation. It simply desired.[40]

Thus, still deep in that primordial night, it begins to go out of itself.[41] "The path is obscure."[42] Prajāpati desired a second and so set out on the way of Sacrifice, of alienation, of the Cross.

b. Sacrifice

Prajāpati desired a second.[43] He could have cried out, like the God of the Mordvines: "If I had a partner, I would make the world!"[44] But the God of Hinduism has no primal matter from which to create the universe.[45] He has no alternative but to sacrifice himself; the dismembering of Prajāpati is the primordial sacrifice by which everything has been made.[46] Creation then is a sacrifice,[47] a giving of oneself,[48] a creative immolation.[49] But there is no one to whom to offer the sacrifice, no one to receive it:[50] Prajāpati must be at once the high-priest,[51] the sacrifice (victim),[52] the one who receives the sacrifice[53] and even its result.[54] He divides himself into as many parts as are necessary to complete the creation. From the sacrifice offered in this total fashion,[55] everything goes forth: strophes and melodies, horses and every animal, the four human castes.[56] His head formed the sky, his chest the atmosphere, his waist the ocean, his feet the earth, the moon is born of his scruples; from his glance is born the sun, from his mouth Indra and Agni, from his breath is born the wind,[57] and so all the rest.[58] Even evil was created by him: "I have surely created evil, since, in creating them (the asuras, malevolent spirits), darkness as it were appeared."[59]

What moved Prajāpati to create? Himself, for an act of God can have neither antecedent cause nor final motivation; Prajāpati is sufficient unto himself. If he decides to sacrifice himself it is neither for someone—who does not exist—nor for something outside himself—which cannot exist either.[60] A single force leads Prajāpati to create: the desire for progeny, the need to multiply himself.[61] Here the texts speak of two mysterious factors that are like the immanent power of Reality and the intimate force that animates Prajāpati: *tapas* and *kāma*.

Whether we speak of the personalist tradition that symbolizes in Prajāpati the origin of all, or of the nonpersonal tradition for which the One comes forth from nothingness, from nonbeing, it is always through these two 'powers' that the creative process originates. It is *tapas*, primordial heat, ardor, initial fire, divine concentration, energy, the creative vitality that sets in motion the entire cosmos:

> Order (*ṛta*) and Truth (*satya*) are born of
> incandescent (*abhīddha*) Heat (*tapas*).
> From it is born Night.
> From it the Ocean and its waves.[62]

So, in the beginning, when other than 'the' One there was nothing whatsoever, when darkness covered darkness like the divine vitality hidden by its own attributes (*guṇa*),[63] the One wrapped in emptiness showed itself by the power of *tapas*.[64]

It is also through *tapas*, by concentrating his heat, his creative energy, that Prajāpati dismembers himself.[65]

But desire (*kāma*) was itself the original reaching out (desire), the first seed (*retas*) of Consciousness (*manas*).[66] And indeed, by searching themselves, the poets surely discover the bond of Being in nonbeing.[67] It is thus that *kāma*, desire or love appears. This love or desire cannot be a desire for something that does not exist. It is concentration on itself and in a certain sense it is connected to *tapas*: It penetrates itself until it implodes and so dismembers itself.

Tapas and *kāma* go together.[68] Love is the ardor that gives the power to create, the energy of *tapas* is actualized by the love that provokes it: "He desired: 'May I become many, may I engender.' He practiced *tapas*. Having practiced *tapas*, he created the whole world, such as it is."[69]

Here is the second moment, the immolation. In order for Being to be, it must immolate itself. Being is much more than a noun, it has the value of a verb, and a transitive verb at that. Even the divine being cannot live without giving itself, without loving, without sacrificing itself (*ad intra* as well as *ad extra*, a certain theology might add).

c. Integration

Prajāpati is dismembered, his body has given birth to all creatures.[70] He has sacrificed himself. But once the sacrifice is performed there is nothing left of him. The creation is such a self-immolation that after having created the world, Prajāpati lay exhausted, old, feeble in spirit; he felt 'emptied' and he feared death.[71] We should not forget that Prajāpati was both mortal and immortal,[72] that although he was mortal he emitted immortals.[73] He can die and he fears death. The price of creation, of a true creation, is death. But only if he immolates himself totally can Prajāpati effectively create. When he had emitted the beings, when he was finished and in pieces, the breath went out from the midst of his body and, when the breath was gone, the Gods left too.[74] In a modern parlance not altogether foreign to that time: God is dead from having created; he has immolated himself so that his creature might be; the World is nothing else but God sacrificed, immolated. He says to Agni: "remake me",[75] he cried out: "Alas, my life!" The waters heard him; with the *agnihotra* they came to his aid, they brought him back his torso,[76] and the Gods carried his limbs back to him. As the consummation of the same sacrifice, Prajāpati is redeemed from death. He had been sacrificed and he lives.[77] He had been dismembered, but he remains the same, literally because the sacrifice has remade him. It is by sacrifice that the Gods have existence and immortality.[78] It is by sacrifice that Prajāpati, benefiting from his own sacrifice, as it were, is rebuilt afresh.[79]

But the creatures, once born, flee from the Creator: Emitted, they departed, turning away from him.[80] The creatures feared their Creator, they fear being reabsorbed by him. But left to themselves, they were in total confusion.[81] They lacked concord and were devouring one another. Desolate,[82] Prajāpati decided to devour them. Knowing his intention, the creatures fled, terrified. He said to them: Come back to me; I will devour you in such a way that, once eaten, you will multiply yourselves in progeny.[83] He lifted a beacon for them; seeing the light, the creatures came back to him.[84]

It is here in the second moment, when creation has taken

place, that the myth of incest comes in.[85] It tells us, not how the cosmos began, but how this same cosmos went on or up or back. The Indian myth of incest appears in two main forms: the incest of God, the father of creation, with his own daughter, often symbolized as Uṣas—the dawn, sky[86]—and the incest of Yama and Yamī, brother and sister, the primordial couple.[87] In this second case the need for incest is clear enough: It is required to perpetuate the human race. And yet the incest taboo is so strong that, in spite of Yamī's arguments, her brother Yama resists the temptation (according to the main texts[88]).

The meaning of the first sort of incest—between God and creature—is obvious: creation, once brought forth, tries to free itself from its Creator, but left to itself it is lifeless and chaotic.[89] God must reenter his creatures in order to give them life.[90] Having created that, he penetrated it. Having penetrated it, he became that which is and that which has been, i.e., that which is (the manifest)—sat—and that which is otherwise (the unmanifest)—tyat—or again the refuge and the lack of it, the knowing and the unknowing, reality and unreality. Reality became all that exists. It is this we call Reality.[91]

This first type of myth presents many variations. Let us simply refer to a few of the most characteristic passages since it is not necessary to give here an exhaustive account. Prajāpati produces, generates, separates from himself a feminine counterpart. With her he copulates in order to create other beings. The creature recognizes her parentage in him, is ashamed and flees. She disguises herself as a cow, but he then becomes a bull and impregnates her; she successively takes on other female forms, and he the corresponding male forms. Thus the couples of the universe are produced.[92]

The most popular form of this myth survives in the Purāṇas, the incest of father and daughter. For creation to continue to exist, it must be fecundated again and again by its Creator, and so Prajāpati pursues the goddess Uṣas or Dyaus, in order to possess her.[93] Now this amounts to incest because everything is his creation, his offspring. The other Gods (his sons) cannot accept this behavior and decide to avenge their sister.[94] In spite of the reproach and contempt of the Gods, however, Prajāpati resolves to commit the incest, to descend again,[95] to render creation fertile and thereby incorporate it into his own life.[96]

Occasionally, because this version seems too crude, the incest is shifted from Prajāpati to his sons.[97] Such moral scruples are to be found not only among contemporary writers who try to explain the myth symbolically; they are present from the beginning. And yet the 'fact', i.e., the myth, is meticulously reported. This implies that for the ṛsis, the ancient seers, incest is more than just a shameful act. The human act is wrong, and even blasphemous, precisely because it imitates a specifically divine act that can be reenacted only mystically, if at all, but not aped. Not only does the modern and the traditional mentality shrink from such behavior, but the Gods themselves share the same repulsion. We may say the reason lies in the fact that the Gods are only supra-anthropomorphic figures; they are not really supreme and their moral code reflects our own. We could equally add that the myth speaks of a primordial natural fact, whereas the Gods belong to human culture. In any case, Prajāpati's action is unique and cannot be reduced to any general paradigm.

The texts to which I have briefly referred cover a wide range of fundamental topics. All of them speak of incest, but the purpose is not always the same. Limiting ourselves to Prajāpati, we find the following motifs:

i. A certain type of anthropomorphic love. The Creator falls in love with his daughter and tries to seduce her; the Gods protest and try to save their sister. Rudra becomes the avenger and pierces Prajāpati with a dart. Afterwards the Gods cure their father[98] and subsequent tradition supplies a ritualistic explanation.[99]

ii. A desire to complete his own creation. The first creatures to issue from Prajāpati were lifeless. A second intervention is required so as to give life—divine life—to the world. Here incest stands for a kind of re-creation, or better said, it symbolizes the completion of the creative act.

iii. A redemptive will. Creation goes astray; all the creatures are dying of hunger. Prajāpati decides to save them. This is the typical scheme of redemption.

iv. The desire to let the creature participate in the divine fecundity, thereby giving creation its own procreative energy. The creature becomes a partner with God in continuing the world. By this the creature is not only 'saved', but also divinized. It shares a divine dynamism, not a static 'nature'.

The central thrust is clear: After the creation by dismemberment, the creature must in one way or another reenter its Creator, return to the point of departure; in short, it must be divinized. Divinization, however, is not an external activity, like throwing a rope of salvation for the world to catch and so be rescued. It has to be a real reconstruction of the divine body, a total liberation from bondage, from creatureliness. For this, only an embrace between Creator and creature, their total reunion, will solve the problem. Nothing short of what is symbolized by the myth of incest will do. Let us not forget that for Hinduism, as for many other religions, redemption is not merely an external act, a moral rescue, but an ontological action, a real regeneration, a new life, indeed a divine life. Alone, the creature is impotent. God must redescend, consume it, unite himself with it, commit incest in order to divinize the creature, in order to bring it to the only end God can have: himself.

The basic sense of this rich and ambivalent mythic complex seems to be the following: the primordial source of everything is even more original than being and nonbeing. Then, by dint of *tapas* and *kāma*, being and nonbeing arise. From the tension between the two (they are compared to two branches[100]), the fundamental principles appear: cosmic order, truth, the primordial elements and the like. In short, the world. And yet this apparition is nothing but the dismembered body of the God who was invisibly enveloped in void, the unmanifest, the ineffable One anterior to being.

Creation thus appears as the sacrifice of God, as the ontological degradation of the Supreme Principle, which produces this intermediate state we call the cosmos, which is neither God, since it is his issue, nor not-God, since it is his own dismembered body.[101]

But this intermediate state is neither stable nor consistent in itself, it is a constitutively transitory state, a true ex-sistence, an *extra causas*, beside itself, so to speak. Creation alone, precisely because it is a *pascha*, a simple passage, is unable to sustain itself and arrive at its appointed destiny. This impotence, this radical weakness, is the original fault and the cause of sin. For sin is nothing other than the creature's wanting to rely solely on itself and cut its bond with God, precisely that link which makes the creature what it is by letting it ex-sist. God descends a 'second' time to remedy this impotence, to recover his creature by diviniz-ing it, making it God with him, reintegrating it with its origin.

It is necessary to reassemble the scattered fragments,[102] to reconstruct the broken unity, to repair the originating fault.[103] This is the myth we shall interpret.

3. THE HERMENEUTIC

Here we do not want to make a simple exegesis of this Indian myth, nor of all the Indian myths concerning the fall or creation by dismemberment or by sacrifice. Besides the myths already mentioned, there would be many other texts to study, like those of the struggle between Indra and the dragon Vṛtra,[104] and indeed many other religions to consider as well, for these myths do not belong only to India.[105] From the Babylonian *Enūma-eliš* to the myths of Australia, there is a whole mythic complex concerning this same problematic and pointing to a similar solution.[106] What interests us here is a hermeneutic through which we may perhaps shed a little light on the problematic of pain in contemporary philosophical thought.

I shall try to remain faithful to the Hindu tradition. If our exegesis goes beyond these limits it is, in the first place, because all tradition exists in order to be handed over, that is, left behind, and in the second place because we see the problems expressed by these myths in a more universal horizon, which also embraces other cultures and religions.

Here I use the term fault and not sin, primarily because in the Hindu myth one cannot properly speak of a sin, since this notion smacks of moralism, and here we are very far indeed from any moralizing.

Moreover, the word 'fault' better expresses the fact of the fall (from the Latin *fallere*) and also the anthropological connotations of the myth without lapsing into a purely voluntary realm of sin. When the Christian tradition speaks of original sin, it underscores that it is not concerned with an exclusively moral conception of sin, but with a blemish, a wound in the creature that penetrates the natural order itself.[107]

a. The Originating Fault

We have already noted that the myth of original sin, however it may be formulated, is a myth that makes Man responsible for his sin and for the ensuing evil. Man has broken the order established by God and he must suffer the consequences. This spares God responsibility for evil and sorrow. Evil is the consequence of Man's fall, and suffering the fruit of a human sin.[108] But this myth exhibits a weak spot to a metaphysically minded culture such as that of India. It is not human solidarity that is problematic for Indian thought, that is, the fact that a Man must bear and pay for the error and sin of another (a problem stemming from an individualism that perhaps did not exist even in mediaeval Europe). The difficulty for Hinduism lies in the fact that the initiative for the sin comes from Man, which seems to contradict the universal rights and absolute power of God. How could Man oppose the will of God? Who is Man to set himself against God? In short, if sin, or anything for that matter, originates in Man—or even in the devil, in any case outside of God—this implies a dualism that is incompatible with the notion of God as the absolute and unique source of everything. Now most myths of the fall are dualistic:[109] The Bible cites the Serpent as the principle of evil prior to Man's sin; the companion desired by the God of the Mordvines is in fact the devil. Christianity has seen this from the very beginning and has attempted to surmount the difficulty by the Christocentric vision of creation and by a Christic conception of the 'real'; sin is only a *felix culpa*, an opportunity for the full unfolding of the

Pantocrator, a moment in the divinization of the cosmos.

But Hinduism cannot accept Man as the original source of anything. If there is an original sin, it must first of all be God's sin, and not Man's alone.[110] But in God there can be neither sin, nor imperfection, nor blemish. The notion of an original sin in God is contradictory. What is original cannot be sin. If there were an original sin in God it would no longer be sin, but something divine, because sin, by definition, is incompatible with the divine nature.

Faced with this impasse, the Hindu myth takes a middle way: The evil existing in the world cannot issue from Man since this would make of him another—evil—God; however, neither can evil be rooted in God, for this would make God the principle of evil. There is no original sin, that is, a sin *in* God, a sin affecting God, but an *originating* fault, a fault of God, coming from God and giving birth to the world. In other words, there is a certain act of God that is not divine—not intratrinitarian, Christians might say—an activity that separates from God, an action that 'produces' not-God, therefore a fault and a sin, in a certain sense: It is the creation, the dismembering of the body of God, the throwing 'outside' himself something that *is* not yet (God), or rather is no longer God. We could leave it at the frailty of all love. If God is love he must want to communicate it, i.e., himself. Finding no one to whom he might give himself, he fabricates, he creates the object of his ardor so that he might desire and realize his love. He goes out of himself, he falls in love, he commits the fault of creating the creature. In brief: We are God's fault.

Looking at it more closely, there is no real original sin according to the myth, but only a provisional originating fault that is on the way to being overcome. Once everything returns to the origin, that is, once the process is finished, once the divine project is realized, the fault will cease to be. The sin is not in the originating, i.e., not *in* God; rather, the fault itself is originating, it gives rise to *saṁsāra*, time, the mortal and decrepit face of the cosmic 'schema'.[111] The fault is provisional. It is real only in time, for those who mistake time for reality, that is, for those who want to possess time, who fossilize it and do not let it flow, for those who stop the flux of ex-sistence, the tensional integrity of the creature. Sin is temporality taken for substance. Existence would indeed be fault and even sin if it were considered and accepted as simple *sistence* cut off from its source and destiny, as a mere fall—into nothingness. Culpable ignorance (*avidyā*) is to consider yourself something 'in itself', to substantialize your self, to vainly believe in a *self*. Creation is sin as a substantive, but not as a verb expressing divine creativity. The Christian scholastics themselves speak of creation *passive et active sumpta*.[112]

The originating fault is that divine act 'unworthy' of God, namely 'creation', at least insofar as it is pure 'creature', for to create means to give existence to what is not-God. Creation is the act by which the world springs forth; or, more precisely, creation is that part of the divine activity—the demi-act of God, so to speak—that gives to the world its initial existence in time in order that it might come to its transtemporal destination. God does not 'produce' exclusively temporal beings. Creation corresponds only to the temporal dimension of beings, but the beings 'produced' by God are in reality more than simple temporality. In Christian language one could say that God 'begets' his Son in whom there will be the new heaven and the new earth, once everything is fully accomplished.[113] The same act by which the Father engenders his Son also 'creates' the world.[114]

The simple and total act of God then is not the creation, but the generation of the total Body—or mystical body, as Christians would put it, i.e., Christ. Using another parlance to express the same intuition, we could say that in creating God simply *continues* to be God. Now just as here 'to be' is the act by which God expresses himself, so God *is* God by stepping beyond himself in pure 'growth', as it were, in an ever new and unedited explosion, without past and without future. The world is nothing else but this demi-reality on the way to becoming God, called to take part in this act of divine 'growth'. Of course, God does not become God, the world becomes him, for its ontological structure is *tempiternal*.[115]

So existence in itself is not sin, but it has its origin in a fault that corresponds morphologically to the *ex nihilo* of the Occidental Christian tradition. Strictly speaking, God does not 'sin', for he has not abandoned the creature midway. In reality, he does not 'create'; better said, he gives his life in a full and total way, although we ought to add that he communicates his life to that which, before this communication, is nothing at all. This is God's growth: not out of some previous 'food', but out of nothing. In time this atemporal action is lived, experienced and thought in fragmentary fashion by Man. Existence is an intermediary passage and is sin only when it takes itself as definitive or consistent. Sin is stopping halfway; it is the *conversio ad creaturam* of the Christian tradition.

In other words, in order to reach its goal, the creature must pass through a stage of sin, a transitory halting place—a trial—which is only as real as one takes it to be; for this reason *avidyā*, ignorance, is the first human sin, just as knowledge is the originating fault of the cosmos. Without divine knowledge the world would not be. This cosmic process is *saṁsāra*, i.e., temporal and inauthentic existence, only if Man has not discovered the whole of Reality. There is therefore an originating fault at the origin of the world; without this there would be neither creature nor Creator. If there is a Creator, there must be a creative act, which, insofar as it produces not-God, constitutes a fault: the originating fault of creation. The creature itself is this fault. Salvation lies in stepping beyond creatureliness.

b. Creative Immolation

All that we have said has been seen and expressed mythically by most religions, the central myth being the sacrifice through which creation comes to be. By sacrifice the world is made and maintains itself in existence;[116] by sacrifice the entire cosmos returns to its source. But here I do not wish to develop a theory of sacrifice in the history of religions. For now, it suffices to continue our hermeneutic.[117]

The originating fault implies the sacrifice of God. The wages of sin is death.[118] God dies, so to speak, in creating his creature; there is no room for two at this level. There is no *nihil ex quo* God can make anything; God can only create by himself. It follows then not that God creates *ex Deo*, but *a Deo*.[119] There is neither an other nor any possible help.[120] Only self-immolation remains. God sacrifices himself, he vanishes, he dismembers himself, he dies in order to reenter, in order to find himself again in his creature. Creation is the altar upon which God sacrifices himself, it is God made victim. The divine love is 'mortified', greater love than this no one has: that he lay down his life for his friends,[121] and there is no greater love than God's. God gives himself to his creation and he dies therein.

Man has in his hands not only his 'private' destiny, but also and preeminently the divine destiny. He is in some ways the successor of God, the agent of divinity. He has not only the power to destroy himself and the ability to explode the material universe; the destiny of God himself is in Man's power. The difference between God and Man is not one of numerical order: They are not two. Neither are they one, for the unity is not yet realized, achieved. Inasmuch as Man *is*, God *is* not; insofar as God is, Man is not; the one means the absence of the other. The relation between the temporal and the eternal cannot be expressed in terms of being. Ultimately 'God' and 'Man', as well as 'Cosmos' are mere abstractions of an all-embracing cosmotheandric reality.

God has annihilated himself, emptied himself,[122] sacrificed himself, offered himself. Offered to whom? To nothing, since there was and is nothing 'outside' of God: He has, so to speak, fallen into nothing, into the void—*in nihilum*. So creation is not only *ex nihilo*, it is also *in nihilum*.[123] The result is Man and the Cosmos; a God plundered, offered up, sacrificed, dead, and now on the way to resurrection by virtue of the divine dynamism itself, which has passed into the hands of Men, the priests of the universe, the mediators between the God who was and the God who will be.[124] Of course, for a substantialist notion of God as an immutable being, other and independent, this last phrase makes no sense, since for this God there is neither past nor future. Nevertheless, the preceding affirmation is valid precisely for Man who finds himself as if floating between a nothing that 'was' and a God who 'will be'. Creation is not an illusion; on the contrary, it is an act proper to God and to Man; in it the destiny of Reality itself is played out. God's sacrifice is a true sacrifice, a real im-

molation, and because of this is itself creative. The world is born
of a sacrifice and by another sacrifice it dies, that is to say it is
reborn into true life, it returns home to God. The cosmic sacrifice
that remakes what had been made in the creative act *in illo tempore*[125] is accomplished in time and space. Creation is illusion,
pure unreality, only when it cuts itself off from its source and
considers itself crystallized on its own, self-sustaining, 'in-itself'.

In fact, the process is complementary and reciprocal: God
constantly dismembers himself and is constantly remade. The
cosmic process is not simply historical, not just a Man-making
process; it is also a theopoetic process, it remakes God. It is not
exclusively temporal, but tempiternal. Man is not a sort of
perishable and despicable worm, a simple dust mote destined to
lose itself in the sidereal spaces. Man is a divine 'spark', a moment in the 're-creation' or restoration of God, an element of the
divine sacrifice that inverts the originating fall. God, from his
side, is not a sort of detached being without a care in the world,
outside of human life and disentangled from human destiny: He is
the God of Man, his divine principle. Thus he infinitely surpasses
the empirical Man, but is not another 'thing', an 'other'. Even as
original sin implies an originating fault, so the creature requires
the Creator. The reality is neither creature nor Creator, taken
separately, but the tension of this very *radical relativity*.

In other words: The whole process of Man, of history and of
the universe is not simply a creatural affair, but belongs to the
creation itself; it is the second act in the drama of creation, and
the inverse complement of the first divine act. This means that the
salvation or failure of Man is much more a divine problem and
responsibility than it is human. Suffering is above all God's suffering, sin is also his sin, the solidarity between Man and God is
total. It is neither an 'other' God who is responsible for human
grief, nor an 'other' Man who must bear the burden of an original
sin; there are the two embarked on the adventure of existence, in
the audacity of creation, on the marvelous path leading through
virgin snow to the construction of the cosmotheandric body of
Reality.[126] The *pati divina* of Helleno-Christian mysticism ought

here to be understood not only as Man 'suffering' the weight of God, but also as the burden of human pain borne by God.[127]

c. Ontic Redemption

Accusing the West of dualism and the East of pantheism will lead us nowhere. We miss the power of the myth of the fall if we think that the West is necessarily dualistic because it attributes an original activity to Man, be it sin or the capacity to sin. We also skirt the depth of the myth of Prajāpati if we make a materialist hermeneutic of his sacrifice and give a pantheistic sense to the dismembering of God.

The vision we have attempted to sketch would leap over this dichotomy: There can be an original sin because it is not Man alone who commits it, God is also involved; there can be an originating fault because it is not the divine essence that perpetrates it.

In other words, what we call creation is only a first moment in the great cosmotheandric drama of reality: To the sacrifice of God, the sacrifice of Man corresponds; to the creation, his divinization.[128] Redemption is not a kind of historical accident in the cosmotheandric adventure, it is not conditioned solely by human affairs, it belongs to the very economy of Reality, it is the bridge that unites the sacrifice of God to that of Man, the road leading to the other shore. It is the way in which God 'lives', unfolds himself, 'creates', loves. The redemption of being is a life-or-death question for all existence. The creature is only a *quasi medium inter Deum et nihil*.[129] If it does not achieve its plenitude, it falls into vacuity. Redemption is the sacrifice of the creature.[130] Being cannot reach its limit except by a redemptive immolation that completes and gives meaning to the creative immolation.[131]

But we must now return to the myth of pain.

Pain, then, does not represent simply purifying some sin. Its deeper sense would be to take part in the redemption of the cosmos.[132] No one has the right to inflict pain on others. This Brahmanic India and the Christian Middle Ages saw quite clearly. They inflicted pain only because they believed—rightly or wrongly—that they were acting in the name of God, that is, that they were sharing in the redemptive pain of the cosmos. A deeper reading of the same myth leads us to say that no one has the right to inflict pain, not even God. The reason is simple: If God punishes it is either because there is a justice superior to him that he must obey, and in this case he would not be supreme; or God punishes because he freely wills it, although he could achieve the same results without making his creatures suffer.[133] One can scarcely see how such a God could be good and benevolent toward Men. Because of this, religions have attempted to convince us that pain either is not an evil, or that Man alone is at the root of it.

Only a myth that does not separate God from the World can justify pain. An independent God, having nothing to do with Men, does not exist. Neither Man nor the cosmos are self-sustaining entities; they are both grounded in God. The myth of pain addresses itself to the level where God and Man commune: the cosmotheandric mystery of reality.

The myth of Prajāpati does not speak to us of sin or pain. It exposes the double dynamism of sacrifice: the creative immolation and the redemptive reconstruction. Pain is the creature's resistance to letting itself con-vert, it is the changing of direction that paves the way to what it is not yet.

After all, what must be redeemed is creatureliness itself, and not merely a moral evil; what must be burned away in the sacrifice is contingency itself, for all that can, in one way or another, cease to be, is fuel for the sacrificial fires.

Redemption is ontic. Pain is the smoke produced by whatever was still too green for the sacrifice.

Notes

1. It is often remarked that κακία as understood in Mt. 6:34 (the citation that opens this chapter), is unique in the New Testament, but we have not given sufficient attention to the problematic of this 'evil' each day carries with it. Evidently this 'pain' has nothing to do with 'moral' evil nor with a pessimistic or dualistic vision of reality. It is enough to recall the proverb popular in several languages: 'Sufficient unto the day

is its own task.' Should we understand this to mean that evil is not at the beginning of the world (original sin), but given with every day?

2. "Culture not only provides the vehicle for expressing pain and the grammar to make of it a challenge, but it also supplies the myth which interprets pain as a God-willed necessity, as a punishment, as vengeance, as redemption, or even as a mystery." I. Illich, 'The Killing of Pain', *Hygenic Nemesis* (CIDOC Cuaderno No. 86, Cuernavaca, Mexico), 1974, p. 40.

3. The greek ποινή properly means: to repair, to repay with good or evil. In addition to reward, it also means punishment. The Latin *poena* also preserves this sense of penalty in juridical terms. Later the same word will pass into most of the Romance languages with the sense of suffering. In Sanskrit 'pain' might be translated textually by *daṇḍa*: staff, rod (cf. the Greek δένδρον, tree); also by *pīdā* which means primarily suffering, pain, and later takes on the sense of torture, correction (cf. *pīdāgṛha*: torture chamber, reformatory). Significantly, the verb *pīd* was originally used to indicate the action of pressing *soma*. So the action of sacrifice would then produce suffering. Sanskrit also uses *vedanā* to express suffering, pain, torture, and also means perception, sensation.

4. "My servants rejoice in suffering; they suffer when they do not suffer," Saint Catherine of Siena heard; *(Dialogues,* tr. Hurtaud, ed. Lethielleux, I:289). "Je ne pensais pas alors qu'il fallait beaucoup souffrir pour arriver à la saintété", adds Saint Thérèse of Jesus *(Histoire d'une âme,* Lisieux, 1944, p. 65). Cf. "pati et contemni pro te" of Saint John of the Cross and a good number of saints, and the definition of "la perfetta letizia" of Saint Francis of Assisi *(Fioretti).* One could also add many other such testimonies from the most diverse traditions.

5. Cf. vgr. D. Thom., *Sum. Theol.* I-II, q. 87, a. 1 sq.

6. Since there is no adequate word to express what we wish to say, we will use 'creation', 'creature' and similar words in the most elementary sense of 'the production of beings', without necessarily implying the notion of *creatio ex nihilo* nor that of a 'personal' God. We prefer 'creation' as the generic term to 'emanation' used by Saint Thomas Aquinas *(Sum. Theol.* I, q. 45). To convey the same notion, Sanskrit uses *sarj*, 'emit' and sometimes also *nir-mā*, 'construct' used in the middle voice. Neither the active nor the passive voice suffices to express the act by which the world proceeds from its source.

7. Cf. a wealth of material in *Guilt or Pollution and Rites of Purification*, Proceedings of the XI International Congress of the International Association for the History of Religions (Claremont, 1965) (Leiden: Brill, 1968), vol. 2.

8. Cf. for example: "And behold, they brought to him a paralytic lying on his bed; and when Jesus saw their faith he said to the paralytic; 'Take heart, my son; your sins are forgiven' " (Mt. 9:2). Cf. also: " 'See,

you are well! Sin no more, that nothing worse befall you.' " (Jn. 5:14) Or again: " 'Rabbi, who sinned, this man or his parents, that he was born blind?' " (Jn. 9:2).

9. "Omnis poena est medicina, sed non semper respectu peccantis", says scholasticism. Cf. vgr. D. Thom., *Sum. Theol.* I-II, q. 87, a. 2 ad 1; a. 3 ad 2; II-II, q. 39, a. 2 ad 1; a. 4 ad 3; etc.

10. Cf. chapter VI.

11. Cf. Gen. 1:27.

12. Cf. Gen. 3:14 sq. Cf. for similar myths, R. Pettazzoni, *Miti e leggende* (Torino: U.T.E.T., 1948-1959), 4 vols.

13. "Poena est bona simpliciter, et mala secundum quid", says a Thomist thesis. Cf. D. Thom., *Sum. Theol.* II-II, q. 19, a. 1, c.

14. Cf. RV X, 129, 2: "The One breathed without breath, by its own impulse. Other than that was nothing else at all"; AV V, 8, 11: "What moves, what flies, what stands quite still, what breathes, what breathes not, blinks the eye, this, concentrated into a single One, though multiple its forms, sustains the earth"; IsU 4: "Unmoving, the One is swifter than the mind. No power can reach him as he speeds on before. Standing still, he outstrips those who run. From him life-power thrills through all things."

15. This is essentially according to the tradition of the Brāhmaṇas. Cf. AV X, 1, 5: "Prajāpati was here being One only in the beginning." In other traditions—at times represented in the Brāhmaṇas themselves—*brahman* takes the place of 'God'. Cf. SB XI, 2, 3, 1 which speaks of *brahman* (*Brahma vai idam agre āsīt tad devān asṛjata*, "In the beginning Brahmâ was this [universe]. He created Gods") in the same words used in TB II, 2, 7, 1 for Prajāpati (*Prajāpatiḥ prajāḥ asṛjata*, "Prajāpati created living beings") (Muir translation).

16. Cf. Homer, *Iliad*, IV, 68 and Plato, *Timaeus*, 37c, where the Supreme God is called the Father of Gods and Men.

17. Cf. the entire Brāhmaṇic tradition. As an example: TB II, 3, 6, 1; GopB II, 3, 9; TMB XXI, 2, 1; XXIV, 11, 2; etc. where the same formula is repeated again and again: *Prajāpatiḥ prajāḥ asṛjata*. Cf. S. Lévi, *La doctrine du sacrifice dans les Brāhmaṇas* (Paris: P.U.F., 2nd ed., 1966), pp. 25 sq.

18. Cf. AV XIX, 17, 9: "May Prajāpati who possesses the procreative energy (*prajananavant*) . . . protect us."

19. RV X, 121, 1-2: "In the beginning arose the Golden Germ: he was, as soon as born, the Lord of being, sustainer of the earth and of this heaven. . . . He who bestows life-force and hardy vigor, whose ordinances even the Gods obey, whose shadow is immortal life—and death—."

20. Cf. SB XI, 1, 6, 14: "Now, these are the deities who were created out of Prajāpati,—Agni, Indra, Soma and Parameshthin

Prājāpatya" (Eggeling translation); TS III, 3, 7, 1: *Prajāpatir devāsurān asrjata*; and also TB I, 4, 11; VIII, 1, 3, 4; TMB XVIII, 1, 1; etc.

21. Cf. SB II, 2, 4, 1: "In the beginning, to be sure, the Lord of Creatures was One only." Cf. note 15.

22. TB II, 1, 2, 1 sq.; MaitS I, 8, 1; SB II, 2, 4, 6; II, 4, 4, 1; VI, 2, 3, 1; etc.

23. Cf. the refrain of RV X, 121, 1-9: "What God (*kah*) shall we adore with our oblation?"; or again: "Prajāpati, who is he?" (TMB VII, 8, 3; AB XII, 10, 1; TS I, 7, 6, 6; SB IV, 5, 6, 4). One legend tells us the origin of the name: "Indra, having slain Vṛtra, having won all victories, said to Prajāpati, 'Let me be what thou art; let me be great.' Prajāpati replied, 'Then *who* am I?' 'Even that which thou hast said', he answered; then indeed did Prajāpati become *Who* by name . . ." (AB XII, 10, 1) (Keith translation). TB II, 2, 10, 1-2 gives a slightly different version: "Prajāpati created Indra, the last born of the Gods, and sent him to rule over the Gods as their sovereign. The Gods said, '*Who* are you? We are better than you.' Indra reported the Gods' words to Prajāpati. Now at this time Prajāpati had the splendor of the sun. He (Indra) said to him, 'Give me this and I will be the Gods' sovereign.' 'And if I give it to you,' he replied, 'then *who* will I be?' 'You will be what you say.' And Prajāpati was named *Ka*." (Cf. S. Lévi, *op. cit.*, p. 17.)

24. Cf. the marvelous hymn addressed to *skambha*, the cosmic pillar, in AV X, 7. Cf. vgr. verse 7: "The One on whom the Lord of Life leant for support when he propped up the world—Tell me of that Support—who may he be?"

25. RV X, 129, 1.

26. *Svadhā* (from *sva* + *dhā*), by his own power.

27. RV X, 129, 2.

28. RV X, 129, 3.

29. Cf. the expression of Tertullian: "Ante omnia enim deus erat solus" (*Adversus Praxean*, 5, 1). Speaking of the intratrinitarian *logos*, he adds: "Tunc igitur etiam ipse sermo speciem et ornatum suum sumit, sonum et uocem cum dicit Deus: *Fiat lux*. Haec est nativitas perfecta Sermonis dum ex deo procedit" (*ibid.* 7, 1).

30. RV X, 129, 3.

31. TB II, 2, 9, 1 (*tad asad eva san mano 'kuruta syām iti*). Cf. TU II, 7.

32. BU I, 4, 1.

33. *Ibid.*

34. Cf. BU I, 4, 2.

35. Cf. CU VIII, 7, 1 sq. (the teaching of Prajāpati on the *ātman*).

36. Cf. BU I, 4, 3: "He found no joy".

37. Cf. Gen. 3:7 sq.

38. Cf. BU I, 4, 2: "He was afraid; so, even today, one who is all

alone is afraid. He thought to himself: 'Since nothing exists except me, of what am I afraid?' Thereupon his fear vanished, for of what should he have been afraid? It is of a second that fear arises."

39. *Id.* "He yearned for a second." Cf. also, for Prajāpati who desired progeny, SB VI, 1, 1, 8; TS VII, 1, 1, 4; TB II, 2, 9, 5; AB X, 1, 5; etc.

40. Cf. CU VI, 2, 3: "It thought: 'Would that I might be many! Would that I might procreate!' " (*tad aikṣata bahu syām prajāyeyeti*).

41. Cf. RV X, 190, 1.

42. RV I, 164, 47. Cf. the commentary in V. S. Agrawala, *Vision in Long Darkness* (Varanasi: Bhargava Bhushan Press, 1963), pp. 184 sq. (cf. note 6 of chapter 3).

43. Cf. BU I, 4, 3; and TMB VI, 5, 1 (*Prajāpatir akāmayata bahu syām prajāyeyeti*); etc. (cf. note 25 of chapter 3).

44. Cf. U. Harva, *Die religiöse Vorstellungen der Mordwinen* (Helsinki, 1954), p. 154 (*apud* M. Eliade, 'Structure et fonction du mythe cosmogonique', in the collective work, *La naissance du monde* [Paris: Ed. du Seuil, 1959], p. 489).

45. It must be emphasized that here Christian theology, despite its disclaimers, relies heavily on a Hellenic idea. The *ex nihilo* makes no sense divorced from a polemic against the notion of a δημιουργός who makes the world, shapes primary matter, converts chaos into cosmos. We know well enough that the word δημιουργός—so popular in Greek literature and Gnostic terminology—is never used in the *Septuagint* to designate the Creator. In the New Testament it appears only in Heb. 11:10.

46. TS VII, 1, 1, 4 sq.: "He meted out the Trivṛt from his mouth. . . . From the breast and arms he meted out the Pañcadaśa Stoma. . . . From the middle he meted out the Saptadaśa Stoma. . . ." (Keith translation); etc.

47. Cf. RV X, 90.

48. Cf. the Sanskrit *sva-dhā* and its sacrificial sense.

49. Cf. the sentence of Plato: τίκτειν ἐπιθυμεῖ ἡμῶν ἡ φύσις (our nature desires to procreate), *Symposium*, 206c.

50. This is not contradictory: The gift has value and consistency in itself. Cf. G. Van Der Leeuw, *Religion in Essence and Manifestation* (New York: Harper, 1963), pp. 13, 50ff.

51. Cf. AB VII, 8, 2; XXXIV, 1, 1; TB II, 1, 2, 1 sq.; SB II, 2, 4, 6; etc.

52. Cf. TB VII, 2, 1: "Prajāpati gave his very self to the Gods in the form of a sacrifice" (*Prajāpatir devebhya ātmānam yajñam kṛtvā prāyacchat*); cf. also SB XI, 1, 8, 2 sq.; etc.; TMB VII, 2, 1; etc.

53. Cf. SB X, 2, 2, 1: "For up to then there existed no other that was worthy of sacrifice."

54. Cf. RV X, 90; cf. also SB XI, 1, 8, 5: "And when (on the following day) he performs the sacrifice, then he redeems himself by sacrifice from the Gods, even as Prajāpati thereby redeemed himself . . ." (Eggeling translation).

55. Cf. RV X, 90, 8.

56. Cf. *id.* 9 sq.

57. RV X, 90, 13.

58. Cf. SB XI, 1, 6, 1 sq.

59. SB XI, 1, 6, 9. Cf. also the interesting Biblical parallels: Is. 45:6-7: "I am the Lord, and there is no other. I form the light and create darkness. I make weal and create woe. I am the Lord, who does all these things"; again Is. 41:23; Am. 3:6; Lam. 3:38; Mic. 1:12; Zeph. 1:12; etc.

60. Cf. Prov. 16:4: "universa propter semetipsum operatus est Dominus"; and the role of this text in Christian scholastic theology. Cf. v.g. D. Thom. *Contra Gentes* III, 17; IV, 34.

61. SB VI, 1, 1, 8 (*Prajāpatir akāmayata bhūyānt syām prajāyeyeti*).

62. RV X, 190, 1.

63. Cf. SU I, 3: "[Sages] well-practised (*yoga*) in meditation have beheld God's native (*ātma-*) power deep-hidden by his attributes (*guṇa*)" (Zaehner translation).

64. Cf. RV X, 129, 2-3.

65. Cf. TB II, 2, 9, 1 sq.: "That became fervent (or practised rigorous abstraction, *atapyata*). From that fervour (or abstraction) smoke was produced. That became again fervent. From that fervour fire was produced . . ." (Muir translation); etc.

66. Cf. RV X, 129, 4. *Retas*, seminal fluid.

67. *Ibid.*

68. Cf. SB VI, 1, 1, 1.

69. TU II, 6.

70. Cf. AV VII, 80, 3: "No one but thou, Prajāpati, none beside thee, pervading, gave to all these forms their being" (Griffith translation). Cf. the translation of L. Silburn, *Instant et Cause. Le discontinu dans la pensée philosophique de l'Inde* (Paris: Vrin, 1955), p. 51.

71. TB I, 2, 6, 1. Cf. also TMB XXV, 17, 3 sq. and SB III, 9, 1, 1 sq.; "Now Prajāpati (the lord of creatures), having created living beings, felt himself as it were exhausted [*riricānaḥ*, lit. 'emptied']. The creatures did not abide with him for his joy and food. He thought within him, 'I have exhausted myself, and the object for which I have created has not been accomplished: my creatures have turned away from me, the creatures have not abode with me for my joy and food' " (Eggeling translation). And again SB X, 4, 2, 2: "Having created all things that exist, he felt like one emptied out, and was afraid of death."

72. Cf. SB X, 1, 3, 2: "Now, one half of that Prajāpati was mortal,

and the other half was immortal: with that part of him which was mortal he was afraid of death" (Eggeling translation). (Cf. Mt. 26:36 sq.)

73. Cf. BU I, 4, 6.

74. Cf. SB VI, 1, 2, 12.

75. SB VI, 1, 2, 13.

76. TB II, 3, 6, 1.

77. Cf. Rev. 5:6 and 12 which speak of "agnum stantem tamquam occisum."

78. Cf. SB VIII, 6, 1, 10; TS VI, 3, 4, 7.

79. SB II, 4, 4, 1 sq.

80. TMB XXI, 2, 1.

81. Cf. TB II, 2, 7, 1.

82. Cf. TMB XXIV, 11, 2.

83. Cf. TMB XXI, 2, 1.

84. Cf. TB I, 1, 5, 4.

85. The problem of incest is well known in the field of anthropology, and there is a rich and complex literature on the subject. For a psychological discussion, cf. E. Neumann, *Ursprungsgeschichte des Bewusstseins* (Zürich: Rascher, 1949); English translation: *The Origins and History of Consciousness* translated by R.F.C. Hill, (London: Routledge & Kegan Paul, 1954). More recently, it has achieved prominence with the rise of structuralism. Cf. Y. Simonis, *Claude Lévi-Strauss ou la "passion de l'inceste"* (Paris: Aubier-Montagne, 1968) for a good summary. Lévi-Strauss would go so far as to say: ". . . avant elle (la prohibition de l'incest), la Culture n'est pas encore donnée; avec elle, la Nature cesse d'exister, chez l'homme, comme un règne souverain. La prohibition de l'incest est le processus par lequel la Nature se depasse elle-même. . . ." *Les structures élémentaires de la parenté* (Paris: P.U.F., 1949), p. 31.

86. Cf. for RV alone: I, 71, 5; I, 164, 33; III, 31, 1; VI, 17, 3 (ambiguous cf. however: X, 61, 7; VI, 12, 4).

87. Later on, Manu will be the first Man and Yama the first Man to die, and thereby the king of the dead in the nether world.

88. Cf. RV X, 10, 1 sq.; AV XVIII, 1, 8 sq. Tempting as it is, I also leave aside a proper consideration of the second type of myth, i.e., that of Yama and Yamī. For a Japanese version of this same myth of brother-sister incest, cf. the Shinto story of Izanaki and Izanami. Cf. Y. Kojima, 'The Myth of the Marriage of Izanaki and Izanami', *Religion East and West*, XXXV/4, No. 171 (Tokyo, March, 1962). Interestingly enough, this ancient myth has been revived in the new Japanese religion Tenrikyō. Cf. Shōzen Nakayama, *A Short History of Tenrikyō* (Tenri: Tenrikyō Kyōkai Honbu, 1960), pp. 15–18. Cf. note 14 of chapter III.

89. TB II, 2, 7, 1.

90. Vgr. TB II, 2, 7, 1; GopB II, 3, 6. Cf. also Gen. 2:7.

91. TU II, 6.

92. Cf. BU I, 4, 3 sq.

93. Cf. the legend of Manu procreating with his daughter (the sacrifice) once she has 'resisted' Mitra and Varuṇa in SB I, 8, 1, 1-10. The passage is the continuation of the Indian version of the flood story.

94. Cf. SB VI, 1, 3, 8; AB XIII, 9; MaitS IV, 2, 12; etc.

95. Cf. TU II, 6.

96. Cf. vgr. TB II, 2, 7, 1; GopB II, 3, 6 (cf. *etiam* Gen. 2:7).

97. KausB VI, 1.

98. Cf. SB I, 7, 4, 1-4.

99. Cf. the Mīmāmsakas for whom *śabda,* the word as ritual, takes the place of the entire creation.

100. Cf. AV X, 7, 21: "The branch of Non-being which is far-extending Men take to be the highest one of all. They reckon as inferior those who worship your other branch, the branch of Being."

101. Cf. the meditating expression of the world as the indeterminate state between being and nonbeing: *sadasatanirvacanīya.*

102. Cf. Jn. 6:12.

103. Cf. the same idea of redemption in the thought of Saint Augustine, *In Psalm. 58*, 10 (P.L., 36, 698): "Divine Mercy gathered up the fragments from every side, forged them in the fire of love, and welded into one what had been broken. . . . He who re-made was himself the Maker, and he who re-fashioned was himself the Fashioner." Cf. other Christian texts on the idea of redemption as the reestablishment of a lost unity, as in the work of H. De Lubac, *Catholicisme* (Paris: Ed. du Cerf, 1952), p. 13.

104. Cf. vgr. RV I, 52; IV, 17; 19; VI, 17; etc.

105. Cf. vgr. the Egyptian God Atun who created the world by dismembering his body. Cf. J.B. Pritchard, *Ancient Near East Texts* (Princeton: Princeton University Press, 1955), pp. 3-5.

106. Cf. vgr. *La naissance du monde,* loc. cit.; A. Heidel, *The Babylonian Genesis* (Chicago: University of Chicago Press, 1963); S.G.F. Brandon, *Creation Legends of the Ancient Near East* (London: Hodder & Stoughton, 1963); S.H. Hooke, *Middle Eastern Mythology* (Baltimore: Penguin, 1963); etc.

107. Cf. vgr. D. Thom., *Sum. Theol.* I, q. 100, a. 1, c.; I-II q. 74, a. 3 and 2; etc.

108. Cf. Gen. 3:19; etc.

109. To which we could add the trickster myths in 'primitive' religions.

110. The idea is not only Hindu. There is a Bulgarian proverb that says: "God is not without sin since he made the world." The concept of original sin in late Zoroastrianism transposes this sin to God. Cf. R.C. Zaehner, *The Convergent Spirit* (London: Routledge & Kegan Paul, 1963), p. 135. Cf. also the Gnostic concept of creation as a fall. Nonethe-

less we think there is a certain originality in the Hindu understanding that distinguishes it from these other myths.

111. Cf. 1 Cor. 7:31; etc.

112. Cf. D. Thom., *Sum. Theol.* I, q. 49, a. 3 ad 2.

113. Cf. Rev. 21:1.

114. "Deus enim cognoscendo se, cognoscit omnem creaturam. . . . Sed quia Deus uno actu et se omnia intelligit, unicum Verbum eius est expressivum non solum Patris, sed etiam creaturarum." D. Thom., *Sum. Theol.* I, a. 34, a. 3, c.

115. Cf. R. Panikkar, 'La tempiternidad', *Sanctum Sacrificium*, Actas del V Congreso Eucarístico de Zaragoza, 1961, pp. 75-93, and more recently: 'El presente tempiterno: Una apostilla a la historia de la salvación y a la teología de la liberación' in A. Vargas-Machuca (ed.), *Teología y mundo contemporaneo* (Madrid: Cristiandad 1975), pp. 133-175, for an elaboration of this idea.

116. Cf. vgr. SB II, 3, 1, 5: "And when he [the priest] offers in the morning before the sunrise, then he produces that (sun-child) and, having become a light, it rises shining. But, assuredly, it would not rise, were he not to make that offering: this is why he performs that offering" (Eggeling translation).

117. On this topic in Hinduism and Christiantiy, cf. R. Panikkar, *Le mystère du culte dans l'hindouisme et le christianisme* (Paris: Cerf, 1970), pp. 83 sq., and as for the Hindu sacred texts, cf. *The Vedic Experience*, (Los Angeles: Univ. of California Press, 1977).

118. Cf. Rom. 6:23.

119. Cf. R. Panikkar, *Māyā e Apocalisse* (Roma: Abete, 1966), pp. 80 sq.

120. Cf. CU VI, 2, 1; BU IV, 3, 32; KaivU 19, etc. Cf. also, in another sense, Sir. 51:10.

121. Cf. Jn. 15:13.

122. Cf. Phil. 2:7; 2 Cor. 8:9. An entire theology of *kenosis* could be developed here. Cf. also: "The moment of creation in time is called *fanā'i-him 'an baqā'i-him* [by Abū'l Qāsim al-Junayd of Baghdad], 'their annihilation out of or after their eternal being', that is to say, their entry into time from eternity." R.C. Zaehner, *Hindu and Muslim Mysticism* (London: The Athlone Press, 1960), p. 147.

123. Cf. the text of Saint Thomas in *De aeternitate mundi*, 7: "Prius enim inest unicuique naturaliter quod convenit sibi in se, quam quod solum ex alio habet. Esse autem non habet creatura nisi ab alio, sibi autem relicta in se considerata *nihil* est: unde *prius naturaliter inest sibi nihil quam esse*" (emphasis added). Cf. also *De pot.* q. 5, a. 1, c., and again *De Veritate*, q. 18, a. 2 ad 5.

124. Cf. Rev. 1:4, 1:8, 4:8; RV X, 90, 2; SB XIII, 4, 2, 2; TS III, 1, 1, 1; and also tradition, vgr. Rāmānuja, *Gītā-bhāṣya,* IX, 19.

125. "La fonction essentielle du sacrifice est de mettre de nouveau ensemble (*samdhā*) ce qui fut morcelé *in illo tempore.*" M. Eliade, *Méphistophélès et l'androgyne* (Paris: Gallimard, 1962), p. 119.

126. Cf. Col. 1:18; etc.

127. An entire theology of incarnation could follow from the idea and would be yet another example of the enrichment deriving from an encounter in the depths between religions. Cf. the work of the Japanese theologian Kazon Kitamori, *Theology of the Pain of God* (Richmond, Va.: John Knox, 1965), which speaks of a suffering God.

128. This idea is traditional in Christianity and may be found in one form or another in almost all religions. Cf. as a single example, Saint Bernard, *De gratia et libero arbitrio*, XIV, n. 49 (P.L., 182, 1027) where he speaks of *creatio*, *reformatio* and *consummatio* as the three moments in the divine action.

129. M. Eckhart, 'Expos. in Io.', *Lateinische Werke*, III, pg. 185, n. 220.

130. "Every sacrifice is a boat to heaven" (SB IV, 2, 5, 10). Cf. JaimB I, 166 which also speaks of sacrifice as the ship of the Gods: *yāṁ ha khalu vai pitāputrau nāvam ajato, na sā riṣyati; daivy eṣā naur yad yajñas* . . . ("The boat which father and son use for transport undergoes no damage. Now sacrifice is the boat of the Gods . . ."). Cf. AB III, 2, 29: "Sacrifice is a reliable ferry."

131. Cf. by contrast the Gnostic myth of Sophia as reported by Irenaeus of Lyon in the beginning of his *Adversus haereses*. Here it is the inverted—and thus wrong—order. Sophia desires the divine Father, but she is severed from him by fifteen pairs of eons. M. Meslin, in *Pour une science des religions* (Paris: Seuil, 1973, pp. 206 sq.), is right in seeing here a psychoanalytical complex, but this would not justify reducing our problematic entirely to Freudian or Jungian categories.

132. Cf. 1 Pet. 4:13.

133. Cf. the Thomist thesis: "Deus potest remittere peccata sine poena", D. Thom., *Sum. Theol.* II-II, q. 67, a. 4 ad 2; III, q. 46, a. 2 ad 3; etc.

V.
Śunaḥśepa.
A Myth of the Human Condition

puruṣo vai yajñaḥ

The sacrifice is Man.
SB I, 3, 2, 1 (+)

puruṣam prathamam ālabhate

Man is the first to be sacrificed.
SB VI, 2, 1, 18

+ Cf. also CU III, 16, 1: *puruṣo vava yajñaḥ*: Man, in truth, is himself a
sacrifice.

1. MYTH AND HISTORY

This study is an attempt to elucidate a crucial double function of myth and to illustrate it with a concrete example. First of all, myth offers the subsoil from which differing philosophical systems may draw sustenance. There are no philosophies *in vacuo*; each philosophy arises in a given context, precisely that furnished by myth. Secondly, due to its philosophical polyvalence, myth is invaluable in the meeting of cultures and the cross-fertilization that can result from it. Concepts are valid in the contexts where they have been conceived, but you cannot purely and simply extrapolate them (without finding laws, etc., to justify extrapolation). Myths, on the contrary, stem from a deeper, and so more universal, human stratum than do the philosophies.

This first section is intended to make the setting of our study explicit.

a. Mythic Facts and Historical Facts

What we currently understand by *fact* is an incontestable given, a reality that presents itself incontestably. Now this incontestability is not a purely objective property; it also includes the subject who considers the fact incontestable. There are no pure facts, facts 'in themselves'; they are always facts for someone. At the very least, every fact implies someone—a person, or even human consciousness in general—for whom the fact is a fact.

A myth seen and lived from within is an ensemble of facts that forms the basic fabric where what is given stands out as if against a horizon. Myth thus serves as the ultimate reference point, the touchstone of truth by which facts are recognized as truths. Myth, when it is believed and lived from inside, does not ask to be plumbed more deeply, i.e., to be transcended in the search for some ulterior ground; it asks only to be made more and more explicit, for it expresses the very foundation of our conviction of truth. Seen from outside, however, the mythical appears a mass of legends, of 'myths' in which others believe, but which have nothing to do with 'factual' truth. Myth then recounts in its own way the ultimate ground of a particular belief: either of others' belief (myth seen from outside), or of our own belief (myth lived from inside). In the latter case we believe the myth without believing *in* the myth, since it is transparent for us, self-evident, integrated into that ensemble of facts in which we believe and which constitute the real.[1]

One of the myths of the modern West is history.[2] History is the landmark to which we refer the incontestability of facts, and in terms of which we criticize other myths.[3] For Western Man, historical facts are the hard and inescapable reality.

The current theological interpretation of Jesus' Resurrection is a striking example of what we are getting at: Because history is the modern myth that gives meaning to reality, we *transmythicize* physical fact into historical fact. We demythicize the myth of the physical or physiological miracle and substitute the myth of the historical miracle. The modern interpretation claims to render the Resurrection comprehensible to us; today the Resurrection is the *historical*—read: real—*fact* of the transformation that occurred among the first Christians who believed in this Resurrection. So, the reality of the Resurrection does not lie in a biological, material or spiritual event, but in a *historical fact*—so moderns will affirm.

Obviously everything depends on how we interpret these two adjectives, historical and mythic. From the contemporary perspective, historical means real, and therefore true; while mythic signifies nonhistorical, thus fantastic, imaginary, unreal. From a myth's ahistorical point of view, historical facts are only transitory examples—often deceptive and always partial—of a reality that is always transhistorical. In the one case, the true Kṛṣṇa, the living and real Kṛṣṇa, is not a historical fact for most of those who believe in him, but a religious fact. In the other case, the true Christ, equally living and real, is not the mystical Christ for most Christians, but the historical fact of Jesus and his continuing presence in history. Christian missionaries who preach this historical Christ in India, for example, must realize that in so doing they preach a docetism and relativism that is exactly contrary to what they intend to proclaim. Except for those who live in the myth of history, historical facts are merely events that have not reached their full reality.

Man cannot live without myths, without indeed a plurality of myths that intertwine and follow upon one another in a way that allows the continual passage from *mythos* to *logos*, and the constant 're-sourcing' of the *logos* in new *mythoi*. Strictly speaking, there is no isolated myth. Each myth lives in a community of myths. Even in the Judeo-Christian-Islamic tradition where the myth of history predominates, especially during the last few centuries, there have always been other myths. But in order for these other myths to be intelligible and acceptable within the mythic world of history, they must assume historical guise. And so *sacred history* emerges. For those who believe in it, it is true and therefore 'history', but in a very special sense because it is also *sacred*, and it is this sacredness that grounds and inspires history, that invests historical facts with their paradigmatic office, and even serves as the key to their deeper meaning. The historical character of sacred *history* constitutes its aspect of truth: It is 'history', so it is true. The sacred character of *sacred* history is its aspect of mystery, i.e., its transhistorical truth: It is 'sacred', so it transcends history. The myth becomes a fact, but every fact is equally a myth; spiritual realities are historical facts, but historical facts are also spiritual realities. So too we discover the myth of history when we pursue the history of myth. And today this latter provides the transition from *sacred myth* to *historical myth*.

To recapitulate our terminology: by *mythos*, I mean that human organ of apprehension on the same level as the *logos* and in constant relation with it. *Mythos* and *logos* are two human modes of awareness, irreducible one to the other, but equally inseparable.

By *myth*, I understand the horizon of intelligibility, or the sense of Reality, disclosed by a certain *mythologumenon*. The *mythologumenon* is the *legein* of the myth, the living voice, the telling of the myth. If the myth is the truth, the reality, then the *mythologumenon* is the expression, the speaking, the language.

Finally, a myth expressed by a *mythologumenon*, i.e., by a mythic narrative, can contain different *mythemes*, which are the themes (mythic and not necessarily conceptual) the myth elucidates.

b. The Pluralism of Ideologies and Myths

Modern Man, bombarded as he is by mass media supplying more and more examples of human plurality, can no longer believe that a world, a religion, a philosophy, a life-style, is *the* world, or *the* exemplar for religion, philosophy or life. He is less and less inclined to ignore, scorn or consider unenlightened those who do not think as he does; 'primitives' arouse new interest, 'natives' are appreciated, 'non-Christians' or 'aliens' are respected, even courted, and (in spite of the shortcomings of grammar), women are no longer considered inferior. Minorities of every sort are assured that they too deserve their place in the sun and their rights in society. But this same openness—even if it is only theoretical—tends to encourage a deceptive belief in my own 'tolerance' and in the superiority of my worldwide and even universal mission. All this leads us to want to go beyond the mere awareness of plurality to an acceptance of *pluralism*. One of the most positive movements of our day is the dynamism, visible almost everywhere, seeking to pass from *de facto* plurality to *de iure* pluralism. But true pluralism does not belong to the order of the *logos*; pluralism cannot be accepted within an ideology. On the ideological level you cannot compromise with error. Just so, two contradictory conceptual statements cannot both be true at the same level, or according to a single perspective. A pluralistic ideology would always place itself above nonpluralistic ideologies. The result would be merely a super-ideology and the worst of paternalisms—I designate myself know-it-all and even tolerate others, provided they remain in the places I have assigned them. Even if we accept a certain perspectivism and the existence of other levels of life and awareness, we can scarcely avoid hierarchizing perspectives and levels according to some third point of view, which still amounts to an ideology, albeit a super-ideology. But true pluralism outstrips both the conceptual and the ideological domains. A purely dialectical solution to the conflict of ideologies cannot call itself pluralist, for it uses only a single criterion that does not allow for true pluralist autonomy. Pluralism is not merely respect for plurality, as a makeshift, or as a pragmatic necessity. Rather pluralism bears witness that one has transcended the *logos* as sole and final arbiter of the real, though without belittling its sway. Pluralism testifies that one has passed beyond *absolutism,* without thereby tumbling into agnostic *relativism.* Pluralism presupposes only a radical *relativity* underlying all human constructs and at the bottom of reality itself.[4]

In brief, pluralism does not stem from the *logos*, but from the *mythos*. Pluralism is grounded in the belief that no single group embraces the totality of human experience. It is based on trust in the other, even though I may not understand him and from my point of view I will have to say he is quite wrong. Pluralism does not absolutize error because it does not absolutize truth either.

This brings us to a methodic consideration that both introduces our subject and justifies our enterprise. It is just this: Dialogue between cultures, and the mutual fecundation that can result from it, must be enacted first of all on a mythic level rather than in the confrontation between *logoi*. This is not in any way to minimize the importance of dialectics. The dialectical method is fruitful in a discussion within a single culture and/or homogeneous civilization, but it operates differently in an encounter between cultures that may have arisen from fundamentally different presuppositions. To assume a priori that a given conceptual form can serve as the framework for an encounter of cultures represents, from the philosophical point of view, an unacceptable, uncritical extrapolation. Sociologically speaking, it represents yet another vestige of a cultural colonialism that supposes that a single culture can formulate the rules of the game for an authentic encounter between cultures. If the *logos* has priority in intracultural confrontation, the *mythos* takes primacy in intercultural encounters. This implies that a purely philosophical methodo-*logy* based on the *logos* is certainly necessary, but not sufficient. We must complete it with a methodic in which the various *mythologumena* also have their decisive role to play.

Instead of elaborating a working hypothesis, I would like to present a concrete example.

c. The Challenge to Philosophy and Theology

To better situate our example let us briefly consider the double challenge that confronts humanist and 'religious' thought in the West. The challenge is the same in both cases, since Western thinking, even when it denies its tie with the Abrahamic traditions, remains grounded in them.[5] Nevertheless, we ought to distinguish between the philosophical and the theological domains, though without separating them.

i. The challenge to philosophy amounts to wondering whether Man can have a pattern of intelligibility other than that created by the encounter and embrace between *rational evidence and historical verification*. The interface between the sky of rational evidence and the earth of historical verification seems to form the horizon under which Western humanity has lived its intellectual, and hence its human, life for at least several centuries and even, perhaps, for some millennia.[6] Is some other mode of intelligibility possible outside this horizon? Can we arrive at profound, human convictions that are not focused on this skyline where reason encounters the exterior (historical) world? Are there no other pillars of truth? Must everything be grounded in history, aided only by reason? For the moment it is enough to pose the problem as a challenge to philosophy.

ii. The challenge to theology could be posed as a question: Must I become, intellectually and spiritually, a Semite if I want to be religiously a Jew, a Christian or a Muslim? Must I be converted to the ways of thinking, and consequently to the life-styles, of these three historical traditions if I recognize and accept Yahweh, Christ or Muhammed as living and valid religious symbols? The problem takes on a keen edge and worrisome dimensions in Islam, the majority of whose adepts are found among peoples having no bond with Arab culture. It has also been posed for a long time in the Christian world, beginning with the efforts of Christianity to distinguish and even separate itself from Christendom. The problem arises even more urgently, and often tragically, for those Jews who do not want to identify themselves with the state of Israel. And, if we are not too touchy about names like 'theology' and 'religion', we will see the same problem posed for the fourth branch of Western culture called Marxism, Humanism or simply Modernity. Is it necessary to take your categories of intelligibility from the Bible, the Gospel, the Koran or *Das Kapital;* must you enter the *Weltanschauungen* of these great traditions, and even their Marxist appendix, in order to call yourself a servant of Yahweh, a brother of Christ, someone who believes in the Seal of the Prophets, or a Man who works for the temporal happiness of humanity? Must an African, an Indian, a Chinese be uprooted from the fertile soil of an age-old culture, its thinking, its myths and its deep human truths, if he or she feels attracted to these three so-called monotheistic religions, or to modern humanist ideology? To know whether modernization implies Westernization is a burning question for two-thirds of today's world. Must we convert to Marxist thought, must we circumcise the African and Asiatic spirit with the blade of technology in order not to miss the appointed communion, assembly, church to which Man today is called? Is there only the one (Helleno-Semitic) path to Christ? These questions are far from rhetorical; they constitute a challenge to theology.

This study does not claim to directly answer questions of such moment. Neither do we wish merely to substitute one myth for another. We would like, first, to introduce to the Western world an Indian myth quite as fundamental as the more familiar Semitic, Hellenic and other myths that recount the human condition. For this it is enough to tell the story. But we would also like to implant it in the open field of occidental myth, today undergoing a radical transformation. Further, we would like to make explicit the importance of this myth in the very heart of the Indian tradition. And finally we would wish to contribute to the modern symbiosis, which is not simply an artificial and superficial eclecticism, and which becomes the more urgent if we want to step beyond the provincialisms of which we are perhaps aware on a planetary scale for the first time. Human destiny is at stake. Either we acquire our global awareness in the cosmotheandric dimensions of this destiny, or we become simple cogs in the wheels of the megamachine. The schizophrenia between a sincere, even deep (but provincial and sectarian) religious belief, and a profane universal technology (which in one sense liberates, but also stupefies and obliterates any variety) is in the long run unbearable.

2. THE SACRED HISTORY OF ŚUNAHŚEPA

The golden rule of all hermeneutic is simply that the interpreted thing can be recognized in the interpretation. This implies that *inter-pretation* must not be *extra-pretation*, but a mediation between the auto-understanding of the interpreted thing and the hetero-understanding realized by the interpreter.[7] The guarantee of a valid interpretation is much like the proofs in elementary mathematical operations: subtraction to prove addition, multiplication to check division. Only if we can retranslate, i.e., reinterpret our interpretation following the original, can we be sure that we are interpreting correctly and not allegorizing.

In order to interpret a myth, we must consider, first, what the myth *says* literally (the text), and, secondly, what it *wants to say*, i.e., we must know the context of the myth in order to know what it means, and finally we must also consider what the myth *has been made to say* over the ages, for past interpretations belong equally to the encompassing context of whatever we interpret.

In short, we must be familiar with (1) the original story, its *mythologumenon*, its *legein*; (2) the context of this telling, its *myth*; and (3) the commentaries, its *logos*.

a. The Narrative (The *Legein* of the *Myth*)

In the myth of Śunahśepa we are dealing with one of the most complete, and probably most ancient, sacred histories of the entire *śruti* or Vedic revelation.[8] It is an exceptional myth from several points of view.[9] The tale alternates simple prose with verse. The verses consist of original strophes (*gāthā*) and quotations from the Ṛg Veda (*ṛc*). They have an epic character and are more grammatically elaborate than the prose texts, which are in more elementary, even rudimentary, Sanskrit. The legend is found in the Aitareya Brāhmaṇa, which was edited between 800 and 600 B.C.; internal evidence and external scholarly criticism, however, indicate that the myth may be very ancient indeed.[10] The legend is inserted into the description of the royal consecration (the *rājasūya*), which leads us to suspect an earlier date for it, and if we take into consideration the reference to human sacrifice, we might even look for a prehistoric origin.[11]

The well-known text has had various publications,[12] and complete[13] or partial[14] translations. After struggling to present a suitable version myself, I have found an excellent French translation by Jean Varenne, from which the following is largely adapted.[15]

Here then is the sacred history of Śunaḥśepa:

Hariścandra Vaidhasa Aikṣvāka was the son of a king; a hundred wives were his, but he had no son from them. In his house dwelt the Brahmins Parvata and Nārada; he asked Nārada:

'Now since men desire a son,[16]
both those with knowledge and those with none,
what does a man gain by a son?
Tell me that, O Nārada.'

Asked in one verse, Nārada replied in ten:

'The father who sees the face
of a son born living
pays a debt in him
and through him attains immortality.[17]

'There is delight in earth,
and delight in fire,
and delight in air. But among the living,
greater still is a father's in a son.

'By the son have fathers ever
passed over the deep darkness;
self born from self,[18]
in sonship the father ferries over.

'What use is dirt or the goat-skin?
What use is long hair or fervor?
Seek a son, O Brahmin,
this is the world's advice.

'Food is breath, clothing a protection,
gold is for ornament, cattle for dowry,
a wife is a friend, a daughter a misery,
and a son a light in the highest heaven.

'The father enters his wife,
as an embryo he dwells in the mother,
in her is he renewed,
and born in the tenth month.

'A wife is called wife
since in her he is born again;
he is seminal, she fruitful,
from here the hidden seed goes forth.

'Together Gods and seers
have brought her bright grandeur;
the Gods said to mortals
"This is your mother again".

' "A sonless one cannot attain heaven",
even the beasts know this;
therefore among them a son mounts
his mother or his sister.

'This is the wide happy path
on which men with sons fare without sorrow;
the birds and the beasts desire this
enough to unite even with a mother.'

So Nārada told Hariścandra. Then he added, 'Have recourse to Varuṇa the king, saying "Let a son be born to me;
with him let me sacrifice to you." '

'So be it,' Hariścandra replied. And he went up to Varuṇa
the king, saying, 'Let a son be born to me; with him let me

sacrifice to you.'

'So be it,' Varuṇa replied. And a son was born to him, Rohita by name.

Then Varuṇa said to Hariścandra, 'A son has been born to you; sacrifice to me with him.' Hariścandra replied, 'Only when a victim is over ten days old is it fit for sacrifice; let my son become over ten days old; then will I sacrifice him to you.'

'So be it,' Varuṇa said. Now when the child was over ten days old, he said to Hariścandra, 'He is over ten days old; sacrifice him to me.' Hariścandra replied, 'Only when the teeth of a victim appear is it fit for sacrifice. Let his teeth appear; then will I sacrifice him to you.'

'So be it,' Varuṇa said. Now when the child's teeth appeared, he said to Hariścandra, 'His teeth have appeared; sacrifice him to me.' Hariścandra replied, 'Only when the teeth of a victim fall is it fit for sacrifice. Let his teeth fall; then will I sacrifice him to you.'

'So be it,' Varuṇa said. Now when the child's teeth fell, he said to Hariścandra, 'His teeth have fallen; sacrifice him to me.' Hariścandra replied, 'Only when the teeth of a victim appear again is it fit for sacrifice. Let his teeth appear again; then will I sacrifice him to you.'

'So be it,' Varuṇa said. Now when the boy's teeth appeared again, he said to Hariścandra, 'His teeth have appeared again; sacrifice him to me.' Hariścandra replied, 'Only when the *kṣatriya* has won his arms is he fit for sacrifice. Let him win his arms; then will I sacrifice him to you.'

'So be it,' Varuṇa said. Now when Rohita had won his arms, he said to Hariścandra, 'He has won his arms; sacrifice him to me.' 'So be it,' Hariścandra replied and addressed his son, 'It is this one, my dear child, who has given you to me. Now let us go; let me sacrifice you to him.'

'No!' cried Rohita, and taking up his bow he went into the wild. For a year he wandered in the wild and Varuṇa seized Hariścandra so that his belly swelled up.

Rohita heard talk of this; he left the forest and returned toward the village. But Indra came to him in human form, saying

> 'Manifold is the splendor of the ascetic,
> so Revelation tells us, Rohita;
> who chooses to live among men does wrong,
> Indra is friend to the wanderer.[19]

So move on.' And Rohita said to himself, 'This brahmin bids me wander,' so he wandered for a second year in the wild. Then he left the forest and returned toward the village. But again Indra came to him in human form, saying

> 'The wanderer's legs are the stems of flowers,
> and his tough body bears fruit.
> His difficult journey
> delivers him from every sin.

So move on.' And Rohita said to himself, 'This brahmin bids me wander,' so he wandered for a third year in the wild. Then he left the forest and returned toward the village. But Indra again came to him in human form, saying

> 'The fortunes of a sitting man also sit;
> if he stands still, so will his fate.
> If he lies down, his luck will fall asleep,
> but if he bestirs himself, his fortunes shall rise indeed.

So move on.' And Rohita said to himself, 'This brahmin bids me wander,' so he wandered for a fourth year in the wild. Then he left the forest and returned toward the village. But Indra came again to him in human form, saying

> 'Who remains reclining becomes Kali,
> who arises becomes Dvāpara.
> Erect, you are Tretā,
> moving, you are Kṛta.[20]

So move on.' And Rohita said to himself, 'This brahmin bids me wander,' so he wandered for a fifth year in the wild. Then he left the forest and returned toward the village. But Indra came to him again in human form, saying

> 'Journeying you find honey,
> and the delicious Udumbara fruit.
> Consider the sun, happiest of beings,
> who never ceases to journey.

So move on.' And Rohita said to himself, 'This brahmin bids me wander,' so he wandered for a sixth year in the wild. He found in the forest one Ajīgarta Sauyavasi, a seer overcome with hunger. This Ajīgarta had three sons, Śunaḥpuccha, Śunaḥśepa and Śunolāṅgūla.

Rohita said to him, 'I will give you a hundred cows, O Seer, if you let me redeem myself with one of these.' Keeping back the eldest, Ajīgarta said, 'Not this one;' 'Nor this one,' cried the mother, keeping back the youngest. So they settled on the middle son, Śunaḥśepa.

Rohita gave the hundred cows, took Śunaḥśepa with him, left the forest and returned to the village. He went to his father and said, 'O my father, let me redeem myself with this one.' Then Hariścandra went to Varuṇa the king, saying 'Let me sacrifice this one to you.' 'So be it,' Varuṇa replied. 'A brahmin is better than a *kṣatriya*.'

Then Hariścandra proclaimed his intention to celebrate the *rājasūya*, the royal consecration, and on the day of anointing chose the boy as victim.

That day, Viśvāmitra was the Oblate, Jamadagni the Acolyte, Vasiṣṭha took the role of Brahman, and Ayāsya that of Cantor.

But when Śunaḥśepa had been brought up they could find no one willing to bind him. Ajīgarta then said, 'Give me another hundred cows and I shall bind him.' They gave him another hundred and he bound his son. When he had been brought up and bound, and the Apri verses had been recited, and the fire readied around him, they could find no one willing to slaughter him.

Then Ajīgarta said, 'Give me another hundred cows and I shall slaughter him.' They gave him another hundred and he, whetting his knife, advanced toward his son.

Then Śunaḥśepa said to himself, 'They are going to kill me as if I were not a human being. I must have recourse to the Gods!'

He first had recourse to Prājapati, since he is first among the Gods, with this verse:

'Which God then? Which immortal's
pleasing name shall we invoke?
Who will restore us to majestic Freedom,[21]
that I may see father and mother again?'[22]

Prajāpati replied, 'Agni is the nearest of the Gods; have recourse to him.' He had recourse to Agni with this verse:

'Agni the God, first of immortals,
let us invoke his pleasing name!
He will restore us to majestic Freedom[23]
that I may see Father and Mother again!'[24]

Agni advised him, 'Savitr is the great Inciter, have recourse to him.' He had recourse to Savitr with this triplet:

'From you, O God Savitr, ever our aid,
Lord of every precious thing,
we beseech good fortune.

'Since fortune—good or bad—
is for you free from desire,
it remains friendly in your two hands.

'May we attain it! With your help
may we reach the summit of prosperity,
our portion from you, O Bhaga!'[25]

Savitr explained, 'It is for Varuna the king that you are bound; have recourse to him.' He had recourse to Varuna with the following thirty-one verses:

'Your dominion, your strength and your passion,
O Varuna, no birds have attained in their flight,
nor waters in their ceaseless flowing,
nor hills resisting wind's might.

'King Varuna of clear understanding
in bottomless space holds the tree's crown,
branches sunk below, roots on high,
deep in us may his radiance grow!

'A broad path above has Varuna cleared
for the sun without feet to traverse.
May he that found a way for the sun,
keep this blade from our heart!

'A hundred solaces are yours, O King!
May your benevolence be equally vast!
Drive this Destruction out of our world,
free us from whatever sin we have committed!

'These stars we see set overhead at night,
where do they go by day? Nothing
transgresses Varuna's laws; the radiant moon
wanders on, seeing us through the night.

'I salute you, I beg with prayer;
with his offerings, the high priest begs:
Do not be angry, O Varuna!
Do not plunder our lives, O renowned one!

'What they tell me night and day,
what my own heart's light reveals to me:
May he to whom Śunahśepa calls in his bonds,
Varuna, King, set us free!

'Tied to the triple pillar he calls,
Śunahśepa calls to the son of Freedom:[26]
Gracious Varuna, King, untie this victim!
Let the unerring sage undo these bonds!

'We would appease your wrath, O Varuna,
with homage, with prayer and offerings.
Wise God reigning over us, attentive
master, free us from our sins!

'Loosen, O Varuna, the bonds that bind us
above and below and from every side.
Make us sinless before your holy law,
unbound for the boundless, O Aditya![27]

'Whatever law of yours, O God Varuna,
we men, being but mortal,
may violate day after day—
do not consign us, we beg

'to be prey to death
or to your own fierce anger,
to be destroyed
by your displeasure.

'As the charioteer
tethers his steed,
so shall my songs
bind your heart, O Varuna.

'My desires fly away
in search of happiness,
just as birds
fly to their nest.

'When shall we move
Varuṇa to mercy,
the Lord of glorious might
whose eye is far-reaching?

'Common to both Mitra and Varuṇa
is the might. Their love
forsakes no worshiper
faithful to Law.

'He knows the path
of birds in the heaven;
as Lord of the sea
he knows each ship.

'True to his Law,
he knows the twelve months
(and the extra month too)
with their offspring the days.

'The path of the wind—
high, sweeping, powerful—
he knows, and the Gods
who reside in the heavens.

'He sits among his people,
consistent to Law.
Most wise, he presides
and governs all things.

'From there, surveying,
he beholds earth's marvels,
both that which has been
and that which shall be.

'May the wise Aditya
prepare for us always
fair paths to tread,
and prolong our lives!

'Varuṇa, wearing
a golden mantle
is clothed in bright garments.
His watchmen sit round him.

'No men of ill-will,
nor evil-doers,
nor those of wrong intent
can harm this our God—

'the One who gives
consummate glory to Men,
imparting this glory
to these our bodies.

'Yearning for him,
wide-seeing Varuṇa,
my thoughts move onward
as cows to their pasture.

'Again let us converse!
The nectar has been brought.
You eat, as a priest,
the food that you love.

'I have seen the One
whom all may behold
and his car passing high!
My songs are accepted!

'Hear, O Varuṇa!
Show us your favor.
Longing for help
I have cried to you.

'Supreme Lord,
ruling the spheres,
hear, O wise God,
as you pass on your way.

'Free us from fetters
of every sort.
Loosen our bonds
that we may live!'[28]

And Varuṇa said to him, 'Agni is first among the immortals, the best friend. Sing his praises, then shall we deliver you.' Śunaḥśepa praised Agni with the next twenty-two verses:

'Put on your cloak of light,
Lord of might, worthy of honors,
O Agni, offer this our sacrifice!

'Be seated, O chosen one, our priest,
youngest of the Gods! With hymns
and luminous words we invoke you, Agni!

'Father sacrifices for son,
friend for friend,
and comrade for chosen comrade.

'Let the mighty lords Varuṇa,
Mitra and Aryaman sit as men
on this our sacred grass.

'Agni, first priest,
rejoice in our friendship!
Attend well our songs!

'Whatever we unceasingly sacrifice
to God after God, to you alone,
O Agni, is the offering given!

'May he be our dear clan lord,
sweet voiced, our chosen priest!
And may we be dear to good Agni!

'For the gods, too, have this bright fire,
and have given us this treasure.
And so our trust is in Agni.

'Let us both, mortals and immortals,
exchange songs of praise,
O deathless Agni!

'With all your fires, O Agni,
bless this sacrifice and these words,
O youngest son of Strength!'[29]

'I will praise you
like a costly horse, O Agni,
Lord of all our sacrifices!

'The far-striding son of Strength,
benevolent, friendly, mighty Agni;
may he be with us!

'Protect us, O Agni, both far and near,
protect us ever from ruthless mortals,
protect us all our days!

'Announce to the Gods
our newest gift, O Agni—
this song of praise!

'Grant us a share in the highest stakes,
and the lowest, and those in between.
Award me the nearest good!

'You are the portioner, the silver flame
on the river's flux,[30] nearest of the near;
you heap wealth upon the giver!

'The mortal you protect in battle,
the Man you inspire, O Agni,
his joy will be forever fresh!

'None will overcome him,
no man vanquish him, O conqueror,
the victor's portion shall be his!

'Renowned in all lands, he shall carry off
the victor's prize on his steeds,
and win the day with the singers!

'O early watcher, shape us a song
to the glory of Rudra,
whom every clan adores!

'Majestic without measure,
with smoke for an ensign, brilliant Agni;
may he spur us to inspiration, and victory!

'Like an opulent chieftain,
banner of the divine, brightlý gleaming,
may Agni hear our songs!'[31]

And Agni said to him, 'Sing the praises of The-All-Gods,[32] then shall we deliver you.' Śunaḥśepa praised The-All-Gods with this verse:

'Homage to the great and to the small,
to the young and to the old!
Let us honor The-All-Gods, if we can!'[33]

The-All-Gods answered, 'Indra is the mightiest, most powerful, strongest, most real and most effective of the Gods. Sing his praises, then shall we deliver you.' Śunaḥśepa praised Indra with this hymn:

'Since we seem to be without hope,
O soma drinker, truthful Indra,
give us hope, O generous one,
hope of handsome cattle and horses by the thousand!

'You who wear helmet and armor,
master of stakes, lord of strength,
give us hope, O generous one,
hope of handsome cattle and horses by the thousand!

'Put to sleep these two evil-doers who eye each other
turn by turn; so that they do not awaken!
And grant us, O gracious one,
hope of handsome cattle and horses by the thousand!

'Put the greedy to sleep, O hero,
but rouse the generous!
And grant us, O gracious one,
hope of handsome cattle and horses by the thousand!

'Crush this ass who brays your praises!
But grant us, O generous Indra,
hope of handsome cattle
and horses by the thousand!

'Spare us the cyclone, let it buffet the forest
far from us, and keep the lizards company!
But grant us, O generous Indra,
hope of handsome cattle and horses by the thousand!

'Strike down the wailers, O Indra!
Strangle the Kṛkādāśu![34]
But grant us, gracious Indra,
hope of handsome cattle and horses by the thousand![35]

'We urge Indra, God of flowing insight,
to come on in glory: Course through us,
O juice of the soma!

'Who drinks draughts of pure soma by the hundred,
and by the thousand mixed with milk;
In whom the soma flows like a river in the abyss!

'When we surge toward him, joy upon us,
in our rapture the vat becomes his belly
and the soma seems to us ocean!

'This soma is yours! You race to it
as the dove wings to his mate;
and you care equally for our song!

'Lord of gifts, we give you this song,
this garland of praises, O hero,
that in return your strong joy may be ours!

'Gird yourself to help us fight this fight,
O God rich in flowing insight, O Indra,
more than all the others, may we two agree!

'O Indra, strongest of the strong,
in every battle, in every way,
we your friends call for your help!

'If he can but hear our cry,
O Indra, let him come now to our aid,
let him bring the prize of victory!

'I call on Indra,
hero of our ancient home, irresistible,
the first our fathers would call!

'O soma drinker, friend to your friends,
who bears the awakening thunderbolt,
we too drink soma with our helmets on!

'What each Man hopes, O soma-friend,
let it be; bring your thunderbolt
and bring to each his own!

'O Indra, may we your table-mates
win wealth and prizes, so that
rich in cattle we too shall rejoice!

'O bold God, so honored in song,
it fits such a hero to welcome our prayer
like a wheel its axle!

'And as your singers had hoped,
O God of intelligence, your welcome
matches their homage in zeal!'[36]

Delighted at heart with Śunaḥśepa's praise, Indra gave to
him a chariot of gold. And Śunaḥśepa sang another verse:

'Forever has Indra celebrated his trophies
With horses who prance and whinny and snort,
Triumphant horses, barded with his armor;
He has given us the victor's chariot of gold!'[37]

Then Indra said to him, 'Sing now the praises of the
Aśvins,[38] then shall we deliver you.' Śunaḥśepa praised the
Aśvins with the following triplet:

'Come Aśvins, with your marvel treasure of horses!
Grant us a hoard of cattle and gold,
O you of wondrous deeds!

'Your immortal chariot
plies the waves without equal,
O Aśvins of wondrous deeds!

'One of its wheels, O Aśvins,
you have fixed in the sun-bull's eye,
while the other covers heaven!'[39]

Then the two Aśvins declared, 'Sing now the praises of
Uṣas[40] the dawn, then shall we deliver you.' Śunaḥśepa
praised Uṣas with the following triplet:

'What mortal can enjoy you, immortal Uṣas?
Who is it your pleasure to love?
Who among us will you choose, O radiance?

'From far, from near,
you brighten our thoughts
like a ruddy mare, O Uṣas!

'Come to us, O daughter of heaven!
Bring us the prize we seek!
Grant us life!'[41]

And at each verse Śunaḥśepa sang, one of his bonds was
loosed and the swollen belly of Hariścandra shrank a little; at
the very last verse, the last bond fell away and Hariścandra
was cured.

Then the priests said, 'Devise for us the performance of
the day.' Śunaḥśepa saw the immediate soma pressing; this he
pressed with these four verses:

'Although at work in every house,
mortar my friend, here you must echo best,
like a drum in the victor's camp!

'Master of the Forest, mortar,
the wind breathes through your crown;
now press the soma for Indra to drink!

'Yield your treasure for the sacrifice,
mortar, devour the stalks
like Indra's bay steeds!

'Press now, Forest Master mortars,
upright with your upright helpers,
press for Indra juice sweet as honey!'[42]

Then he carried it to the wooden receiving vat with the verse:

'Take up in bowls whatever remains,
and pour the soma through the seive;
on the cowhide set the dregs!'[43]

Then, taking hold of the high priest from behind, he offered the following four verses with cries of *Svāhā!* (Hail!):

'Where the broad-based mortar sets,
where the pestle rises to press the soma,
come there, O Indra!
Drink what we have crushed! *Svāhā!*

'Where mortar and pestle squeeze together
as if to make love,
come there, O Indra!
Drink what we have crushed! *Svāhā!*

'Where women pound true,
forwards and back,
come there, O Indra!
Drink what we have crushed! *Svāhā!*

'Where they bind up the pestle
as we rein in a horse,
come there, O Indra!
Drink what we have crushed! *Svāhā!*'[44]

Then he led the high priest to the final bath with the two
verses:

'O Agni, knowing one, we pray you
ward off the wrath of Varuṇa!
Shining one, best of priests and guides;
drive far from us every evil-doer!

'Draw close, O Agni, and help us,
be very near to us as this day dawns!
Sacrifice for us, make offering to Varuṇa,
gain us his favor and we shall bless you!'[45]

Next he had the high priest pay reverence to the hearth
with the verse:

'Śunaḥśepa was bound, from these thousand stakes
you have freed him when he was in pain!
We also will you free from our bonds,
O wise Agni who put us here!'[46]

Then, the sacrifice concluded, Śunaḥśepa sat on Viśvāmitra's lap. Ajīgarta Sauyavasi demanded, 'O seer, give
back to me my son!' 'No,' said Viśvāmitra, 'the Gods have
given him again to life, and to me.' And so Śunaḥśepa came to
be called Devarāta Viśvāmitrasuta,[47] and his descendants are
the Kāpileya and the Bābhrava.
    Ajīgarta Sauyavasi tried again. 'Come now, let us both[48]
invite him,' he said:

'You are an Āṅgiras by birth,
famed as a sage, son of Ajīgarta;
O seer, do not abandon your ancestors;
return to me!'

To which Śunaḥśepa replied:

'They have seen you knife in hand,
a thing not found even among *śūdras*.
Three hundred cattle, O Āṅgiras,
You preferred to my life!'

And Ajīgarta Sauyavasi answered:

'This evil deed I have done
causes me great remorse, dear one.[49]
I would obliterate it in your eyes;
the three hundred cattle are yours!'

But Śunaḥśepa said:

'He who once does evil
will do that evil again;
you have not abandoned your *śūdra* ways;
what you have done is irreparable!'[50]

At the word 'irreparable' Viśvāmitra joined in, saying:

'Dread indeed was Sauyavasi
when he stood knife in hand,
ready to kill; give him up!
Become a son of mine, Śunahśepa!'

Śunahśepa asked:

'I wish what you have said,
O king's son, but say how,
being an Āṅgiras,
I can become a son of yours.'

Viśvāmitra replied:

'You would be the eldest of my sons,
your children would hold the highest place.
Accept my divine inheritance,
to this I invite you!'

And Śunahśepa said:

'Bid your sons agree
to friendship and prosperity for me,
then may I become your son,
O bull of the Bharatas!'

So Viśvāmitra addressed his sons:

'Listen Madhuchandas,
Ṛṣabha, Reṇu, Aṣṭaka
and all your brothers;
do you accept his precedence?'

Viśvāmitra had a hundred and one sons, fifty older than
Madhuchandas, fifty younger. The older ones did not think
this right. These Viśvāmitra cursed, saying 'Your offspring
shall inherit the outlands of the earth!' These are the Andhra,
the Puṇḍra, the Sabara, the Pulinda and the Mūtiba who live
in large numbers beyond the borders; most of the Dasyu are
descendants of Viśvāmitra.
Madhuchandas with the other fifty said:

'What our father has decided, we accept;
we place you at our head
and we all will follow you.'

At which the delighted Viśvāmitra praised his sons:

'O my children, who by your obedience
have given me a hero for a son,
you shall be rich in cattle
and in your turn have heros for sons!

'With Devarāta, a hero,
to lead you, O Gāthina,
you shall all prosper, my sons;
he shall see truth for you!

'Here is your chief, O Kuśika!
Follow Devarāta!
You yourselves shall be his patrimony,
and all the knowledge we know!'

And for this it is said:

'Thus the sons of Viśvāmitra, the Gāthina,
all together with pleasure
accepted Devarāta
as their chief and eldest.

'So Devarāta, the seer,
had two patrimonies:
the lordship of the Jahnus,
and the sacred lore of the Gāthina.'

This is the tale of Śunaḥśepa, with a hundred Ṛc verses
as well as Gāthās. This the Oblate tells to the king after the
ritual Anointing. He tells it seated on a golden cushion and his
Acolyte, also seated on a golden cushion, responds: Gold is
glory, thus the Oblate makes the king prosper by glory.

'Om' is the response to a Ṛc, 'So be it' to a Gāthā. 'Om'
is divine, 'So be it' human.[51] Thus with what is divine and
what is human are we freed from all evil and every sin.

Therefore a victorious king, even when not sacrificing,

should have this tale of Śunaḥśepa narrated; not the faintest shadow of sin will remain in him.

A thousand he should give to the Narrator, a hundred to the Respondent; the golden cushion and a white mule chariot should also be given to the Oblate who tells the tale.

Those who wish sons can also ask for this legend to be recited. They will have sons.[52]

b. The Context (The *Myth* of the *Legein*)

To situate the context of Śunaḥśepa, we will mention (a) the myth's immediate past, its milieu, which centers on the notion of sacrifice; (b) its present state, its *Sitz im Leben*; and (c) its future, its continuation within the tradition, its vectorial tension, so to speak. We shall not, however, pursue details (interesting as they may be) that belong to a more specialized investigation.[53]

The study of a myth's context is important from a double point of view. First, it is only by situating the myth in its proper context that we can interpret it correctly. Secondly, knowing the context also makes it possible to justify extrapolation, i.e., to apply the myth to situations that differ from the original. We do not transplant a plant with its roots awash in potassium permanganate; we transplant it with an optimum of native soil, so that it can take root together with its own ground in a new milieu.

i. The Sacrifice (Past)

One of the central intuitions of the entire Vedic tradition consists in seeing all life, divine as well as cosmic, in terms of a dynamism rooted in the sacrificial character of reality itself. Sacrifice is the primordial energy, prior to everything. It was by sacrificing himself, by offering himself as victim, that Prajāpati created the world.[54] And, when exhausted by his creative act, it is again through the sacrifice (offered in turn by his creatures) that he regains his power.[55] By sacrifice the Gods win immortality.[56] From the sacrifice of the cosmic Man (*puruṣa*) by the Gods, Men and animals and the cosmos are born.[57] By sacrifice Men obtain heaven.[58] Sacrifice is the fundamental law that regulates absolutely everything: cosmic, divine, human life. 'The sacrifice is Man.'[59] Sacrifice is the total oblation of all we have and all we are; By this offering, life unfolds and we are redeemed from death.[60]

Although the notion of sacrifice may have been modified, refined and interiorized down the ages, the underlying Vedic intuition remains vital. We might express the essence of sacrifice as that action which effectively creates, i.e., which *is* effective, potent, which attains the end it sets itself. Sacrifice is that action which directly links the activity and its result in the selfsame act. It is not a merely ephemeral action which, once accomplished, would disappear as if no longer needed; it is rather an action that is an integral element in every activity. It is the act sustaining the action of whatever acts.

Sacrifice then is communication, and communication constitutes the very structure of the universe. Reality is neither self-subsistent nor purely contingent. It is not necessary that beings, or even Being exist; beings, because they are certainly contingent; Being, because nothing guarantees its existence except itself and it can, if it so please, destroy itself. This is out of our hands, we know nothing about it. Absolutely nothing can prevent a slip back into pure nothingness. We have no guarantee, no certainty, that time will always continue, that the world will not destroy itself one day, or even that Being will not cease to be.[61] The whole of reality maintains itself, it does not lean for support on something else. It is so to speak a divine contingency, a contingency of the second degree. There is no other, ulterior reason for existence, it is its own *raison d'être*. Hence it is for no other reason than itself that Being continues to be. This rationale suffices for an immutable and static notion of Being, but for a dynamic conception, the problem of the ontological continuity of Being becomes crucial. The fundamental question is not: Why is there being rather than nothing, since there is being; but rather: Why will there always be being, why must Being perdure be-ing? We must realize that time on the one hand, and freedom on the other, are at the root of Being.

This universe has no other structure than its own, and here we discover the place and the function of sacrifice. Sacrifice is what conserves and perpetuates life, what gives life and gives it hope. It is what lets Being be. Sacrifice is that act which makes and sustains the universe—not via an external intermediary, be-

cause there is nothing outside the universe, but rather by the
ontological cooperation of the universe with its own subsistence,
that is, by the energy and the love upholding the Being there is.[62]
Man alone cannot accomplish this, and the Gods left to themselves are equally impotent. Alone, the Supreme Being is also
incapable of accomplishing this act, since it is not God for itself,
but for the 'creatures'. To offer sacrifice is not to take part in a
profitable exchange, or to please the Gods, or humanity, or oneself; to sacrifice means to live, to contribute to one's own survival
and to that of the entire universe. It is the act par excellence by
which the universe continues to exist.

Our myth does not stop for such considerations, but sacrifice
plays a central role in it. The God Varuṇa demands a sacrifice,
Śunahśepa is about to be sacrificed, afterwards the priests offer
the *soma* sacrifice, and the myth is realized in the setting of the
rājasūya, another ritual based on sacrifice. Although these sacrifices are more concrete and of lesser scope than the primordial
sacrifice we have been discussing, they actualize it and celebrate
it in part.

ii. The Royal Consecration (Present)

This *mythologumenon* is found in the part of the Aitareya
Brāhmaṇa dedicated to the royal consecration (*rājasūya*). It introduces the consecration[63] and thus plays an integral role in a
Vedic ceremony and even, perhaps, in one of mankind's most
ancient rites.[64] In any case, the *rājasūya* is the rite of Varuṇa,
who is also the God of our myth.[65]

Within the Indian tradition, this sacred history has a
paradigmatic value: It must be recited during the royal consecration so that all the world might hear. It thus fits thematically into
the very heart of human life.[66] The setting of the *rājasūya* gives
the myth its social significance. Although it is recited before the
general assembly, it underscores the superiority of the priest—
the brahmins—over the royalty—the *kṣatriyas*—by the fact that
the hero is a brahmin who, by being offered as a substitute, saves
the life of the king's son. So the context is eminently sacerdotal.
On the other hand, the priestly group is not blameless; the unpar-

donable sin of betraying one's own son is committed by a
brahmin.

In short, the solemn ambience in which this sacred history
unfolds seems to justify speaking of it as a central myth in classical Indian culture. We are thus led to wonder whether this sacred
history is not a myth that reveals an important awakening of
human consciousness.

We have here a very striking example of the old dispute
about the priority of myth over rite, or vice versa. We need not
take sides for or against the 'myth and ritual theory',[67] but only
note the interesting contribution this sacred history could bring to
the question.[68] Our myth clearly shows the interdependence of
rite and myth; but interdependence does not mean subordination.
From one angle, myth and rite seem autonomous. In fact, the rite
of the *rājasūya* has no need of our myth; it could very well take
place without it.[69] Moreover, even if the myth may have been a
later interpolation—simply added by the compiler of the Aitareya
Brāhmaṇa with a view to setting the *rājasūya* in further relief—
the sacred history of Śunaḥśepa is complete in itself and has no
need of the *rājasūya*.[70]

From another angle, myth and rite belong together. The
rājasūya, as a rite unfolding within the cosmic order of history (it
is the consecration of a Man, the king, with historical duties and
cosmic repercussions), cannot content itself with the *aśvamedha*
celebration, i.e., the horse sacrifice.[71] It must one way or another
integrate the *puruṣamedha*, the human sacrifice.[72] Without the
cosmic sacrifice of Man, the royal consecration is not complete
and the king cannot attain the summits of cosmic and universal
sovereignty, for 'the human sacrifice is everything'.[73] But if Man
kills and eats Man, it is no longer the cosmic sacrifice of the
puruṣa, but a debauch.[74] This is why one text tells us that a voice
cried out not to kill the Man, but to free the victim.[75] Here is a link
with our myth. On the one hand, we ought to offer a sacrifice
worthy of Man, and therefore human. On the other, we feel we
must not do it. Śunaḥśepa is the ideal solution. Man recognizes
his total dependence, he immolates himself without compromise,
but also without homicide or suicide. The myth and the rite need

each other. Without the *puruṣamedha* solemnly celebrated in the *rājasūya*, our story could quickly degenerate into pious legend.[76] A myth without its rite is only a cold orthodoxy. But a rite without its myth is pure superstition.

There is therefore a radical interdependence between myth and rite. Every myth is related to a rite, and vice versa, but often in an *existentielle* and extrinsic fashion. The myth need not narrate the rite, nor the rite enact the myth. There is a *sui generis ontonomy* between the two. Myth and rite are both constitutives of human culture.

There is no subordination of action to contemplation, of orthopraxis to orthodoxy, of rite to myth. This would be mythology. Neither is there subordination of practice to theory, or life to principles, of *mythos* to *logos*. This would be rationalism.

But there is even more: Independently of the *rājasūya*, our myth still centers on sacrifice, and contains in itself all the elements of a rite. Here an interesting tension comes to light. Everything revolves around the theme of human sacrifice, but events unfold in such a way that each in its fashion shows why the human sacrifice does not after all take place. The rite is essential to our myth, but it is the myth that leads to an interiorization and spiritualization of the rite. And when all is said and done, no one is sacrificed.

This leads us to consider this myth as the vestige of a primordial initiation rite, probably pre-Vedic and tribal, as we shall yet have occasion to see. Here we need only stress the myth-rite unity that our story reveals.

iii. The Sacredness of the Theme (Future)

Subsequent tradition has not forgotten this sacred history, and we find an almost uninterrupted series of tales about the different characters of our *mythologumenon*.[77] Already in the Rāmāyaṇa, we have another version of the myth:[78] Ambarīṣa, the king of Ayodhyā, was in the midst of offering the royal sacrifice of the *aśvamedha* when, there too, Indra intervened and carried off the victim. Now such a crucial sacrifice cannot be left unfinished; this would entail a major catastrophe. The celebrant priest declared that only a human victim would save the situation. They began searching and finally discovered a brahmin who had three sons. The father wanted to preserve the eldest and the mother wanted the youngest; the one in the middle, Śunahśepa, agreed to serve as the victim for a great sum of gold, jewels and cows.[79] Then he went off to find his maternal uncle Viśvāmitra, to whom he said: "I have neither father nor mother. Arrange it so that the king may be able to offer the sacrifice, but save my life."[80] So the great sage taught him two verses that Śunahśepa uttered when the occasion arrived and was delivered.[81]

Here one should underscore the fact that Śunahśepa offers himself as the victim voluntarily; the sin of paternal betrayal is thereby evaded. On the other hand, Śunahśepa allows himself to be led to the sacrifice knowing he will be spared. The entire sacrificial *mytheme* is thus enfeebled.

The Purāṇas and the Mahābhārata also give us different versions.[82] In chapters VII and VIII of the Mārkaṇḍeya Purāṇa (one of the oldest and most important purāṇas[83]), we read the savory and quixotic narrative of Hariścandra, the famous king lauded in the Mahābhārata for the generosity with which he celebrated the royal consecration, and for which he afterwards pays dearly. His rival is the brahmin Viśvāmitra, whose supremacy Hariścandra bemoans as the downfall of the 'sciences' (*śāstras*). The priest is victorious however, and after reducing Hariścandra to a poverty bordering on misery, still requires from him the ritual honoraria due a brahmin at the *rājasūya*. Hariścandra must sell his kingdom and dispose of all his riches in order to satisfy the debt. Then, with the queen Saibyā and their son, he leaves for Varanasi. But Viśvāmitra has preceded the family to that city and now demands that Hariścandra pay the remainder of his debt at once. The king must sell his wife and child, and then sells himself to a *caṇḍāla* who assigns him the most humiliating tasks, even to the point of making him steal the garments of the dead that people bring to be burned. One night, after a year of this abject work, he recognizes a child brought to be cremated, and the woman who brings him, as his son and his wife. And the king, a model of patience and nonviolence, decides to die with his wife on the pyre of their only son. But he is not free to do so, he must first ask permission of his master the outcaste. He obtains permission, places his son on the pyre and then, before lying there together with his queen, collects his thoughts by meditating on the Supreme Atman, Śiva, Viṣṇu, Brahmā and Kṛṣṇa. At this point, the assembled celestial court intervenes and declares him to be a truly righteous Man who has won heaven by his good works. Even the *caṇḍāla* reveals himself to be none other than the God Dharma. But Hariścandra, the perfect king, refuses to go to heaven unless all his subjects can accompany him. Because of his poverty he had deserted them in suffering, but he cannot abandon them now. He wishes them to share his happiness. So Indra descends from heaven with ten thousand celestial chariots to transport all the king's people. And Hariścandra, having made the necessary arrangements for his resurrected son to succeed him, ascends to heaven with the queen and all his servants and people.

The Mārkaṇḍeya Purāṇa ends the story by praising the patience and generosity of Hariścandra, striking but one melancholy note by alluding to the catastrophic results of the unfinished *rājasūya*.[84] Subsequent legends introduce more complications into the narrative, as if to emphasize the human character of our hero.[85] Thus, for example, the later literature paints for us a Hariścandra who is induced to vaunt his virtues by the brahmin Nārada. As a result, he and his subjects fall from the celestial paradise. Midway, however, he repents and the Gods check his fall and create for the king and his subjects *saubha*, the aerial city between heaven and earth that, following popular belief, can still be seen on special occasions.[86] Even today, this story is a living part of North Indian culture.[87]

c. The Commentaries (The *Logos* of the *Myth*)

Our concern here is not to study the numerous commentaries of Indian and occidental authors on this text. Besides the classical commentary of Sāyana, there are other, earlier commentaries.[88] To the extent that I was able to consult these, I noticed

that they supply precious hints on details and allegorical interpretation,[89] but offer no general interpretation. There is no need—
for these commentators the meaning of the myth goes without
saying, it is self-evident. The majority of commentaries made by
Indologists, on the other hand, are preoccupied with technical
questions or historical problems like human sacrifice, but I have
found no study along the lines of the present interpretation.[90] This
silence bears me out in believing that this is a living myth and so,
for some, it has never been interpreted as a myth while, for
others, it has been offered as a simple legend. To the former, you
give the straightforward account, i.e., the *legein*, not the *logos*, of
the *myth* (you tell the story, but make no hermeneutic of it). For
the latter group, you analyze the *logos* of the story and not the
legein of the *myth* (you reduce it to its literary content, but again
make no hermeneutic of it). Here you are substituting the *logos*,
the interpretation, for the *myth*.

Is it possible to make a hermeneutic of a myth as myth? Do
we not condemn our own effort, since we are trying precisely to
interpret this myth? Do we kill the myth by interpreting it? My
reply here must be as carefully nuanced as it is sincere. The
moment someone feels the need to interpret a myth he cannot, by
this very fact, accept it without his interpretation. But then the
myth has crossed over from the invisible horizon to the visible
object, from the background canvas to the figure in relief, from
the context to the text. When we cease to believe *the myth*, when
it no longer 'goes without saying', we try to believe *in* it by means
of our interpretation. But in so doing we distance ourselves from
it; the myth is no longer connatural to us, transparent. Its interpretation inter-poses itself between the myth and us. Was Socrates not condemned to death for daring to interpret myth?[91]

Clearly, there is a whole *methodic* latent here, quite different
from any traditional methodology. I have already hinted at it but,
as I have said, I prefer giving an example to elaborating a theory.
Therefore I shall mention only a few of the problems raised by
Indologists, in order to round out the setting of our myth.

i. The Elements of the Sacred History

An analysis of this sacred history leads us to think that it
arises from the conjunction of three motifs and three stories.[92]

The first motif, probably the oldest, goes back to the Ṛg Vedic texts that recount Śunahśepa's liberation from affliction and death due to the bounty and generosity of the Gods. There is here an element of piety, of *bhakti*, and trust in God—one of the rare Vedic examples of such devotion tinged with love. From this angle it seems to be a purely religious text, ripe for any spiritual or spiritualist interpretation: It is divine grace that frees Men from anguish and danger. The sacred history becomes a theology that recounts the relations between Man and the Gods. The hero is Śunahśepa: Man in distress, or simply *homo religiosus* (the brahmin).

The second element centers on the story of Hariścandra and his son Rohita.[93] Śunahśepa appears only as the substitute. The theme here is confronting one's destiny, and fleeing it. The sacred history becomes a cosmology that underscores the solidarity of the entire universe. The hero is Rohita: Man in the world, or simply *homo saecularis* (the *kṣatriya*).

The latest text furnishes the third element; here the accent is on Śunahśepa[94], above all on his relationship with Viśvāmitra, since this affects the whole skein of relations between the *gotra* (clans) of different families. The theme is more ritualistic and sociologically important for India. The sacred history becomes an anthropology—or a sociology—showing the ethico-historical dimension of these human ties. The hero is Devarāta: Man in his historical role, or simply *homo politicus*.

One thing seems clear: This sacred history, conveyed to us over nearly three millennia, reveals older and in a sense deeper strata of human awareness than we find in the historical era of the written document. It has been composed with extreme care, placed in an appropriate setting, and worded in such a detailed way that it seems written for posterity—for us.

Whatever our *mythologumenon*'s gestation period may have been, we ought to stress the myth's functional unity. A myth is not a historical narrative. We must see it whole in order to understand it. Besides his importance in the Brāhmaṇic tradition, Śunahśepa is also a seer, a Vedic *ṛṣi*.[95] In the Ṛg Veda we find the hymns he composed at the sacrificial stake together with others attributed to him as well.[96]

ii. The Human Sacrifice

Our story is a *locus classicus* of discussion on human sacrifice in Vedic India,[97] a required study among Indologists of the
last century.[98] Those who subscribed to an interpretation favoring the existence of human sacrifice alleged, above all, that such a
story could not have been told if human sacrifice had not been a
practice current, or at least familiar, during that epoch.[99] Others,
in our century as well, lean heavily on parallels within the overall
Indian tradition.[100]

On the other hand some authors, probably the most numerous, tell us that human sacrifice is certainly not Vedic.[101] Indeed,
our text in general seems to hold human sacrifice in disfavor—the
general narrative tone, the denouement of the plot, the four
priests who refuse to sacrifice a human victim, the fact that
Ajīgarta, Śunahśepa's father, is punished to the point of losing his
paternity for having consented to bind his son for the sacrifice,
Śunahśepa's cry of surprise and anguish when he discovers they
want to kill him like an animal; a great deal supports the negative
thesis concerning human sacrifice.

Other authors see in the tale an end to this custom and,
according to these scholars, the legend was composed with this in
mind. Still another sort of interpretation that favors the existence
of human sacrifice makes the strong and crucial point that if the
danger were not real, the story would be meaningless.[102]

Parenthetically, perhaps, one might also wonder why a king
who lacks an heir would pray for a son only to sacrifice him.[103]
Are we to conclude that the customs of the time demanded sacrifice of the firstborn?[104]

However these matters may stand, the central problem is not
merely a problem for historico-religious research, but also and
above all a truly human question, with which we must now come
to grips.

3. THE MYTH OF THE HUMAN CONDITION

Can we present this myth in such a way as to express the
deep convictions, the horizon, of the culture that gave it birth,

and at the same time discover it as a sacred history able to offer to other cultures a guidepost to where they may find a thinking deeper, or even fresher, than their own? Has this myth a transcultural value, and consequently a role to play in the encounter and eventual enrichment of human traditions?

This is not only, nor principally, a question of appropriate translation into another idiom, i.e., it is not just transposing one system of signs into another system of signs in order to express in a different way what one already knows. Here it is a question of *language*, not merely of idiom. Our problem is not translation. We can only translate what can be translated into another system. All true translation presupposes, first, that the elements we are going to transpose retain their identity in the transaction, and, second, that there are meaningful signs for these elements already present in the idiom into which we are translating.

Here we see the fundamental difference in method between translating concepts and interpreting myths. The hermeneutic of myths resembles a liturgical act, a sacred action, which is the true office of Hermes—not an intermediary, a simple go-between, but a priest, a mediator between worlds.

Our own function is consequently that of priest, celebrant, even prophet. What concerns us is whether this myth can be celebrated on soil not its own, whether it can realize in another culture a function similar to the one it has fulfilled in its original culture. Can we sing the psalm of Śunaḥśepa on foreign soil?[105] Can this *mythologumenon* be truly revealing, as every genuine myth is? Any myth, to be sure, offers us a horizon over against which we can voice whatever we discover; but at the same time, every myth sets us a course, opens certain doors, unveils dimensions of the real that without this contact might not be dis-covered (myth as revelation) or even heard (myth as *śruti*). No revelation manifests something utterly new, which we would find incomprehensible. Every revelation unveils what we have already glimpsed, foreseen and even in a way believed.

The thrust of our interpretation comes down to what I could call an anthropological theory of myth. This theory does not deny any other approach to myth: psychological, morphological, structuralist, historical or theological. The contributions of contemporary scholarship are too abundant to ignore.[106] Rather it emphasizes a trait common to most of these theories: In myth Man discovers himself, myth expresses what Man is.

Myth entices and intimates, it gives pause, it excites and fascinates, because in myth Man discovers his roots, his origins, as integral parts of his own being. He discovers in myth his true memory, which is not only the conscious reminiscence of events in his individual lifetime, but a memory that extends over thousands of years, back at least to the origins of his language. Whatever the question—Man's psychological, personal or social dimension, his historical agency, his reflection on being human, or his response to the sacred—in every case, we discover in myth what Man is. In this perspective we will situate ourselves.

The method we will use is not directly comparative; i.e., we shall not compare the Indian myth of Śunahśepa with, say, the biblical myth of Adam or Abraham or even Job. We will pursue a more simple, although more difficult, course: to clarify the myth by itself, to place it in a larger context that will render it intelligible given the horizon of understanding provided by contemporary Western language. *In obliquo*, we will find here points of contact as well as disparities, but these depend on our personal contexts. Strictly speaking, the *mythologumenon* needs a *ṛṣi*, a bard, in order to be sung, recited; and a *hotṛ*, a priest, in order to be performed, consummated.

I have called this sacred history a myth of the human condition for two reasons. First, from the phenomenological point of view, it depicts the factual situation of Man on earth. I hope to show this by analyzing respectively (1) the characters of the *mythologumenon*, and (2) several *mythemes*, present and absent. Secondly, from the philosophical point of view, the myth presents the human condition by bringing it to a climax in the deconditioning of human liberation itself, i.e., by really freeing freedom from the compulsion to be.

a. The Characters

Before us parade the representatives of the three worlds: Gods, Men and Cosmos. It is worth recalling that the cosmotheandric vision of reality is an almost universal cultural invariant. I know of no culture where heaven-earth-hell, past-present-future, Gods-Men-World, and pronouns I-you-it, and even the intellectual triad of yes, no and their embrace, are not found in one form or another.

Here I can only capsulize this cosmotheandric principle, which I have developed at length elsewhere, by noting that the divine, the human and the earthly—however we prefer to call them—are three real and different dimensions that constitute the real, i.e., any reality inasmuch as it is real. We can, we sometimes even must, make distinctions, but we cannot close communication between spheres of the real. What this principle emphasizes is that the three dimensions of Reality are neither three modes of a monolithic indistinguishable Reality, nor are they three elements of a pluralistic system. They are rather one, though intrinsically threefold, relation that expresses the ultimate constitution of Reality.

The central theme of our myth is the human condition, not the divine situation or the destiny of cosmos. But it depicts an all-embracing, and not a solipsistic, human condition. The humans here occupy the foreground, but they are not alone. The myth is centered on a complete Man, not closed in on an abstraction 'man' lacking any constitutive relation to the entire reality.

i. The Humans

A. *Śunaḥśepa* is without doubt the central figure, the hero of our myth. He is flanked right and left by two pairs of characters whose roles change according to circumstances. First, on his right are the king Hariścandra and his son Rohita, the dual cause of his trial; on his left are Ajīgarta and the priest Viśvāmitra, the two fathers who claim him. Next, at his right are the ailing Hariścandra and Viśvāmitra who refuses to sacrifice Śunaḥśepa, both together being the secondary cause of his deliverance; and at his left, Rohita, egoist or anguished son, and Ajīgarta, miser or coward, both being the secondary cause of his ordeal. Throughout the drama we find this ambivalence of roles.

His name is just revolting: Śunaḥśepa, 'the penis of a dog',[107] the most shameful part of an accursed animal. (His brothers have similar names.[108]) But neither the name nor the form (which, as *nāmarūpa*, generally go together in Indian literature) represents the thing or its function, even less its essence. The notion is midway between realism and nominalism: The *nāma* is exterior, but it must be interiorized until it is completely transformed. But change cannot come before initiation, conversion, purification. And the process must be total. The name will not change until the very end, until the victory in the trial-by-fire with death. Śunahśepa's name changes only when Viśvāmitra explains what has happened: The Gods have given him back to life, and to Viśvāmitra—Devarāta, God-given (Deodatus, Theodorus). Man must live his life with a humble, even humiliating name until he is free.

All India recalls the teaching of the Chāndogya Upaniṣad[109] that name and form are not the essence, not the being, and of no importance in arriving at wisdom, which is not to know all things, but to understand that by which all things are known.[110]

Śunahśepa is a brahmin, son of a brahmin of the Āṅgiras line.[111] It befits a brahmin to be poor, but not to be miserable in this poverty or harried by hunger. Śunahśepa's only worth, his wealth, is his life, most of which is still to be lived.[112] And this life they would strip from him in the most inhuman way. He is not the hero who fights, who risks life and limb for a noble cause, nor the one who abandons this world's goods to seek better. He is not an exceptional, extraordinary fellow. To the contrary, he incarnates the most banal, the most common, human condition: the son of a poor family who yet retains the dignity of knowing himself to be a person.

Śunahśepa is alone, without ties: pure victim. His father looks out for the eldest son, and his mother watches over the youngest; but he belongs to no one. He has neither father nor mother nor possessions.[113] He has only himself.[114]

Śunahśepa does nothing; bad luck finds him. He approaches the pyre and allows himself to be tied to the triple stake.[115] Is this not the human destiny of the common Man; Śunahśepa, the Man whose life is controlled by circumstance, the Man brought to bay at death's door? Śunahśepa is seized unawares. Nothing has prepared him for the role he is to play. Only at the last moment, when he realizes they are about to sacrifice him like an animal, when there is no other way out, does he have recourse to prayer as a final entreaty.

Śunaḥśepa's mission is not the fruit of a choice or an option: It is a given, or rather an unexpected and seemingly paradoxical gift that takes protean form, now as a menace, now as a curse. In any case, it is not a mission chosen nor a conflict sought. There is no willfulness here. The ordinary Man does not choose his vocation, he has neither the luxury, nor the occasion, to torment himself by asking whether he could not be more useful elsewhere, or whether he could do something else. Destiny hits us like a thunderbolt; it corners us and leaves no door open, no alternative but a leap into transcendence. The moment of *salto morale* comes only when existence is menaced, when life itself is at stake. Here is where prayer is most authentic.

The prayer of Śunaḥśepa is not primarily an intellectual elucubration, nor is it an outpouring of the heart. It is sincere, but neither directly willed nor reflexively reasoned out. It is the final attempt, the supreme request, by groping, searching. He knows neither whom to address nor how. He tries again and again, he perseveres without being discouraged. His patience, his endurance, will save him.

Śunaḥśepa's prayer is not a superfluity. It is neither the effusion of a loving heart, nor the profusion of a spirit in quest of supreme knowledge. It is much more elementary, terrestrial, urgent. It is the simple cry of a Man who is 'without hope', as Śunaḥśepa himself puts it.[116] This prayer is the cry of a Man in misery, the human spirit's spontaneous impulse toward something more powerful than itself or the whims of Men. When you have recourse to other, more direct means for obtaining what you want, prayer is not authentic, above all if you make it an excuse for not using these other means. You only really pray in a 'limit situation'. Prayer is the very frontier of life, not a simple human activity alongside all the others, but the final and most fundamental human act, by which Man recovers life when all else fails. Prayer wells up spontaneously from the very fount of our being, almost in spite of us: It hollows us out through and through, as if issuing from a hidden immanence we did not suspect and flowing into an infinite transcendence we cannot even imagine.

We tend to forget that the very word 'prayer' does not mean only a request, but a *precarious* supplication—uncertain, unassured, impoverished, lacking any basis or support other than that which it invokes.[117] Magic, not prayer, claims to be effective by itself.

Once free, Śunahśepa remains within the ritual world. He reenters the realm of the sacred and must perform his new office. The true high priest is always also the victim.[118] Since the sacrifice cannot remain unfinished, he must complete it. He becomes the *rṣi*, the seer, the poet, the priest. Now he is the whole sacrifice, 'Man is the sacrifice.'[119]

Śunahśepa is Man, the victim of destiny—of the Gods, of society, of human privilege and power. He is the average Man, the Man of this exploited, starving, enslaved, alienated majority present since the world began, the victim of the sacrifice. He is the poor Man called 'a dog's penis'. But he is also—and here we find all the ambivalence of the sacred—the victim who by his sacrifice gives life. He is the savior, the pure one, the one who pays, because he is the only one who has the wherewithal, something to pay with—namely his life. Śunahśepa is the one who atones for and redeems the powerful, the nobles, warriors, rich Men, Men of action, and all the Rohitas of the world. He is the true brahmin, the real priest—the 'royal' priest, not a class or a caste, but the common human being with an unembellished humanness that truly mediates between the Gods and the rest of the World.

Some have wanted to see in Śunahśepa a fettered solar divinity.[120] He thus becomes a cosmic figure fastened to the triple-rooted[121] cosmic tree.[122] It is not for us to interpret Śunahśepa by way of a full-blown hypothesis on Vedic divinities. Our human interpretation is valuable for the myth in itself, even if the cosmic and solar hypothesis should prove accurate.

B. Rohita, after Śunahśepa, is the richest character in the myth. His name too is significant. It means "the reddish one", a double reference to the sun (often called by this name), and to the earth ('the red'). Rohita, like *adamah*, means the reddish inhabitant of earth; the active Man par excellence.[123] He incarnates historical Man, the one who makes history, *homo activus*.

If Śunaḥśepa is the Man marked by destiny, who bears his burden by sacred calling, Rohita is preeminently the secular Man, the one who chooses, who finds himself confronted by life-or-death options. He is the Man of will, above all of a will to life. The passivity and nonviolence of the brahmin Śunaḥśepa contrasts with the activity and aggression of the *kṣatriya* Rohita.

Rohita is born of an impossibility. He is exceptional. Even a hundred wives could not engender him. Just so, human life is the exception in nature, it realizes the minimum probability. Life is indeed a gift, but we hoard it, we resist giving it back; it is too precious, too exceptional. There is a Rohita in everyone.

The life of Rohita is an obstacle course run around death. He flees death, he runs in the opposite direction. In childhood, his father decides for him; later, he himself says no! and leaves for the forest. He cannot live among Men because he fears they may recognize him, trap him. But his fear does not paralyze him; he is ready to take up his bow and assume his responsibilities; he slinks only from death. When he hears talk of his father's affliction, he is prepared to go to him; but each time he seems about to yield to filial piety, Indra appears in the form of a brahmin and counsels him not to bury himself in his kingdom, not to go home to his village. He must wander like the sun: *Homo viator!* Has he succumbed to temptation or followed good advice? We cannot answer this question without denying its validity (as we shall see a little later).

Rohita's first act once he reaches the age of reason is to say no, and leave for the wild. This no is not a mere figure of speech. Rohita does not justify himself, he argues against nobody. He says no, picks up his bow and escapes. This no is repeated successively throughout his wandering life; the five times he seems ready to give in, his no is reinforced by Indra's arguments. What is Man? The *ascetic* of life, the animal who says no?[124] Is he the *rebel* in the universe, the one who collapses under the burden of his humanity?[125] Is he the *itinerant*, not yet mature enough or wise enough to accept human contingency?[126]

In any case, Rohita's life gravitates around this no. It is a no to death, but also to obedience and submission. Does he say no to *dharma* and ultimately to *ṛta*? Or does he only repudiate tradition's burden and ultimately injustice?

In the first instance Rohita would be a blasphemer: In order to save his own skin he defies the cosmic order, tries to avoid it, and finally coerces Ajīgarta to sell his son. But the narrative gives no clue that would permit this interpretation. Not a single line pronounces judgment against Rohita. His actions appear irreproachable. Such a hermeneutic is also impossible given the Indian context of our story. The *kṣatriya* (as we read in the Gītā) must set his own life to protect others.[127]

In the second instance Rohita would be the hero of our myth, he would represent Man, the reddish one, the earthly, the secular one, who, bow in hand, confronts the fixed, petrified tradition and tries to free himself from the Gods' crushing grip. It is then hardly surprising that he should choose a brahmin, the living incarnation of tradition, as his substitute. From this angle, Rohita represents a mankind come of age that, freed from paternal tutelage, seeks to protect itself by taking in hand its own destiny.

But it is important to keep from seeing Rohita's attempts at emancipation as a revolution in the modern sense of the word. Rohita does not revolt against his father, nor does he rebel against the Gods. He is not a Prometheus struggling against Zeus. Rohita denounces nothing and nobody. Throughout the narrative there is an atmosphere of serenity that keeps Rohita from being turned into a Western-style prophet like Jonah, for instance. He says no, and afterwards keeps silent, flees and tries to defend himself.

Rohita is spared death, but he also misses true life. The silence of the text is freighted with meaning. There is nothing more to say about Rohita; he lived to escape death and in this he succeeded, but is this evasion authentic life? In any case, emancipation remains a central consideration to which we shall return.

C. Hariścandra, of whom later legend will speak so abundantly, is in this myth a peculiar, rather eclipsed character. Here we shall

note only the essential traits that characterize his role. Hariścandra has but a single desire: to have a son and keep him alive.
He symbolizes the wish for immortality, represented in this case
by the desire for a male descendant. He wants to live on, he
knows he himself cannot exhaust all the vitality he possesses. He
still has projects to realize, dreams to dream, pleasures to try,
powers to exercise. Hariścandra is the Man for whom life is too
short, or too full. He cannot live by halves, nor leave any desire
unsated. He needs to prolong his life. It is the son who continues
the life of the father, and so saves him. Hariścandra has feelings
common to everyone. He embarks on an affair without knowing
how he will ever get out of it; and when he finds himself driven
into a corner, he continually puts off any decision. He wants only
to avoid the humiliation of not having an heir.

Hariścandra cannot escape the destiny he has forged for himself. He falls ill because he does not keep his promise to offer his
son in sacrifice to Varuṇa. He has power, but not freedom; he is a
king, possesses a kingdom, but he is sick and impotent.

It is significant that later tradition has focused the myth more
and more on Hariścandra, nearly forgetting the other characters.
Does this indicate merely a change in the social climate favoring
the monarchy, to which the court scribes bear witness? We might
instead venture two hypotheses. The first is the tendency to convert tragedy into drama. Although the myth may not have the
literary form of a tragedy, it presents certain tragic elements.
Śunaḥśepa and Rohita are seized by destiny, they represent Man,
they incarnate us, each in his fashion. On the other hand, the
legends of Hariścandra are dramas. Hariścandra is a king; we can
look at him, even pity him, but from a distance. He is not us, we
cannot identify with him.

Our second hypothesis would be that while the mythic
strength of Śunaḥśepa and Rohita has remained buried over the
centuries, only to flower in our own day, the evocative strength of
the drama surrounding Hariścandra, the nobleman with his faith
in Men and the Gods, harmonized more readily with the atmosphere of times past. Hariścandra would then be the hero of a
bygone social order.

D. Ajīgarta, so the text tells us, was starving. Hunger is a poor counselor, but also a valid excuse. He should nevertheless have been content with selling his son, but he seems to have caught a taste for silver. He comes forward a second, then a third time, to bind and to sacrifice Śunaḥśepa, in return for which he adds to his riches. If Hariścandra wants a son at any price, Ajīgarta is hardly anxious to keep his. Certainly, he has two other sons, but, as Śunaḥśepa himself reproaches him, to prefer three hundred cows to the life of his son is unthinkable, even among people of the lowest class. Ajīgarta the brahmin behaves worse than a *śūdra*. The value of the person is measured here by his acts, not by his birth. Rather a revolutionary vision for a society on the way to petrifying its caste system.

It is noteworthy that the myth speaks of the sin of Ajīgarta, and even of an unforgivable act. His own son indicts him. But in later tradition the great code of Manu justifies acts committed in order to save life that is menaced by starvation and even cites Ajīgarta as a pertinent example:

> Ajīgarta, suffering from hunger, comes close to sacrificing his son, but he committed no sin, since he sought to cure hunger.[128]

We note here the radical change of valuation when passing from the ontological regime we have been considering to the juridical regime of the *śāstras*. In this latter world Ajīgarta's action is not considered sinful—and many a court of justice would probably agree with Manu (at least regarding the first hundred cows). In the realm of ontological sacrifice, on the other hand, which is the context of our myth, Ajīgarta is the villain indispensable for the sacrifice, the traitor necessary to complete the sacrifice; he is in a way the true high priest of the sacrifice: the 'hangman'. And in another sense he is the 'victim' who makes it possible. Śunaḥśepa is the victim immolated for Men, which is why he is spared and does not die. Rohita is in a certain sense the victim chosen by the Gods and the victim of circumstances, who is also saved by Śunaḥśepa. But Ajīgarta is the true victim, the one who is not spared. He is the victim of cosmic destiny, *rta*, and is condemned without pardon. And yet it is Ajīgarta who, as Śunaḥśepa's father, but above all by his triple acceptance, renders the sacrifice possible. Is there not in every sacrifice an irreducible, unpardonable element which cannot be integrated into the sacrifice and which is precisely what makes the sacrifice possible? It seems there must be a sin, hence a sinner, a fall, a disorder at the origin of any sacrifice. Even more, it seems there is an originating fault at the origin of the universe itself.[129] Unhappy the one through whom the scandal comes, accursed he who commits the crime, or causes it, but through his sin, by his crime, deliverance comes and the sacrifice is effective. Ajīgarta represents the ontological condition for sacrifice, that act for which no reparation is possible. He is both the stumbling block and the starting block. Thanks to his sin, virtue triumphs.

E. Viśvāmitra is among the most famous *ṛṣis* of the Vedas, and the author of the Gāyatrī; this *kṣatriya* (or even, according to some, this *śūdra*) who merits the rank of brahmin[130] by his austerities and by his life, here plays a double role. On the one hand, he represents the liturgical and sacred element, the complete sacerdotal order in its dimension of charisma and institution. He is the Man of rite, of sacred history. Despite the abomination of the human sacrifice, he and his fellow priests cannot ignore the vitality of sacrifice and implore Śunaḥśepa to continue the ceremony after he is no longer its victim. One can neither interrupt the sacrifice, nor leave it unfinished, as the 'rubrics' of practically all religious traditions tell us.[131]

On the other hand, Viśvāmitra is the Man of the Establishment, of History. He not only adopts Śunaḥśepa, but installs him as the eldest of his sons, as the chief of the *gotra,* the clans that make up the elite of the Aryan race. We can speak of the unity between sacred and profane, or of the continuum between sacred history and secular history, or of the institutional and charismatic character of the priesthood; in any case, Viśvāmitra stands for sacred and historical continuity, as the whole tradition surrounding this Vedic seer confirms.

F. Vasiṣṭha

Vasiṣṭha, the great brahmin and foe of Viśvāmitra, hardly appears in our history. Important as he is in other contexts, here he would only figure in a 'historical' and 'naturalistic' interpretation. According to this exegesis, everything is reduced to a political plot of Vasiṣṭha in order to inherit Hariścandra's kingdom: As the royal priest, he first suggested the vow to the king and then, clothed as Indra, tried to dissuade Rohita from going back.[132]

G. The People

Although these five characters may be the myth's central figures, all of humanity is represented as well.

The women have a role best described as subdued; the hundred wives of Hariścandra and the mother of Śunaḥśepa are mentioned, but Rohita's mother is not identified.[133]

The two brahmins Parvata and Nārada are the voice of purest orthodoxy. It is Nārada who expounds the traditional doctrine of immortality and who advises the king to have recourse to Varuṇa by promising to offer his son in sacrifice. It is Nārada who tells us of the incest between animals in order to obtain descendants and of the traditional notion of human debts.

The names of the three other priests officiating at the sacrifice are also mentioned. Viśvāmitra is the Oblate, Vasiṣṭha, his traditional enemy, plays the role of Brahman,[134] and Jamadagni is the Acolyte. The liturgical, sacramental and sacred setting is thus complete.

Śunaḥśepa's two brothers are mentioned as well. Their presence underscores both Śunaḥśepa's solitude and his ties with the community. Solitude, because he is alone, he is not the favorite, saved by his parents like his brothers; his communal ties, since he is one among the sons of Ajīgarta, a 'young man of good family'.

Finally, history is represented by the hundred and one sons of Viśvāmitra. Here, as in any historical realm, we have a division into two groups, the elders who are cursed by their father for not accepting Śunaḥśepa, and the younger ones who are blessed and from whom the pure clans of the Aryan race will descend. It is very clear here that the origin of castes 'beyond the pale' lies in a disobedience and a curse; the *dasyu*, slaves or non-Aryans are also descendants of Viśvāmitra. The myth seems to want to justify history and sociology, so it emphasizes the fact that both Aryans and non-Aryans are sons of the same father. Here is myth seeking to vindicate history.

ii. The Gods

The human condition is not complete if it does not include the mysterious forces that envelop human life. In this myth we find three very significant patterns of divine intervention.

A. Varuṇa, the great God of the Ṛg Veda, is the supreme Lord of life and death. He watches over all that lives. Now every human birth modifies the universal *status quo.* Man must thus reestablish the equilibrium his existence has disrupted. In Vedic terms: Human life carries with it a fourfold obligation on the part of the new being towards all reality, a debt that accompanies one throughout life.[135] These obligations are not the results of chance, but constitutive of human life: the debt to the Gods, to the *ṛsis*, to the ancestors and to humanity. Accordingly, one offers sacrifice (to cooperate with the Gods in sustaining the world), studies the Vedas (to acquire wisdom and so live a full life), prolongs the life one has received, i.e., has children (each of us is the link between our ancestors and our descendants), and finally welcomes one's contemporaries, practices hospitality and the other civic virtues (without which life would be a failure).[136]

It is within this context that we must understand the role of Varuṇa. Rohita's birth, like any human birth, is the fruit of a longing and a natural improbability. Man does not belong to the Gods like some sort of private property of which they may dispose at will. *Ṛta*, cosmic order, governs the dynamism of all Reality. Man belongs to the entire universe. The Gods also have their role—a divine role—to play. Varuṇa, the guardian of *ṛta*, enters our tale not as a capricious and powerful sovereign; he does not take the initiative, he simply agrees to Hariścandra's proposition. He does not accept Hariścandra's promise in order to test him, tempt him, or toy with him by putting him in an impossible situation. Varuṇa is not an anthropomorphic God. In spite of Śunaḥśepa's prayer, it is not Varuṇa who delivers him.

He need not justify himself before Men, nor explain death and evil to them. As Lord of the cosmic order, he knows very well that human life is transitory and that one must offer it in sacrifice. The mystery of life is the mystery of solidarity, the law of *karma* stands always in the background. Each of us has to face his own *karma*. Rohita must die like any Man. So must Śunaḥśepa. Only the manner of death differs. In this common destiny, the real state of things, which is normally unseen, becomes visible. Varuṇa is but its living symbol.

B. Indra is always a God who strikes; but this time he does not strike with his *vajra*, his thunderbolt, but by his unexpected intervention, which brings to light an important facet of this sacred history. Rohita refuses five consecutive times to return home so that Hariścandra might keep his promise to Varuṇa and be cured. The temptation, if we can call it that, does not come from demons, but from God. Rohita never feels compelled. Indra takes human form precisely in order to let Rohita choose for himself. Rohita does not have to decide between filial duty and divine command. He must decide by virtue of his own convictions. Nevertheless, Indra seems opposed to the justice that is due to Varuṇa. A monolithic conception of divinity would have temptation come only from the devil; but then where does the devil come from? In a pluralistic conception of divinity (not to be confounded with so-called polytheistic plurality), temptation comes from the very core of the divinity. But temptation is certainly not an evil per se, and Man must recognize in it an immense potential to be developed. Temptation is not a trap, neither is it a sort of low blow from an enemy. Temptation is intrinsic to life, it belongs to the very nature of things and to the divinity; it is at once the test and the proof; it proffers different courses of action and confronts us with the full constitutive ambivalence of the human situation. It thus creates a space where human will can unfold. This is not the function of an evil spirit, but of God himself. Such is Indra's role in our story.

The temptation instigated by Indra is the ordeal all adults must undergo in making decisions. Death lurks everywhere. Can we escape it? In the village, at home, death is certain; but in the wild, life is not a human life. Clearly, the true *saṁnyāsin* must forsake the village, even if his father is dying, and even if he, the son, has caused it. The exigency of the absolute is absolute. Indra offers Rohita the opportunity to convert his evasion into a sublimation. Let us examine this more closely.

Although the *Sūtra* narrative, which postdates the Brāhmaṇa version, speaks of yet a sixth encounter with Indra, the five temptations of our text offer an interesting typology of human ordeals, and consequently of what Man is.[137]

The key theme is always pilgrimage, movement: 'Move on, move on!' The leitmotif of all Indra's interventions is to emphasize that action, the life of wandering, of continual pilgrimage—in a word, dynamism—is superior to all static conformity. We should recall the situation: Rohita has pangs of conscience and decides to return to his father and face his destiny. Indra, disguised as a brahmin, goes to meet him and convinces him otherwise; he must continue to live, to wander, to follow his path.[138]

The reasons comprising the five temptations are drawn from different depths: The first is grounded in the superiority of the *saṁnyāsin*, of asceticism over the townsman's life, since 'he who chooses to live among Men does wrong'. This is the traditional rationale and Indra mentions *śruti*, Revelation, in order to lend weight to his argument. He does not propose disobedience, but fidelity to tradition.

The second temptation goes a step further. Deliverance is not easy; Man is a sinner and must be redeemed. All his efforts must be directed to this end. Personal salvation is the supreme law.

The third temptation alleges a reason that appears more egoistic, but at bottom may also be deeper. Life is not merely a struggle to purify yourself of sin, but a matter of realizing yourself fully, of making your fortune, of not letting your talents go to waste without bringing them to fruition. For this it is necessary to 'traffic' with them, by 'pressing on'. Human plenitude does not come to us without effort, by 'sitting down on it'. We must move along, we must go to meet our salvation.

The fourth temptation may be explained by either a cosmic

or a social rationale.[139] From the former point of view, there are four cosmic ages. Our conduct can reflect each of these ages or it can condition them. If Rohita wants to model himself on the age of *kali*, the worst of all, he can relax, do just as he likes; if, on the contrary, he wants to express the best of times, he must keep active. In other words, the reason here is that in order to collaborate with cosmic history, each of us must step beyond individualistic problems and awaken to our cosmic vocation. If, on the other hand, it refers only to a game of dice, this reason seems much like the preceding one, and could be interpreted as symbolizing the different qualities of human life.

The fifth temptation seems to combine human, personal, even egoistical, elements with the dynamism of the universe, represented by the sun, ever active, ever journeying, the happiest of beings. Man goes on his way together with the seasons and the stars.

Must we call these temptations? Has Rohita done well to listen to them? Has he acted according to *dharma* or not? Should he not have gone back to the village immediately to keep the promise made to Varuna and save his father from affliction?

Here again the myth is original and, indeed, scarcely intelligible outside the Indian context.

In order to understand, we must consider the symbolism of Varuna and Indra. They stand for two poles of the divine. Varuna is called the ethical God, the one who sees, scrutinizes, judges and pardons the actions of Men, the one whom nothing escapes. Varuna represents justice and truth, the internal correlation of things (*rta*) and at the same time forgiveness, i.e., the power of redressing the broken order. Indra, on the contrary, stands for power, warlike strength and victorious force, the one who liberates and delivers from enemies. If Varuna is the moral God par excellence, Indra is the prototype of the one 'beyond good and evil'. Varuna is King[140] by virtue of his intimate relation with the cosmic order, because of his fidelity and his pardon. Indra is King because he is the victor in celestial and earthly battles.

What is Man? The nexus, the *kṣetra* or battlefield between the two most powerful symbols of the divine in the Ṛg Veda:

Indra and Varuṇa. Without going into Indological details, we can sum up this way: There is in Man a constitutive tension between the development of his personality, his own life, and his integration with the cosmos, with society. Man is made from this tension between fidelity to the social and cosmic order and authenticity toward himself. Which must he obey? What must Rohita do? The conflict takes place within him; the Gods are interiorized in this case, since he sees only his father's life in danger and his own menaced. So Rohita moves on until he finds a substitute. Has he done well? Can we reconcile Indra with Varuṇa? Rohita is powerless, but there is Śunaḥśepa, the mediator, and there is prayer, the transhuman dimension in life. It is from the ensemble of characters that the web of life is spun.

C. The Vedic Pantheon plays an important role in this myth. Varuṇa has agreed to accept Śunaḥśepa as the substitute for Rohita and the boy is to be sacrificed during the *rājasūya*. But now, as the rite is being celebrated, the victim cries out for deliverance. Who can save him? Should he not resign himself to a higher order of things? Should someone not die in order to save the king, the kingdom and the world? Is there any justifiable escape? Here too our myth is revealing. Śunaḥśepa's oration is neither a prayer of resignation, nor an acceptance of superior divine will. He is unaware of his redemptive mission; he does not consciously reflect on the value of his act. His hands are bound; prayer is all that is left him. The accent here is not on Śunaḥśepa's personal power as a savior, but on the suprahuman power of prayer. Prayer is presented here as the art of the impossible. If you pray for something that is possible for you to obtain, then should you not rather be busy obtaining it? Nor is prayer a matter of projecting a psychological anthropomorphism into the superhuman world; having recourse to one particular God, or one saint in order to thwart the influence of another 'supernatural' being. Śunaḥśepa does not dream of winning the favor of one God against another. True prayer is not an instrument of power, or a weapon. He does not even ask that justice be done, as if it were unjust to die for others or to be sacrificed; prayer does not judge.

The whole situation takes place on another plane altogether; it concerns freedom. True freedom does not mean a choice between alternatives that, once made, would deprive us of other freedoms. The realm of choice is the world of *karma*. *Karma* is subject to human decision, but once this decision is exercised it is inexorable and follows a *sui generis* law of causality.[141] The sphere of true freedom lies outside the causal, rational or karmic structure of the world; it does not contradict these earthly structures, but it oversteps them by far. The sphere of freedom is the sphere of hope against all hope, the sphere of impossibility, of the incomprehensible and nonmanipulable. Śunaḥśepa wants to know if he has any chance of being freed because freedom is the supreme value. His liberation is from every point of view impossible. Here is where prayer intervenes, here and only here is its proper place.

We see now why Śunaḥśepa has recourse to the Gods one after the other. He begins by invoking Prajāpati, Lord of all the Gods. He asks to be delivered to Aditi, the personification of freedom, the limitless; he prays for release from his bonds, and to see heaven and earth, father and mother once again.[142] Prajāpati sends him to Agni, the God nearest to the celestial inhabitants and to mortals, the high priest of sacrifice, and the boy repeats his prayer for freedom. The entire celestial world hears Śunaḥśepa's oration, but there is no favoritism here. Prayer is not a privilege, but a higher activity of the spirit that unlocks a new degree of freedom and makes possible what is ordinarily impossible. Obviously this is not an ontological impossibility which prayer surpasses. Prayer is not a power hidden in the Man of prayer that he can utilize, like a weapon, when the moment comes. This would be magic or at least some other power that has nothing to do with prayer. True prayer is uncertain, and unaware of its power. We don't know, the Gods themselves don't know. Nothing is fixed, there are no rules in the world of prayer. Its reality is always new; the mandate of prayer is pure spontaneity; to congeal it leads to idolatry. Śunaḥśepa is, so to speak, carried away by the spirit of prayer; he tirelessly implores the Gods one after another, each time according to the directions he receives. Agni quite naturally redirects him to Savitṛ, the great inciter, who alone might impart him the necessary inspiration. And Savitṛ counsels him to address Varuṇa, since it is Varuṇa who had him bound (something which Śunaḥśepa did not know). A first circle closes. Śunaḥśepa sings one of the most beautiful prayers of the Ṛg Veda to Varuṇa, who sends him again to the God of sacrifice, Agni. But Agni can do nothing all alone (we are beyond any voluntarism), and must this time induce Śunaḥśepa to call on The-All-Gods, viśve-devāḥ.

One particular deity has been involved in the adventure all along, and has not yet been specially invoked as he ought to be. This is why The-All-Gods tell Śunaḥśepa to address himself to Indra. A second circle closes. Indra offers a chariot of gold to poor Śunaḥśepa, but he wants his freedom. So he entreats Indra once more, who answers by telling him to sing the praises of the twin precursors of light, the Aśvins. Indra directs him to where cosmic novelty sees daylight: Uṣas, Aurora, the dawn, ever new and unforeseeable, an innovation never repeated, for today is never the simple repetition of yesterday. God is not sheer inactivity. Each day the creation is new, and runs the absolutely incalculable risk of whatever will come of it. And with each strophe Śunaḥśepa sings to the breaking day, to Uṣas, one of his three bonds falls away. The new day's new light sets him free.

iii. The Cosmos

Hariścandra is a king, and consequently has a kingdom. He is not an isolated individual but a point of convergence, so to speak, the summit of one order of the real. His entire kingdom is engaged in the adventure, as we learn in the later tradition that speaks of the aerial city of *saubha*. But the cosmos of the original myth is not a fantastic world, it is neither anthropomorphized nor divinized. Things are as they are. Nature is neither spiritualized nor allegorized. The forest is the forest, and hunger is hunger. The cows are real and have their full value: One hundred cows are well worth a human life.[143] The cosmos here does not overwhelm the other domains of reality. The cosmotheandric equilibrium is carefully maintained. Things are in their proper place; there is no need to make them play an unfamiliar role, which would in any case be secondary. As we have said, this myth of the human

condition is centered first and foremost on Man. So it naturally
presents a cosmos seen by Man. It tells us of honey and the
delicious Udumbara fruit, and mentions the village as well, always alluring for its rich human intercourse.

The vision of the cosmos is rather detailed: Human generation is described with care—even the ten lunar months of gestation are mentioned—as well as food, dress and riches. The sacrificial altar, knife and fire are also noted, each in its place and its
role.

The verses abound in the pictorial richness typical of the Ṛg
Veda—the Soma with mortar, pestle and sieve, the containers
and the cowhide, the abundance of livestock, the chariot of gold
given to Śunaḥśepa and Varuṇa's golden cloak, as also the songs,
the stars, the moon and the sun. The cosmos is real, it shares in
the human adventure.

It is interesting to note in passing the tension between nature
and culture, symbolized by the pair forest/village. Contrary to
what might at first glance be supposed, neither is unequivocal:
The village represents culture, but equally the danger of death;
and while the forest represents nature, it also offers the only hope
of life. For Rohita, the village means Men, civic duties and death,
whereas the forest means continual pilgrimage, adventure, the
unknown, the flight from Men and escape from death.

In this section I have sought to describe the characters of the
myth by trying to render them comprehensible without uprooting
them from their context. It remains for us now to penetrate the
myth itself.

b. The Mythemes

To analyze a myth means to reduce it to its basic mythic
elements, much as in chemical analysis we seek the simplest elements that make up a substance. The process with regard to myth
is difficult since we do not know the appropriate reagents, nor
how the myth will react to different reagents. We do not yet have
a critical method for mythical research. The process is also delicate, for we risk being unable to reconstruct the myth once it is
analyzed. The living elements of a myth are not merely the concepts it may contain, just as a compound is more than the simple

juxtaposition of its elements. Any *mythologumenon* is composed
of symbols that combine to form more or less complex *mythemes*.
Each *mytheme*, although complete in itself insofar as it expresses
a definite problematic, is also a fragment of the larger horizon
illuminated by the myth.

To better understand the meaning and also the limits of this
myth, we shall mention three *mythemes* that are *not* found in the
myth in addition to discussing three fundamental *mythemes* that
are present.

i. The Present Mythemes

The *mythemes* we may discover in a *mythologumenon* must
always be understood in terms of the myth's context. The three
we shall point out represent what the myth had to say to Men of
its time and, moreover, what it may still say to us today, for they
convey three invariants of human existence.

A. *Presence of Death*

We have said that a *mytheme* is not a thesis. Consequently,
this first *mytheme* does not speculate on the nature of death. It is
content to show how life on earth is a constant confrontation with
death, and this at every level: the biological, where Ajīgarta
wants to elude death from starvation; the social, where Hariścandra wants to continue his life through his son; the psychological, where Rohita wants to escape death at any cost; and at the
personal level of Śunaḥśepa, from whom life is about to be
snatched prematurely.[144]

To face death is inherent to the human condition. Death is on
all sides, it lies in wait for Man wherever he is, whatever he does.
But does this mean that Man must face death, or merely seek
escape from it? Our *mytheme* does more than simply state the
problematic; it suggests a certain typology for death. We have
already hinted at this. The presence of death is a universal fact in
nature as in culture. Is culture in general not a sort of sophistica-
tion of natural law, of the law of the jungle? Culture regulates how
Man ought to face death, and yet these rules always derive from
the law of the strongest. Culture by and large suppresses only
total anarchy and the tyranny of naked force, so that the survival

of the strongest comes about a little less brutally.

This *mytheme* shows us the different ways in which Men seek to escape death. Each in his own way wants to evade death; the difference lies in the price one is willing to pay. Ajīgarta sells his son; Hariścandra is willing to pay with the life of his son; Rohita seeks another's life to save his own. And finally there is Śunahśepa: he also wants to live, but he is cornered, despite himself, in a dead end. He can neither retreat nor look for a substitute. *Saṁsāra*, the cycle of inauthentic lives, ends with him. Life here is victory over death, not merely a reprieve.

So we find here two types of life: a horizontal life that can be lived solely by passing it on, so to speak, to another; and a vertical life that leaps over the first and reengages itself in the temporal. Both types confront death, and both wish to overcome it.

The first type is dominated by competition, another form of the law of the jungle; the survival of the strongest is paid for by eliminating everyone else. This is *saṁsāra*, existence exclusively in time and space.[145]

The second type of life is no longer conditioned by flight or substitution, nor obtained at the expense of others (although it may become a bone of contention, as the revolt of Viśvāmitra's elder sons illustrates). It is a life that in a sense recapitulates the life of all Men, and that of the world. It is not an 'other' life beside, or above, or even after, this temporal life. On the contrary, it dwells in the very heart of the temporal and material realms, but without confining itself to spatio-temporal coordinates.

Strictly speaking, the issue here is not two discrete types, but two dimensions of human life in tension and constant exchange. But our *mytheme* does not speculate; it recounts the complexity and richness of human life.

B. Solidarity of Life

Following on this, a second *mytheme* emerges at once. The death one flees is nothing but the danger inherent to life. Life is precarious, it can end at any time. Now this life is not any individual's private property; rather it is a bond between the living, a link stronger than the individuals it connects. We live only because we bear and express this supra-individual life. Life takes primacy over any living individual. What matters is the quality of life, not the quantity, because life as such is a qualitative value and consequently unquantifiable, ontologically *in solidum*, 'for the whole', interdependent.

It is precisely this solidarity that permits substitution, that allows an inauthentic life to be replaced by another's life. We can become unworthy bearers of life only when we do not live it, i.e., when at bottom we do not bear it. So then we get rid of it by giving it to others. On the other hand, authentic life is neither conserved nor passed on to others, but burned off, lived out, which means constantly renewed, at the risk of death and new birth.

Now this solidarity of life makes itself known at different levels. The father's life is continued in the son; the brahmin Śunaḥśepa's life is well worth that of the *kṣatriya* Rohita. The promised sacrifice of Rohita to Varuṇa rests on substitution, a law that corresponds to the most intimate nature of reality and must not be understood in quantitative categories. The solidarity of life that permits substitution for an inauthentic life does not mean that all life is interchangeable, or that the important thing is to conserve the quantity of life on earth, whoever its bearer might be. 'I will offer him in sacrifice', Hariścandra said, meaning that in pledging his son's life, he offers his own. When the son flees, the father falls ill (probably dropsy). Life is the bond that unites us, but this bond is placed in our hands. We can hold it back, release it, or even break it.

With Śunaḥśepa this *mytheme* attains its apex. He is sold for a goodly sum but derives no advantage from the exchange. On the contrary, the transaction nearly costs him his life, and his father is the beneficiary. But Śunaḥśepa, the substitute victim accepted by Varuṇa, redeems Rohita, who was not ready to give up his life.[146] And the redemption is genuine, since once Śunaḥśepa is saved, Varuṇa does not demand that Rohita be sacrificed. Śunaḥśepa continues the traditional Vedic sacrifice without human victim. Rohita is thus saved from a premature death.

Here the originality of this *mytheme* appears most clearly. The solidarity of life is not a physical, or even a material, notion of life like the conservation of energy law. It is neither a question of an eye for an eye, nor of *jīva* for *jīva* (soul for soul).

In contrast to other heroes and saviors, Śunaḥśepa does not die biologically, he does not pay as it were a physical debt. In fact, nobody dies in this myth—which is remarkable. The solidarity of life is of an order higher than and irreducible to quantitative standards. There is something above the realm of causality and necessity. The second *mytheme*, then, does not just say that all life is equal; you cannot play with life. Ajīgarta is charged with having committed a hideous crime. Rather, the *mytheme* affirms that this law of solidarity is vital, governed by freedom and not by determinism. Here we are rather far from juridical notions of compensation and material substitution. To be sure, Śunaḥśepa has been legally purchased, but his redemptive action is effective not because he has been sacrificed, or because of any decision on his part. The relation is neither juridical nor material; nor, moreover, does the redemptive value of his act stem from the individual will. The relation is *sui generis*, embracing all humanity and the Gods as well.[147] Śunaḥśepa is neither a chosen hero, nor a Man of superior willpower; he is but an ordinary Man grappling with existence and ready to play his last card in the game of human interdependence. Śunaḥśepa is anyone who finds his back to the wall because this solidarity of life has made him the last link in the chain of human lives. Basically he cannot do like the others and postpone the true confrontation of human existence with reality by leaving the responsibility to another and letting the circle of *saṁsāra* revolve again. He must face death by accepting the solidarity of life and preparing to leap into transcendence.

This *mytheme* tells us that the real human condition is one of such dependence upon others that we can be completely cornered and have no other recourse but to leap into a brand new sphere that transcends the spatio-temporal individual. In more popular language, the just must pay for the sinners since they are the only ones who can pay. They are called just precisely for this, that they do not mutter out of a misplaced sense of individualistic propriety, and so do not find their fate unjust (or else they would no longer be just).

This solidarity of life—which was self-evident for the myth's contemporaries, but which we need to recall—is a solidarity of all life, involving even the Gods. Man is not a solitary in the universe, not an individual cut from his roots and stripped of his purest fruits. Man could perhaps be defined as the nexus, as the visible intersection where the domains of reality cross one another. He is the crossroads of a reality that traverses every being, embracing Gods as well as material things.

Once again, we would do well to recall that this is not a mono-dimensional myth, not a strictly 'humanist' tale, but a myth in three dimensions, for the *puruṣa* is not only what we call 'man', and still less the individual, but the total cosmotheandric person reflected to different degrees in each human being.[148]

C. Transcendental Desire

Hariścandra desires a son; Rohita desires to preserve his life; Ajīgarta desires to live without hunger; Śunaḥśepa desires his freedom; Viśvāmitra desires to continue the sacrifice and to place Devarāta (Śunaḥśepa) at the head of his descendants. Desire is present throughout. In every case it appears not as a superficial whim or autonomous will, but rather as the manifestation of each being's deepest dynamism. Desire in these cases is neither caprice nor the consequence of a reasoning intellect, but the result of an integral situation. Each one desires that which engages his entire being. It would be perhaps more proper to speak of the ontological tendency of every being. Or we might recall Śunaḥśepa's hard words to his father: "He who once does evil will do that evil again!" This is not true of an action born of covetousness, of psychological desire, but only of an action springing from that ontological desire which expresses the very core of our being.[149]

Where the first two *mythemes* in a sense go beyond the individual Man, where they attune him to what limits him from below (death) and from on high (life), this third *mytheme* places us at the very heart of the human condition: Man is not described here as intelligence or will, but as this desire *to be*, as the very desire for being. Clearly, this is no matter of mere piecemeal appetites, but a deep-seated desire for existence. I can conquer my appetite for possession or for vengeance by mastering it with a deeper conviction; e.g., that possession will not enrich me, or vengeance give me peace. I can purify my appetites, sublimate them, but I cannot eliminate the constitutive desire of my being that enables me to overcome them. Every sublimation depends upon a deeper desire that takes up and transforms the particular appetites.[150] In this realm of transcendental desire there can be no ontological pretense. The myth situates us at a depth where we cannot be deceived by acts that can be retracted, or by more or less superficial appetites, or by whatever notions we might have of ourselves. Here we cannot pretend; simplicity will not countenance a two-faced attitude.

In the depths of this ontological desire true human freedom dwells, not merely in the psychological domain of possible choice. What good is it for you to put on a mask, upheld by the will or by the reason, that lets you act contrary to your own nature? Either freedom is rooted in our very being, or it is just so much superstructure. Freedom comes to light in being able to free itself from exterior constraint. This is why you must be aware, be yourself, master yourself, in order to be free.

Human being, this *mytheme* tells us, has a profound desire, which belongs to its very constitution, and which is always a desire for transcendence. (In a sense this is a tautology—but, like any true principle, a qualified tautology.) The transcendence of this ontological desire goes well beyond the death of the individual.

We should properly call this a transcendental desire, one constitutive of being. And, if we concentrate on human being as the myth does, we could see in it an expression of desire as a fundamental *existenzial*, since it expresses the ontological structure of human existence.

Whatever our philosophical categories may be, this *mytheme* seems to voice a deep-seated invariant found in practically every religious tradition: the desire to open oneself to a more authentic life, a life that escapes the banal, a life where we go beyond the limits of time and space that seem to so imprison human existence. This desire is generally linked with the conviction that we

need a sacred act, a sacrifice, in order to realize it. We are thinking here of what historians of religion are accustomed to call
initiation, a rite by which one passes from appearance to reality,
from illusion to truth, from adolescent life to life in its fullness;
initiation as the true or second birth.[151]

In fact we find in this sacred history all the elements of an
initiatory rite, which may incidentally be its likeliest historical
origin. The myth presents several characteristics appropriate to
initiation.

As we have time and again observed, this is above all a myth
centered on Man. It tells the tale of Man's life on earth, not a story
about the Gods or a cosmic narrative. Initiation is a human experience par excellence.

The myth is also focused on overcoming death and entering a
higher life. For this one has to vanquish death, to be sacrificed
and reborn to new life. Śunaḥśepa has earned a new life. It is
symbolized in his new name, his new father, his new role, and
above all by his second birth on the altar. The *mytheme* does not
theorize on the *dvijātva*, the state of being reborn; it tells us the
facts.

This new birth, in the third place, does not come about automatically. It is not a physical birth but an anthropological one.
For this some action is needed, the sacred action of a rite, which
the myth unfolds before us.

The myth, in the fourth place, recounts a rite that runs the
risk of life and death, and where substitution takes place only
after a withdrawal to the wild—traits we find in most initiatory
rites.

But this is clearly not an initiation practiced in the epoch
when the myth was composed. The myth does not deal with
traditional Indian initiation; besides, both the brahmin and the
kṣatriya are already initiates, *dvijās*. Nor is it a matter of explicat-
ing or justifying the social situation of the time. The castes are
accepted here; in fact, the caste system is taken for granted. Even
śūdras are talked about in the most conventional manner.

We are not concerned with a social initiation already crystallized in a ritual structure, but with a third birth if you will:[152] the

true personal birth, which is unlike either biological or sociological birth and located on another plane altogether. We would like to emphasize this important nuance. True life is immortal; only what is mortal ever dies, only the husk of life as it were, like the skin shed by a serpent.[153] This means that the tension here is not so much between death and resurrection as between inauthentic life and real life. Thus the victim need not really be killed, since death is never real. Śunaḥśepa is not resuscitated, he is *suscitated* to a new life. This means, further, that we must not await an 'other' life or a 'beyond' to this life, but that we can realize it here and now, once we have been liberated like Śunaḥśepa on the altar of sacrifice. We awaken to true life.

So this *mytheme* means that there is a life hidden in Man, a new life that we can awaken by a rite centered on prayer, on the existential cry of Man faced with death. Man is then raised up, awakened, *suscitated* to a new life that *will* not be in another existence, but that *is* in this very life, once we have crossed the threshold of our egocentrism.

ii. The Absent Mythemes

A myth is a living myth if it still depicts a horizon where we can fit in our experience of Reality. No doubt our myth describes an essential part of the human condition as it is still lived and suffered by contemporary humanity. Nevertheless we find important absences in it that might lead us to suspect that our sacred history is perhaps too limited to serve as a myth for today. In this case, it might serve to accentuate several aspects of human life and then to integrate them into a new myth that has yet to unfold. But by paying special attention to the *mythemes* we feel are lacking, we may perhaps find a deeper meaning in their absence.

Our course here, our enterprise, delicate as any argument *ex silentio*, seems justified in that we are trying to understand this sacred history over against the background of contemporary mythic sensitivity. Three *mythemes* are symptomatically missing, but once again we should try to understand them before criticizing or drawing conclusions for our era.

A. Sexuality

The story tells us of the hundred wives of Hariścandra, and the introductory verses speak of procreation,[154] but the myth as such remains unacquainted with any anthropological notion of sex. Man is presented as complete from a monosexual, or rather a masculine, point of view. Where the woman's role is concerned, and even the man's insofar as he is male, it is an asexual myth. The values of intimacy and love are also lacking, and it is difficult to find in the myth motivations, and likewise perhaps interpretations, that go back to human sexuality.

The importance of this absence is remarkable as much for the myth itself as for our theories on human nature, particularly after Freud and Jung.

But our myth does not completely ignore sex; in fact, it specifically notes the sexual meanings of the names of Ajīgarta's three sons. And we remember that the entire myth unfolds because Hariścandra desires a son. On the other hand, the children's names seem to be mentioned only to show more clearly the family's painful and degraded situation,[155] and Hariścandra's desire is explicitly interpreted as the great human desire for immortality.[156]

Neither is there any trace of sexual complexes. Uṣas, the dawn, the divinity who grants Śunaḥśepa's prayer, is indeed a gracious Goddess, but we would introduce foreign elements into the myth, and so constrain it, by trying to see in the dawn a symptom of the sexual problematic.

To be sure, we can hardly expect to find the notion of sexual equality, or women taking an active part in social life, in the sociological context of the myth. Nonetheless, India has never disregarded the function of sex, nor the indispensable role of the feminine (even if sociologically she remains subordinate to the male). Nor has India ignored a metaphysic, even a cosmology, of sex.[157]

Consequently this absence is more striking than it would be in another culture, and one suspects that it is not casual.[158]

So here is a myth that identifies Man with the male, but that does not deal with the male as such, but only insofar as he is human. Someone could certainly retort that the myth then speaks only to a truncated human condition, that it does not claim to give us a complete likeness of human life or society but restricts itself to one aspect.

The absence of sexuality is nevertheless not without significance, especially given a certain modern tendency toward pansexualism. The themes of death, life and desire are treated here without reference to sexuality.

Sexuality is the *synchronic complement*, it is desire for the time being. Freud was perhaps right to think of pathological troubles when this synchrony cannot be realized, which is when you kill your father, etc.

To desire a son, on the contrary, is the *diachronic supplement*; you desire a child for the future, for the continuation of life when you are no longer there. The child will fill this unhappy absence. Obviously *kāma*, love, is at the root of both synchronic attraction (sexual love) and diachronic desire (paternal and maternal love), as we see in Hariścandra and Ajīgarta.

Here is the proper place to consider celibacy, which is not founded on the pragmatic argument of having more time, or detachment, or interest in things spiritual. Neither is it based on the ascetic argument of renunciation, purity, the greater unity that should not be dispersed. In brief, the rationale for celibacy is not directly linked to sexuality, curious as this might sound. The orthodox rationale for Hindu celibacy is based on the socio-anthropological argument of the law of *karma*. Only the *saṁnyāsin*, the monk who has already burned away all his *karmas*, who has nothing left to continue, to achieve, to undergo, is celibate. Because he has lived his life totally, because he has used up the quantity of temporal life he has inherited, because he does not desire 'horizontal' immortality (and therefore has no need of sons to continue his unfinished life and his unrealized dreams)—only such a one, a saint who has lived his final life on this spatio-temporal earth, is celibate.[159]

But our myth does not talk about saints. So why this silence where sex is concerned? Can we speak of death, life and desire without including sexuality? We would like to suggest a hypothesis that is perhaps subtle from the exegetical point of view, but plausible given the Indian context, and that will perhaps enrich the Western perspective.

Hariścandra has a hundred wives and we can suppose that Viśvāmitra's situation is similar since he has a hundred and one sons. We might say that their sexual needs were filled to overflowing. Consequently sex is not a problem, at least not an urgent one. But sex is not only an elementary genital desire. The Indian context would retort here that a hundred wives are not solely for the pleasure of the body and that to confound the sexual impulse with ontological desire is simply an error. The great human problems, the three we have disclosed in our myth, are sexual problems only for those who have not yet quietened or sublimated their primary instincts and so let them overrun all other domains. Our hypothesis suggests that sex does not belong to the human order in its ultimacy. Sex is an element, and even a condition, but not the substance of human being in its plenitude. We could cite an analogy with hunger. Unless it is mastered, you become Ajīgarta; if you are starving, everything is tainted by this problem, everything is food. We cannot minimalize the anguishing problems of hunger, nor ignore the driving force it has in the lives of Men and civilizations; but to suppose that everything can or should be reduced to satisfying the fundamental need for food would surely oversimplify the question. If you have not sublimated sexuality, you find it everywhere. To be sure, we neither can nor should ignore the importance of the sexual impulse, but from there to pansexual reductionism is a considerable distance.

There is then in this myth an element of novelty even for India, a culture still highly exuberant in conceiving sexuality. The exceptional character of our myth comes through once again.

In sum we can only seek to understand this notion within the horizon afforded by contemporary experience and so note the cathartic effect it could have for our era. What this negative *mytheme* in effect tells us is that the great problems of human existence and the meaning of Man's life on earth are not necessarily connected with sexuality. Could we even say that our myth demythicizes the modern sexual myth?

B. Political Perspective

In our myth Man hardly seems engrossed in establishing a better or more equitable society. Rather, society seems to be an unalterable given, like a fact of nature we do not worry about changing. We find no rebellion. Hariścandra does not question Varuṇa's decree, Rohita does not revolt against his father, he simply flees, and always with some remorse. Ajīgarta does not appear a nonconformist, and even Śunaḥśepa seems unconscious of any injustice. It is true we are dealing with a situation in which the Gods play a part, but divine mandate does not mean immutability, as many another myth demonstrates.[160]

This absence should not be interpreted in the modern terms of a class struggle or a revolutionary *Geist*. We must veto any such *katachronic* interpretation, i.e., projecting today's categories of understanding in order to grasp events that belong to another order of things. Just as the problematic of sexuality was not unknown to the India of that time, there could also be a certain social consciousness within the cultural milieu of our myth. Still, it does not deal with war, political struggles or economic problems. The social is absent from it, and surprisingly so. Excepting the final reference to Viśvāmitra's descendants, there is in fact no reference to a consciousness of Man in the world; of Man who, by the very fact of being human, is susceptible to change, growth, improvement. The myth seems to imply that the purpose of life lies in each one's playing his or her role, but not in changing either society or the people who compose it.

We could say that given the social order of the time, one could not do otherwise than conform to it or escape from it. Now although this may not be totally accurate,[161] we find no indication of social concern or rebellion against the established social order. Further, Indra himself in counseling Rohita seems almost to scorn everything social. And Rohita takes the God's advice to live his life spiting every divine and human convention.

Nevertheless, the myth is not asocial; it does not focus solely on the isolated individual. All society is in a way reflected in it: the kingdom, the castes, the poor, commerce, patrimonies. So we can hardly say it pertains to another species. And yet not a word betrays historical perspective.

Here, as for the *mytheme* of sexuality, we must try to understand before we criticize.

This myth deals with salvation, the salvation of the Man who escapes death, who lives his life and seeks above all to surpass it. Not surprisingly, this salvation is depicted in the sociological terms common to its era, while at the same time remaining utterly indifferent to them. The fact of salvation, the presence of death, the reality of life, the possibility of authentic life, seem to be autonomous values with respect to the social situation in which Man finds himself immersed.

Along with the modern bent toward sexual reductionism, we could cite here the trend of other contemporary currents toward politicization and socialization. Man is reduced to a *sociological animal* who has no other substance; his salvation is political liberation, his felicity economic independence, his good fortune to participate in the democratic process.

But the myth does not say whether the social order of its day is just or unjust. It tells us only that human salvation is to some extent independent, autonomous—I prefer *ontonomous*—and consequently that human plenitude, the initiation to authentic life, is not reducible to its socio-political parameters. The issue is not ignoring the dangers of social escapism, the abuse of established religions, the inertia of history and human exploitation; it is rather a question of bearing in mind that human liberation also has a dimension that is more fundamentally constitutive than the social factors involved.[162]

We have here then another absence full of meaning, and another challenge to contemporary Man.

C. Eschatology

Our third absent *mytheme*, all the more astonishing in an Indian myth, is a double one: that of Man's beginning and final end. In this myth there is no attempt to elucidate the eschatological problem, neither from the temporal nor the metaphysical points of view.[163] It looks like a fragment of human film, clipped in mid-reel, not fully unraveled. It seems to say that whatever Man's origins may be, and independent of his end, human life unfolds according to a design in which eschatological opinions on the matter seem irrelevant.

This is a very intriguing silence, which once again marks this myth as exceptional and strikingly original. It recounts a human situation and even how to go beyond it without, however, having recourse to a cosmology of origins or a metaphysic of ends. Doubtless we can always retrace the cosmosgonic and metaphysical presuppositions in any human narrative. But it is remarkable that our myth does not depend on these presuppositions to say what it has to say.

Death, life and authentic existence can be faced independently of our particular cosmological and metaphysical persuasions. So here is a myth of Man that does not philosophize (although philosophy may underpin it as it does any other human construct).

And here again, this absence is meaningful especially today when we tend to couch everything in ideological terms. This sacred history seems to make the extraordinary claim to speak to us of human deliverance without being bound to a formal doctrinal system. This is the advantage of myth, to be sure, but in this case we have, further, the fact that the very language of the story does not rely on fixed preconceived philosophical notions.

It deals with the Gods and with sacrifice; we find the whole Vedic ambiance reflected in it. But the sacred history itself can easily be disengaged from these concrete images on which it rests or by which it expresses itself. The interpretation we have suggested is valuable for an atheist, as well as for a theist or a pantheist (and equally valid whether one acknowledges or rejects the notions of creation and a heaven 'to come').

It may perhaps be said that if one refutes transcendence and invocation, for example, the myth loses all meaning. Far be it from me to be noncritically irenic, or even to claim to have a myth of universal value, free from any presupposition. We should not analyze a *mytheme*, and still less an absent *mytheme*, as we do philosophical theses or concepts. Nor am I asserting that our *mytheme* is free from all conceptual baggage; I am simply pointing out that the absence of eschatology entitles the myth to claim to be acceptable to several metaphysics and cosmologies; the absence itself symbolizes this possibility.

c. Deconditioning Man

Until this point, our interpretation has been primarily phenomenological and in line with the history and science of religions. It has disclosed three *mythemes* present and three absent that have enabled us to propose a hermeneutic of the myth for our epoch. The present *mythemes* we have seen like colors over against the backdrop that our myth itself forms. Accustomed as we are to seeing other tints as well as these 'primary' colors, we have remarked their absence and sought to explicate it. We have presented the absent *mythemes* as a default and a challenge. A default, since their absence makes it difficult to consider this as a myth of today's human condition. A challenge, since the myth situates Man on a plane that seems able to dispense with the *mythemes* modern Man considers so important. We must in any case admit that a myth that does not speak to Man qua Man is not a myth but only a peculiar, perhaps pedagogical, legend.

In voicing the absent *mythemes*, I have tried to represent a certain contemporary mentality. This should be kept in mind, and I should apologize for my role of devil's advocate in stressing the absence of certain *mythemes*. If this absence were total and these themes central to being human per se, our myth would not qualify as a real myth.

The fact is, however, that what is absent in our myth is a certain—modern—interpretation of the topics represented in the three supposedly absent *mythemes*. As for a more contextual interpretation, we could say that the three absent *mythemes* are not really absent; quite the contrary, they are clearly present in the three *mythemes* we have revealed. What is sexuality if not an expression of transcendental desire? Is death not the substructure of any eschatology? And again, does the solidarity of life not represent social and political awareness in its deepest stratum? Modern Man may have a different understanding of sex, politics and eschatology, and he may be right or wrong. But in any case, these three topics, together with another—perhaps deeper, though undifferentiated—understanding are also present in the story of Śunahśepa.

Let us simply say that a deepened meditation on the myth reveals still another fundamental trait that permits us to list it among the myths of mankind that have not yet lost their validity. In seeking the meaning of the human condition depicted in this myth we have tried to fathom the depths of its simplicity. And it seems that the myth describes the human condition in order to present the deconditioning of Man as its quintessential message.

This puts our myth in rather a special light. Man is this being who knows himself to be conditioned, by birth, by habit, by circumstance and position; in short, by nature and culture. Precisely because he is conscious of this, he must learn to live in the gaps left by his conditioning. Is education, modern education in particular, not centered mainly on the effort to teach the new generation how to manage within the conditionings we call society, civilization, technology, scientific knowledge, etc.?[164]

The proper sense of the human condition is certainly to be conditioned. Hariścandra is conditioned by his desire and his promise, Rohita is conditioned by his fate (Indra, it is true, tries to decondition him—and the temptation he instigates rescues Rohita, but this deconditioning succeeds only partially). Ajīgarta is so conditioned by his famished predicament that he is hardly free to choose. Śunahśepa is the very expression of conditioning carried to the extreme, since this conditioning is not due to limitations of his own making, from which he could extricate himself; no, he is conditioned by external agencies, and in the most brutal manner. He no longer has any freedom of choice or movement and he finds himself in imminent danger of losing his life.

This then is the center of the myth: the deconditioning of Man, his liberation, his *freedom*. Our hermeneutic now takes a new course, a second approach, more philosophical and anthropological than the first, which will allow us to see the core of the myth in the *protomytheme* of deconditioning. For this it should be enough to read the hundred *rcs* Śunaḥśepa recites,[165] to hear his prayers and to listen to the myth in its entirety. We often leave aside the central aspect of a myth in the rush to decipher the threads of the sacred history, the rubrics, so to speak, thus neglecting the content, the prayers, the *nigrics* as I have called them.[166] The central prayers of the myth are all freedom hymns, variations on the theme of deconditioning the very human condition imposed on us by other people, by the Gods, or by ourselves.

From this angle, our myth is complete and simple: It is necessary to decondition Man from every conditioning. It matters little whether what binds us is life, or death. Man is conditioned by fear of death, by attachment to life, and by his desires, which bind rather than release him. This myth reveals the essence of religion as an unbinding rather than a *'religatio'*.[167]

By deconditioning, we mean this *freedom* from every conditioning that enables each of us to acquire the liberty to realize without bound or limit whatever we are capable of being. Now this liberation is at once a *freedom from* (our bonds) and a *freedom to* (realize ourselves in our plenitude). The example of Śunaḥśepa is clear. He is freed *from* death *to* realize his being (symbolized here by the performance of the Vedic sacrifice, and by his engagement in a new life as Viśvāmitra's son).

Here again we discover a human invariant found under different names in every culture: *mokṣa*, or, literally, liberation according to the entire Indian tradition.[168] *Soteria*, *salus*, liberty, emancipation, independence, deliverance, and so on, are so many words for it in various traditions.

Man finds himself conditioned, mediatized, annexed, exploited and abused by the Gods, fate, nature, society, others and himself. He feels in him the desire, even the capacity to be free, but he suffers from his lack of freedom, he desires liberation. This is the *protomytheme* of our sacred history. It tells us that the desire for liberation is the fundamental human impulse. It adds that this liberation is possible in any circumstance, since Śunaḥśepa realizes it in the most desperate predicament. It emphasizes that this emancipation belongs to the deepest stratum of the human person. And it mutely stresses that the need for freedom is plainly more basic than sexual desires, political opinions, economic situations or human ideologies. Our *protomytheme* further reveals that the price of this true freedom is our own life, which must be redeemed, reconquered after death is vanquished.

Modern Man, Man of the moment, of the *modus*, Man of the current and so fugitive instant, does he not live more conditioned than ever by the forces of alienation? Civilized life, and above all modern 'developed' life—still obsessed by development—does it not mean conditioned life? conditioned by others, by society, by the innumerable webs we weave and that bind us not only to others, but also to the megamachine Man has constructed and without which, or outside of which, he can no longer live? Contemporary Man does not know how to live without his technological diving suit, and very soon he will no longer know how to breathe without it.

Every myth does more than offer a horizon where we may insert our thoughts by giving them a backdrop and furnishing them a context: It also orients our thinking and incites us to follow one approach instead of another; it invites us to think in a certain direction. And in this way our *mythologumenon* offers an invitation to modern Man. A double invitation: not to allow himself to be crushed by culture and nature, by Men, society and the Gods, and also not to dream of a denouement in a horizontal future that nobody will ever see, but rather to envision a transhistorical present that neither denies the temporal nor drowns in it. Our sacred history is assuredly a challenge to the myth of history. Human freedom is possible and real, not merely for our successors, or in an *other* life; but now, in the *tempiternal* present, the deepest core of the *humanum*.[169]

Notes

1. Cf. the distinction made by the Christian patristics and scholastics between *credere in Deum*, *Deum* and *Deo*.

2. Cf. W.T. Stevenson, *History as Myth* (New York: Seabury Press, 1969), and his article: 'History as Myth: Some Implications for History

and Theology', *Cross Currents* (Winter, 1970), XX, 1:15-28, as an example of the blossoming of this idea in the West.

3. Cf. the assertions made by C. Lévi-Strauss in the final chapter of *La pensée sauvage* (Paris: Plon, 1962): ". . . dans le système de Sartre, l'histoire joue très précisement le rôle du mythe" (336). "Peut-être cet âge d'or de la conscience historique est-il déjà révolu" (337). "Par conséquent le fait historique n'est pas plus *donné* que les autres" (340). "L'histoire n'est donc jamais l'histoire, mais l'histoire-pour" (341). And he makes note of "une sorte de cannibalisme intellectuel de la 'raison historique' " (341 n.).

4. Cf. chapter II.

5. Cf. the well-known overstatement: "Wir Abendländer alle sind Christen," K. Jaspers, *Der philosophische Glaube angesichts der Offenbarung* (München: R. Piper, 1962), p. 52.

6. Is it perhaps this which P. Ricoeur names "le geste philosophique de base" in describing "le geste herméneutique" as "l'aveu des conditions historiques auxquelles toute compréhension humaine est soumise sous le régime de la finitude"? and in characterizing "le geste de la critique des idéologies" as "un geste critique indéfiniment repris et indéfiniment tourné contre la 'fausse conscience', contre les distortions de la communication humaine derrière lesquelles se dissimule l'exercise permanent de la domination et de la violence"? 'Herméneutique et critique des idéologies', *Demythisation et Idéologie,* edited by E. Castelli, (Paris: Aubier, 1973), pp. 25 and 46. Ricoeur remarks quite correctly that the problematic cannot be put in terms of an alternative: hermeneutic *or* critical consciousness, even though he himself is unwilling to leave the terrain of hermeneutics in the process of enriching it. We would like to locate the problem we are going to examine along the same lines, but taking a step forward, i.e., can we study the universal conditions of human understanding without limiting ourselves to our understanding of the question itself? Cf. also J. Habermas, 'Der Universalitätsanspruch der Hermeneutik', in *Hermeneutik und Dialektik*, edited by R. Bubner, K. Cramer and R. Wiehl (Tübingen: J.C.B. Mohr, 1970), I:73-103.

7. It is interesting to note that the *pres*, *pretis* of interpretation comes from the Sanskrit root *prath* (the verb: *prathati* or *prathate*): stretch, spread, scatter, extend, increase, enlarge (cf. *pṛthivī*, the extended one, i.e., the earth). Interpretation, then, would be the act of extending, spreading, lengthening, distending, enlarging the meaning, not only *diachronically* (through time) but also *diatopically* (in different places and cultures). This study hopes to present such a *diatopical interpretation*.

8. Our text is AB VII, 13-18 (XXXIII, 1-6), which is practically the same as SSS XV, 17-27. ASS IX, 3 repeats the ending of AB VII, 18, where it speaks of ritual instructions.

9. "La seule exception", says Jean Varenne, *Mythes et légendes*

extraits des Brāhmaṇa (Paris: Gallimard, 1967), 11, referring to the fact that, unlike other myths, here the entire text is given and not shortened or reduced to a schematic form. "Là encore, l'histoire de Śunaḥśepa, déjà insolite quant à sa forme, fait figure d'exception" (*ibid.*, p. 13) he adds, with respect to *bhakti* spirituality which, except in this myth, is at least 'quasi-clandestine' in the Brāhmaṇas.

10. Cf. A.B. Keith, *Rigveda Brahmanas: The Aitareya and Kauṣītaki Brāhmaṇas of the Rigveda*, Harvard Oriental Series (Cambridge: Harvard University Press, vol. 25, 1920); reprinted, Delhi and Varanasi: Motilal Banarsidass, 1971, pp. 42-50.

11. Cf. M. Winternitz, *A History of Indian Literature*, Calcutta: University of Calcutta, 1962, revised English edition, I, 1: 184-188.

12. The editions of M. Haug (Bombay, 1863), of Kāśinātha Śāstry Āgāśe (Poona, Anandāśrama Series, No. 32, 1896), of Vāsudevaśarman Paṇśīkara and Kṛṣṇambhaṭṭa Gore (Bombay: Nirṇaya Sāgara Press, 1911); that of Satyavrata Sāmaśramī in *Bibliotheca Indica;* that of Aufrecht, etc. The second edition of O. Böhtlingk's *Chrestomathie* also gives the original text in a revised version; we find it likewise in the appendix of Max Müller's classic *A History of Ancient Sanskrit Literature* (Varanasi: The Chowkhamba Sanskrit Series Office, 1968, a new edition revised by S.N. Śāstrī that incorporates the SSS variations).

13. The first English translation of the entire AB is that of Haug, which ought to be read in the light of the important critical review of A. Weber, *Indische Studien* IX (1865). Cf. also the translation of H.H. Wilson, JRAS, XIII (1851), pp. 96 sq. There is a German translation by R. Roth, IS I:457 sq. and II:112 sq., etc.

14. For example, Max Müller, *op. cit.*, pp. 370-376; J. Muir, *Original Sanskrit Texts* (London: Trubner & Co., 1868-1874, 5 vols.; new revised edition, Amsterdam: Oriental Press, 1967), I: 355-360. S. Lévi, *La doctrine du sacrifice dans les Brāhmaṇas* (Paris: E. Leroux, 1898; 2nd edition, Presses Universitaires de France, 1966), pp. 134-136, etc.

15. The text of the AB here is adapted from the versions of Keith, *op. cit.*, pp. 299-309 and Varenne, *op. cit.* In his translation, Varenne had the excellent idea of also translating the hundred RV verses the original text only mentions. The reader can thus follow the complete story. Varenne's version was quoted with permission in the original French of this chapter. Having checked the original Sanskrit at that time, the author has made no new translation here, except in a few passages.

16. *Putram icchanti.* Cf. also Plato, *Symp.* 206-207.

17. Important and common idea. Cf. RV V, 4, 10; TB I, 5, 5, 6; MB I, 74, 111; VisnP IV, 19, 3; etc. Cf. also Sir. 30:4, "The father may die, and yet he is not dead, for he has left behind him one like himself." Debt here is the translation of the capital Vedic notion of *ṛṇa* (cf. note 135). We

may give the following as an example of the entire text:

rṇam asmin saṃnayaty
amṛtatvaṃ ca gachati /
pitā putrasya jātasya
paśyec cej jīvato mukham //

The conviction that the father lives on in the son is older than the idea of transmigration. Cf. SB XI, 6, 2, 10 and the entire ritual of the father's blessing before dying in BU I, 5, 17-20.

18. Literally: "the *ātman* is born from the *ātman*", or equally, "he himself (the father) is born again". Cf. Keith, Winternitz, etc., *loc. cit.*

19. Nānā śrāntāya śrīr asti
iti Rohita śuśruma /
pāpo nṛṣadvaro jana
Indra ic caratah sakhā //

Some read with Sāyaṇa: *na-anāśrantāya*. Revelation: *śuśruma*, what we have heard or are hearing, Tradition. Indra is here the representative of tradition and friend of the ascetic wander-monk. Cf. AV XX, 127, 11. The hero figure is often a wayfarer.

20. Cf. Keith, *h. l.* on the interpretation of this passage. He asserts that in this context, the throws of dice—not the four Yugas (i.e., the cosmic ages) are meant (*pace* Sāyaṇa with whom Müller and Weber agree): the notion of ages is not Vedic, nor can Manu IX, 302, stand as evidence for the AB. Muir seems to follow Müller and Weber in thinking that the names refer to the Yugas, although he notes that it is but a brief allusion and doubts that the system was fully developed (see *op. cit.* I:46-49).

21. Literally: Aditi, the great mother Goddess who often personifies freedom. Cf. note 142.

22. RV I, 24, 1. Father and Mother: heaven and earth.

23. Aditi.

24. RV I, 24, 2.

25. RV I, 24, 3-5.

26. As above, Aditi here personifies freedom.

27. 'Aditya', i.e. Varuṇa, one of the sons of Aditi. Up to here RV I, 24, 6-25.

28. RV I, 25, 1-21.

29. RV I, 26, 1-10.

30. Literally: Sindhu, i.e., the Indus River, which stands for any river.

31. RV I, 27, 1-12.

32. Literally: Viśvedevas, a term used to designate the 'all Gods', a particular class of Gods forming one of the nine Gaṇas, enumerated under gaṇadevatā.

33. RV I, 27, 13.
34. A kind of evil spirit.
35. RV I, 29, 1-7.
36. RV I, 30, 1-15.
37. RV I, 30, 16.
38. Aśvins, the twin Gods, literally 'the two charioteers' who drive their golden chariot across the sky at dawn; friendly to men, they bring wealth and avert illness.
39. RV I, 30, 17-19.
40. Uṣas, Goddess of the dawn and daughter of Prajāpati (the lord of creatures). For the myth of the divine incest of Uṣas and Prajāpati, see above, chapter 4.
41. RV I, 30, 20-22. The word we have translated here as 'life' is *rayi*, goods, wealth, riches.
42. RV I, 28, 5-8.
43. RV I, 28, 9.
44. RV I, 28, 1-4.
45. RV IV, 1, 4-5. This hymn is not by the *ṛṣi* Śunaḥśepa.
46. RV V, 2, 7. Another *ṛc* not attributed to the *ṛṣi*.
47. I.e., God-given ('Deo-datus'), son of Viśvāmitra.
48. I.e., Ajīgarta and Viśvāmitra—both claim paternity over Śunaḥśepa.
49. The text reads:

    tad vai mā tāta tapati
    pāpaṃ karma mayā kṛtam /

Tapas here connotes not only passive remorse but the will to do penance and the ways towards purification.

50. Because of my interpretation I give here the entire stanza:

    yaḥ sakṛt pāpakaṃ kuryāt
    kuryād enat tato 'param /
    nāpāgāḥ saudrān nyāyād
    asaṃdheyaṃ tvayā kṛtam / /

51. Om ity ṛcaḥ pratigara
    evaṃ tatheti gāthāyāḥ /
    om iti vai daivam
    tatheti mānuṣam / /

Some authors see here the clear differentiation between the sacred (and sacred language) and the profane (secular language). The almost identical sentence occurs in ASS IX, 3; SSS XV, 27. Cf. also ЅB I, 1, 1, 4; I, 1, 2, 17; III, 3, 2, 2.

52. Thus far AB VII, 13-18.
53. The various footnotes of this chapter may serve as an introduction to a more specifically Indological study.
54. Cf. SB XIII, 7, 1.

55. Cf. TB II, 3, 6, 1.

56. Cf. SB II, 2, 2, 8-14.

57. Cf. RV X, 90; cf. also RV X, 130; AV VII, 5; SB X, 2, 2, 1.

58. Cf. SB VIII, 6, 1, 10; VIII, 7, 4, 6; IX, 2, 3, 27; IX, 4, 4, 15.

59. SB I, 3, 2, 1. Cf. SB I, 7, 2, 1-5.

60. Cf. SB III, 6, 2, 16.

61. In anthropological terms, not only do Men have to face death, Man also is mortal. Personal meditation on death is today reacquiring its ecological dimension.

62. Cf. RV X, 129, 3-4; AV IX, 2; XIX, 52, 1.

63. The conclusion of the AB (VII and VIII) is devoted to the *rājasūya* or royal consecration. It begins by explaining how to divide the sacrificial victim, followed by a long list of expiations for errors committed during the sacrificial oblations (VII, 1-12). The story of Śunaḥśepa (VII, 13-18) follows immediately. Then a description is given of the preparations for the royal consecration (VII, 19-26); next a description of the royal food and drink (in lieu of *soma*) (VII, 27-34). In VIII the different rites of anointing are described. The final section deals with the priest ("The Gods eat not the food of a king without a *purohita* [priest]", *VIII*, 24) and his duties.

64. It is quite probably an example of an annual rite of cosmic regeneration. Cf. A. Weber, 'Über die Königsweihe, den Rājasūya', ABAW (Berlin, 1893); J.C. Heesterman, *The Ancient Indian Royal Consecration: The Rājasūya described according to the Yajus texts and annotated* ('s-Gravenhage: Mouton, 1957), pp. 158-161.

65. Cf. SB V, 4, 3, 2, and the importance of this notion in linking our myth with the *rājasūya*.

66. Although the myth is complete in itself, it is difficult to consider it isolated from the *rājasūya*, an opinion shared by J. Gonda, *Die Religionen Indiens* (Stuttgart: Kohlhammer, 1960), I:167 and F. Weller, 'Die Legend von Śunaḥśepa im Aitareyabrâhmaṇa und Śânkhâyanaśrautasûtra', VSAW (Phil.-Hist. Klasse, Berlin, 1956) for example. On the other hand P. Horsch is right in affirming in his beautiful chapter on Śunaḥśepa that: "Ursprünglich hatte sie" our legend with the *rājasūya* "nichts zu tun", *Die vedische Gāthā-und Śloka-Literatur* (Bern: Franke, 1966), p. 286.

67. Cf. a good collection of texts in *Reader in Comparative Religion, An Anthropological Approach*, edited by W.A. Lessa and E.Z. Vogt (New York: Harper and Row, 2nd edition, 1965), pp. 142-202.

68. As far as I know, this myth has never been studied from this perspective.

69. YV IX and X also contain formulae and prayers for the *rājasūya*, but without referring to the myth of Śunaḥśepa.

70. Even today it forms part of a living rite performed in order to obtain children.

71. Cf. AB VIII, 21-23. For the *aśvamedha*, cf. SB XIII, 1-5.

72. Cf. YV XXX-XXXI, with all the references in this text to the *puruṣasūkta*: RV X, 90 and AV XIX, 6; SB XIII, 6.

73. SB XIII, 6, 2, 20 (cf. XIII, 6, 1, 11).

74. Cf. P. Horsch, *op. cit.*, pp. 286 sq. for further discussion and literature on the problem of human sacrifice.

75. Cf. SB XIII, 6, 2, 13.

76. This could shed light on the problem of the human sacrifice as the paradigm and prototype for the horse sacrifice. Cf. the paper of W. Kirfel, 'Der Aśvamedha und der Puruṣamedha' in W. Schubring, *Beiträge zur indischen Philologie und Altertumskunde* (Hamburg: Cram, De Gruyter, 1951), pp. 39-50, showing that the human sacrifice is the "sinnovollere und verständlichere" (p. 46).

77. Cf. MB XIII, 186, besides the texts on which we are going to comment.

78. Ram I, 61 and 62.

79. The agreement speaks of one hundred thousand cows (Ram I, 61, 12), but in addition the king gives "tens of millions of gold and silver pieces and heaps of precious stones" (I, 61, 22)—a clear indication of the hyperbolic character of the gift, and of monetary and religious inflation.

80. Ram I, 62, 4.

81. The episode with the sons of Viśvāmitra is also mentioned here (I, 62, 13-17).

82. Cf., e.g., MB II, 489 sq.

83. Cf. *Markaṇḍeya Purāṇa*, translated by F. Eden Pargiter (Calcutta: Bibliotheca Indica, 1904; reprinted: Varanasi: Indological Book House, 1969).

84. Cf. MarkP VIII, 270.

85. Cf. vgr. BhagP IX, 7 and also 16; VisnP IV, 7, 22 (only mentioned).

86. Concerning the story of Hariścandra, cf. also: F.E. Pargiter, 'Viśvāmitra, Vasiṣṭha, Hariścandra and Śunaḥśepa', JRAS (1917), pp. 37 sq.; J. Muir, *op. cit.*, I:379; B.H. Wortham, JRAS (1881), pp. 355 sq. Hariścandra is often compared to the Biblical Job.

87. Bhārtendu Hariścandra, a writer from Varanasi who at the beginning of this century struggled for the renaissance and independence of Hindi literature, wrote a popular play based on the Purāṇic narrative, *Satya Hariścandra*, by now a classic, still performed in Varanasi and containing strikingly realistic descriptions of the ghat where the dead are burned. (Hariścandraghat, adjacent to Hanumanghat).

88. Cf. the introduction to Keith's translation, *op. cit.*, pp. 101-102.

89. Cf. for example, Sāyaṇa's, regarding the four *yugas* mentioned in the fourth verse recited by Indra in AB VII, 15.

90. Cf. among others, the classic studies of F. Streiter, *Dissertatio*

de Sunahsepo (Berlin, 1861); A. Weber, SBAW (1891), pp. 776 sq., *Id.*, ZDMG, 18, pp. 262 sq.; W.H. Robinson, *The Golden Legend of India* (London, 1911); A.B. Keith, JRAS (1911), pp. 988 sq.; G. Dumézil, *Flamen-Brahman* (Paris: Geuthner, 1935), pp. 13-42; 97-113; R. Roth, IS I:457 sq., II:112 sq.

91. Cf. Socrates saying that he believes in the Gods "in a sense higher than any of my accusers" (*Apology* 35d).

92. Cf. A.B. Keith, *op. cit.*, pp. 63-67, who describes these three levels. In this study I have inverted the order between the second and third elements following the text of AB and seeking a *leitmotif* in each case. Cf. also the study of R. Roth, IS II: 112-123, commented on by J. Muir, *op. cit.*, I:359 sq.

93. This is found in AB VII, 13-16.

94. This will be found in AB VII, 17-18.

95. Eight hymns in the RV are attributed to the *ṛṣi* Śunaḥśepa: RV I, 24-30; IX, 3. The story in AB cites RV I, 24-30 and also RV IV, 1, 4-5; V, 2, 7; the latter two are not by the *ṛṣi*. At the closing of the *ṛc* RV V, 2, 7, the name of Śunaḥśepa is recalled to Agni in order to obtain deliverance.

96. Cf. C. Kunhan Raja, *Poet-Philosophers of the Ṛgveda. Vedic and Prevedic* (Madras: Ganesh, 1963), pp. 80-96 for a study of the *ṛṣi*.

97. As for the other passages, cf. YV XXX-XXXI; SB XIII, 6; SSS XVI, 10-16; VSS XXXVII, sq.; etc.

98. Other than the studies cited, cf. H. Oldenberg, *Die Religion des Veda* (Berlin, 3rd edition, 1923), p. 365; R. Mitra, 'On Human Sacrifice in Ancient India', JAS XLV (Bengal, 1876); A. Weber, *Indische Streifen* (Berlin, 1868-1879), I:54 sq.; J. Eggeling, *The Śatapatha Brāhmaṇa*, SBE (Oxford: Clarendon Press, 1900, reprinted Delhi: Motilal Banarsidass, 1966 second edition), vol. XLIV, which offers a very useful study on the *śrautic* problem (pp. xxxiii-xlvi).

99. Cf. the concurring opinion of A. Hillebrandt, *Ritual-literatur* (Strassburg, 1897, 2nd edition, Breslau, 1927), p. 145. Cf. also *id.*, *Vedische Mythologie*, iii, p. 32, criticized by A.B. Keith, JRAS (1908), p. 846.

100. Cf. vgr. E.A. Gait, 'Human Sacrifice (Indian)', ERE, *sub hac voce*.

101. Cf. vgr. A.B. Keith, *Rigveda Brāhmaṇas*, *op. cit.*, p. 62; *id.*, JRAS (1907), pp. 844 sq.; J. Eggeling, *loc cit*.

102. Cf. H. Lommel, 'Die Śunaḥśepa-Legende', ZDMG, 114, 1 (1964), p. 157 sq., which examines the relation between Hariścandra's vow and Jephthah's vow: "If thou wilt deliver the Ammonites into my hands, then the first creature that comes out of the door of my house to meet me when I return from them in peace shall be the Lord's; I will offer that as a whole-offering" Jg. 11:30 (NEB). In fact, in the Bible Jephthah's daughter, his only child, was sacrificed! Cf. also 2 Kg. 3:27, etc.

103. Cf. J. Eggeling, *op. cit.*, p. xxxvi. One could answer that the humiliation of a father—let alone a king—without children suffices to explain the conduct of Hariścandra.

104. And must we also conclude that the command of Yahweh to Abraham requiring the sacrifice of his son proves that human sacrifice was practiced at that time? Eggeling himself notes the parallelism. Cf. also P. Horsch, *op. cit.*, pp. 287 sq.

105. Cf. Ps. 137:4.

106. Cf. as the most recent example, M. Meslin, *Pour une science des religions* (Paris: Seuil, 1973) where, contrary to other older works, the problem of myths and symbols becomes the central problem of religious studies.

107. Or even, 'one who has a dog's penis (or tail)'. Cf. Pāṇini VI, iii, 21 for the grammatical sense. Utilizing the word-play that Sanskrit permits, C.K. Raja writes that the word implies 'one who cannot be altered in his views' or 'one who is always crooked in his ways', *op. cit.*, p. 94.

108. Śunaḥpuccha, 'the tail end of a dog' and Śunolāṅgūla, 'dog's tail (penis)'. Cf. the German *Hundsfott* (Old Nordic: *fudh-hundr*) properly meaning *cunnus canis*. The German root *fu* (cf. *faul,*) comes from the Indo-European root *pu* (cf. Sanskrit *pūyati,* he stinks, Latin *puteo* [*pus*]. πύον, to stink) and means *cunnus,* vulva.

109. Cf. CU VI, 1, 4; etc.

110. Cf. CU VI, 1, 3.

111. He is also the renowned poet of the same name; here we are dealing with a juxtaposition—or even more simply we could say that Śunaḥśepa becomes a *ṛṣi* later on.

112. Tradition considers Śunaḥśepa still a boy.

113. Cf. Ram I, 62, 4.

114. Cf. the intriguing figure of Melchizedek (Gen. 14:18; Heb. 7:1) and my study on him in *Kairos*, No. 1 (1959), pp. 5-12.

115. Indologists argue about the meaning of *dru-pada* (tripod) and *yūpa* (the sacrificial stake); one could equally elaborate on the underlying trinitarian symbolism.

116. RV I, 29, 1.

117. Prayer, cf. Latin *precāri* (*poscere*, to demand), Sanskrit *prechati* (*praśna,* a question), means certainly to ask, request, entreat (cf. also German *fragen* from *prāgēn*), which already implies the penury (cf. Greek πένης, poor, Latin *pēnūrias*, poverty) of not having, not knowing the answer. *Precārius*, strictly speaking, means that which is not assured (not certain) because it is obtainable only by prayer and thus does not depend on oneself or on automatic laws (of nature or culture). The extremely rich Indo-European root is *perk-*, (*prek-* and *pṛk-*), to ask. Cf. *postulō* and *templum.*

118. Cf. Heb. 9:11-28 for the Christian interpretation of this general fact in the history of religions.

119. SB I, 3, 2, 1 (the citation that opens this chapter).

120. Cf. L. Silburn, *Instant et cause* (Paris: Vrin, 1955), pp. 23, n.4; 29-30.

121. *Id.*, p. 23.

122. *Id.*, p. 401.

123. Both the Semitic and Sanskrit roots have the same meaning: 'red', and refer to both Man and earth.

124. Cf. Max Scheler, *Wesen und Formen der Sympathie* (Bonn: F. Cohen, 2nd ed. 1923); etc.

125. Cf. Albert Camus, *L'homme revolté* (Paris: Gallimard, 1951).

126. Cf. Gabriel Marcel, *Homo viator* (Paris: Aubier, 1944) and the essay on Camus' *L'homme revolté* in the appendix of the 1963 edition.

127. BG II, 31-38: "Hold pleasure and pain, profit and loss, victory and defeat to be the same: then brace yourself for the fight. So you will bring no evil upon yourself (38)." R.C. Zaehner trans., *The Bhagavad-Gita* (London: Oxford, 1969).

128. Manu X, 105.

129. Cf. the creative sacrifice of Prajāpati in chapter IV.

130. Cf. Manu VII, 42.

131. With this in mind, cf. the rather revolutionary injunction of Mt. 5:23-24.

132. Cf. F.E. Pargiter, 'Viśvāmitra . . .' *art. cit.* who despite his customary scholarship betrays here the spirit of his time by refusing to accept any truth found in myth unless it is historical.

133. Given this silence, I am not concluding—as is so often done in similar circumstances—that Rohita's birth is somehow 'supernatural'. The text does not mention whether Hariścandra had daughters. We might suppose he did have, however, since nothing in the story implies either the impotence of the king or the sterility of his wives. The myth takes place in the realm of the normal.

134. These two traditional enemies are here in full accord, a fact of interest with regard to both chronology and the location of the myth in the complex of Vedic relationships.

135. Cf. the notion of *ṛna*, debt, duty, obligation (cf. the Latin *reus*). The root *ṛn* (going, movement) denotes that dynamism called forth by an omission or 'privation'.

136. Cf. for example SB I, 7, 2, 1-5; III, 6, 2, 16.

137. In SSS the order is also different (1, 3, 4, 2, 5 and a 6th verse). I am well aware that one cannot construct theories on texts that are more or less contingent. On the other hand, neither need we have recourse to a collective unconscious in order to justify this interpretation. I am basing it on the contents of the texts, without insisting on the order of the five temptations.

138. Cf. the arguments used by Kṛṣṇa to convince Arjuna he ought to fight in BG II and III.

139. That is, are we talking about the four ages of the world (Max Müller, A. Weber) or a simple dice game (A.B. Keith)? An argument in favor of the latter view is that the four *yugas* or cosmic cycles are not Vedic. Cf. Keith, *h.l.*, etc.

140. MaitS I, 6, 11; II, 2, 1; TB II, 5, 7, 6; etc.

141. *Sui generis* since we cannot summarily reduce the karmic process to Aristotelian categories and still less to modern scientific chains of causality.

142. Cf. RV I, 24, 1: Aditi, translated by freedom, also means infinite, without boundaries or limits, the integrality of all being. In the RV she is usually personified and divinized.

143. Cf. the rather different implication of the gift of one hundred thousand cows in the Ram.

144. Cf. the Vedic conception of *āyus* (Greek αἰών, eon). After a life lived fully (*dirghāyus*), death is not a death properly speaking. Real death is premature death (*akālamṛtyu*), in one's youth, by accident, etc.

145. We could perhaps translate it by *exo-sistence*, i.e., no longer *ek-sistence* (the tension existing between fullness and nothingness; the tensional dynamic stretched over nothing and subsisting below infinity), but the outward extension, the 'sistence' in two dimensions, viz. in a corporal space and in a time, which imprisons movement itself. "Quid est enim existere, nisi ex aliquo sistere", says Richard of St. Victor, *De Trinitate* IV, 12 (P.L. 196, 937).

146. In the text already cited of Ram I, 61, 21, Śunahśepa declares that he, unlike his elder and younger brothers (the two preferred by his parents) is ready to die.

147. *Ṛta*, generally translated as cosmic order, is not a physical or natural law, but the very expression of the factual behavior of all reality, the sheer freedom of the real, or of divine spontaneity if you wish— doubtless something different from divine caprice. Cf. RV I, 23, 5; II, 28, 4-5; V, 62, 1; V, 63, 1 and 7; V, 68, 3; X, 190, 1; AV IV, 1, 4; X, 7, 11; XII, 1, 1; etc.

148. Cf. RV X, 90, the famous *puruṣa-sūkta*.

149. Cf. RV X, 129, 4 where *kāma*, desire or love, is described as the original force that initiates the dynamism of creation and being. Together with *tapas*, heat or energy, it forms one of the two elements of existence. Cf. TB III, 11, 86; AB IV, 23, 1; V, 32, 1; SB VI, 1, 1, 8; X, 5, 3, 3; XI, 5, 8, 1; etc.

150. Modern European languages have significantly enough lost the desiderative form of the verb (and in English even the future). Future and desiderative are not extrinsic modes or simple constructions of the human mind that can be expressed with mere auxiliary forms or verbs. They belong to the very structure of our being.

151. It was common at the beginning of this century to consider

initiation as a simple *rite de passage*. We use the word in a deeper and broader sense. Unfortunately, the narrow conception of initiation as a phenomenon typifying 'primitive' religion has not yet entirely disappeared from modern writing. Cf. *sub hac voce* ERE and, in comparison, the progress of RGG.

152. Cf. SB XI, 2, 1, 1: "Verily, Man is born thrice, namely in this way:—first he is born from his mother and father; and when he to whom the sacrifice inclines performs offering he is born a second time; and when he dies, and they place him on the fire, and when he thereupon comes into existence again, he is born a third time;—wherefore they say, 'Man is born thrice' " (Eggeling trans.).

153. Cf. BU IV, 4, 7. Cf. also with regard to this Hegel's words: "Das Individuum ist Sohn seines Volkes, seiner Welt; der Einzelne mag sich ausspreizen, wie er will, er geht nicht über sie hinaus. Denn er gehört dem einen allgemeinen Geiste an, der seine Substanz und Wesen ist; wie sollte er aus diesem herauskommen?" *Vorlesungen über die Geschichte der Philosophie* (Stuttgart: Frommann, 1928), p. 75. 'Jumping out of one's skin' is precisely what concerns us here. Cf. incidentally the thrust of this metaphor in most Western languages as the expression of an impossibility.

154. Cf. Manu IX, 8 which seems to refer to Nārada's introductory verses in AB VII, 13.

155. Even if these names have a 'phallic connotation' (J.C. Heesterman, *op. cit.*, p. 159), here they hardly play what could be called a significant role.

156. I agree with P. Horsch (*op. cit.*, p. 290) who notes that "trotz der Vorliebe der alten Inder für Namendeutung, die Etymologie von Śunaḥśepa nirgend eine Rolle spielt."

157. It is not a question of ignorance or naiveté or even innocence. Cf. the myths of Prajāpati (SB I, 7, 4); of Yama and Yamī (RV X, 10); of Purūravas and Urvaśī (RV X, 95; SB XI, 5, 1); etc.

158. Could this be another factor favoring an interpretation of the myth as a myth of initiation?

159. Cf. BU IV, 4, 22, where it is said that because sages know the *ātman* to be the true realm of salvation, they do not desire children or wealth, which are only aids to salvation. For the Western and Christian tradition, cf. Ton H.C. Van Ejk, 'Marriage and Virginity, Death and Immortality', *Epektasis*, Mélanges J. Daniélou (Paris: Beauchesne, 1972), pp. 209-235.

160. Sf. SB II, 2, 2, 8-14.

161. It is enough to cite the entire MB and BG in order to note the difference.

162. I can't help thinking here that someone like Solzhenitsyn, who describes the 'glimmering light' at the center of a person even in a prison

camp, in the 'first circle' of condemned Men or in a cancer ward, understands very well what this myth says.

163. Cf., e.g., the famous cosmogonic hymns: RV X, 90; 121; 129; 190.

164. I am tempted to quote here from another tradition and cite Tsze Sze's first thesis (I,1) in the *Chung Yung*, the second of the *Four Classics* of Chinese wisdom, which Ezra Pound rendered as *The Unwobbling Pivot* (and whose version I reproduce):

> What heaven has disposed and sealed is called the inborn nature. The realization of this nature is called the process. The clarification of this process (the understanding or making intelligible of this process) is called education.

The translation can be found in Pound's *Confucius* (New York: New Directions, 1969).

165. There are exactly 97 *r̥cs* and 31 *gāthās*.

166. If *rubrics*, printed in *rubrum*, red, explain the ceremonies, what I call *nigrics*, generally printed in *nigrum*, black, constitute the very substance of the rites. Cf. R. Panikkar, *Worship and Secular Man* (London: Darton, Longman & Todd and Maryknoll, New York: Orbis Books, 1973), pp. 69 sq.

167. Cf. chapter XVI.

168. From the root *muc* (*mokṣ-*) meaning liberate, set free.

169. Cf. R. Panikkar, 'El presente tempiterno. Una apostilla a la historia de la salvación y a la teología de la liberación', edited by A. Vargas-Machuca, *Teología y mundo contemporaneo. Homenaje a K. Rahner* (Madrid: Cristiandad, 1975), pp. 133–175, where these ideas are further developed.

Part II

FAITH

Πίστει νοοῦμεν κατηρτίσθαι
τοὺς αἰῶνας ῥήματι θεοῦ εἰς τὸ μὴ ἐκ
φαινομένον τὸ βλεπόμενον γεγονέναι

*Fide intelligimus aptata esse
saecula verbo Dei: ut ex invisibilibus
visibilia fierent.*

By faith we understand that the
secular worlds have been formed by the speech
of God, so that from the invisible the
visible came to be.

Heb. 11:3

VI.
Faith as a Constitutive Human Dimension

καὶ ἐάν μὴ πιστεύσετε,
οὐδὲ μὴ συνῆτε

If you do not believe,
you will not exist.
Is. 7:9+

+ Before commenting on the text, I will give some of its most common translations: "Nisi credideritis, non intelligetis" (LXX, the version generally employed by mediaeval theologians); "Si non credideritis, non permanebitis" (Vulgate); "Vosotros, si no tuviereis fé, no permanecereis" (Nacar-Colunga); "Si no creéis, no podréis subsistir" (Martin Nieto); "Se non avrete fede, non starete saldi" (Istituto Biblico); "Se non crederete, non resterete saldi" (Nardoni); "Mais si vous ne tenez à moi, vous ne tiendrez pas" (*Bible de Jérusalem*, but in a note: "Si vous ne croyez pas"); "Gläubt ihr nicht, so bleibt ihr nicht" (Luther); "If you lose courage, your cause is lost" (Knox); "If ye will not believe, surely ye shall not be established" (*AV* & *RV*); (RSV changes only ye for you); "Have firm faith, or you will not stand firm" (NEB).

I am deeply aware of the responsibility as well as the risk and incongruity of breaking silence to speak of what is lived and contemplated only in silence: faith and myth, both sucklings of silence.

When celebrating the mystery of the *Logos* made flesh during Christmas, the Christian liturgy chants: *Dum medium silentium tenerent omnia . . .* —'For while gentle silence enveloped all things. . . .'[1] To speak of faith translates it into belief; the original vanishes, but only for a little while. Myth is myth because it is μύειν and not λέγειν, mute and not speaking.

Having broken the silence, I only wish to be able to reenter it afresh, this time perhaps not alone. . . .[2]

1. THE STATE OF THE PROBLEM

a. Crede ut intelligas[3]

'Without faith you cannot exist.' In this way I interpret this key passage in traditional Christian theological speculation.[4] The Hebrew word play is significant: if you do not believe, *ta'aminu*, you will not exist, *te'amenu*.[5] *Aman* (cf. *amen*, *emet*) is one of the two expressions for faith. If on the one hand *betah* (*batah*) brings out the aspect of confidence, *emet* (*aman*) on the other indicates firmness, solidarity, subsistence and consequently consistence.[6] Thus faith appears as the real foundation for human existence.[7]

Contemporary human experience—followed, not always without delay, by theologians—clearly shows that Man, when deprived of faith, does not know how to bear the weight of an existence torn by internal struggles, nor can he sustain the continual demand to surmount the tensions created by communal life. Deprived of faith, Man collapses. From a phenomenological point of view, one could say that Man is a being 'designed' to function in the realm of faith: whoever alienates himself from this sphere ends up destroying himself.

Such an anthropology is plausible not only phenomenologically but also within traditional theology. If on the one hand Man depends on God—and this dependence belongs to the so-called 'supernatural' order presupposed by faith—and if, on the other hand, Man is through and through a rational animal whose being is a conscious being, he can only be founded in truth—and ultimately *be*—if, in some way or other, he can see, intuit, comprehend, believe that his existential situation has a foundation that is not (yet?) himself.[8] Without this awareness his existence is mutilated. A plant lives as long as sap runs in its stalk; Man needs that ontic sap, which gives him his being, runs up to his head and heart. Any 'theology' uses similar arguments. Hindus and Buddhists would say empirical Man is not his own foundation. Faith is precisely that *x* in Man which makes possible the 'recognition' of the foundation, for by it Man is united (at least intentionally) to this foundation. A human being cannot attain his destiny if he does not 'recognize' the foundation of his being. Now faith is precisely what manifests this foundation. Without faith Man cannot live an authentic human life.

A passage from the *Bhagavad Gītā* seems to express what I wish to say: Just as there are three kinds of Man according to classical Indian anthropology, there are three types of faith, one corresponding to each of these fundamental human types. 'Man is made by faith: As the faith so the Man.'[9] Without now investigating the notion of *śraddhā*[10] (faith)—which originally signified the theandric condition essential to the efficacy of the sacrifice—it can be said that our thesis is in harmony with the spirit of the Indian religions[11] and in general with every religion.[12]

Yet I may go further: The mediaeval Christian said, *Crede ut intelligas.*[13] By this expression he did not wish to indicate just the ontological priority of faith with respect to reason, i.e., the existential situation in which Man cannot understand if he does not believe. Rather he suspected something more, and it is this intuition I wish to clarify in this study.[14]

b. Crede ut sis[15]

I dare to say 'Believe in order that you may be'. Faith is not only necessary in order to understand, but also to reach full humanity, to be. In other words, faith is a constitutive human dimension. By faith Man is *distinguished* from other beings. But precisely because of this, faith is a human characteristic that *unites* mankind. Thus faith is not the privilege of some individuals or the monopoly of certain defined groups, however large their membership. Faith is not a superfluous luxury, but an anthropological dimension of the full human being on earth.[16]

Our thesis maintains that if creatureliness can be said to be simple *relation* to God, to the Source or whatever name we give the foundation of beings, faith is another name for the *ontological relation* to this absolute that characterizes Man, distinguishing him from all other beings. If beings as such are nothing but this relation (the creature neither is nor has its foundation in itself), Man is that unique being whose rapport with the foundation becomes the *ontological link* that constitutes him as Man.

In saying 'relation' to 'God' I am not assuming a kind of merely 'private' link with an exclusivistic and anthropomorphic God, but the constitutive radical relativity of all things, so that this link is not a solitary 'relation' to an only transcendent 'God' but a relation of solidarity with the whole of Reality. The traditional way of expressing this view would be to say that the 'theological virtues' are also *cosmological* ones, or in a word *cosmotheandric*. Faith, Hope and Love are not only vertical, but also horizontal.[17]

If religion (from *religare*) is what binds Man to his foundation, faith is what frees him from mere cosmic existence, from being simply a thing. Freedom arises in this opening to or rupture from his subjection to the realm of objects.[18] By his freedom Man is placed at the heart of the personal Trinitarian relation. The relation between God and Man can in no way be free unless there is freedom within the Godhead itself and Man is somehow integrated into that intra-divine free-play. This is what the idea of the Trinity, in any of its forms, is saying.[19]

It seems to me unnecessary, but it may be important to add that this thesis, although expressed in a particular language, need not be linked to a single philosophy or religious tradition. It claims to be as valid for a Buddhist as for one who calls himself an atheist. The meaning of words depends not simply upon the semantic expression, but also upon a whole collection of cultural connections that should not obscure our central theme or turn us aside from it. On the other hand, I may be excused from not undertaking excursions into other cultural worlds and not utilizing other frames of reference. All terminology is just the concrete objectification of a cultural system. A discourse in totally abstract terms, i.e., lacking any cultural connections or reference, is impossible. The reader may find it easier to understand what I am saying if he translates my words into those of his own personal frame of reference. I hope it will become clearer as we proceed.

c. The Consequences

This thesis has important consequences. If it is true, it provides the key to one of the most important problems of our time: the encounter of religions. In other words, it delivers us from the impasse in which the science of religions currently finds itself. It suggests the astonishing possibility that the encounter of religions might be a religious dialogue—even at the level of faith—rather than a mere rational dispute. It may also serve to free religion from its exclusivistic aspects, its frequent sectarian character and from an archaic unilateralism incompatible with the process of universalization in which humanity is engaged. Recognizing faith as an anthropological dimension situates the encounter between people on a fully human plane and does not exclude religion from the dialogue.[20] In a human encounter worthy of the name, it is not enough that Men recognize their brotherhood in shared biological functions or elemental needs while raising barriers when it is a question of a deeper embrace.

One cannot put faith in parentheses any more than one can bracket reason when truly human understanding is at stake, unless one would castrate Man and render him not only infertile but

monstrous.[21] Faith is the foundation and guarantee of human relations. Banishing it would inevitably condemn us to solipsism by
destroying the last possible foundation for a path to any transcendence, beginning with that transcendence which allows Man to
'go out' of himself and meet his fellow-being without alienation.

Understood in this way faith is also a condition for love and
guarantees its creativity. Faith cannot be ignored in considering
the deepest realities of human life; it is part of a fully human
existence on earth. Every profound human encounter in which
faith is left to one side can only appear hypocritical to someone
who does not think he has faith, for in such a meeting, the so-
called nonbeliever does not meet the believer on the same level if
the latter has bracketed his faith; what is ultimate and definitive
for the first is only penultimate and provisional for the second.
And vice versa: for the Man of faith, there is no real encounter
because by putting his faith in parentheses he shuts away precisely what the 'nonbeliever' would like to put on the table.

Further, we can suggest that in and by faith the believer
'communicates' and fraternizes with the Man who calls himself a
nonbeliever. Removed from this deep level of faith, human
fraternity becomes an infra-human communication of the biological order or even an artificial contact, like a computer that always
gives the same results when fed the same data. Reason does not
get us out of this situation, because it divides, decides and distinguishes but does not unite.

For several centuries, Western Man has been indoctrinated
that his humanity (and consequently his universality) was
grounded in reason. The effort to discard theology, and faith
along with it, to reduce the latter to a corner in humanity's sac-
risty so that the real human encounter can be realized in the
domain of pure reason, of true and uncontaminated philosophy,
has characterized 'modern' philosophy since Descartes.[22] According to this view, faith would be a privilege gratuitously given
by God to the few. Faith would then separate Men while reason
would unite them and provide the possibility for universal human
communication. Theologies differ, it is said, precisely because
they are based on something 'more than human'. As a result,

philosophy becomes the universal science and following the judgments of reason appears the only way to attain, if not a celestial, at least a terrestrial paradise. 'Two and two make four anywhere' is the popular summary of this attitude. 'Religion divides people while reason unites them' is its sociological translation. As the only source of universal knowledge, philosophy is thus opposed to theology, which it construes as merely exegesis of gratuitous propositions.

The recent historical and philosophical evolution has put Man, mostly Western Man, on guard against a naive rationalistic optimism. Today, after two world wars, a cold war in progress (détente notwithstanding), and at least two atrocious wars before our own eyes, after the failure of idealism and the ensuing chaos of philosophy, faced with an almost worldwide revolution of an entire generation against another, our confidence in reason has been thoroughly shaken. We are actually beginning to suspect that 'two and two do not make four' except in a purely ideal and abstract realm. It is the revolt of life, of the concrete, which refuses to be imprisoned or paralyzed in reason's formalism. Two roses and two violets make four flowers, to be sure; but completely different from two lilies and two jasmines, although these are also four flowers. Is love for a mother plus love for God the same as love for a car plus love for a garden? Reality cannot be so simply manipulated.

Faced with the nonreasonable situation of the world, the defenders of 'pure reason' advance the argument of contamination. The failure of reason, they say, is due to something for which reason itself is not responsible: In itself reason is infallible, but in operation, desires, passions and feelings mutilate it, render it impotent. The argument, however, is not convincing. First of all, it begs the question and demands a far greater leap of logic than that of the famous and so often misunderstood 'ontological argument'. In fact it represents a jump from the 'real order', which we experience as fallible and nonrational, to the 'ideal order' of pure reason by postulating the infallibility of reason. Further, the argument is unconvincing because, even if it were to prove anything, it would be useless: A reason that is theoretically infallible and practically impotent cannot help us. We are not concerned with knowing the theoretical rights of 'pure' reason, but with what can actually guide Man. Reason verifies and criticizes; it does not discover and guide. Perhaps we have been seduced by a distorted definition of Man, by removing its most salient element, animality, and so converting Man into a 'logical' being.[23] In addition, *logos* is often interpreted in an excessively rationalistic fashion.[24] But I am not interested in attacking reason or bringing the analysis of critical philosophy to bear on it.

It goes without saying that the word reason does not need to stand only for a merely Cartesian reason and that today under this word one would include the entire mediaeval meaning of intellect and even more.

The urgency of our problematic, however, lies in another direction, whose importance and gravity we discover when we confront it. One of the most striking phenomena of our age is atheism. The various manifestations of contemporary atheism generally coincide with denying the *object* of religious faith: Such atheism denies the Christian affirmation of the existence of God, rejects the theistic affirmation of transcendence, etc. Today, a Man is often declared an unbeliever because he refuses to objectivize his faith and does not wish to limit the possibilities of his existence by being recognized as a member of a part of humanity—more or less great—but nevertheless only a part. We could say that a certain monopoly of faith on the part of some groups has taken from him the possibility of believing.[25]

At this point the gravity of our theme appears: Faith can be recovered because it was never lost.[26] It is purified because its content is questioned as being ever inadequate.

We might mention in passing two connected problems: the 'loss of faith' and 'conversion'. Does one really lose faith or is it simply an abandoning of certain beliefs?[27] Does faith disappear or does Man flee the light?[28] We refer to the so-called great crises of faith that beset our epoch. Have the Catholics of post-Vatican II lost their 'faith' because they no longer believe what their ancestors held to be the case? Have the neo-Marxists and contemporary Eurocommunists to lose their identity because they no longer agree with orthodox party lines? And conversion: Is it a real change of faith or a return to an interiority enabling us to discover what we, in an inadequate or unconscious way, already believed? Would not every conversion be a *gnosis*, a knowing, a *metanoia*, a change of mind, which reveals to us the true name or the authentic relief of what we already believed? We refer to the great traumas caused by conversion into other religious 'creeds' that no longer need imply a rupture from and abjuration of the previous tradition. Has a Hindu becoming Christian to denounce all his Hindu past? Or has a Christian becoming Buddhist to forego what he still believes is valid in the Christian tradition? Or has an Indonesian becoming Muslim to sponsor the Arab cause? Has conversion necessarily to entail alienation? Should we then not distinguish between faith and belief?[29]

2. THE THREE INSTANCES OF FAITH

To elaborate a little further I wish to bring to mind two conceptions of faith that illustrate this inexhaustible problematic.

The discovery of writing began a new cultural stage for humanity: It showed Man the power he could draw from his rationality. Although sporadic experiences of the almost diabolical character of his volitional capacity have redeemed Man from the wonder and near self-adoration into which he often fell once he left prehistory behind, mankind has nonetheless practically identified his humanity with intelligence and will. As a result, the theology of faith has insisted first on the intellectual aspect of the act of faith and second on its volitional and thus free dimension.[30] If faith then is the supreme value it will have to be anchored in the supreme human faculties: intellect and will.

The first conception, founded on the primacy of an essentialistic conception of Truth, leads one to identify faith with *orthodoxy*, i.e., with correct doctrine properly formulated. The second insists on the moral character of the religious act, based on the supremacy of the Good, and consequently leads one to identify faith with *orthopoiesis*, with the attitude and moral deportment that lead Man to his destiny. If the first risks 'dogmatism', the second skirts 'moralism'. From Paul and James in the first Christian generation to Maritain and Russell in our times we could draw an interminable list. Complementing these two interpretations, which do not seem false but only one-sided, we offer the concept of faith as *orthopraxis*.

This hypothesis does not center orthopraxis in another particular faculty of Man, but links it to his very being seen as act. If Man as Man is a religious animal, his religion cannot be a sect, his religiousness cannot be one element among others or a mere 'virtue'.[31] Rather his religion must be based on this free movement that penetrates the totality of his being, rejoining his most profound existence to its source. Faith is what gives him this freedom.[32]

a. Orthodoxy

The presupposition that Man is above all a 'rational animal' has caused the problem of faith to be centered on an almost exclusively intellectual dimension; whence the tendency to consider true faith synonymous with orthodoxy, i.e., to link the essence of the act of faith with its conceptually 'correct' expression.

This perspective enables us to recognize various degrees in the awareness of faith, since a concept that expresses the content of faith may be more, or less, adequate. Nevertheless it is here maintained that formulation is essential to correct faith. In this way concepts like 'erroneous faith' or 'infidelity' arise to mark what is not recognized as 'orthodox'.

It follows that although in principle it is possible to have different formulations of faith, the formulation is in a certain sense intrinsic to the faith itself. So, one cannot have faith if one does not adhere to a definite doctrine. Faith is fundamentally considered a definite understanding. Certainly, faith can be expressed in several formulae, leaving room for a certain doctrinal pluralism. But here the justification of pluralism does not consist in accepting that the different conceptions may express the same existential situation, but in recognizing that in the last analysis they are all equivalent to the heart of the doctrine itself. If the different formulations were not analogous or at least mutually reducible who would judge whether they are really equivalent? In other words, the only possible pluralism orthodoxy allows is the manifold expression of one and the same doctrine (and this only insofar as one expression is less adequate than another). But there is no place for a pluralism in which the different expressions represent really different doctrines of one ever-transcending reality not reducible to the *logos*.

Now this is only detectable once we jump outside the cultural world in which we usually move. Otherwise, we are existentially unable to distinguish because orthodoxy claims exactly to express (with precision, if imperfectly) the right view on a particular or general religious truth. Orthodoxy makes sense only in the context of one specific and homogeneous culture, i.e., under the assumption that one takes for granted the premises necessary to link Reality unequivocally to a fixed conceptual expression. If, in a given culture—always under the assumption that Man is a 'rational animal'—one finds a bi-univocal system of references between Reality and its expression, then all dissension on the conceptual plane will also indicate dissension on the objectively real plane. It is for this reason that in a closed culture one must consider the 'heretic' not only mistaken but also in bad faith.[33]

Let me give an example. I may accept and you may deny the attribute of 'substantiality' to the Godhead. This is within the limits permitted by orthodoxy as long as neither of us denies the possibility for the other to think (although erroneously, each of us will assume) of God with or without that attribute. But if I cannot admit as even thinkable a God without substantiality, the moment you deny this attribute I shall suppose you deny God altogether. And this is no longer tolerable, for God is here the very symbol for my tolerance of 'you'. If substance for me means Being and Being, Reality (and Truth), then there is no place within orthodoxy for the true atheist, for someone who denies the 'being' of God, and thus the Reality of the entire universe; but this is not necessarily the case in the other two attitudes we have still to describe.

One cannot deny the intellectual character of faith without denying faith itself; however, faith cannot be identified with any of its parameters. In this we see both the strength and the weakness of orthodoxy.

The distinction between both the act of faith and its conceptual formulation, on the one hand, and between faith as a salvific act and belief as its intellectual expression, on the other, characterizes the purest scholastic theology.[34] According to one such theology, the act of faith grasps things in themselves. Its formulation is only a conceptualization of some 'thing' that transcends it.[35] The formulation of faith cannot be essentially linked to its content without violating its transcendent, supernatural character.[36] This is why the Orthodox and Catholic Churches only condemn doctrinal affirmations that seem contrary to truth: They do not correctly express the ever-transcendent mystery of faith. And faith is a mystery that cannot be tied to a definitive form of expression or related univocally to any intellectual formulation. As long as Man is *viator*, faith can only be 'itinerant'.

Attempting to immobilize the act of faith by making it depend on unalterable formulations would not only be treason against history but would also deny what faith claims to be: the ontological link relating Man to the transcendent. Faith is not essentially tied to a fixed doctrine, but it does need an intellectual vehicle or even, in most cases, a conceptual system to express it.[37] One faith can crystallize in several systems of belief.

The importance of the so-called 'articles of faith' lies in the fact that although no formulation is exhaustive, not every formula is necessarily true. An article of faith can attain greater or lesser conceptual perfection. This formal perfection comes from either of two sources: the (more or less perfect) philosophical system it uses, or the intuition expressing (with greater or lesser profundity) the ineffable and transcendent content of faith, what Christian theology calls 'first truth', the unique and ultimate object of all faith.[38]

The role of orthodoxy is to defend the rights of the intellect in the ontological 'linking' of Man to God.[39] It is not, however, I would submit, the feebleness of our intellect that leads us to proceed beyond it, but the fact that the intellectual element does not exhaust the nature of faith. Even in contemporary speech we speak of a Man in good faith to indicate one who, although far from orthodoxy, is not outside its effective sphere.

In defending the community of faith between Men and angels, and in considering the formal object of faith above materially believable truths, i.e., in underscoring the subjectively formal aspect of faith, scholastic theology wishes to say, it seems to me, just what I want to show here,[40] namely, that faith is unique, even if its conceptual translations and vital manifestations are multiple.[41]

An analogy from the physical world could perhaps symbolize this: A crystal prism decomposes light into different monochromatic components; another prism, placed at a different angle, re-collects all the wave lengths into a single beam of light. Likewise the 'object' of faith, considered the ultimate term of the ontological intentionality of the act of faith, is unique; there is only one Absolute. When the single light beam of faith is refracted in the prism of our consciousness, it is decomposed into as many conceptual beams as there are intellectual structures by which the pure act of faith is expressed. The 'colors' and the angles of the rays are different, to be sure, but their source is one and they can be reunited. Heterodoxy is the mixture of colors or the confusion of angles. Orthodoxy does not need to maintain there can be only a single, monochromatic beam. Numerous colors can appear on the doctrinal screen. Light is faith, the act of faith is the refraction of light (not absorbing it altogether) under its 'proper' angle. Colors are the symbols of belief. The color depends on the wavelength or on the nature of the body; yet no color is without light—nor light without color.

b. Orthopoiesis

Perhaps a reference to the Protestant Reformation will help clarify our point. To the intellectual and, in a certain sense, static and objective aspect of faith, the Reformation opposed a more dynamic notion, predominantly subjective, stressing the voluntarist character of the act of faith. If one does not live in conformity with the exigencies of the act of faith one is not Christian, Protestant theology tells us; the sacraments are not efficacious if one is not worthy of them. If the community of Christians by and large does not live its faith, it ceases to be the Church founded by

Christ, etc. Only faith can save,[42] and consequently it cannot be reduced to a mere intellectual assent separate from life: Faith without works is dead faith,[43] and in every believing will there is an inclination to live in accord with faith.

Whatever it is, faith doubtless contains a practical and volitive element: Its end is not merely the Truth but also the Good. Certainly it is insufficient to identify religion with ethics or reduce faith just to moral deportment, but one cannot deny that it is precisely faith that makes possible the unity of life in Man's daily existence.[44]

In order to understand the diverse facets of the problem in their real complexity, we must distinguish between the transcendent plane where faith moves and the terrestrial plane where ethics resides. It is not rigorously exact to say, following the famous Augustinian diatribe, that the virtues of the pagans were *splendida vitia*, 'splendid vices', but we cannot deny that if faith is reduced to orthopoiesis one destroys the very foundation of religion, which claims to be more than mere 'perfectionism'.

Like orthodoxy, orthopoiesis has its place in a global conception of faith. However, the relation is not reversible: Negative moral deportment could be an obstacle to a real life of faith, but an irreproachable ethical life is not equivalent to a life of faith.

Furthermore, just as faith can be expressed in more than one orthodox formulation, it can also be manifest in differing ethical behavior. This consideration is important since it enables us to understand other religions and cultures whose customs, even today, are considered by many people intrinsically immoral. Just as there is doctrinal pluralism, so there is also ethical pluralism. And just as doctrinal pluralism does not mean conceptual chaos, so ethical pluralism does not imply moral anarchy. To decipher a code we must have a clue; to confront several different ethics, we must ascend 'even higher'.

The positive value of orthopoiesis is the accentuation of faith as love, as a personal offering, as a decision about life, as freely assumed human freedom. A faith that is mere conviction, unexpressed in life, is incomplete.

Faith shapes human existence: It rules the destiny of Man. It is the necessary condition for 'right action'.[45]

Through this understanding of faith Man becomes the artist of his own life and the life he constructs is above all terrestrial: In a certain sense, it is a construction exterior to his being. Through faith, Man the artist expresses himself through his *poietic* capacity. Without faith, not only would no cathedrals have been built, but we would have neither atomic weapons nor artificial hearts.

It should be clear by now that we have taken the Aristotelian concepts 'poiesis' and 'praxis' as relevant for our distinctions. By the first we understand human activity whose result falls on the external object to which the act is directed; in the second, the act reverts on the agent himself and transforms him.[46]

c. Orthopraxis

Man possesses intelligence and will. He rushes forward drawn toward the Truth and the Good. But he is not exhausted there, or, better said, these primordial activities spring from an even more radical source: his very being, his being as *act*. Human life is not exhausted either in the thought process or in extrinsic constructions: Man is much more than a spectator or constructor of the world. Above all he is an actor; fundamentally he enacts himself through his capacity—not exhausted by his *facere*—to embrace his *agere* as well. His activity is not simply *poiesis,* but above all *praxis*. Herein lies the meaning of the sacred action that all religions recognize: the horizon of orthopraxis.

Through faith Man becomes himself; in other words, he is saved, completed, attains his fullness, obtains liberation, his final end, by whatever name he may call it.

Religions do not claim primarily to teach a doctrine or provide a technique. They claim to save Man, i.e., to liberate him or, in other words, to open for him the way to the fullness of his being, whatever this fullness may be. When this end is interpreted as an intellectual vision, the doctrinal aspect comes to the fore. If, on the other hand, it is seen as a reward for a life, for moral conduct, the practical values have the primacy. But in both cases, one presupposes that human fullness consists in acquiring this value that lies at the center of human finality.

Orthopraxis illuminates a fact common to all doctrine and all deportment: Man should reach his goal and fullness, however he may interpret these expressions.[47]

We have introduced the term "orthopraxis" not as a sign of our dependence on a particular philosophical system, but as a concentrated expression of what we mean. *Praxis* is that human activity which modifies and fashions not only Man's exterior existence but also the interior dimension of his life. The effect of praxis is part of Man's very being: It is the salvific activity par excellence. Within a certain metaphysical framework, praxis is that activity which actualizes the potentiality of the human being. "Work out your salvation with diligence," said Gautama just before his death.

Now we should not mistake the concept of praxis for praxis itself, not only in the obvious sense in which no concept is the 'conceptualized' thing, but in a very peculiar way, inasmuch as here the very concept does not stand for some 'thing' about which we may have a more or less adequate concept, but as 'anything' which, in a given frame of reference, may stand for that praxis. In this way, if the end of Man is to become God, he is divinized by orthopraxis. If human fullness consists in the individual's contribution to future society, orthopraxis constitutes the actions that lead to this contribution. If the goal of human life is to annihilate the contingent and the existent, the actions that deliver Man from his earthly condition represent orthopraxis, and so on.

The quintessence of faith, then, reflects this aspect of Man that moves him towards fullness, this dimension by which Man is not closed up in his present state but open to perfection, to his goal or destiny, according to the schema one adopts. Faith is not fundamentally the adhesion to a doctrine or an ethic. Rather, it is manifest as an act that opens to us the possibility of perfection, permitting us to attain to what we are not yet. The concept of orthopraxis does not eliminate the possibility of erroneous actions, but it excludes the possibility of interpreting them only in terms of doctrine or morality.

Every action that leads to the perfection of Man in his concrete existential situation, every action that leads Man to his realization, is authentic praxis, way to salvation.[48]

Just as error is possible in the doctrinal order and mistakes occur in human conduct, so pseudo-praxis is possible: It is an action that does not build Man up. Human liberty and dignity are based on the fact that Man is a required factor in constructing his own destiny. But being the constructor or at least co-constructor of his own destiny, Man risks failure. He can reach his goal or he can become lost on the way and not arrive, stop in his becoming (being); and this, viewed after the fact, leads one to say this person never had being.[49] It is not a question of Man's being presented with homogeneous alternatives—heaven or hell, to be or not to be.[50] It is more a question of the possibility of fulfillment offered to every Man than a Manichean dichotomy of standing before the alternative of not realizing the destiny to which the individual seemed called. I say 'seemed' because if we move from a general and essential problematic to a concrete and ontic consideration of existence, the individual who does not reach his end proves by this very fact that he did not have being, since the not-yet-being that characterizes his terrestrial existence has not been realized. If Man is not-yet-being (for he is still *be-ing*, still on his way to fulfillment), the individual who does not reach his destination (his being), can in truth be said not to have been, since we *are* only insofar as we shall be.[51] Hindu *karma*, Christian predestination, Humanist religion, etc., could offer us many ways of solving the same question.

An important but different problem (which does not render invalid what I have just said) is the possible interpretation of orthopraxis as hetero-praxis or auto-praxis. In the former case, the saving act comes from above or outside the individual; in the latter, salvation comes from within. A certain type of Buddhism and a certain contemporary Existentialism could serve as example of auto-praxis. Most traditional interpretations of religions bear witness to hetero-praxis. A deeper understanding of person (in contrast to individual) could perhaps offer a new solution to this almost 'chronic' problem—but we should refrain now from elaborating further.[52]

3. FAITH AS A HUMAN INVARIANT

a. Theological Consideration

An introductory theological consideration seems opportune now, to point out the horizon where this reflection on the nature of faith as a constitutive human dimension emerges. I could utilize the schema of any 'theology,' Buddhist or Hindu, for example. But to be better understood by the Western reader and because the problem has become particularly agonizing within Christianity, I shall use Christian terminology.

Christianity considers faith absolutely necessary for salvation.[53] Without faith we cannot reach God, because by definition it is the bridge that links us to Him.[54] This affirmation seems axiomatic since, whatever the destiny of Man, that by which it is attained or discovered constitutes the structural morphology of faith. The faith of an atheist, for example, is what permits him to discover himself entirely divorced from any theistic transcendence. This faith alone, he says, offers him the possibility of realizing his life's destiny. Some may call it conviction, intuition, discovery. *Sed de nominibus non est disputandum*. It comes to the same, something that frees Man from inauthentic existence. Here Christian theology cannot escape the alternative: Either only those who have the Christian faith are saved or salvific faith can also be found among so-called 'nonbelievers'.[55]

The classic distinction between implicit and explicit Christian faith shows that tradition has admitted that the essence of faith does not consist in its explication but in what causes it to arise. This already represents a relaxation of too rigid an orthodoxy, but the recognition of implicit faith as a condition of salvation is often interpreted as a fact of the doctrinal order, i.e., within the intellectual domain. In effect, the recognition that God exists and that he rewards was said to constitute the indispensable foundation for the explication of true doctrine.[56] And yet the accepted salvation of baptized infants makes it possible to recognize, by virtue of the ontological change introduced by baptism, an implicit faith not simply in the doctrinal order, but also outside this order. The salvific faith of the infants cannot be at all intellectual.

Both of these—the doctrinal insufficiency of the ignorant and the doctrinal incapacity of baptized infants—offer a point of support within the tradition that we now continue by going beyond it. They lead us to reexamine widespread opinion that faith is the privilege of Christians alone and the exception for anyone else. If we admit what is commonly accepted—that the Man who acts in good faith according to his conscience is saved—it follows that since this conscience generally moves him to follow his own religion, in doing so he reaches salvation. In some way, then, salvific faith is included in this good faith, for without faith there is no salvation.

Further, it follows that faith must be something common to Men, whatever their religious beliefs. Denying this amounts to saying that the vast majority of Men do not reach salvation and are damned. At least quantitatively, human creation would be an almost total failure.

But, beyond orthodoxy and orthopoiesis, we can still ask what comprises the real essence of faith.

Having posed the theological problem in this way, we are led to seek the structure of faith belonging to the very constitution of Man. Now a critique of an exclusivistic faith should not cause us to go to the other extreme and defend a universality that excludes all discrimination and difference. This directs us to another theological consideration.

What has just been said does not impugn the validity of various classical doctrines on faith that emphasize its differential aspect. If faith is a gift from God,[57] nothing prevents it from being a universal gift, like nature or existence. There is, however, a fundamental difference between the gift of being (as traditional creationist terminology calls it) and the gift of faith. The former is conceived of as the gift of substance, more or less complete, but basically subsistent, consistent. The gift of faith, on the contrary, cannot be interpreted substantially: It is a gift inviting response, a challenging call, a door that is opened[58]—all of this implies freedom and the possibility of refusal, for a gift is not a gift if it is not accepted, if there is not a positive response. Faith is that a-substantial dimension of Man that makes it possible for him not to stop midway, or to become paralyzed in time, locked into the past. Faith is fundamentally dynamic, functional, 'that which one hopes'. It is that gift which makes fullness possible because it elicits a response to an appeal, to the call to be human. But this appeal has been made once and for all—$\ddot{\alpha}\pi\alpha\zeta$—to all Men.[59]

Traditional Christian theology would say the act of faith responds to supernatural grace and gratuity, but this does not deny that the structure of faith and the act of faith may be of the order I have tried to describe. Without analyzing the concrete functioning of faith or the conditions required for the act of faith, we could already conclude that many different notions of faith have their place in the fundamental structure I am going to describe and, notably, the doctrine of the act of faith as a supernatural act is not necessarily or directly contested.

Venturing a hypothesis on how the act of faith functions amounts to having already entered the realm of theories that, to be accepted, demand that one recognize their supporting philosophical foundations. In Christian language one could say: Man's destiny is divinization, that is, becoming God. But how? We might find in the idea of the Trinity an answer to the paradox of integral union with God on the one hand and distinction from Him on the other. Just as the Son and the Spirit are identical with regard to the Father, they are also infinitely different—for nothing finite exists in the Trinity. Strictly speaking, we cannot talk of equality or difference in the heart of the divinity; these categories presuppose either an independent, exterior criterion of measurement (inadmissible here) or a higher referent with which, or in which, this equality or inequality is confronted (impossible in the realm of the Absolute).

On earth Man is not perfect: He is neither fully Man nor truly God; he is not yet what he is called to be. He has (or has received) the capacity to become what he must be in order to realize his destiny; in fact, he must actualize it concretely. The first capacity we call 'faith', the second 'act of faith'. Whether or not the grace of God is necessary to freely decide an act of faith raises a problem of a different order, but not one incompatible with what we are saying. If God is the end of Man, it seems plausible that to attain him, the *terminus a quo* (starting point) as well as the *terminus ad quem* (end point) participate in the act that conducts Man to his goal. At the same time, however, it does not follow from these principles that the same grace cannot inspire doctrinally unequal acts of faith; in other words, we cannot affirm that heterodoxy—doctrinal heterodoxy—is a univocal sign of lack of faith (which would amount to saying that one who does not know the true doctrine cannot be saved). The Christian tenet that true faith is faith in God and consequently in Christ is not incompatible with what we are elaborating,[60] but our subject is not directly concerned with this problem.[61]

b. Philosophical Reflection

Our investigation seeks something in Man that links him to transcendence, brings him to his end (Absolute, God, Nothingness or whatever); in other words something that makes progress possible toward what Man is not yet, the bridge connecting him with his destiny. This 'something' must be sufficiently ample and universal to constitute the foundation of salvation for Man as Man. It must justify our affirmation that the very fact of being human means that Man has the real possibility of attaining the end proper to him. This end—however we may characterize it—is what we have called salvation.

Evidently, this 'something' cannot belong to the purely doctrinal order since the world of concepts depends upon the possibilities offered by the different cultures through which it is expressed. In fact there is no universal culture in either time or space. And a concept is meaningful, and hence valid, only where it has been conceived.

This fundamental 'something' we seek can only be found as a constitutive dimension rooted in the very existence of Man. Our task is to try to describe it, and we say 'describe' because, in speaking of a fundamental human dimension, we lack any external overview for a rigorous definition.

We could describe faith as *existential openness toward transcendence* or, if this seems too loaded, more simply as *existential openness*. This openness implies a bottomless capacity to be filled without closing. Were it to close, it would cease to be faith. The openness is always to a *plus ultra*, to an ever farther, which we may call transcendence and in a certain sense transcendental.

One is open to what one is not or, rather, to what one has not yet become. Real openness means the possibility of being: openness to Being. It implies a capacity to be ever more and more filled, an 'in-finite' receptivity, because Man is not 'finished', finite. Man is open because he is not closed, he is not complete because he is itinerant, not definite, not 'finished', in-complete. The existential openness of faith represents Man's capacity for his non-finitude, that is, his in-finity. No person considers himself as finished, as having exhausted the possibilities of becoming. The opening of which we speak is constitutive of the human being, the other side of what we call contingency. This latter appears when we look backwards, to our foundation, thus discovering that we do not have in and of ourselves the ground of our own existence. The former, i.e., the existential opening, appears when we look forward, towards the goal, the end, the transcendent, etc., and discover that we are not complete.

We should not affirm a priori that all religions say the same. An important branch of the Buddhist tradition will object to the language I have just used. And in fact the Buddhist insight obliges us to go a step further, towards a kind of metaontology. Nevertheless, hardly any other religious tradition has more forcefully underscored the fact that *we are not*, so much so that it will say that we should not subreptitiously intercalate a *yet*. The way to *nirvāṇa* implies precisely the total openness without qualifications.

Recognizing Man's openness means admitting he is not God, i.e., not (yet?) finished, absolute, definitive. It means admitting there is something in him that must evolve; it also affirms the capacity for such evolution.[62] The openness of faith is Man's capacity to proceed towards his fullness.

This openness is not primordially a capacity of the intelligence as the faculty of the infinite, but rather an openness we call existential to indicate that it does not primarily belong to the realms of intellect or will, but to a prior level given in the very existence of Man. Only the naked existential order, previous to intellect and will, offers the desired universality.[63]

Thanks to this dimension of faith Man recognizes that he is not finished, he needs completion; better, he needs definite aid to attain the goal. Thanks to faith Man discovers his indigence. Faith is precisely the base underpinning both human precariousness and the possibility of overcoming it. Further, Man's grandeur and his supreme dignity are expressed by faith, since its existential openness does not signify merely need but complementarily indicates an unlimited capacity for growth. Finally it represents a much firmer foundation than human autonomy or self-sufficiency, and expresses the supreme ontic richness possible; we recognize that no 'human' or limited value whatsoever can fill it.

Existential anxiety, modern gnoseological atheism and certain social ideologies today are various manifestations of this fundamental attitude of faith that is not satisfied with anything closed, limited, finished. Prefabricated responses, previously given solutions—always things of the past—are inadmissible on the plane of faith. Human dignity resides precisely in the anthropological dimension of faith: Man is an ever open, infinite being.

In a word, faith is rooted in the Absolute; consequently it is the foundation of freedom, an important theme that, for the moment, we can only mention.[64] Without faith Man would not, could not be free; he would have neither the constitutive ambiguity that permits decision, nor the spontaneity necessary for the human act to go beyond—not against—the dialectical possibilities given in the data. True freedom does not consist in manipulating possibilities but in creating them. God creates and his creation is the real; human freedom also participates in this power and Man's creation is the possible. Freedom is not simply the power of option, but the power of creating possibilities.

The openness of faith is a constitutive openness. It cannot be closed; it is infinite, neither limited nor limitable. Faith is like a hole in the human being that is never filled, saturated, or turned into a kind of substantivity that would represent the supreme religious blasphemy and sever Man from any relation with the infinite. Through this hole he reaches the infinite (cf. *śūnyatā*).

As the bridge between us and the Absolute, faith is a ὑπόσ-τάσις (hypostasis) whose στάσις (stand) resides in the hope for what is not yet and whose ὑπο (base) is found in what can never appear, i.e., in the radical apophatism of what—as such—can never have epiphany, because its φαινόμενον (*phenomenon*), its epiphany is already the εἰκών (icon, image), the λόγος (*logos*, word).[65]

For still another reason we call faith 'openness' and, as we shall see in what follows, 'question', since it is essential to faith to be a powerless capacity, an ontological thirst that cannot be quenched, an anthropological desire that cannot be satisfied and that—if it could—would annihilate Man by destroying this constitutive tension that thrusts him ever toward the Absolute (whatever we call it: God, nothing, Man, society, future). Faith is constitutive of humanity's itinerant condition.

Returning to the distinction between faith as 'opening' and the act of faith as 'response to this opening', we will add a new consideration.

Philosophical reflection on the essence of faith emerges, it seems to me, from an analysis of the inquisitive nature of Man.[66] Man is an inquiring being who *desires*, *seeks*, *questions*.

This triple articulation of the inquisitive nature of Man seems important. Above all, Man *desires*.[67] In considering the centrality of desire let us not forget the prominent place it occupies in Buddhism, Hinduism and Christianity, to cite only three traditions. In Man there is a connatural movement toward the 'farther', the 'yet more', toward something distinct from himself that can complete him and satisfy his incessant thirst for transcendence, his yearning to go ever *plus ultra*, ever beyond, never to stop. We know the typical reaction of Buddha, Saint Augustine and many others: to interiorize desire, to purify the factor of alienation that all desire seems to bear with it.

Desire not only drives us to satisfy it, but also to *seek* and pursue the search endlessly, even when its immediate object has been attained. In Man there is not only the romantic desire to listen to the beating of a heart filled with longing; Man is an active being who hunts the object of his desire, tracks it, smells it out, directs himself to what completes him, throws himself toward the terrestrial, and even the temporal frontiers, seeking perhaps not any particular object but simply what he does not have, what he is not. This search constitutes Man. What we call God, Man, Truth, the Good, Pleasure, Life or Nothing is but the terminus of this desire.

This human search presents a characteristic dimension: *the question*.[68] Man's first question is directed not to what things are or to what he himself *is*, but to what lies behind his very search. Man seeks what he has not, or is not. He always seeks his completion, his God.[69] Anthropologically speaking, God is the final goal of desire,[70] the end of every desire—in both senses of the expression.[71]

Faith relates to Man's inquisitive structure. He asks because he does not know *yet*, but—and this makes him truly an inquiring being—he also asks because he knows that he does not know yet and because he knows that in knowing he will obtain not only the answer but that on which the answer is based.[72] The question also provides the frame within which the answer can appear as an answer:[73] Ontically the answer is contained in the question. The question, then, is nothing other than the ontological condition for the answer. Consequently every question is an inquiry about God and Man.[74] No question ever obtains an adequate response, since at bottom every question is about the infinite.[75] We speak, of course, of human questioning and not of mere asking for information. Each authentic question is a human incursion into nothingness.[76]

Revelation from the side of transcendence without a previous question from our side would not be re-velation, nor would it be intelligible since it would not be the manifestation, the epiphany of what one asks, seeks, desires. Complete heterogeneity would be indiscernible and from every point of view inefficacious. Even the most metaphysical nothingness can only be a negation of being.[77] The question about nothingness is only meaningful within the horizon of being.

Until now more philosophical importance has been given to the ontological than to the ontic and, as a result, faith has been considered a response rather than a question. According to this understanding, faith belongs to those who give the correct (doctrinal) answers or those who at least act morally. All others were 'infidels' because they did not know the orthodox formulae or the path of orthopoiesis. My thesis does not claim to diminish the merit of either of these two responses, but intends to inscribe them in a larger sphere that includes Man as Man and not only those who know the right answers or follow the moral path— important as these are.

The essence of faith seems to me to lie in the question rather than in the answer, in the inquisitive stance, in the desire rather than in the concrete response one gives. Faith is more the existential 'container' than the intellectual content of 'that thing' we try to describe. It belongs not only to those who respond correctly, but to all who authentically seek, desire, love, wish—to those of 'good will'. The proper realm of faith is orthopraxis, the right actions Men believe they must perform in order to be what they believe they must be.

We have, moreover, distinguished between faith and the act of faith. The latter is the free response to faith, is Man's reaction to this capacity that instills in him the thirst for the Absolute; it is his decision to respond to the possibilities presented him in daily life or in the particularly serious moments of his existence.

If faith is an existential opening, a vital questioning, the act of faith is equally an existential response. It is however part of the perfection of the act of faith that it also possesses an intellectual and volitional aspect. The human response to the thirst for perfection, the desire for transcendence, the free reaction to what several schools see as an appeal from transcendence—this constitutes the act of faith.

Everybody 'has' faith, every human being is endowed with this constitutive dimension; but no one is forced to live *ex fide*, out of faith or from faith.[78] Such a life characterizes the 'just Man'. In other words faith is not the act of faith; the latter can be positive or negative and of different degrees of purity and intensity. Our conception of faith does not imply that Man cannot 'sin' against it or perform a negative act of faith, but these are aspects of the problematic we do not need to investigate further here.[79]

4. EXCURSUS ON GOOD FAITH

'Good faith' is an expression common to quite a few languages. Obviously this cannot be identified with theological faith, but we think some pertinent observations on this subject are possible in the overall problematic of the relations between *mythos* and *logos*.

Before analyzing the concept, I wish to emphasize that I am not thinking of any particular doctrine, nor shall I consider this notion as understood in Roman law or in the thought of J. P. Sartre. I refer to the simple human experience of what we still call 'good faith'.

Speaking of 'good faith' implies there is also a 'bad faith'. In common parlance, 'bad faith' seems to imply more reflection, more intellectualizing, more will than good faith. A ticketless traveler who is of good faith knows nothing of what the abusive (ticketless) traveler of bad faith must know. Good faith appears innocent, deprived of all knowledge. Bad faith is full of science and knowledge. Popular speech, then, invites us to interpret faith that is nonreflective as 'good faith', while it calls 'bad' that which recognizes itself as faith. Good faith cannot be proved.[80] If the traveler of good faith were to give too convincing a proof of his good faith, this very proof would accuse him of bad faith. Good faith cannot defend itself at the tribunal of reason. In other words: Reason cannot defend good faith because in so doing it profanes good faith. The only defense of good faith is its weakness before reason. In short, good faith does not support any hermeneutic. Interpreted, it ceases to be 'good', i.e., 'pure'; it becomes adulterated by other ingredients. A faith that needs interpretation ceases to be 'good faith'.

Perhaps some will ask what is the connection between this faith, apparently part of quotidian banality, and the saving faith of theologians. I would respond, first, that our effort is to bring faith down from the altitudes of a privileged monopoly and to install it on the earth of common understanding, on the level of fundamental human structures. Second, we certainly admit the legitimacy and truth of that aspect of faith which is intellectual, volitive, sentimental.[81] One does not exclude the other.[82] Our attempt might be summed up as a meditation on the first beatitude: 'Blessed are the poor.'[83]

Quite recently, reacting to a purely rationalistic, sentimental or voluntaristic naturalism, the maximalist position has been emphasized: This attitude wishes to have nothing to do with a general concept of faith, fearing it will dilute the exigencies of 'supernatural' Christian faith.[84] We understand this position well and we would almost say that because of it we take the opposite position. Faith is not the privilege of orthodox Christians but a gift, universally given to humanity. The free response to faith may be negative, but this does not mean it must be uniform or unisonant.

Doubtless, as soon as good faith tries to justify itself, it begins to disintegrate: If it wants to prove its ignorance or defend its position, it automatically ceases to be good faith.[85] Good faith can be brought to light as an ingredient of all faith only from above, from the side of a faith *oculata* as tradition says.[86] This primordial element of 'good faith' implies that faith is faith in what we do not see,[87] in the future,[88] in what we do not know[89] and also, perhaps, taking the paradox to the extreme, in what we do not believe.[90]

Good faith is unique, it has no plural.[91] The Man of good faith is not presented with two or several possibilities. He is free precisely because he does not feel constrained to choose. Rather the Man of good faith feels chosen and elect, but not at all forced. He finds himself in a situation and he simply accepts it. His freedom does not result from deliberations on how to escape the hold of the different possibilities presented to him and that, menacing, force him in some way to decide, but it is the fruit of an inner maturation or of an unconscious spontaneity; unconscious not as such, but as regards its intellectual content or ob-ject. It is about this latter that decision is necessary. Good faith is so unitary that it permits no reflection. When, taking account of what has happened in a second moment, a Man of good faith realizes he has performed a good or bad action, he invariably discovers he *did not know* his action was good or bad.[92]

This necessary loss of 'good faith' seems to be the crisis of the modern world. It is a process in which we are still plunged.[93]

Good faith exists where reflection has not yet entered. It is undeniable that 'science' always progresses at the expense of 'faith'. When faith has defended itself and become science, it has often given the impression of 'bad faith', or at least of abandoning its greatest value in the face of reason, a value reason secretly envies. Thus the Christian Middle Ages had good reason to maintain that faith that could be proved ceased to be faith, since faith is faith in the invisible, the nonevident; it sees but cannot be seen.[94] *Unum idemque non potest esse scitum et creditum.*[95]

As soon as good faith submits to judgment, as soon as it becomes problematic and wishes to justify itself, to be proven, to defend itself instead of turning the other cheek,[96] it ceases to be 'good faith' and becomes good (or bad) science or even 'bad faith' should it insist on being called faith.[97]

The loss of good faith is necessary for two reasons. First by virtue of the *kairos* of our culture. Not only can we not march behind the progress of human history, but the forward march bears what is in the process of being produced everywhere, in every culture: the advance of reason, reflection and knowledge at the expense of 'good faith'. Knowledge is always a tree of the knowledge of good and evil.[98] Faith is the tree of life.[99]

The contemporary world is engaged not only in industry, machinery, socialization, the intercommunication of all sorts of values, but is inexorably committed to conceptualization, to leveling, demythicizing, to the growth of reflexive consciousness. More and more Man takes his daily existence in hand and for this he needs to know more and more and to believe less and less. Or, better said, human knowledge advances because it usurps the domain of belief, the realm of 'good faith'. They were two separate trees in paradise and separate they remain in the exile.

The second reason is even more serious because it does not belong to a fixed moment in a single culture, but to the very history of humanity. This history suggests that the peregrination of Man over the course of time corresponds to the awakening of his reflexive consciousness at the expense of his ecstatic consciousness, to the accumulation in the conscious realm of what was hidden in the unconscious, to the loss of good faith, which is replaced by science—as if, to speak theologically, the original fall were an originating fall and original sin an originating sin, which is repeated in each person and each generation in an eschatological crescendo. Man wishes to know but does not trust in God; he wishes to be like God, but does not have the patience to wait and become God. Human progress is tied to the loss of good faith. This crisis makes Man proceed, makes him gamble on what he is not.[100]

'Believe in order to understand', Christian tradition said; but it seems that once one has understood, believing is no longer necessary. Lightning rods have successfully replaced candles to Saint Barbara, and antibiotics, Extreme Unction; the psychoanalyst supplants the spiritual director and even γνῶσις, knowledge, is on the way to replacing πίστις, faith. Every attempt since Kant[101] to 'make room for faith' has resulted in a new mutilation of its territory. Faith is the presupposition of understanding, but understanding seems to offer faith no support.

Are we at a dead-end? Is there only good or bad faith? I do not think so. There is faith that is neither good nor bad, because it is a constitutive human dimension and, theologically speaking, a redeemed faith. This is our final point.

Good faith can be saved only by recognizing it has ceased to be good and repenting of it. *Metanoia* is the condition for entering the kingdom of heaven, change of νοῦς, of mind, of direction.[102] Good faith can be saved only by recognizing that in ceasing to be 'good' it is still 'faith', since it has no other place to find the words of eternal life.[103] Bad faith is 'bad' because it has ceased to be faith in order to become science. Bad faith does not believe: It knows. On the other hand, if Man recognizes that he has come into this world without a ticket, if he admits the fault of not having a ticket that would enable him to travel in this world without danger, if he does not seek to justify himself or say he has lost it, but simply that he does not have it—if faith does not claim to defend itself, it can be saved, not as 'good' faith but as redeemed faith, as a faith that, discovering itself to be 'bad', finds therein the possibility of redemption.[104]

The redemption of faith: This is a typical Christian problem. Christian faith is not one that wishes to supplant others. If it were only that it would be the faith of a sect with an unjustifiable claim to universality. But this is not part of our present theme.

In reality good faith is not the *best* faith. In the final analysis it is a faith that does not know it is faith. It is an implicit faith that does not possess the element of 'impurity', of evil, sin or redemption; in short, the existentially human factor, the opening that enables faith to be fertilized by the only thing that lets it bear fruit in a saving act.[105] Good faith is 'good' because it is not yet open to the air, the world, the sun, the stars. It is innocent but not existentially human. Real Man—Man as we know him—has lost his first innocence.

Whoever possesses good faith will be saved by it, but whoever knows he possesses it and trusts in his possible good faith will be accused of bad faith and voluntary incredulity by that very faith. One does not speculate with good faith. The new innocence is the fruit of redeemed faith, but not an object of the mind or of the will. It is not born of Man, but reborn of the Spirit.

Now we return to the very beginning of this meditation. It seems the only way to speak of faith, to 'save' faith (some would say), is to discover its mythic character. Authentic faith, so it seems, cannot question itself. Real faith is always unsatisfied with the answer; it is always a question so virgin that it does not even know if there is an answer. So faith is a myth. But when faith is known as a myth, it appears insufficient; and yet when it ceases to be myth it seems to vanish.

This is the dilemma. Mythic faith is good faith, but good faith does not recognize itself as mythic, nor will it claim to be. Myth is not and cannot be the object of faith because it is by its very constitution the vehicle of faith. A demythologized faith is empty, it becomes reason, changes into *logos*. Undoubtedly, good faith is a myth, but it seems that without myth faith is not even possible.

The myth of faith is constitutively linked with the faith in myth. Thought demythologizes but life is mythopoietic. Faith also mediates here—between thought and life. A myth is something we believe in without believing that we believe in it. The moment that this second degree of consciousness appears, i.e., the self-reflexion on belief, the myth gives way either to the *logos* or to an unbelievable mythology. Modern Western culture, which is too accustomed to manipulating ideas, parameters and people, understandably resists accepting the absolutely nonnegotiable, nonmanipulable factors in life. But the principle of property is hardly supreme. There are things we cannot 'have' because having or even intending to have them amounts to annihilating them. Faith is one of these. We cannot *have* faith the way we have money, property or friends. We live by faith and from faith; it is always underneath or above but, like any horizon of reality, always just beyond our grasp. It flashes for a timeless instant; you know neither where it comes from nor where it goes, it lifts you from isolation, you weep with joy and find a deeper silence. And then it lets you believe in anything. 'All things are possible to him who believes!'[106] What you cannot do is believe at your whim,[107] just as we cannot master the core of our own being—who would do it? Faith is like our existence (and the two are linked): They are *gifts*, the theologian will say; they are *given*, the more reluctant philosopher might echo. It all depends on how we receive the present.

Notes

1. From the Latin liturgy of the Sunday after Christmas applying the text of Wis. 18:14-15 (referring to the first Passover) to the Incarnation of Christ (cf. Jn. 1:1-18, though the text is closer to Rev. 19:13).

2. I have kept this spoken introduction of my original French lecture because I feel that it equally applies to the written word—though some of its connotations (it was the first paper of the Colloquium, the title of the meeting had been suggested by me the previous year, many of the participants were 'unbelievers' in any 'religious faith', it was after Christmas, etc.) may no longer 'speak' to the reader. Nevertheless it is

only by carrying the others along that one is both stopped in his journey and helped to carry fellow-pilgrims on their way.

3. "Believe so that you may understand" was a commonplace for at least half of the twenty centuries of Christian history.

4. For over a thousand years in the West and *mutatis mutandis* also in the East, the central philosophical problem has been that of clarifying the relationship between 'faith' and 'reason'.

5. Cf. 2 Chr. 20:20 with the same play on words: "Trust (*haaminu*) in the Lord your God and you will remain *entrusted* (*ta amenu*)." The LXX says: ἐμπιστεύσατε εν Κυρίῳ θεῷ ἡμῶν, καὶ ἐμπιστευθήσεσθε. The Vg.: "Credite in Domino Deo vestro, et securi eritis." The NEB: "Hold firmly to your faith in the Lord your God and you will be upheld."

6. Cf. Qur'ān, XLVII, *passim*, where *āmanū* (verbal form of *mu'min*, the believer), 'those who have faith' (*imān*) play an important role in Islam.

7. For the Hebrew, cf. L. Bouyer, *Dictionnaire théologique* (Tournai: Desclée, 1966), v. 'foi'; A.G. Herbert, ' "Faithful" and "Faith" ', *Theology*, No. 424 (October 1955), pp. 373-79. For an interesting discussion of the Hebrew concept of faith, cf. T.F. Torrance, 'One Aspect of the Biblical Conception of Faith', *Expository Times*, LVIII (1956/1957), 111-14, reprinted in his book: *Conflict and Agreement in the Church* (London: Lutterworth, 1959-60), II, pp. 74-82. A very severe critical judgment is found in chapter VII (' "Faith" and "Truth"—An Examination of Some Linguistic Arguments') of J. Barr, *The Semantics of Biblical Language* (London: Oxford University Press, 1961), pp. 161-205. Barr does not think such concepts as 'faith' and 'to create' are used only of God, not of Men. Further he thinks the so-called 'fundamental concept' of 'firmness and stability' suffices to explain the Hebrew notion of faith. See also the important article in Kittel's *Theologisches Wörterbuch des Neuen Testaments, s.v.*, and Jepsen's article *'āman* (1971) in the not yet finished *Theologisches Wörterbuch zum Alten Testament* (Stuttgart: Kohlhammer) *s.v.* (I, 313-348).

8. He can lean on *betah*, if he allows himself to be guided by *emunah*.

9. BG XVII, 3; cf. also IV, 39; XVII, 17; etc.

10. Cf. BU III, 9, 21. Cf. K.L. Seshagiri Rao, *The Concept of Śraddhā* (Delhi: M. Banarsidass 1971 [1974]), and P. Hacker, '*Śraddhā*', *Wiener Zeitsch. Kunde S-O-Asiens* VII (1963).

11. Cf. the little known text of the Kṛṣṇa Yajurveda: "Faith envelops the Gods, faith envelops the entire universe. For this offering I am augmenting this faith, mother of desires." TB II, 8, 8, 8. Or again the entire chapter 6 of the Tripurā-rahasya dedicated to faith: ". . . faith is the ultimate resort of the whole world. . . . Everyone is able to communicate

with the other because he believes the other. . . . faith is the way to attain the ultimate good. . . ." Cf. A.U. Vasavada translation (Varanasi: Chowkhamba Sanskrit Studies, vol. L, 1965).

12. Cf. G. Widengren, 'Mythe et foi à la lumière de la phénoménologie religieuse', *Mythe et Foi*, edited by E. Castelli (Paris: Aubier, 1966), pp. 315-32.

13. Cf. Th. Heitz, *Essai historique sur les rapports entre la philosophie et la foi: de Bérenger de Tours à Thomas d'Aquin* (Paris: Gabalda, 1909); E. Gilson, *Reason and Revelation in the Middle Ages* (New York: Scribner's Sons, 1954).

14. Cf. some characteristic texts: Aristotle: "Whoever wishes to understand must believe" (*Adv. Soph.*, II, 2:165b2 [although one could translate: "he who wants to learn has to trust", later tradition has interpreted it in the former sense]); S. Leo: "Nisi fides credat, sermo non explicat" (*Sermo*, 29, 1 P. L., 54, 226); S. Augustine: "Crede ut intelligas: praecedet fides, sequitur intellectus" (*Sermo*, CXVIII, 1, *Opuscula*, VI, 498); "Intellectui fides aditum aperit, infidelitas clausit" (*Sermo*, CXXXVII, 15); "Intelligere vis? Crede. . . . Intellectus enim merces est fidei. Ergo noli quaerere, intelligere ut credas, sed crede ut intelligas" (*In Ioan. Tract.*, XXIX, 16, *Opuscula*, VI, 498); "Sic credite ut mereamini intelligere: fides enim debet praecedere intellectum ut sit intellectus fidei praemium" (*Sermo*, CXXXIX, *Opuscula*, VI, 498); "Ergo intellige ut credas, crede ut intelligas" (*Epist.*, 120, I, 3, P. L., 33, 453-454); "Nullus quippe credit aliquid, nisi prius cogitaverit esse credendum" (*De praed. sanct.*, II, 5, P. L., 44, 962-963); "Quaequam et ipsum credere, nihil aliud est, quam cum assensione cogitare. Non enim omnis qui cogitat credit; cum ideo cogitent plerique non credant: sed cogitat omnis qui credit, et credendo cogitat, et cogitando credit. . . . Fides, si non cogitetur, nulla est" (*De praed. sanct.*, II, 5, P. L., 44, 963); "Sed ego quid sciam quaero, non quid credam. Omne autem quod scimus, recte fortasse etiam credere dicimur; at non omne quod credimus, etiam scire" (*Solil.* I, 3, 8); "Credimus ut cognoscamus, non cognoscimus ut credeamus" (*In Ioan. Tract.*, 40, 9); cf. etiam *Sermo* XLIII, 7, 9; *De Trinitate* VII, 5, 5; etc.; Peter Lombard: "Unde colligitur non posse sciri et intelligi credenda quaedam, nisi prius credantur; et quaedam non credi, nisi prius intelligantur, et ipsa per fidem amplius intelligi. Nec ea quae prius creduntur quam intelligantur, penitus ignorantur, cum fides sit ex auditu. Ignorantur tamen ex parte quia non sciuntur" (*Sent.*, 24, 3; P. L., 192, 809); S. Anselm: "Necque enim quaero intelligere, ut credam, sed credo, ut intelligam" (*Proslogion*, I, P. L., 158, 227); D. Thomas: "Et inde est quod Augustinus dicit [*Super Ioan.*, XVII, 7, P. L., 35, 1618], quod per fidem venitur ad cognitionem, et non e converso" (*Sum. Theol.*, I, q. 32, a. 1 ad 2); "Fides est in nobis ut perveniamus ad intelligendum quae credimus" (*In Boeth. de Trinitate*, q. 11, a. 2 ad 7);

Hugh of St. Victor: "Ideo enim credimus, ut aliquando sciamus" (*Summ. Sent.*, tract. I, 1, P. L., 176, 43): "Credimus ut cognoscamus; non cognoscimus, ut credamus" (*ibid.*, I, 2, P. L., 176, 44); and also in the *Imitatio Christi*: "Omnis ratio et naturalis investigatio fidem sequi debet, non praecedere" (IV, 18, 5).

15. "Believe so that you may be." I am not using this sentence only in a post-Cartesian way: "Credo ergo sum," as a Ferdinand Ebner would do. Cf. his collected works, *Fragmente, Aufsätze, Aphorismen* (München: Kösel, 1963), pp. 481, 486, 495, 558.

16. It is worth pointing out in this context the traditional idea that loss of faith is, in a certain sense, *contra naturam*. (Cf. D. Thomas, *Sum. Theol.*, II-II, q. 10, a. 1 ad 1.)

17. Cf. my contribution to the Theological Congress of the Eucharistic Congress of Bombay in 1964, 'The Relation of Christians to their Non-christian Surroundings' in J. Neuner (ed.), *Christian Revelation and World Religions* (London: Burns & Oates, 1967), pp. 143-184; republished in *Cross Currents:* 'Christians and So-called "Non-christians" ', XXI, 3, 281-308.

18. Cf. chapter XVI.

19. Cf. R. Panikkar, *The Trinity and the Religious Experience of Man* (London: Darton, Longman & Todd and Maryknoll, N.Y.: Orbis Books, 1973), esp. pp. 40 sq.

20. The religious encounter, we have said time and again, is neither a private meeting of isolated individuals nor a meeting of abstract generalities, but the concrete meeting in time and space, among living persons, each of whom carries in a more or less complete and conscious way the burden of an entire tradition.

21. Cf. R. Panikkar, *The Intrareligious Dialogue* (New York: Paulist Press, 1978), chapter IV.

22. Cf. Descartes, *Discours de la Méthode* (Paris: Gallimard, 1932), p. 14: "Je révérais notre théologie et pretendais autant qu'aucun autre à gagner le ciel; mais, ayant appris comme chose très assurée que le chemin n'en est pas moins ouvert aux plus ignorants qu'aux plus doctes, et que les vérités révélées qui y conduisent sont au-dessus de notre intelligence, je n'eusse osé les soumettre à la faiblesse de mes raisonnements, et je pensais que, pour entreprendre de les examiner, et y réussir, il était besoin d'avoir quelque extraordinaire assistance du Ciel et d'être plus qu'homme."

23. The famous Aristotelian dictum of Man: λόγον δε μόνον ἄνθρωπος ἔχει τῶν ζῴων, i.e., as 'animale rationale' (a rational animal) means, in fact "Man is the only animal whom [nature] has endowed with *logos* (the gift of speech)" (*Polit.* I, 2, 1253a 9 sq.; cf. VII, 13, 1332b 5), which is a totally different matter.

24. One could write a history of a good part of Western (and Chris-

tian) civilization by following the evolution of the concept of 'logos' as 'verbum dei' (Word of God, his Son), as 'verbum entis' (the rationality of being), 'verbum mentis' (word of the mind, as an expression of the rational truth of everything), down to 'verbum mundi' (word of the world) and 'verbum ventus' (word of the wind, i.e., words as mere labels, pragmatic designations of things).

25. "Today the faculty of faith lies hidden in innumerable human beings", is the beginning of K. Jasper's important study *Der philosophische Glaube angesichts der Offenbarung* (München: Piper, 1963), p. 7. [*Philosophical Faith and Revelation* (New York: Harper and Row, 1967), p. xxv.]

26. Cf. today almost as a curiosum, G. Baroni, *È possibile perdere la fede cattolica senza peccato?*—Dottrina dei teologhi dei secoli XVII-XVIII (Dissertatio ad Lauream—Gregorianum) (Romae: Gregoriana, 1936).

27. "Faith is not a thing one 'loses', we merely cease to shape our lives by it." G. Bernanos, *Journal d'un curé de campagne*, (Paris: Plon), p. 108, [*The Diary of a Country Priest* (New York: Macmillan, 1937), p. 109.]

28. "Deus namque sua gratia semel iustificatos non deserit, nisi ab eius prius deseratur", said Augustine, *De natura et gratia*, c. 26, n. 29, P. L., 44, 261, and was quoted by the Council of Trent (Sess. VI, c. 11, Denz. Schön. 1537) and repeated by Vatican I (Denz. Schön. 3014).

29. Cf. R. Panikkar, *The Intrareligious Dialogue*, chapter II. Cf. also W. C. Smith, *Belief and History* (Charlottesville, Va.: University Press of Virginia, 1977), speaking on faith rather than belief as "the fundamental religious category."

30. Cf. R. Aubert, *Le problème de l'acte de foi* (Louvain: Warny, 1958); J. Pieper, *Ueber den Glauben* (München: Kösel, 1962); J. Mouroux, *Je crois en toi* (Paris: Cerf, 1949), English translation: *I Believe: the Personal Structure of Faith* (New York: Sheed and Ward, 1959). Cf. *etiam* T. Izutsu, *The Concept of Belief in Islamic Theology* (Tokyo: Keio Institute, 1965).

31. Cf. D. Thomas, *Sum. Theol.*, I-II, q. 60, a. 3, though the Divus Thomas has a more elaborated theory than that which identifies religion solely with a virtue. Cf. for instance, *Sum. Theol.*, II-II, q. 81, a. 1.

32. For a descriptive formulation of the New Testament concept of faith, cf. S. Lyonnet, *Les Épîtres de saint Paul aux Galates et aux Romains* (Paris: Ed. du Cerf, 1959): "It is the adherence of the intellect to truths (Rom. 10:9), but even more, it is the adherence of the entire soul to a Person (Rom. 3:22, 26; 10:14; etc; Gal. 2; 16; etc.). It is an essentially active faith (Gal. 5:6; cf. Eph. 2; 10), which, while remaining an activity of Man, is even more God's acting in him (Gal. 2:20), fruit of the Spirit (Gal. 5:25; 6:8; Rom. 8:14; cf. 1 Cor. 15:10; etc.)" (p. 61).

33. Cf. the efforts of C. Journet in *L'Eglise du Verbe incarné* (Paris: Desclée, 1941) to distinguish two types of heresy: one, simple heterodoxy; the other, infidelity. Scholastic tradition has long distinguished between formal and material heresy, without thinking there was a movement of the will in formal heresy.

34. Cf. the stanza of the hymn of the *Feria II ad Vesperas* in the Roman Breviary, attributed to Pope St. Gregory the Great (540-604):

Lucem fides adaugeat
Sic luminis iubar ferat:
Haec vana cuncta proterat:
Hanc falsa nulla comprimant.

Faith is a light—an increasing light, that illumines the light of reason—it is the leading light, for life; it discovers the vanity of things, that they are really vain, viz. empty; it is irrefutable since no arguments can prove it to be false.

35. "Actus autem credentis non terminatur ad enuntiabile, sed ad rem." ("Now the act of the believer does not terminate in the proposition, but in the thing."), D. Thomas, *Sum. Theol.*, II-II, q. 1, a. 2 ad 2.

36. Cf. the well-known distinction between "id quo et id quod creditur", as, for example, in Cajetan, *In* II-II, q. 1, a. 1, n. 11 ("credo Deo—revelanti—et Deum—revelatum").

37. "Fides non potest exire in actum, nisi aliquid determinate et expresse credendo", D. Thomas, *In III Sent.*, dist. 25, q. 1, art. 1, sol 1 ad 3.

38. "Sed contra est quod Dionysius dicit (*De Div. Nom.* c. 7, 4, lect. 5), quod 'fides est circa simplicem et semper existentem veritatem'. Haec autem est veritas prima. Ergo obiectum fidei est veritas prima." ("On the contrary, Dionysius says that 'faith is about the simple and everlasting truth.' Now this is the First Truth. Therefore the object of faith is the First Truth."), D. thomas, *Sum. Theol.*, II-II, q. 1, a.1. Cf. the words of Augustine: "Sic amatur veritas, ut quicumque aliud amant, hoc quod amant velint esse veritatem." *Confess.*, X, 23, n. 34 (quoted by Meister Eckhart, *Expos. in Io.*, I, 1–2, Nr. 48).

39. "Veritatis prima se habet in fide et ut medium et obiectum", D. Thomas, *De veritate*, q. 14, a. 8 ad 3.

40. "Sed tamen considerandum est quod in obiecto fidei est aliquid quasi formale, scilicet veritas prima super omnem naturalem cogitationem creaturae existens; et aliquid materiale, sicut id cui assentimus, inhaerendo primae veritati. Quantum ergo ad primum horum, communiter fides est in omnibus habentibus cognitionem de Deo, futura beatitudine nondum adepta, inhaerendo primae veritati: sed quantum ad ea quae materialiter credenda proponuntur, quaedum sunt credita ab uno quae sunt manifeste scita ab alio . . ." ("Nevertheless we must observe that in the object of faith, there is something formal, as it were, namely

the First Truth surpassing all the natural knowledge of the creature, and something material, namely, the thing to which we assent while adhering to the First Truth. With regard to the former, before obtaining the happiness to come, faith is common to all who have knowledge of God, by adhering to the First Truth. But with regard to the things which are proposed as the material object of faith, some are believed by one, and known plainly by another . . .'"), D. Thomas, *Sum. Theol.*, II-II, q. 5, a. 1 c.

41. "Formale autem obiectum fidei est unum et simplex, scilicet veritas prima. . . . Unde ex hac partes fides non diversificatur in credentibus, sed est una specie in omnibus. . . . Sed ea quae materialiter credenda proponuntur sunt plura, et possunt accipi vel magis vel minus explicite; et secundom hoc potest unus homo plura explicite credere quam alius. . . ." ("Now the formal object of faith is one and simple, namely the First Truth. . . . Hence in this respect there is no diversity of faith among believers, but it is specifically one in all. . . . But the things which are proposed as the matter of our belief are many and can be received more or less explicitly. And in this respect one man can believe explicitly more things than another. . . ."), D. Thomas, *Sum. Theol.*, II-II, q. 5, a. 4 c.

42. Cf. Rom. 1:16; 3:28, 30; Gal. 2:16; 5:6; etc.

43. Cf. Jas. 2:17.

44. Cf. Jn. 7:17 and also S. Gregory the Great, *Hom. 23 in Ev.* (as in the Roman Breviary, for Monday within the octave of Easter, lesson iii): "Quisquis ergo vult audita intelligere festinet ea quae jam audire potuit, opere implere." ("Whoever, then, desires to understand the lessons he has heard, let him hasten to put in practice what he has already been able to hear.")

45. Cf. the Buddhist problematic on this issue, which undoubtedly transcends the realm of orthopoiesis.

46. Here is not the place to elaborate further on this distinction, which played an important role in the whole of ancient and mediaeval anthropology. Cf. vgr. the scholastic *actio immanens* (or *operatio*) over against *actio transiens* (or *factio*). Our distinction does not, nevertheless, coalesce with the simple scheme represented, for instance, in the commonly repeated text: "Duplex est actio, una, quae transit in exteriorem materiam, ut calefacere et secare; alia, quae manet in agente, ut intelligere, sentire et velle. Quarum haec est differentia, quia prima actio non est perfectio agentis, quod movet, sed ipsius moti, secunda autem actio est perfectio agentis." (". . . action is two-fold. Actions of one kind pass out to external matter, as to heat or to cut, whilst actions of the other kind remain in the agent, as to understand, to sense and to will. The difference between them is this, that the former action is the perfection not of the agent that moves, but of the thing moved, while the latter

action is the perfection of the agent."). *Sum Theol.*, I, q. 18, a. 3, ad 1.

47. It does not seem necessary to insist that 'salvation', 'liberation', 'goal', 'fullness', are terms that do not necessarily have a specific content or need to be interpreted only in the light of the so-called salvific-religions. Here all these words stand for the *x* at the term of human life—individually, collectively, cosmically or in whatever sense this life might be understood.

48. For a more complete elaboration of this theme, cf. R. Panikkar, *Le mystère du culte dans l'hindouisme et le christianisme* (Paris: Cerf, 1970).

49. Cf. the dictum: "peccatores in quantum peccatores non sunt" in agreement with the optimistic metaphysical view of evil as a *privatio*. This sentence is the obliged answer to the query that if God is love, he has to love everything (cf. Wis. 11:25) and thus cannot hate sin (cf. Ps. 5:7). St. Thomas's answer is worth quoting: "Deus autem peccatores, inquantum sunt naturae quaedam, amat: sic enim et sunt, et ab ipso sunt. Inquantum vero peccatores sunt, non sunt, sed ab esse deficiunt: et hoc in eis a Deo non est" (*Sum. Theol.* I, q. 20, a. 2, ad 4). Hence in pure Thomism hell is merely an ontic abortion!

50. It should not be forgotten that the congruent mediaeval conception of 'hell' is not just the dialectical counterpart of heaven, but a failure to become, a hole, as it were, in the 'new heaven and the new earth', a kind of abortion of 'eternal life'. Cf. the previous footnote.

51. Cf. R. Panikkar, *El concepto de naturaleza* (Madrid: C.S.I.C., 1972, 2nd edition), pp. 225-232, where the teleological conception of contingent being is developed.

52. Cf. regarding the entrance into the Kingdom of God, the suggestive saying of the *Gospel of Thomas*, 22, seen in this light: "When you make the two one, and make the inside like the outside, and the outside like the inside, and the upper side like the under side, and when you make the male and the female into a single one, . . . you shall enter [the kingdom]."

53. Cf. note 42.

54. "Humanae salutis initium, fundamentum et radix omnis iustificationis." Thus the Council of Trent summarized the New Testament doctrine (Denz. Schön. 1532).

55. No need to recall the incongruency of retaining today the old nomenclature of 'nonbelievers' (which, incidentally, derives from translation of 'infideles') while at the same time maintaining the idea common to biblical and other religions in general, that faith is necessary for salvation. Either they are not 'unbelievers' or they are not saved (or, following the other line, faith is a mere label for a particular 'sect' of people). Or should we already advance our distinction? They may be unbelievers but not unfaithful.

56. Cf. Heb. 11:6 and the interpretation of the Council of Trent, Session VI, cap. 6 (Denz. Schön. 1526).

57. Cf. Eph. 2:8 which shows the instrumental character of faith. We may understand it: "For by grace you have been saved through faith; and this is not your own doing, it is the gift of God."

58. Cf. Acts 14:27.

59. Cf. Heb. 11. The sense of this 'semel' (Heb. 9:12 and 26) like that of the sacrifice of Christ (Heb. 7:26, 27) is not simply temporal but *tempiternal*.

60. We may quote what Origen says concerning faith in the name of Jesus—εἰς τὸ ὄνομα αὐτοῦ—and faith in him—εἰς αὐτόν. *Comm. in Jo.* X, 44. Obviously it is not a question of two faiths.

61. Cf. R. Panikkar, 'The Meaning of Christ's Name in the Universal Economy of Salvation', *Evangelization, Dialogue and Development.* -Documenta Missionalia, 5- Roma (1972), pp. 195-218.

62. Cf. the remark of Teilhard de Chardin: ". . . la foi néo-humaine au Monde, dans la mesure même où elle est *foi* (c'est-à-dire don et abandon, pour toujours, à un plus grand que soi), implique nécessairement un élément d'adoration, c'est-à-dire l'admission de quelque 'Dieu'." 'Le coeur du problème' (1949) in *L'Avenir de l'Homme, Oeuvres* (Paris: Seuil, 1959), vol. V, 346.

63. This would be my comment on the definition of faith as 'an act of existential understanding' given by S.M. Ogden, 'The Christian Proclamation of God to Men of the so-called "Atheistic Age" ', *Concilium*, VI, 2 (June 1966), 46, although it seems to me we are both going in the same direction. Cf. in this regard the words of Clemens. Alex. who was "the first to combine the Aristotelian term faith with the Stoic term assent" (*apud* H.A. Wolfson, *The Philosophy of the Church Fathers* [Cambridge, Harvard University Press, 1970, 3rd ed.], p. 120): "Jam vero fides, et si est voluntaria animae assensio, est tamen bonorum operatrix, et justae fundamentum actionis" (*Strom.* V, 13, 86, P. G., 9, 128A).

64. Cf. chapter XVI.

65. Cf. Heb. 1:2 sq. in connection with 11:1; etc.

66. "So ist das fragenmüssende Sein Nichtsein, ist in seinem innersten Seinsgrund schwach. Seinsmächtigkeit ist endlich, darum muss es fragen, darum ist es nicht schlechthin bei sich." K. Rahner, *Geist in der Welt*, (München, 1957, p. 85); ("Thus the being that must ask is non-being, is deficient in its innermost ground of being. The intensity of its being is finite, and therefore it must ask, therefore it is not absolutely present-to-itself." K. Rahner, *Spirit in the World* [New York: Herder and Herder, 1968], p. 72).

67. Cf. Dan. 9:23.

68. The reader will forgive us for not elaborating here on the

metaphysical reflections of M. Heidegger, R. Bultmann, K. Rahner, E. Coreth, H.-G. Gadamer, etc., on the problematic of the question. Cf. also H-D. Bastian, *Theologie der Frage* (München: Kaiser, 1969).

69. "Omnis igitur appetunt quasi ultimum finem Deo assimilari." D. Thomas, *C. Gentes* III, 19.

70. "Deus quem amat omne quod potest amare, sive sciens sive nesciens" ("O God, whom everything loves which is capable of loving, whether knowingly or unknowingly"), Augustine, *Solil.* II, 1, 2 (P. L., 32, 869).

71. "Nemo potest venire ad me, nisi Pater, qui nisit me, traxerit eum." Jn. 6:44.

72. "Console-toi, tu ne me chercherais pas, si tu ne m'avais pas trouvé" ("Console thyself, thou wouldst not seek me, if thou hadst not found me"), Pascal, *Pensées* (New York: Washington Square Press, 1965), n. 553, p. 158.

73. "Nemo te quaerere valet, nisi qui prius invenerit." S. Bernard, *De dil. Deo*, VII, 22, P. L., 182, 987.

74. "Im menschlichen Dasein ist ein existentielles Wissen um Gott lebendig als die Frage nach 'Glück', nach 'Heil', nach dem Sinn von Welt und Geschichte, als die Frage nach der Eigentlichkeit des je eigenen Seins." R. Bultmann, *Glauben und Verstehen* (Tübingen, J.C.B. Mohr [P. Siebeck], 1965), II, 232.

75. "The question of God and the question of myself are identical." R. Bultmann, *Jesus Christ and Mythology* (New York: Scribner's Sons, 1960), p. 53. For Bultmann's theological problematic, cf. G. Hasenhüttl, *Der Glaubensvollzug* (Essen: Ludgerus, 1963), pp. 31-61.

76. Cf. R. Panikkar, *El silencio del Dios* (Madrid: Guadiana, 1970), pp. 162 sq.

77. Cf. chapter VIII.

78. Cf. Rom. 3 sq.

79. This last paragraph seems necessary as a response to the query that if everybody has faith, nobody has it, or the worry that failure, tragedy, sin, damnation and the like are not possible. They are indeed possible precisely because the act of faith is a free act.

80. Significantly enough, this mere phenomenological analysis tallies with the later and much discussed canons 13 and 14 of the VI Session of the Council of Trent (1547) on Justification, which state that nobody in ordinary circumstances can be absolutely sure and have reflexive consciousness of being in the 'state of grace', forgiven, predestined and the like. ". . . cum nullus scire valeat certitudine fidei, cui non potest subesse falsum, se gratiam Dei esse consecutum" (Denz. Schön. 1534). Cf. the famous text 1 Cor. 4:4 *et etiam* Denz. Schön. 1540, 1565-1566.

81. "Der Glaube als religiöser Akt oder religiöse Haltung ist zunächst ein Akt oder eine Haltung des ganzen Menschen . . . des Ver-

standes, des Willens, des Gefühls . . . Glaube als Erkenntnis, Ueber-zeugung und Bekenntnis (Bezeugung). . . ." A. Rademacher, *Die innere Einheit des Glaubens* (Bonn, 1937), pp. 32-33.

82. ". . . der Glaube ist nicht eine mysteriöse supernaturale Qual-ität, sondern er ist die Haltung echter Menschlichkeit." R. Bultmann, *Keryma und Mythos* (Hamburg: Reich, 1948), I, p. 34.

83. Mt. 5:3.

84. Cf. R. Garrigou-Lagrange and Gaudeau, cited by R. Aubert, *op. cit.*, n. 15, pp. 689 sq.

85. Cf. Rom. 12:16.

86. 'Oculata fide'. See D. Thomas, *Sum. Theol.*, III, q. 55, a. 2 ad 1. Cf. the beautiful mediaeval expression: "Ipsa caritas est oculus quo videtur Deus." William of S. Thierry, *De natura et dignitate amoris*, VI, 15, (P. L., 184, 390).

87. Cf. Heb. 11:27. Cf. also M. Schmaus, *Katholische Domatik* (München: Hueber, 1956), III, p. 175: "Dieses Schauen im Nichtschauen, dieses Ueberzeugstein von noch verborgener Wirklichkeit nennen wir Glauben."

88. Cf. Heb. 11:1.

89. "Glaube aber ist stets Ueberwindung des Aergernisses durch Gehorsam." Th. Steinbüchel, *Religion und Moral im Lichte personaler christlicher Existenz* (Frankfurt: Knecht-Carolusdruckerei, 1951), p. 115. But cf. the words of Clemens Alex.: "Fides ergo, ut ita dicam, est brevis et compendiosa eorum quae necessaria sunt cognitio. Cognitio autem est firma ac stabilis demonstratio eorum quae assumpta sunt per fidem. . . ." ("Faith is, then, so to speak, an epitomized knowledge [σύντομός . . . γνῶσις] of the essentials; and knowledge is a strong and sure demonstra-tion of what is received by faith [πίστεως].") (*Strom.* VII, 10, 57, [P. G., 9, 481A]) *et etiam*: "Aristoteles autem, id, quod consequitur scientiam, judicium, quo verum esse hoc aut illud judicamus, dicit esse fidem. Est ergo fides scientia praestantior, et ejus criterium." ("Aristotle says that the judgment (κρῖμα) which follows scientific knowledge (ἐπιστήμης) by which we judge this or that to be true is faith. Accordingly, faith is scientific knowledge, and is its criterion.") (*Strom.* II, 4, 15, [P. G., 8, 948A]).

90. Cf. Mk. 9:24 and the commentaries on the passage: 'In fide dubitavit', Gregory the Great, *Homilia XXVIII in Ev.*, in the Roman Breviary, at Matins, on the Twentieth Sunday after Pentecost. Cyril of Jerusalem (*Catech.*, V, [P. G., 33, 505 sq.]) had already seen that faith admits of incredulity. Cf. in this regard: J. Mouroux, *L'expérience chrétienne* (Paris: Aubier, 1952), p. 59. Cf. the abundant modern literature on 'Unbelief'.

91. Cf. E. Castelli, 'Mythe et foi', in *Mythe et Foi*, edited by E. Castelli (Paris: Aubier, 1966), p. 13.

92. Cf. Mt. 25:37-40, 44-45.

93. It is the passage from *myth* to *logos* about which we spoke in the previous chapter.

94. Cf. the very profound (personalist?) passage, Heb. 11:27 and the various commentaries on it, both classical and modern.

95. Cf. D. Thomas, *Sum. Theol.*, I, q. 1, a. 1 ad 2; *C. Gentes* I, 4; etc.

96. Mt. 5:39.

97. Cf. Rom. 14:22 sq. The *Bible de Jérusalem* translates: "Mais celui qui mange malgré ses doutes est condamné, parce qu'il agit sans bonne foi et ce qui ne procède pas de bonne foi est peché." The translation, however, is misleading on this point, since the text of Rom. 14:23 reads 'faith' and not 'good faith'.

98. Cf. Gen. 2:9 and 3:6.

99. Cf. Gen. 2:9.

100. Cf. the reflections of R. Araud on this subject in *L'homme devant Dieu,* Mélanges H. de Lubac (Paris: Aubier, 1963), vol. I, p. 127 sq. Cf. also chapter III of this book.

101. I. Kant, *Critique of Pure Reason*, preface to the second edition (1787).

102. Cf. Mt. 3:2; etc.

103. Cf. Jn. 6:68.

104. Is this not the only possible way of understanding the parable of Lk. 18:9-14? There seems no other way out than a real forgiveness of real sins: If I 'know' myself to be without sin, I am by this very fact damned. If I have sinned, I am sinful. But if I am aware of sin and not of forgiveness (because in this case I am already feeling 'justified'), then I may return home righteous. Real value is always spontaneous and unconscious. To pretend here is metaphysically impossible. This is what I would like to call the existential argument: one that destroys itself in the very act of its setting.

105. Cf. Rom. 11:32.

106. Mk. 9:23.

107. But we may be able to cry: 'I believe, help my unbelief!' (Mk. 9:24).

VII.
Witness and Dialogue

Ἀναστάντες μάρτυρες ἄδικοι,
ἃ οὐκ ἐγίνωσκον,
ἐπηρώτων με.

Surrexerunt testes violenti:
quorum non eram conscius,
a me quaerebant.

Violent witnesses did rise up:
on matters of which I am not conscious,
they question me.
Ps. 35:11 (+)

+ LXX and Vulgata: Ps. 34. The Latin version is that of the New Psalter.

1. PROLOGUE

Witness (testimony) has been considered the purest, the most sublime expression of faith. Almost all religions (in the widest sense of this word) commemorate their witnesses, their martyrs, and very often cite them as motives for credibility. In the Christian tradition the martyr is the perfect Man, the perfect imitator of the Lord.

Dialogue—the exchange of views, the encounter of beliefs on equal grounds with mutual confidence, complete frankness and without ulterior motives—is today considered an indispensable element in the search for truth and the realization of justice. Our contemporary world feels the need to base itself on dialogue. Only dialogue makes pluralism, coexistence, democracy, even justice and peace possible. Dialogue is the essence of freedom of speech. Politically it incarnates in parliamentarianism, ecclesially it manifests in the dialogue with the 'world', with 'non-Christians', and even so-called 'nonbelievers' (as the Vatican, Geneva and Phanar testify). Contemporary ecumenism is founded on dialogue and even evangelization cannot ignore it.[1] One could summarize the last twenty centuries of Western Church history in the following kairological moments: *Witness* (until Arius), *Conversion* (until the impact of Islam), *Crusade* (until the discovery of America), *Mission* (until the end of the colonial era) and *Dialogue* (today).[2]

What is the relation between witness (testimony) and dialogue? Is testimony possible when we admit dialogue? At a certain point, does the witness not refuse dialogue? Don't communist and inquisitorial methods, while claiming to engage in dialogue—albeit as interrogation—represent a refusal of dialogue? Both the goal and the end of some dialogues seem to be the defendant's confession.

2. A DOUBLE DIALOGUE: 'EARLY CHRISTIAN' AND 'MODERN POLITICAL'

Before analyzing the relationship between witness and dialogue in order to discover its underlying myth, we would like to show a double dialogue, 'early Christian' and 'modern political', presented side-by-side to make the differences and analogies plainly visible. We do not dramatize here, nor do we suppose the interrogators are in bad faith. The acts of martyrs, contemporary literature—need we do more than mention A. I. Solzhenitsyn?— and the history of every period furnish sufficient examples to allow this concentrated presentation.

A	B
Judge: Are you an enemy of the State?	Judge: Are you an enemy of the State?
Christian: No.	Citizen: No.
J: Well then, why don't you obey its laws?	J: Well then, why don't you obey its laws?
C: I obey my conscience.	C: I obey my conscience.
J: You must bow down and offer incense to the Emperor.	J: Then collaborate with the State.
C: That would mean I recognize him as God.	C: That would mean I recognize it as omnipotent and infallible.
J: So?	J: So?
C: I recognize only one God, the Father of our Lord, Jesus Christ.	C: I recognize no absolute power.
J: Yes or no: Will you obey the State?	J: Yes or no: Will you obey the State?
C: Of course, but this act of adoration is not part of that obedience.	C: Of course, but not through a servile, blind, unconditional fear that yields only injustice.

J: Who is the judge here, the State or you?

C: I cannot *not* obey God . . .

J: According to your personal interpretation?

C: According to my faith.

J: Then you divinize yourself.

C: I obey Caesar in his own domain.

J: And you decide what that is.

C: I follow Jesus Christ and his teachings do not permit idolatry.

J: We don't ask much, not even what you believe. Just submit to the law: Sacrifice at the altar in honor of the Emperor.

C: In whose name?

J: The Emperor's.

C: I obey God before Caesar.

J: Don't you see this is sheer obstinacy?

C: I pray only to have the strength to remain truthful.

J: Don't you realize your behavior is irrational?

C: Why?

J: As a result of this small act, you will suffer greatly and then die.

C: True life is not on earth.

J: Who is the judge here, the State or you?

C: I cannot *not* obey my conscience . . .

J: According to your personal interpretation?

C: According to my convictions.

J: Then you consider yourself above the State?

C: I obey the State in its own domain.

J: And you decide what that is.

C: I stand by the human—or humanist if you prefer— tradition of personal dignity.

J: No one wants to strip you of your dignity. We only want to reeducate you, destroy this ill-fated individualism and pride in thinking yourself truthful.

C: In whose name?

J: The Party's. That means the People, Men like me. You know very well that the will of the people and truth manifest themselves in the process the Party incarnates.

C: No, I don't believe that.

J: Don't you see this is sheer obstinacy?

C: I'm tempted to say the same thing to you.

J: Don't you see that such individual behavior is an aberration?

C: Why?

J: Because it means chaos, because the group must determine what is truth; only the group counts.

C: So?

J: Can't you understand we seek your own good? We just want to make you see your mistake.

C: Mistake?

J: Just this: if you want to realize your ideal, you need to live in order to convince others you have the truth.

C: Merely existing is not the supreme value. Besides, arguments cannot persuade any one to believe; this is the work of grace.

J: But dead you can do nothing.

C: You cannot kill real life.

J: You're just a fanatic.

C: Not at all.

J: Yes! You refuse dialogue.

C: We're obviously not talking about the same thing.

J: Have you anything to add?

C: God is my witness:
    I follow my conscience and Jesus Christ.

J: So realistically speaking, the group wants to rehabilitate you, it invites you to collaborate with its goals and admit your mistakes. We want only your good.

C: You want only the group's good, chopping off the true fulfillment of the human person.

J: But you're part of this collectivity. This is what gives you all your rights.

C: But the group is not necessarily uniform . . .

J: No, but it is united . . .

C: To accomplish goals that are not convincing and stifle the human being.

J: Then your selfishness condemns yourself and excommunicates you from the community. You are a blind fanatic.

C: I should like to speak with this community.

J: All your life it has listened to you and now has handed you over to us. No one would listen to you: they might put you in an asylum.

C: I would still like to explain my point of view.

J: What good is it to listen to a madman? Would you like to answer once again?

C: Let me be heard by witnesses.

J: History will prove you wrong.

C: You're not the judge of history.

J: In any case history is on our side.

C: Small victory: There is a Providence that will judge even you, since you ignore truth.

J: What is truth?

C: Our Master did not answer this question.

J: And you?

C: The disciple is not above his Master.

J: Let's leave these speculations. Give witness of your submission to Caesar.

C: I bear witness to my faith which is action, a way of life more than a doctrine or an interpretation.

J: That's just sectarian fanaticism talking.

C: I believe in Jesus Christ.

J: But this Christ did not forbid you to obey Caesar.

C: I witness to truth . . .

J: Abstract . . .

C: Concrete . . .

J: Which?

C: Christ.

J: He, it seems, would prevent you from being an ordinary citizen.

C: He taught us to reject idolatry.

J: One last effort: Interpret this any way you wish, but render public witness to the Emperor.

C: It would be false witness (testimony).

J: History will witness against you.

C: You're not the judge of history.

J: More than you are in any case.

C: Only because you are in power.

J: Because we are right and know the truth.

C: What is truth?

J: The Will and Welfare of the People.

C: But who determines this?

J: The People themselves.

C: I believe in something less volatile, more stable and solid.

J: That's just religious fanaticism talking.

C: I don't believe in God.

J: But you do believe in something that goes above and beyond the group.

C: I witness to truth . . .

J: Abstract . . .

C: Concrete . . .

J: Which?

C: My conscience.

J: We'll have to reeducate it.

C: By force?

J: One last effort: help us to reeducate you.

C: That would betray my convictions.

J: To refuse means death.

C: No, it means real witness.
J: To whom?
C: To God.
J: Where is that?

J: Very well. To refuse means death.

C: No, it means real witness.
J: To whom?
C: To Man.
J: Where is that?

3. THESIS: TESTIMONY IS POSSIBLE ONLY IN A MYTHIC COMMUNION

These two colloquies, which in a certain sense represent the beginning and the end of a historical era, illustrate my thesis concerning witness in our time of dialogue: *testimony is possible only in a mythic communion*. Only this mythic communion—participation in a common myth—makes testimony possible. Outside the horizon provided by a common myth, testimony becomes meaningless. Further, we perceive this preexistent mythic communion only when dialogue is ruptured or when testimony produces dialogue.

To illuminate our thesis, we will divide it into three parts:

Testimony is only possible if there is an *audience*, i.e., somebody to witness to (the witnessed) distinct from the witness. So testimony is essentially a relation, but not a dialectical one. Neither is it mere dialogue in the traditional sense of the word. It is one element of the *dialogical dialogue*, but even this does not exhaust it.

Testimony belongs to the order of myth, not of *logos*. Strictly speaking, you bear witness to a loyalty, not to a truth.

The direct intention to witness destroys the force of the testimony. Further, any hermeneutic of the testimony by the witness makes it vanish. One cannot be a witness and an exegete at the same time. Should the witness try, however, and should a semblance of his testimony still remain, this would rather be confession. A witness does not bear witness to himself; whereas a confessor confesses his belief.

4. SEMANTIC REFLECTIONS

Before developing these three points, we shall situate the problem with a few semantic reflections. 'Testimony' and words from the same root come from the Latin *testimonium*, which derives from *testis*, i.e., *tri-stans*, literally he who 'stands for the third', he who can really witness, attest, give evidence because he is an impartial third party outside the litigations.[3]

On the other hand, the Greek μάρτυς gives primacy to the anthropological, as opposed to the juridical, dimension. Μάρτυς comes from *mrtu*, whence μέρμηρα, anguish, care, anxiety, and μερμηρίζω, preoccupied, concerned, anxious, μέρμερος, requiring much deliberation; μεριμνάω, to think, meditate, be anxious for, whence μέριμνα, anxiety, thought, and μερμαίρω, to consider, reflect, deliberate, etc.

The underlying Indo-European root is *smer* (*mer*) which means to reflect, think, remember, take care of, be anxious, recollect (cf. in Sanskrit *smṛti:* that which one entrusts to memory, i.e., tradition).[4] The root is also connected with *men* (cf. μένω), to think, remain (cf. in Sanskrit *manas*, in Latin *mens* and *manere*).[5] The Anglo-Saxon word *witness* also springs from the order of knowledge (*wit*, *wisdom*).[6]

Following its etymology and history, we reach the following description:[7]

Μαρτυρία, witness (testimony) is the act or result of witnessing, of attesting, giving evidence of a conviction one holds, about which one cares, which one recollects and for which one is concerned. The witness knows, understands, recollects, is anxious for, concerned about; he thinks, considers, is preoccupied with what he will manifest to another in his testimony.

To testify then would be the act of 'recollecting' in one's own 'thought' through 'concern' for that very reality to which one bears witness. Contrary to what one might think, neither the word 'witness' nor 'testimony' denotes an existential or volitional attitude, but both are clearly rooted in the order of the intellect, the memory, thought. Nor do the words suggest action or will; rather they belong to the realm of consciousness. Now consciousness has at times been hastily identified with the *logos*; myth also belongs here and with full rights. We want to show that the character of testimony is to reveal myth. Myth reveals itself in dialogue just as the *logos* liberates itself in dialectics.

We end these considerations now to study the problematic of witness (testimony) in the particular and precise viewpoint of our thesis.[8]

5. TESTIMONY AS A RELATION

The fact that testimony implies a *mythic communion* between the witness and the witnessed (audience) means, in the first place, that testimony entails a special relationship between the act of witnessing and the witnessed (audience). By *witnessing* we mean the witness in the act of testifying; by *witnessed* or *audience* the one to whom the witness testifies, the one who recognizes, in order to accept or reject, the witness and his testimony. We must distinguish *witness*, the *audience* and the *testimony*; the last being the contents or meaning, i.e., what the witness testifies. The audience is the one for whom the witness discloses himself as such. The audience means a person, a fact, the object on whose behalf one testifies (God, truth, an event, a friend, etc.); even what or who receives and recognizes the testimony of the witness (the judge, society, humanity, a group, the future, etc.). We shall try to be as precise as possible in order to avoid confusion and so use witness to mean almost exclusively the one who gives the testimony; exceptions to this usage will be clearly indicated.

Above all, testimony is a relation. It occurs whenever a witness is recognized as testifying to something by an audience. In the final analysis, the audience must recognize the witness or there is no witnessing; at the very least the witness must believe in the existence of an audience. Without this recognition (between the witness and the audience)—be it mutual or only unilateral—witnessing is not possible. The *testis*, 'the third', is essential to testimony, even when removed from the juridical sphere; a third part is also necessary in the anthropological order of knowledge for testimony to exist as such. The witness is not someone who knows something, but one who communicates this something to another. Witnessing is a phenomenon of the third power (witnessing, audience, testimony), reflexive consciousness of the second (knowing and known), and immediate perception a phenomenon of the first (the perceived).

a. Now this relation between witnessing and the audience is *not dialectical*, that is, it does not derive from the order of the *logos*. By the order of the *logos* we understand that epistemologically verifiable domain of consciousness, the critical realm.[9] Could the witness testify via the *logos*, he would be an expert, a lawyer, a *savant*, a sophist or a sage, but not a witness. If you can prove with reason or furnish evidence, you are not, strictly speaking, testifying, you are not witnessing but demonstrating. You do not testify to a geometric theorem, you prove it. You do not testify to a mathematical axiom, you postulate it. You do not testify to some fact accessible to others; you point it out. You do not testify to acquired knowledge, you indicate it. You testify only to what is inaccessible to the audience outside the testimony itself. The witness has an inherent authority that is at once his strength and his weakness. You cannot criticize the witness by attacking his testimony as such, i.e., by an internal principle of verification— except, of course, self-contradiction. You must be content with extrinsic criteria: The witness is honest, loyal, intelligent; he has reasons or motives for his testimony, etc.

Testimony does not present the structure of *A is B* or *A is not B*. Its form is rather *M says that A is B* or *M is in favor of A is B* (or their respective negatives). There is an element that escapes dialectics, an element that is not of the order of the *logos*, the logic-al realm. There is no need to testify when the other can experience or confirm the testimony by himself—although very often the higher human experiences are inaccessible except through the mediation of a witness. The tutor or the teacher demonstrates, proves, communicates learning; he makes one aware of new facts or helps uncover previously hidden relations; but he does not bear witness, or rather he witnesses only insofar as the students are not able to realize by themselves what he is *instruct-*

ing. The instructor is a dialectician, not a witness. On the other hand, the true master is one who testifies to something the disciple cannot yet obtain by himself. One can testify only to transcendence, vertical as well as horizontal: The ultimate place of testimony is not dialectics. In this realm testimony is only provisional and must give way to reasons verifiable by the intellect.

Strictly speaking, the interface between dialectics (that acquired through critical knowledge) and testimony (that requiring the mediation of a witness in order to be accepted) cannot be defined a priori. Without the witness of the ancestors, elders, scholars, wise Men and saints, human life would remain banal. It is through authentic martyrs—through witnesses—in every field that humanity does not wander aimlessly but journeys toward a positive eschatology. The master testifies to the invisible in the hope that eventually his testimony will become superfluous, that one day we shall see face to face.

In any case, testimony does not belong to dialectics.

b. Witnessing certainly implies a relation but not one of mere dialogue in the sense of dialogue as a dialectical tool. As long as dialogue is dialectical, i.e., an intellectual arena where one contends by means of reason to confront the adversary, testimony has no place in it. As long as the dialectical dialogue remains open, as long as one continues to inquire, to question oneself but to admit only reason, dialogue does not allow any witness to testify, for the witness testifies precisely to something that escapes the grasp of dialectics. Otherwise witnessing is out of place. This is why testimony always takes the form of an apodictic affirmation (or negation): 'This is what happened', 'these are the facts', 'I state or swear this', 'I attest this', *non possumus*, etc. The witness ends, shatters, dialectical dialogue by placing himself on what he believes to be another level. His testimony uncovers depths that de facto pure dialectics or simple dialectical dialogue do not achieve. To every dialectical argument, he responds that things are a certain way because this is how he has heard, seen, experienced or believed them. The witness also ultimately takes exception to dialectical dialogue: He does not remain indefinitely involved in dialogue, but declares that he has a different source of knowledge that forces him to give testimony to what he believes to be true.

Testimony ends dialectical dialogue and, in turn, such dialogue allows no room for witnessing. As long as the process is open, as long as the dialogue goes on, no testimony is possible because there is no witnessing nor any audience, but only partners in dialogue, equally open to each other in a confrontation that accepts only the constraint of logic. Each one is seeking; there is no room here for the apodictic affirmation of testimony that, when it comes, can only either be dismissed or end such dialogue. The place of testimony is at the end of the dialogue and so finishes any dialogue. But when do we know that there is no longer place for dialogue or that there is the time for accepting the witness?

Now the dialectical dialogue is not the only, nor even the most important, form of dialogue. Discovering the capital importance of dialogical dialogue represents an important cultural mutation in our times.[10] Until recently dialogue has been mainly a dialectical tool; now, disengaged from dialectics, it has its own justification. This dialogue is neither a tool nor a *pis-aller*, that is, a purely extrinsic aid that acts as a catalyst to invigorate my introspection. Dialogical dialogue is not the external reinforcement of a monologue in the belief that 'two heads are better than one'. Dialogue here is not like procedure of the 'great executive's' subordinates whose critical collaboration enables their boss to deploy his best dialectical skills. In its critical form it is a novelty of contemporary culture and it befits the *kairos* of our times to have liberated dialogue from the tutelege of dialectics. No longer does dialogue necessarily belong to dialectics; hence it does not exist to convert another, to evangelize;[11] it is not merely a method to know the other and his point of view, nor is it a better test of his dialectical skill. Dialogue is, fundamentally, opening myself to another so that he might speak and reveal my myth that I cannot know by myself because it is transparent to me, self-evident. Dialogue is a way of knowing myself and of disentangling my own point of view from other viewpoints and from me, because it is grounded so deeply in my own roots as to be utterly hidden from me. It is the other who through our encounter awakens this human depth latent in me in an endeavor that surpasses both of us. In authentic dialogue this process is reciprocal. Dialogue sees the other not as an extrinsic, accidental aid, but as the indispensable, personal element in our search for truth, because I am not a self-sufficient, autonomous individual. In this sense, dialogue is a religious act par excellence because it recognizes my *religatio* to another, my individual poverty, the need to get out of myself, transcend myself, in order to save myself.

Dialogue seeks truth by trusting the other, just as dialectics pursues truth by trusting the order of things, the value of reason and weighty arguments. Dialectics is the optimism of reason. Dialogue is the optimism of the heart. Dialectics believes it can approach truth by relying on the objective consistency of ideas. Dialogue believes it can advance along the way to truth by relying on the subjective consistency of the dialogical partners. Dialogue does not seek to be primarily *duo-logue*, a duet of two *logoi*, which could still be dialectical; but a *dia-logos*, a piercing of the *logos* to attain a truth that transcends it.

We call this *dialogical dialogue* and we add that the relational nature of all witnessing belongs to this dialogue.

Now the problematic is more complex since this mutation in the concept of dialogue corresponds to a certain mutation in the concept of the testimony. If dialogue is more than a dialectical technique, it cannot dispense with a certain testimony, i.e., with the nonapodictic testimony of the other that communicates his experience and does not merely criticize my views. Without this testimony we cannot establish the true dialogue we have described. If I can learn some new truth on my own, even if eventually helped by another, I do not yet leave the territory of dialectics and my partner is only a critic. But if I cannot know my own myth, cannot discover my own prejudices and above all cannot recognize my presuppositions by myself, then I need the arguments and criticisms of my partner as well as his testimony. His testimony says to me (without proof until we share a common language and homogeneous categories) that there are other points of view, other possibilities, that what is self-evident to me may not be to another. This new sort of dialogue can proceed only by mutually integrating our testimonies within a larger horizon, a new myth.[12] What the other bears is not a critique of my ideas but witness to his own experience, which then enters our dialogue, flows with it and awaits a new fecundation.

Where this dialogue today is perhaps most plausible, most delicate and also difficult—but most necessary—is between religious traditions, between world views and between ideologies. The working attitude of this dialogue is fundamentally different from that of dialectical dialogue. The Christian will speak with the Buddhist, for example, not to convert or merely to know *him* but to better understand himself in the radical sense of an understanding that goes far beyond a simple development or a broadened outlook on oneself or one's religion. He approaches the Buddhist to integrate on a new horizon human experiences that until the dialogue were irreconcilable, inscribed on different skylines, and that permitted the game of dialectics only as a second instance.[13]

There are then different kinds of dialogue, just as there are different kinds of testimony. There is dialectical dialogue and the 'monological' witness who refuses all dialogue. But there is also dialogical dialogue and the dialogical witness who welcomes dialogue, both barely experienced on the global scale in which they present themselves today as one of the greatest challenges of our times.[14] Dialogical dialogue accepts the witness of the other and together with him seeks to integrate this testimony in a new experience no less concrete but more universal than the original starting point.

c. Nevertheless, witnessing cannot be reduced to a component of dialogue. It presents its own consistency over and above any dialogue. We have no guarantee that the witness accepts the rules of the game of dialogue—even of dialogical dialogue. There is a 'divine madness', a 'foolishness of the Cross' in most religions.

Doubtless there are pathological forms of witnessing just as there are diabolical and fanatical forms that refuse all dialogue and any analysis; but history and experience show—no need to cite the *Phaedrus*[15] — that there are authentic forms of witnessing that do not spring from dialogue and cannot be inscribed in the dialogical process. We might call them revelatory forms: They reveal a transcendent message and bear their own authority. One hears, loves and accepts them or one ignores, hates and refuses them. They have nothing to do with dialogue; wanting to 'co-opt' them dialogically would vulgarize, deform and finally destroy them. Francis of Assisi could not give reasons for his message any more than Camus' stranger could testify to his innocence. Jesus spoke with the Roman and Gentile Pilate, but was silent before his compatriot and fellow-believer Herod, with whom he shared not only the same idioms but the same language.

Wanting to master the witness, to reduce his testimony to dialectics or even to dialogue, suffocates the Spirit, straitjackets the freedom of God and Man. Wanting to dictate the rules of witnessing, to manipulate its reality, may succeed for a while— until asses[16] and even stones[17] begin to testify!

To be sure, testimony enables dialogue to be more than a mere dialectical strategy; on the other hand, it is no less true that the witness constantly challenges dialogue and only in certain cases does he allow dialogue to continue without destroying it. But testimony is not a simple provisional working hypothesis. Even in the most perfect form of dialogue, the witness will not be accepted if his testimony does not present a certain homogeneity indispensable to dialogue, a mythic homogeneity. This needs to be analyzed more precisely.

6. THE RELATION BETWEEN THE WITNESS AND THE AUDIENCE

We have said that the relation between the witness and the witnessed, the audience, is a relation *sui generis*. It is neither dialogical nor dialectical, but rather mythical. It arises from a mythic communion: Testimony makes sense only to those who share a common myth. And it is precisely this myth to which the witness testifies. The crisis that today confronts testimony from every side is not due to a lack of convinced people or a lack of heroism, but more properly to the crumbling of traditional communal myths. The testimony's very foundation—the myth held in common by the witness and his audience—is disappearing. For example, the Christian priest used to witness to the ongoing process of redemption. The witnesses are still there, but their testimony is scarcely visible; they have ceased to witness because that particular myth of the Church that made their witnessing possible no longer holds. The anticlericalists of last century arose precisely in countries of traditional beliefs because people thought that priests were giving a bad or even a false testimony of what they still believed the Church to be. Today people no longer discuss what kind of witnesses priests are, because they no longer recognize the context—the myth—of the Church within which the testimony of priests was inscribed. The context having changed, anticlericalism today makes no sense. To give another example: Today we are undergoing not a crisis of patriotism, but the dissolution of the myth of the fatherland that heretofore made a certain patriotism positively or negatively meaningful.

Indeed, for the testimony to exist, the witness must be able to testify to someone and have this receiver, the audience, receive his testimony. This person need not be a judge or someone actually present in favor of the witness or not; the audience can be God, Society, History, the Future, etc. But someone must be *there* to receive the testimony; the witness proclaims his testimony to *him*. To live in the presence of God, for example, means to take him as witness of our actions and to be able to say: 'I do not receive glory from Men.'[18]

In any case there must be a certain communication, even a certain communion, between the witness and the audience. Authentic witnessing begins when the audience recognizes that the witness is actually testifying, affirming, revealing, uncovering, manifesting, something not given in either a dialectical relation (in argument) or a dialogical one (in trusting the other).

In certain cases, it may be that the audience exists in the mind of the witness alone, but this does not contradict our thesis. There will be no actual witnessing until an audience appears; yet the witness can be an authentic witness because he believes in the existence of an audience.

One accepts (or rejects) the witness when one enters into a mythic communion with him and accepts (or rejects) his testimony to the degree of this communion. The first Christian martyrs, for instance, testified to the truth of Christianity for Christians of subsequent generations; they testified to the strength of their convictions or their faith for historians of religion; they testified to their fanaticism or their blindness for Marxist or Maoist adepts. Testimony appears only at the level of the audience's communion of myth with the witness; the latter testifies only to something we ourselves can accept as attestable. Witnesses testify to miracles to the extent that the audience believes in miracles; otherwise they testify to their superstition and gullibility.[19] Christ's Resurrection was pondered, proven, attested to by the primitive Church in exact proportion to one's belief in the possibility of resurrection. Christian witnesses repeat the same thing for twenty centuries, but we accept them only to the extent that we share a common myth with them.[20] Contemporary theological reflection of Jesus' Resurrection provides a striking instance. We accept as authentic the witnessing of the early Christians insofar as we believe in what they testified to and this belief is provided by the mythical horizon we still hold in common with them.[21]

Be this as it may, you witness to a loyalty, not a truth. The witness does not need to reveal a hitherto unknown truth—which would always remain foreign and incomprehensible—but a loyalty to a certain situation we may already know. In the example we gave earlier, the Christian martyr witnesses to the Christian 'truth' to Christians, to the 'truth' of heroic courage to historians of religion and to the 'truth' that religion is the opium of the people and the enemy of progress to Marxist and Maoist ideological adepts. In each case we admit witnessing to a loyalty—to something we believe to be the case.

In general, the witness has been studied within the framework of a specific context—precisely because a witness makes sense only within one context. As long as we live in a given culture, in a particular mythical context or a particular horizon of intelligibility and experience, we are not aware that our witness makes absolutely no sense outside this given horizon.[22] The task of our epoch is to expand this horizon to include a transcultural perspective as well. Only then shall we become aware that each concrete witnessing does not have universal meaning.

It is in fact the notable silence of witnesses today that leads us to discover our broken myths and prompts us to reconsider the true unity of humanity on a broader basis.

We have said that the place of the witness is within a mythic communion. Witnessing belongs indeed to the realm of consciousness, but not at the level of the *logos*. One could almost assume, by process of elimination, that what remains in consciousness and is not *logos* is myth. But here we are not concerned to argue semantics. We could call myth that invisible common horizon that allows communication.

To recapitulate, we might say that there is no testimony without a hermeneutic of that testimony by an audience. This hermeneutic implies a common horizon we have called the mythic communion between the witness and the audience. Otherwise the would-be witness is sent to an asylum for the insane.

7. INTERPRETING THE WITNESS

One characteristic of a genuine witness already discovered in the light of what we have said is that the hermeneutic necessary to accept his testimony comes from the audience and not from the witness.

To clarify our thesis, we would add that voluntary manipulation of the testimony by the witness would invalidate the testimony. The true witness bears testimony in spite of himself, without intending to, strictly speaking. He bears witness knowingly, but he does not testify for the purpose of witnessing. He witnesses because he is compelled to do so, impelled to give witness, so to speak, by his conviction and the power of the truth in which he believes.[23] It is the audience that discovers the testimony of the witness. The reflective consciousness that may elicit in me the will to testify would destroy the value of the testimony, for then it would no longer represent the irruption of something higher, the rupture of endless dialogue or the over-

stepping of a dialectical argument incapable of reaching any conclusion. It would no longer represent the epiphany of a *testis*, a
third, but the deliberate influence on a second, i.e., a proof presented to an audience. In this way, testimony becomes dialectics
or dialogue, or worse yet, didactic; but it disappears as testimony.
It becomes sophistry.

I do not really testify of any authentic love for my neighbor if
I love him in order to bear witness of this love to him or anyone
else—my friends or my brothers. I do not testify to a true love, if
I love someone, in order to bear witness of my obedience or my
loyalty to God. I do not bear witness to the truth of my faith if I
proclaim it in order to be a witness. In other words, the witness
cannot intend to witness without becoming inauthentic. Of course
falsehood is also possible here. As long as the audience believes
the testimony of the witness, he bears true witness—*ex opere
operantis*—but he ceases to do so when the audience discovers
that he—rather than the testimony itself—intends to speak, to
bear witness.

In fact, the will to bear witness implies wanting to show, to
prove the truth of my witness to another, to convince him, to
convert him because I myself am convinced that the contents of
my testimony are proper for him too. By this very fact I cease to
be a witness, because my testimony ceases to be the testimonial
of a third, the affirmation of a conviction, the expression of a
concern, the manifestation of something within, that one
cherishes in itself and for oneself, the spontaneous epiphany of an
experience. Instead it becomes a conscious act that intends to
make the other share my convictions; the purpose is no longer the
passive blossoming of a grace that the audience freely discovers,
but the active communication of a value I consider proper for
others. The motive is no longer in the 'thing' testified (the testimony itself), but in the reason one wishes to testify.[24]

So we can shift the emphasis of witnessing and this dis-
placement changes its nature and transforms it into a duty, a
charitable act and the like, depending upon how we interpret it.
The intention to bear witness implies that you are convinced not
only of your 'truth', but also of its value for another. Moreover,

this value does not consist in the truth of the testimony per se, but in its utility for the audience to whom one intends to testify. It is justified, then, in pragmatic terms and not by virtue of the demands that genuine witnessing itself makes; you have the audience in mind. A good doctor—one who is a living witness to medical knowledge—prescribes a remedy or a treatment not to testify to the efficacy but to cure the patient. An honest lawyer argues a case not to testify to his debating skill but to obtain justice for his client. True social service does its job not to testify to the superiority of the society that commissions it or the techniques it uses, but to assist in a concrete human situation. The businessman does not testify to the excellence of his enterprise, he seeks to convince the buyer of the utility of his merchandise or services.[25]

A simple example serves to reinforce what we have been developing: as is evident in any courtroom, testimony that considers the effects it will have on others by this very fact loses value. A witness who testifies only when his testimony is agreeable to his ideas or friends loses credibility as a witness.[26]

We might go further still and assert that any hermeneutic by the witness himself destroys his testimony. If the left hand knows what the right hand is doing. . . .[27] Indeed, many passages from the Gospel fit here;[28] the parable of the pharisee and the publican is another example.[29] If, having understood the parable, the pharisee no longer boasts of his fasting nor proclaims how good he considers himself to be nor judges the publican because he fears the parable's condemnation, he is twice cursed. If, in turn, the publican proclaims himself a sinner knowing he will thereby be justified, he shall be twice cast out. As the text adds,[30] this means that whoever exalts himself will be humbled and whoever humbles himself will be exalted. But if you accuse and abase yourself in order to be pardoned and raised up, you will find neither pardon nor honor.[31] We cannot escape this impasse by dint of reflection or will power. We cannot manipulate faith, nor dispose of myth at will or by thought.

We bear witness to something we cannot indicate in any other way or prove by reason; that is why witnessing engages the

entire life of the witness. We bear witness not by reason or sentiment, but through our life. Ultimately we can bear witness only
with our life. Now, life is given to be lived, i.e., to be given up,
and as we pass on this gift we also give life, transmit, continue,
immortalize it.[32] Do we mean by all this that reflecting on one's
life is inherently inauthentic? an instance of original sin in Man?[33]
Are we not saying that interpreting one's life as witness destroys
its authenticity? What shall we think then of Christ who said: "For
this I have come into the world, to bear witness to the truth"?[34]

Certainly I can know my life bears witness in the sense that I
am aware that I communicate what I have seen, experienced or
realized, and can be expressed only in lived testimony.[35] But
when I lose sight of the third party testifying in and through me,
when I fall back on myself as a witness, I destroy my testimony.
In this sense Christ said: "If I bear witness to myself, my testimony is not true; there is another who bears witness to me, and I
know that the testimony which he bears me is true."[36]

Does this constant prayer, in one form or another, "Thy will
be done",[37] "not as I will, but as thou wilt",[38] not characterize
an authentic life? Is liberation not primarily liberation from the
ego? We do not witness in or by our life except as an expression of
loyalty to a 'third', to the Spirit, however we may call it, which
alone enables us to say that a higher power guides us.[39] Or again,
to express this with profound wisdom:

> By whom it is unthought, by him it is thought;
> By whom it is thought, he does not see.
> Not understood by whom it is known;
> Understood by whom it is not known.[40]

This is not paradox but literal truth: The mystery of life is not
understood by those who understand it or think they understand
it. Just as understanding the mystery destroys it, understanding
Reality renders it inauthentic; it is no longer incomprehensible but
understood only in a limited way. What is understood is not
Reality at all, but the object of understanding. Nor is the mystery
of life truly understood by those who understand they cannot

understand it; not by the pharisees of the intellect (even if they call themselves philosophers); nor by those aware of their ignorance, who understand their ignorance or understand that they do not understand. Rather, it is understood by those who really do not understand—and in not understanding, do not understand that they do not understand. Only infinite ignorance is a blessing. This is why it was later proclaimed: 'Blessed are the poor in spirit'.[41]

In brief, the hermeneutic belongs to the audience, not to the witness. Some will then discover that this hermeneutic is itself a testimony the audience has given without being aware of it. Thus life continues in the encounter of witnesses. Our thesis says that the witness exists only in the framework of a mythic communion with the audience and so it goes on. It is history as dialogue. A witness arises and the acceptance or refusal of his testimony penetrates as if by osmosis into human experience to the extent that the witness lives in communion with Man.

8. WITNESS AND MYTH

The place of the witness is in myth. When we live in the same myth, we are open and receptive to the witness. The *logos* does not need witnessing: At the very least this would be an insult. Truth must be proven or demonstrated according to its intrinsic evidence. Witnessing to anything belonging to the order of the *logos* is out of place, although such 'déplacement' constitutes one of life's tensions. Intellectual authority is only for those who have not yet discovered the logical character of the truth proclaimed by authority. The *logos* properly functions in dialectics.

Today dialogue distinguishes itself from dialectics and seeks to accept the witness. In thus accepting the witness in dialogue, we seek to reintroduce testimony into the realm of the *logos*. If we do not succeed, dialogue will not proceed further; but if we succeed, we shall continue to search dialectically and dialogically, the more enriched by the various witnesses. In this process there are martyrs and conversions, bungled dialogues and successful syntheses; ancient myths crumble and are demythicized; others, more meaningful, arise and penetrate humanity. We pass from myth to *logos*; we enrich the second, we change the first—but we do not exhaust it.

So testimony itself stands in a dialectical relation with dialogue. On the one hand, it nourishes dialogue by the contributing witnesses; on the other hand, testimony represents the end of dialogue, because as long as it offers testimony and only that, it remains impenetrable to the *logos*.

NOTES

1. Cf. the International Congress of Theology on Evangelization held in October 1971 at Nagpur, India, where the major items discussed were dialogue and development. The recent Roman Synod (October-November 1974), convened under the general title of Evangelization in the Modern World, dedicated many of its sessions to the question of Dialogue.

2. Cf. my chapter, 'Christianity and World Religions', in *Christianity* (Patiala: Punjabi University, 1969), pp. 78-127, esp. 85-98.

3. Cf. also *testamentum*, testament, *testificari*, to give evidence, to certify, *testari*, to attest, etc. Cf. C.D. Buck, *A Dictionary of Selected Synonyms in the Principal Indo-European Languages* (Chicago: University of Chicago Press, 1949), *sub voce witness* (§21.23), pp. 1435-1436. The riches of this root include giving meaning to context, detest, protest, testament, etc., as well as testicle (witness to virility). Cf. v.g. E. Partridge's English etymological dictionary *Origins* (London: Routledge & Kegan -Paul, 1966, 4th ed.).

4. Cf. *etiam* the Latin *memor*, *memoria*, *mora*; the old German *mornen* and the English *mourn*.

5. Cf. J.B. Hofmann, *Etymologisches Wörterbuch des Griechischen* (München: Oldenbourg, 1966), *sub hac voce*. H. Grassmann, *Wörterbuch zum Rig-veda* (Wiesbaden: Harrassowitz, 1964), col. 1614 for *smṛ* and *smar* in the sense of remember, memory, think, recollect. It also appears with the prefixes *anu* and *prati*, although the root appears only rarely in the Ṛg Veda, etc.

6. Cf. C.T. Onions, *The Oxford Dictionary of English Etymology* (Oxford: Clarendon Press, 1966, rep. 1967), *sub voce*. Cf. the Latin *videre*, to see and the Sanskrit *veda*, see, understand, know, *vidyā*, knowledge, etc. The witness is he who knows (cf. the German *wissen*).

7. Cf. also H. Strathmann, in Kittel, *Theologishes Wörterbuch zum Neuen Testament* (Stuttgart: Kolhammer), *sub hac voce*. J.H. Moulton

and G. Milligan, *The Vocabulary of the Greek Testament* (London: Hodder & Stoughton, 1930, rep. 1963), *sub his vocibus*. G.W.H. Lampe, *A Patristic Greek Lexicon* (Oxford: Clarendon Press, 1961), for the use of these words by the Patristic Fathers, pp. 838 sq., etc.

8. For some information supplementary to the bibliography given in Strathmann, *op. cit.*, in the *RGG* and in *Sacramentum Mundi*, see also B. Trepanier, 'Contribution à une recherche sur l'idée de témoin dans les écrits johanniques', *Revue de l'Université d'Ottawa,* 15 (1945), 5-63. I. de la Potterie, 'La notion de témoignage dans saint Jean', *Sacra Pagina* (Gembloux, Ed. J. Duculot, 1959), II:193-208. A Vanhoye, 'Témoignage et vie en Dieu selon le quatrième évangile', *Cristus* (avril 1965), 16, 155-171.

9. Cf. chapter X.

10. Cf. the dialogue between Heidegger and a Japanese: 'Ein Sprechen *von* der Sprache könnte nur ein Gespräch sein.' M. Heidegger, *Unterwegs zur Sprache* (Pfullingen: Neske, 1959) p. 150. Cf. also: '*Dialectik* weist zurück auf den Dialog und kennzeichnet die Methode des dialogische Denkens', *RGG* (Tübingen: J.C.B. Mohr [P. Siebeck], 1958), II:167.

11. "We reject the idea that dialogue is by itself a means to evangelization", is found in the final declaration of the Nagpur Conference cited above, although the editing committee took the liberty (!) of eliminating this sentence approved by the entire Congress—perhaps because of the ambiguity of 'evangelization'.

12. We could compare this with what H.-G. Gadamer says about *Horizontverschmelzung* as the process of understanding, in *Wahrheit und Methode* (Tübingen: J.C.B. Mohr [P. Siebeck], 1972), pp. 289-290, 375, etc.

13. Cf. R. Panikkar, *The Intrareligious Dialogue* (New York: Paulist Press, 1978), chapter IV.

14. When I initially wrote these lines (1972), Josef Cardinal Mindszenty was just arriving in Rome after twenty-three years of seclusion. Was he to be considered a martyr for having refused dialectical dialogue or will history judge him a failed witness who refused dialogical dialogue? Cf. his subsequent (and foreseeable) conflicts with the Roman milieu.

15. 244a sq.

16. Cf. Num. 22:28 sq.

17. Cf. Lk. 19:40.

18. Cf. Jn. 5:41 (after acknowledging that the Scriptures bore witness to him).

19. Cf. Lk. 16:31: "If they do not hear Moses and the prophets, neither will they be convinced if some one should rise from the dead." Cf. also Jn. 5:46-47 for a similar problematic.

20. Cf. Chapter XI for the problematic of fundamental theology today.

21. Cf. 1 Cor. 15:13: "But if there is no resurrection of the dead, then Christ has not been raised."

22. These days we have striking—often tragic—examples of congregations and other religious groups that, sincerely tired of propaganda and activism, feel themselves called to a humble, silent testimony, unaware that their testimony does not exist and is even revolting outside the mythical boundaries of a culture where the concrete values of testimony are still accepted.

23. Cf. 1 Cor. 9:16-17: "For if I preach the gospel, that gives me no ground for boasting. For necessity is laid upon me. Woe to me if I do not preach the gospel! . . . I am entrusted with a commission."

24. A principal text of Christian testimony (Acts 1:8) does not only say the disciples of Jesus ought to witness to the ends of the earth; it explicitly underlines that this witness results from the disciples' having received the power of the Holy Spirit—that is, from a third—which makes them witnesses.

25. We do not enter here into the important and delicate problem of Christian missions that have too often confused testimony with proclamation, evangelization and conversion.

26. Paradoxically, one could say that the Christian missionary who testifies to Christ while convinced that this makes the situation more precarious or even renders salvation more difficult is a more authentic witness than the missionary who testifies to Christ in order to save 'souls' or assist persons to lead more human lives. Here, of course, we are limiting ourselves to the problem of witnessing.

27. Cf. Mt. 6:3. Cf. *etiam* 6:5: "ut videantur ab hominibus".

28. Cf. vgr., Mt. 6:1-6, 17-20; Mk. 13:9-13; or also Lk. 21:12-15: ". . . you will be brought before kings and governors for my name's sake. This will be a time for you to bear testimony. Settle it therefore in your minds, not to meditate beforehand how to answer; for I will give you a mouth and wisdom, which none of your adversaries will be able to withstand or contradict."

29. Cf. Lk. 18:9-14.

30. Cf. Lk. 18:14; Mt. 23:12; Lk. 14:11.

31. Cf. on this problem chapter 3.

32. This phrase would like to express what the historian of religions would call heaven, grace, liberation, salvation, immortality.

33. This is an idea current in the history of religions, most recently revived by the late R.C. Zaehner, *The Convergent Spirit* (London: Routledge & Kegan Paul, 1963); etc. Cf. chapters 3 and 4.

34. Jn. 18:37. Cf. *etiam* 3:11.

35. In the same sense one could cite A. Gide: "Chaque être est né

pour témoigner . . ." (*Attendu que* . . ., Paris: Charlot, 1943, p. 109) (*apud* P. Robert, *Dictionnaire alphabétique et analogique de la langue française* [Paris: Nouveau Littré-Le Robert, 1969], VI:494).

36. Jn. 5:31-32. Cf. *etiam* 5:33-34.
37. Mt. 6:10; etc.
38. Mt. 26:39; etc.
39. Cf. Jn. 4:34, 6:38; etc.
40. KenU II, 2-3.
41. Mt. 5:3. One could also translate: "Blessed those who are poor through the Spirit." Cf. *etiam*: "for the Son of Man is coming at an hour you do not expect" (οὐ δοκεῖτε) Lk. 12:40.

VIII.
Silence and the Word.
The Smile of the Buddha

When you are gathered together, monks,
there are two things to be done:
either talk about *dhamma* or the
ariyan silence.
Majjhima-nikāya I, 161 (+)

+ I.B. Horner's translation of the famous *Ariyapariyesanasutta* or *Discourse on the Aryan Quest*. Cf. the common Buddhist expression of *noble silence*: *ariyo tuṇhībhāvo*; love of quiet: *appasadda-kāmo* (vg. *Dīgha-nikāya* I, 208; etc.). Cf. Candrakīrti's beautiful saying: *pāsamartho hy āryāṇām tuṣṇim bhāvah*, "The most noble truth is silence" (*Prasannapadā* LVII, 8).

1. INTRODUCTION: THE SPIRIT, THE WORD AND THE NAME OF GOD

There have been many attempts to express the awareness of the Absolute. Two of the main attitudes could be summed up in the expression *transcendent transcendence*, symbolizing the Semitic trend proper to the Jewish-Christian-Islamic and modern post-Christian tradition, and *immanent transcendence* proper to the bundle of religions we call Hinduism.

The Buddhist approach is startling. It does not fit into this typology. It would rather say the true awareness of the Absolute is to have none.

Let us quote a passage that dates probably from pre-Buddhist times:

> —Now once there was a dispute between the Spirit (*manas*) and the Word (*vāc*). 'I am excellent,' said the Spirit and the Word said: 'I am excellent.'
> —The Spirit said: 'I am certainly better than you, because you do not utter anything which is not previously understood by me. So, as you just imitate what I am doing and simply follow me, I am certainly better than you.'
> —The Word said: 'I am certainly better than you, because whatever you know, I make it known, I communicate it.'
> —They went to Prajāpati, asking for his decision. Prajāpati spoke in favor of the Spirit, saying (to the Word): 'The Spirit is certainly better, because you only imitate and follow what the Spirit is doing; and he who is imitating and following what another does is undoubtedly inferior.'

—As the Word was thus refuted, she became ashamed
and miscarried. The Word spoke to Prajāpati: 'I shall never
become the carrier of your oblation, I whom you have thus
refuted!'
Therefore, whatever in the sacrifice is performed for
Prajāpati is done in a low voice, because the Word refused to
carry the oblation to Prajāpati.'[1]

This was a fundamental option. By and large, I would
daresay India decided in favor of the Spirit while the West opted
for the Word. The consequences are far-reaching. The Word is
powerful, is articulate, leads to clarity and distinction, to science
and technology, is sure of itself once it has assumed a critical
stance; the word organizes, commands, expresses and even cries.
The Spirit is helpless outside its inner realm, it is unstructured
and insecure for it blows now one way, now another, in a total
freedom that often amounts to disorientation and anarchy; the
Spirit feels, is concerned, contemplates and is easily satisfied at
the price of being blind to externals; it is joyful and happy.
Perhaps the time has come when the twins will have to meet if our
world is to survive, but I am not now writing a full commentary
on this passage of Scripture. I would like to exemplify a single
consequence, and would beg that what follows be understood in
the light of the just-quoted text.

Most traditional religions are concerned with God to such an
extent that to speak of an atheistic religion seems a contradiction
in terms. Yet around the sixth century before Christ, at a time
when humanity seemed to be awakening to reflexive self-
consciousness, when Men began to develop a critical attitude,
there appeared religious reforms—Jainism and Buddhism—that
claimed to establish an entire way of life with no reference to
God. These reforms, although excluding the existence, essence,
name and reality of God, soon became authentic religions. It
could even be said that, for the Buddha, eliminating the name of
God is the supreme religious undertaking.

Much has been written about so-called Buddhist atheism and
many hypotheses seeking to explain the silence of the Buddha
have been proposed.[2] I would like simply to indicate here what

seems to me the fundamental attitude of the Buddha on the problem of the name of God, an attitude at the origin of the whole
Buddhist tradition, one that could well have exceptional importance for our time.

To be brief, I shall introduce the problem without referring to
the *brahmanism*, the religious ferment and the multiplicity of
Gods at the time of the Buddha. I would only cite one verse of the
Bible that will situate us *in media res*: "You shall not utter the
name of Yahweh your God in vain."[3]

Why?

Because one cannot speak of God but may only invoke him,
because talk about God does not belong to current language,
because his name is justified only in the vocative, because he is
not an object like others, his name cannot be linked to other
names, and because respect and adoration are due him. This is
the traditional answer of nearly every religion.

Now the Buddha goes further. He tells us that any speaking
of the name of God, any talk and even any thought about God is
just so much blasphemy. According to the spirit of the Buddha it
would be pure hypocrisy to forbid making images of God or
speaking his name if we are at the same time permitted to think of
'him'. The purification must reach to the very heart of the matter.
What use is it to cast God from the imagination, from the pen, the
lips or the walls, if one retains the thought of 'him'? The Buddha
tells us that God can only be named in vain, that every name of
God is a vain name (a false name, if we follow the modern translation), that no name attains to God, who is beyond all possible
naming.

Now all that is, can be named—in one way or another—and
being is the final object (or the ultimate subject if one prefers) of
all that is named. God cannot be named, nor can 'he' even be
called 'being'; this would kill him, destroy him as God by situating 'him' among the things of this world. God does not *have* a
name because 'he' *is* not. Buddhism will defend this in all its
consequences.

"Why do you ask my name?"[4] says the Man, the angel or the
God who wrestles with Jacob. We should perhaps emphasize the

importance of this text and others like it throughout the Christian tradition.[5]

We cannot ask the name of God either because we do not have the right to do so, for God has a hidden name, a secret name that he reveals only to the initiate, etc. (this seems to have been the line followed by the Christian and Islamic traditions), or else because he has no name. The Buddha chose the second alternative. We shall now attempt to examine it.

2. THE DOUBLE SILENCE OF THE BUDDHA

The Buddha's attitude is known. He does not answer questions on the ultimate nature of things. He refuses to be dragged into purely speculative discussions, for they do not lead to deliverance from suffering and so distract us from the existential and concrete meaning of life. The famous parable is well known: when a Man is pierced by an arrow, to concern himself with conjectures on the direction whence it came, its nature, the possible motives for which it was shot, the identity of the guilty Man, whether he was right, etc., will cause the wounded Man's death long before there is time to answer the questions that were raised.

To understand the Buddha's attitude we may distinguish a double level in his silence.

a. First-Degree Silence: The Silence of the Answer

There is no possible answer to the question on the nature of the absolute since the question itself cannot be absolute—for we are relative, limited, contingent—and so it cannot give the desired information. If it is said that *nirvāṇa* does not exist, one falls into the existential contradiction of trying to show and follow a path to something that does not exist. If one says *nirvāṇa* exists, one falls into a whole series of insurmountable difficulties. Basically this would deal a fatal blow to transcendence, it would render transcendence accessible to our thought or to our speech. At the same time one falls into a speculative contradiction, for the existence of an absolute should explain the burning questions

Man raises, resolve his difficulties and save him from contradiction.[6] Yet life and philosophy, experience as well as thought, bear witness that this is not the case. So we must remain silent if we do not want to fall into a contradiction. Silence is the sole response.

Nevertheless, it is not out of fear of committing himself or of falling into logical contradiction that the Buddha remains silent. Quite the contrary, his silence is irksome to people and, given the spirit of his time, it can well be said that his failure to elaborate a new theory amounted to casting himself from the company of cultivated and spiritual Men. His silence is an even greater commitment and more eloquent than any theory.

The Buddha wishes to teach us to know silence, to love it and to grasp its message. He speaks of noble silence and says the monk is a lover of silence. He thereby indicates that the reality of speech, the world of signs and expressions, can be surpassed. Concerning God total silence must be kept. Neither affirming nor negating him can lead us to attain the threshold where divinity is found (or where it is also not found). His message invites us to go beyond the world of signs, words, speech, the realm of the *logos*. You will come to divinize the *logos*, he would have said, if you persist in trying to penetrate everything with the *logos* and go everywhere by the power of your discourse. This is what has happened in the West where, in reaction, Man has gone to the other extreme: antitheism. Without myth, the *logos* becomes absolute, it divinizes itself, and a divinized *logos* destroys itself.

As for the excuse that the *logos* speaks only of the existence and not the essence of God, the 'back' of God and not his 'face', an indication and not a localization, an analogy and not a univocal concept, an image and not a notion, a name and not a reality; or that we can grasp the name of God as an ersatz, since we cannot understand his being, etc.—this the Buddha would refute as the worst example of spiritual and intellectual hypocrisy, as a religious farce that speaks of something affirmed to be unknown. The game must be played clearly, the Buddha would say, and he was to attract crowds who were tired of complicated religiosities.

To say that for God everything is clear, to affirm that the contradictions, the ruptures of human life, its injustices, its sufferings and its scandals are only appearances that have been deformed by our ignorance or by our sin (since all goes well, all is just and good for God in his happiness), to try to convince ourselves we must blindly accept that, in God, all the contradictions are resolved, that we must content ourselves with knowing only his existence—all this is for the Buddha a striking example of the weakness of the established religions that perpetuate a state of things (organization, cult, castes, etc.) for very mixed motives. Buddhism would add that defending the possibility of knowing the existence of God while closing off the content of his essence amounts to postulating his existence from motives that have nothing to do with God, but that stem from the human desire to find a crutch outside reality. Buddhism says it can very well do without the God hypothesis and does so without falling into the contradiction that affirms the most important thing about God—his existence—and yet denies knowledge of his essence. What is the meaning of an existence whose essence cannot be known?—and whose essence, in a way, cannot be different from his existence?

But the Buddha does not stop here. He does not prétend that his silence is the adequate answer. He does not fall into the trap—as has so often happened in the history of human thought—of believing that everybody up to his time has been wrong and that he brings the true solution. In a word, silence is not the Buddha's answer. He does not answer with silence. To think this would be to misunderstand him and to follow him only out of intellectual curiosity as if he were a simple philosopher.

To ask the name of God means to ask his identity, to enclose him in our categories, even if one says his name is secret and unknowable. According to the Buddha God has no name because there *is* nothing that *has* this name. There is not even any meaning in saying that God is identical to himself: Because he has no identity, he cannot be identified by a name. The principle of identity would destroy him. There can be no God identical to God—to himself. But the Buddha is not an agnostic; he is an Enlightened One. It is here that the modern age and contemporary scholarly studies generally fail to grasp his spirit, reducing him to a thinker, a philosopher or a great humanist, and forgetting that he was above all a prophet, a mystic, a saint. I would propose to call his silence a silence of the second degree.

b. Second-Degree Silence: The Silence of the Question

The Buddha's silence is neither a methodology nor an answer; it is not a new theological or philosophical system. The Buddha does not answer by silence: He does not answer. He remains silent and gives no hermeneutic of his silence but only of his refusal to answer. He explains why he does not rally to the views of this party or that, he gives reasons why he does not share the belief of those who say the soul exists after death, and also why he is not of the contrary opinion. He gives reasons for his refusal, but he does not expand upon his silence. He says categorically that he is not of the opinion of those who say A, nor of those who say non-A, nor of those who at once affirm both A and non-A or deny both A and non-A.[7] He does not give a positive opinion, he goes over every possible opinion and denies holding any of them. But he does not give any opinion of his own. He is silent, but his silence is not an answer to the question.

What the Buddha does is to silence the question, to pacify the questioner by showing him that his question has no meaning, or rather that he does not have the power—hence the right—to put such a question. In a way he puts the question, and thereby the questioner, in crisis. He puts the question in question, and thereby also the questioner who had unduly identified himself with his question. The question becomes anguishing only when Man identifies himself with his reason and loses the global perspective of his human situation. The entire message of Gautama is to make Men understand that torturing oneself over the so-called major questions of life is the great human fallacy, the source of misery and the price paid for the utopia of believing one has the right, or worse yet the duty, to pierce the mystery of existence. An ideal like this is the fruit of human pride. What the Buddha requires is a realistic sense of acceptance of reality just as it presents itself, a total confidence in life, in what is given to us, without seeking to replace Reality with our own ideas. His faith is a cosmological faith, his hope is the elimination of any future, and his love is a compassion for Men of flesh and bone, our contemporaries, not an ideal entelechy that exists nowhere.

When Man discovers by himself that he has nothing to ask,

that a question about ultimate Reality has no meaning, and yet in spite of this finds himself neither a rebel nor discouraged nor despairing, then will he begin to understand the liberating message of primitive Buddhism: the total acceptance of our human condition, of the real contingency in which we find ourselves. It is not a matter of resigning oneself to never surpassing the human condition; it is rather understanding that what we must do is better it. If it must be surpassed, this does not depend absolutely on us, and if it must not be surpassed, every effort to do so will lead us to alienation and only increase our misery. The whole message of the Buddha tends to render us silent, to silence our desires. It is often said (but easily forgotten) that the most intense desire or, as the Buddha himself says, thirst is to transgress Reality, to evade the human situation: to attach oneself to life is just as unreal and deadly as to long for death, no matter what the motive. The thirst for nonexistence is to be eliminated as well as the desire for existence.

'Blessed are the poor in spirit', not the poor who seek and beg, but the poor in spirit, those who do not want to jump beyond themselves spiritually nor believe they can become as Gods. The Buddha does not discourage human and secular initiatives, but he does not recognize evading the human condition by whatever means as a true religious undertaking.

We might sum up the Buddha's message thus: If there is a transcendence, it will take care of itself. And if it does not exist, it is useless to deceive oneself. But there is more to it. If it 'exists', transcendence is so transcendent that it surpasses both our thought and our being, and thus also any attempt to name it. For the Buddha, to name the Absolute would be the great blasphemy. The Buddhist apophasis is at once ontic and ontological. Silence is taken seriously, not as another form of expression or speech. In the last part of this chapter I try to explain this with a dialectic borrowed from the Buddhist tradition.

3. THE DIALECTICAL GAME

"Is the principle of sufficient reason insufficient to name God?" Castelli asks us in his introduction to the Colloquium on

The Name of God.[8] Here then is the Buddha's genial answer according to the Buddhist tradition.[9]

Without hesitation Buddhism tells us that by virtue of this very principle we must renounce naming God, and also asking anything whatsoever about him. He cannot even be named without sinning against this basic principle of all rationality. How can we postulate a sufficient reason that is other than and superior or exterior (God) to that very principle of sufficient reason, without presupposing an infinite series of such principles? Before trying to grasp the Buddhist dialectic, I would like to make a brief excursus to situate the problem in the history of religions.

a. The Dialectic of the Name of God

I shall summarize my point.[10] We can discover a sort of dialectical play regarding human relations with this superior principle we agree to call God.

I would like to highlight the following moments. I would request that they not be considered chronological milestones but, if I may use the more accurate expression, *kairological* moments.

i. Before the cultural and religious complexity of the so-called great religions, each God is a local God with a local name, his proper name. To know the God is to know his name, and vice versa. The act of faith is the act of invoking the name. This name has usually been revealed in myth.

ii. There is an early realization, either through encountering different traditions or by deepening the mystery of God, that God has several names. The first reaction is to postulate a plurality of Gods corresponding to the plurality of names. Thus the harmony between the name and the thing is not ruptured. To each name corresponds (one) God. But we should not confuse real(istic) polynomy with the so-called polytheism.

iii. True polyonomy, however, cannot be maintained for very long. A plurality of Gods guaranteed by a plurality of names leads to the discovery that there is a basic unity among the Gods, that they are, in one way or another, only different manifestations of a single and unique supreme power. The innocence of the name begins to waver. Each name of God does not exhaust the divinity, since there are other names that also refer to the divinity. Men begin to suspect that the name of God is not God, or rather that his name is not *the* name of God, but *a* name of *one God*. The name of God does not express God, so to speak. A break, a hiatus appears between the name and the thing. Truth bridges the gap.

iv. At the same moment the divine name suffers its first crisis, i.e., when the plurality of names suggests a plurality of gods, the tradition of the hidden name of God appears. The names of God are not his true name. His true name is hidden, secret, and reveals itself only to him to whom God wants to reveal it. The divinity uncovers his true name to his devotees. The revelation is the revelation of this name.

v. The essence of the secret name is that it is unknown. In the beginning Man could be content to say that it is unknown to the uninitiated, but soon he becomes aware that the secret name represents something more than the divine whim to remain hidden or the selection (by the divinity) of a small group to whom the name would be revealed. Man is aware that God has a name that is in itself intrinsically hidden, as it were. One thus arrives at the highly suggestive formulation that the name of God is simply an interrogation. God is the question that is always open, his name is the simple question about him, to find him means to seek him; to know him means not to know him (to name him means to invoke him as an unknown God with an unknown name), for his name is the question, pure and simple. God is not a substance and has no name, but he is a question, a simple pronoun, an interrogative: *Who?*

vi. The next moment of the kairological dialectic is of more than historico-religious interest. A good deal of mankind's contemporary reflection revolves around this point. If God is the transcendent, the nonanthropomorphic, the ever Other, the interrogative pronoun, the question, the search, the road ever open and beyond, a suspicion enters the mind of Man: At bottom is he not really questioning himself rather than interrogating God? Is the question about God in its depth not the question about Man? Is anthropology not the true theology? Is the question about God not the anguished quest or the hope-filled question of Man concerning himself, the meaning of his life and destiny? Is it not really the Self that is sought?

vii. The dialectical process does not end here. At this point Buddhism brings us its contribution. Since there is no appeasing answer to the question about God or Man, no explanation of the meaning of life or the mystery of existence, will silence not then be the true response? Does he alone who knows how to be silent understand the mystery of the real? We have already reached this point in our presentation and even the following point.

viii. As an answer silence remains nonetheless suspect, since every question requires a decision and a choice. Silence can appear cowardly, a lack of courage to take a position and rid oneself of atavisms. If silence is a sign, it is a very weak and vague one. It is acceptable as a transition inasmuch as we dare not destroy all the idols at once, but it does not satisfy the human mind. It is here that our last point appears: silence as a question and not an answer. Man comes to silence the question: It lacks meaning. He no longer asks, he lives and has regained innocence on a higher plane.

ix. This would be the last moment of this sort of dialectical circle. One returns to daily living, as the tenth Zen painting, the seventh mansion of Saint Teresa or any affirmation of nearly every mysticism shows. God is immanent and transcendent, existent and nonexistent; and at the same time he is not. There is nothing more to be said. God is that about which there can be no talk. Discourse on God is basically inauthentic; only in the interior cell where the *logos* is silent can the Father be adored in spirit and truth.

    This is not irrationalism, fideism or religious romanticism: The Buddha leads us by the hand. I would like very briefly to develop his dialectic further.

b. Reduction to the Sublime

In many instances the Buddha does not impose silence, but wins over his adversaries, converting them to his way not by reducing their reasoning to absurdity, but by what I would like to call a reduction to the sublime. It is for this reason that those who come to question him are not only won over but converted, and very often enter the order of the mendicant brothers (*bhikkhu*, in Sanskrit *bhiksu*). Nevertheless, on rare occasions he reveals the dialectic of his thought by directing the attention of his interrogator to the meaning of the question itself.

'When a bhiksu, Sirs, knows thus and sees thus, would that make him ready to take up this question as intelligent (and intelligible)?" he often asks after a long discourse on the absurdity of holding any opinion whatever on the ultimate problems of the human condition.[11]

I would like to analyze just one text. To the question repeated a thousand times in the dialogues of the Buddha concerning the meaning of life, the Buddha answers the monk Rādha in this way:

"Rādha, you can grasp no limit to this question."[12] "That question is beyond the compass of an answer."[13]

But it is worth translating the text in full.

'Thus have I heard:—The Exalted One was once staying near Savatthi, in the Deer Park.

'Then the venerable Rādha came to the Exalted One. Having done so, he saluted the Exalted One and sat down to one side.

'So seated, the venerable Rādha thus addressed the Exalted One:—

"They say, 'Māra! Māra! lord. Pray, lord, how far is there Māra?' "[14]

"Where a body is, Rādha, there would be Māra or things like Māra, or at any rate what is perishing. Therefore, Rādha, regard the body as Māra; regard it as of the nature of Māra; regard it as perishing, as an imposthume, as a dart, as pain, as a source of pain. They who regard it thus rightly regard it.

" And the same is to be said of feeling, perception, the activities and consciousness."

"But rightly regarding, lord,—for what purpose?"

"Rightly regarding, Rādha, for the sake of disgust."

"But disgust, lord—for what purpose it is?"

"Disgust, Rādha, is to bring about dispassion."

"But dispassion, lord—for what purpose is it?"

"Dispassion, Rādha, is to get release."

"But release, lord—what is it for?"
"Release, Rādha, means *Nibbāna*."
"But *Nibbāna*, lord—what is the aim of that?"
"This question, Rādha, goes too far. You can grasp no limit to this question.[15] Rooted in *Nibbāna*, Rādha, the holy life is lived.[16] *Nibbāna* is its goal, *Nibbāna* is its end." '[17]

This is reduction to the sublime. He does not say the question has no meaning. How could he say this when it is the most anguishing question for a good part of mankind and the very torture from which, according to the Buddha himself, he has come to liberate us, the torment of useless anguish and suffering without reason? It is not an absurd question.

It is not a false question either. There are no false questions, properly speaking. It could be contradictory and in that sense false: a question that negates itself in the asking because it is founded on a contradiction. But here this is not the case.

Those who ask this question are not considered weak-minded by the Buddha nor do they sin against logic. The most profound parallel I can find is between the Buddha's attitude and the cry of Jesus: "Father, forgive them for they know not what they do!" When confronting the Absolute, Man truly does not know what he is saying or doing.

Let us imagine the question: 'What is God?' for this is basically the question at issue although *nirvāna* is the problem in the dialogue quoted above. The Buddha answers that the question itself cannot grasp its proper limits, that the question does not know what it is asking. We must be careful in our exegesis. The Buddha does not say the Man who raises the question does not have something very definite in mind when he asks. He believes he knows it. He is asking about the Absolute, about God, about the last things, eternity, *nirvāna*, etc. And he who asks will never be mistaken in his asking. He knows very well what he wishes to know. What is truth? Pilate asked this question of him whom he called 'Man' and he too obtained only silence.

What the Buddha is saying is that the question itself is not capable of defining its limits, that the question asks nothing, for it does not know where the request leads or what it asks for. Suppose I answer the question 'what is God?' by saying 'Mu!' How would I know this answer is not satisfactory if the question itself does not know, and cannot know, what it takes in and what it leaves out? If I ask the color of the stone hidden in Śākyamuni's pocket, I have some idea of the question's limits. I do not know the color of the stone, nor even all the colors, but I do know what a color is and I can distinguish a color from a sound or anything else. And I know that stones have colors. The question, in a word, already contains the answer ontically; the question determines the very level at which the answer is an answer and through which the answer must pass, so to speak. The question fixes the limits of the answer and also gives the conditions of its intelligibility. Only what is possible to ask is asked because the limits of the answer are already known.

For this reason many religious traditions admit that to seek God implies having already found him, to ask about him means, in a way, to know him already. The unquestionable cannot be questioned, and if the Absolute is questionable it is no longer absolute. In other words, a real question about the nature of the Absolute cannot grasp its limits, can offer no criteria by which the answer might be verified, as modern parlance would put it. The question does not know what it is asking; it is not a question.

This comes down to saying that I am asking nothing, and not just nothingness. This in effect destroys the question, for in asking nothing there is no question. All the meaning I find in the question is the meaning I inject into it, a meaning the questioner gives, but certainly not the meaning of the question itself.

And now we near the end of the Buddha's catharsis. The meaning of the question is not the question's meaning, but the meaning the questioner gives it, his anguish, his insecurity, his doubts. He projects into a question a problem the question does not contain and cannot contain or support. So what is to be done?

What the Buddha does is very clear. He makes us understand that the real question destroys itself and in so doing ceases to be a question and frees us to go directly onto the path of deliverance. To be sure, by destroying the question he has also destroyed the questioner, the little ego who had identified himself with his ques-

tion. What is to be done then? To make Man aware of his limits, to
center him on what he can do, not to distract him from his human
task, not to allow him to become dissipated by and in his speculation, to make him lose the ego that would have him believe himself a little God. The Tathāgata repeats his theme constantly: to
show Man the path to deliverance. He removes Man's obsession
with orthodoxy in order to return him to *orthopraxis*, to the
eightfold path that leads him to liberation because it eliminates
the obstacles—the contingency—and is not preoccupied with the
rest.

Must we then renounce all intelligibility? Neither the Buddha
nor Buddhism would say that. I have just sought the dialectic of
the matter: The very question destroys itself as a question. But
this is an existential operation in which reason by itself can do
very little. How does one silence the *logos*? Certainly the *logos*
does not silence itself. The *logos* must not be silenced outright, it
must simply recognize that there is a gate it must not cross, that it
can eat of all the fruits of paradise save one: God cannot be
named. Much more: Man must recognize that there is no need to
name God, that the question is not even raised and that, if raised,
it shows I am falling into the *hybris* of believing myself to be a
little God who can question God and ask him to justify or explain
himself.

These are all metaphors. The question is raised as well at the
altogether deeper level of being and Being. God certainly *is* not in
any sense we can give this concept. But the Buddha does not say
it in this way for he never loses sight of the existential and personal level on which he speaks. He sets forth no theory. The
problem of God does not lie in the realm of theory. It does not
belong to the realm of the word, but to the kingdom of silence.

I would answer our philosophical query in this way on behalf
of the Buddha: The principle of sufficient reason forbids us to
name God in any way whatsoever.

The new question would be: Is the Man who no longer questions still a Man, or has he become an angel? or a beast? Is pure
quest not the quintessence of the *humanum*?

The Buddha does not reduce the word to silence, nor does he

speak of a word of silence; rather he helps us discover the silence of the word: *The Buddha smiles!*

4. THREE REMAINING PROBLEMS AND ONE HYPOTHESIS

Is it still meaningful to speak of God when one has understood what the Buddha says? Can we consider the name of God a stage in the awakening of human consciousness? Can there be faith without an object?

Can we regain lost innocence? Is salvation possible without thought of God? Can Man cease to raise the ultimate and definite question?

Would the Buddha agree with someone who does not speak of God, but who adds that the word (*logos*), the image (*icon*), is the pole required for dialogue and is called 'Man'? Can there be a cross-fertilization between silence and the word? Would it be the smile? The lurking hypothesis is the following. Since that extraordinary affirmation of Aristotle,[18] transformed by Augustine,[19] commented on in his own way by Lessing[20] and underscored by Heidegger,[21] the West seems to see the human condition as the constant search asking what Being is: Man is a questioning being.[22] Since the no less extraordinary affirmation of the Buddha, matched by the Upanishads, the Tao and later traditions, the East seems to see the human condition as the ontological confidence in a Reality that has No-way of approach: Man is real when he shares in that Reality which does not allow for the alienation that the mere questioning would create. Man realizes his proper status only when all words have been spoken and he re-enters into the Silence.

NOTES
1. SB I, 4, 5, 8-12.
2. Cf. R. Panikkar, *El Silencio del Dios* (Madrid: Guadiana, 1970). The reader will find the appropriate scholarly notes and historico-religious apparatus in this work.

3. Ex. 20:7. The translation of the Jerusalem Bible is very significant: "You shall not utter the name of Yahweh your God to *misuse* it, for Yahweh will not leave unpunished the man who utters his name to *misuse* it." The Vulgate gives: "Non assumes nomen Domini Dei tui *in vanum*: nec enim habebit insontem Dominus eum, qui assumpserit nomen Domini Dei sui frustra" (emphasis added). The Septuagint uses the same expression in both cases. Cf. as points of reference: Lev. 19:12, 24:16; Deut. 5:11; Sir. 23:9; Mt. 5:33-35; Jas. 5:12.

4. Gen. 32:29: "Cur quaeris nomen meum?" Cf. M. Eckhart's commentary in I *Expos. Genes.* Opera Omnia: Lat. Werke (Stuttgart: Kohlhammer, 1938), vol. I, 95-96, nn. 298-300.

5. Cf. Jg. 13:18: "Cur quaeris nomen meum, quod est mirabile," and the relation that Christian thought has found between these two texts and those of Ps. 8:1 and 9, and Is. 9:6; etc. The Jerusalem Bible translates 'mirabile' (θαυμαστόν) as 'mysterious', the OAB 'wonderful'.

6. I can't resist the temptation to quote the 'Buddhist' answer of Jesus in refusing to say by what authority he acted, when even the 'chief priests and the elders of the people' did not know if the Baptism of John was by heaven or by Man. Cf. Mt. 21:23-27.

7. The fourteen propositions that the tradition attributes to the Buddha and that he refuses to uphold are the following:
1-4:   the world is/is not/is and is not/neither is nor is not/finite in time;
5-8:   the world is/is not/is and is not/neither is nor is not/finite in space;
9-12:   the Tathāgata exists/does not exist/exists and does not exist/ neither exists nor does not exist/after death;
13-14:   the soul is/is not/identical with the body.

8. Cf. *L'Analyse du langage théologique. Le nom de Dieu*, edited by E. Castelli (Paris: Aubier, 1969), p. 22.

9. Even if these texts were not spoken by Gautama himself, they are ancient texts of the purest Buddhist tradition.

10. Cf. the contributions of Bettina Bäumer, 'Le nom secret dans l'hindouisme', and Marina Vesci, 'Ka, le nom de Dieu comme pronom interrogatif dans les Véda. La démythisation du nom de Dieu' in the above-mentioned volume edited by E. Castelli (pp. 135-144, 145-154 respectively), which furnish the details of what is here condensed in a dialectic of nine points. Cf. also my chapter 'Betrachtungen über die monotheistischen und polytheistischen Religionen' in *Die vielen Götter und der eine Herr* (Weilheim Obb., O.W. Barth, 1963), pp. 43-51.

11. Cf. for example, *Mahali-sutta* 16, 19, i.e., *Dīgha-nikāya* VI (16 and 19).

12. *Saṁyutta-nikāya* III, 189. F.L. Woodward (tr.), *The Book of Kindred Sayings*, The Pali Text Society (ed. Mrs. Rhys Davids, London, 1954), vol. II, p. 156.

13. *Saṁyutta-nikāya* V, 218: *Mahā-vagga* IV, 5. *Jaravaggo* 42,

2-Unnabho Brahmano. Cf. the translation of F.L. Woodward, *op. cit.*, vol. V, p. 193:

"Nibbāna, brahmin, is the resort of release."

"But, Master Gotama, what is the resort of Nibbāna?"

"The question goes too far, brahmin. That question is beyond the compass of an answer. The aim of living the holy life, brahmin, is to plunge into Nibbāna. It has Nibbāna for its goal, Nibbāna for its ending."

Here the Pali text says: *ajjha-parām, brāhmaṇa, panham, na-sakkhi parayantam gahetum.* Other texts say: *accasarām* (i.e., transcendental), instead of *ajjhaparām.* The Nalanda edition in Devanāgarī says: *accayāsi.* Cf. the analysis of the text in the following notes.

14. Māra is a mythical personage in the life of the Buddha, the evil one, the tempter and also death.

15. Cf. the Pali: *accayāsi, rādha, panham, nāsakkhi panhassa pariyantam gahetum.* Nalanda edition. The Pali Text Society gives *assa* instead of *accayāsi.*

16. *Nibbāna gadham hi, rādha, brahmacariyam vussati.* It is interesting to note that what translations render as the 'holy life' (pure life, in the text) is *brahmacariyā.*

17. *Saṁyutta-nikāya* III, 187/189 (*Khandha-vagga* II, 1). I have relied on the translation of F.L. Woodward in the volumes of the Pali Text Society, *op. cit.*, III, pp. 155-156.

18. Cf. Arist. Metaph., VII, 2 (1028 b 2-4): καὶ δὴ καὶ τὸ πάλαι τε καὶ νῦν καὶ ἀεὶ ζητούμενον καὶ αεὶ ἀπορούμενον, τὶ τὸ ὄν, τοῦτό ἐστι τίς ἡ οὐσία. "Et quod olim et nunc et semper quaesitum est et semper dubitandum, quid est ens, hoc est quae substantia." "And indeed, that which was searched for since antiquity, but which is also now and always will be, which is at the same time always without a way out [an aporia, in doubt]: that is, what is being? viz. what is substance?"

Heidegger's translation is interesting (and significantly enough he does not quote the second interrogation): "Und so bleibt also von altersher und so auch jetzt und immerfort ein Gesuchtes und damit ein solches, das keine Auswege bietet (dies): was ist das Seiende . . .?"

I may give two standard translations of this "längst vergessenen Satz" (Heidegger): "And indeed the question which was raised of old and is raised now and always, and is always the subject of doubt, viz. what being is, is just the question, what is substance?" (R. McKeon). "Y en efecto, lo que antiguamente y ahora y siempre se ha buscado y siempre ha sido objeto de duda: ¿qué es el Ente?, equivale a: ¿qué es la Substancia?" (V. García Yebra).

19. Cf. his famous "Quaestio mihi factus sum."

20. Cf. his often-quoted passage of *Eine Duplik* that if God would hold in his right hand all truth and in his left the constant struggling for it

he would choose the latter (*Gesammelte Werke*, ed. K. Lachmann and F. Muncker, XIII, 23).

21. Cf. M. Heidegger, *Was heisst Denken?* (Tübingen: Niemeyer, 1954), p. 128, where he quotes Aristotle and refers to his previous comments on the passage in his previous work *Kant und das Problem der Metaphysik*.

22. Cf. Heidegger's *Einführung in die Metaphysik* (1953) (Tübingen: Niemeyer, 1966): "Die Leidenschaft des Wissens ist das Fragen" (p. 122), and again: "Das Fragen ist die echte und *einzige* Weise der Würdigung dessen, was aus höchstem Rang unser Dasein in der Macht hält" (p. 63; emphasis added). I may copy here my own marginal notes on those two pages wondering about other possible 'Grundhaltungen': "Leidenschaft des Wissens oder des Noch-nicht wissens? Es gibt keine letzte Frage (es wäre ein Widerspruch), es gibt aber eine *sancta ignorantia*." And "Warum nicht die Anbetung? oder die Stille? oder die nichts- und nicht-fragende Beschauung? oder sogar liebender Gehorsam?" To smile is not the same as to laugh!

Heidegger would probably agree that the "Leidenschaft des Fragens" and "das Fragen als ein Grundgeschehnis des geschichtlichen Seins" (p. 109) belongs to the "Grundstellungen des Geistes des Abendlandes" (p. 89) and cannot be called a human invariant. Or had he second thoughts when he coined that famous phrase at the very end of his lecture 'Die Frage nach der Technik': "Denn das Fragen ist die Frömmigkeit des Denkens"? (*Vorträge und Aufsätze* [Pfullingen: Neske, 1954], vol. I, p. 36).

Or again would Heidegger say that *Besinnung* is the wisdom I have been speaking about when he concedes that such contemplation "den Charakter des Fragens verliert und zum einfachen Sagen wird"? (*op. cit.* p. 62). That Heidegger was almost obsessed with the question of the question is patent since the first pages of *Sein und Zeit*. Cf. also the last sentences of *Der Satz vom Grund* (Pfullingen: Neske, 1957), both the course (p. 188) and the lecture (p. 211) referring to "die Frage". And yet later on (December 1957) he quotes again the same sentence, "Questioning is the piety of thinking," and adds that this phrase is already in the wake of what I would consider his more 'oriental' attitude, namely, "Dass das Fragen nicht die eigentliche Gebärde des Denkens ist, sondern das Hören der Zusage dessen, was in die Frage kommen soll." *Unterwegs zur Sprache* (Pfullingen: Neske, 1975, 5th ed.), p. 175. Is this totally compatible with the by now totally 'Indian' assertion: "Das Denken ist kein Mittel für das Erkennen" (p. 173)? I am saying this because he did not put a full stop after 'Zusage'. And this is what he really says a few pages below (180 sq.). The later Heidegger seems to subscribe to the metaphor: "Das Denken zieht Furchen in den Acker des Seins." (173).

IX.
Advaita and Bhakti.
A Hindu-Christian Dialogue

priyo hi jñānino 'tyartham aham,
sa ca mama priyaḥ

I am much loved by the sage
and he is loved by me.
BG VII, 17

1. INTRODUCTION

A dialogue between Hinduism and Christianity very often gets stuck and cannot proceed further, with the consequent sense of frustration, because of fundamental misunderstandings based sometimes on mutual prejudices or lack of proper knowledge. To mention only a few points: Hinduism is supposed neither to believe in a personal God nor to consider charity the first of religious duties. The concept of Person, which seems essential and indispensable for any exposition of Christian faith, is apparently unknown to the Hindu mind, and so on. From the other side, the more 'realized' Hindu who mostly professes *advaita*[1] considers Christianity an inferior religion because it takes God to be essentially the 'other', allowing no union or identification with him. For the *advaitin* the concept of person would seem secondary, and so applying it to the Absolute is tantamount to idolatry.

These problems are certainly more than semantic—although fundamental terminological clarifications are urgently needed before a real dialogue can take place. The following letter hopes simply to show some implications of such a dialogue, which I have called an 'intrareligious dialogue', as distinguished from an interreligious one.[2] 'Dialogue' is not just an external meeting with somebody who has other ideas than I have. Dialogue in the real sense arises precisely where I (or we) discover the same currents and problems within the religion of the 'other' as I (or we) find in my (or our) own religious world. In this chapter I do not intend to talk about the Hindu's opinions or the Christian's ideas, but rather to enter straight into the problem at hand—love and identity, certainly one of the major issues in a Hindu-Christian dialogue. In this way, we can help each other face our own, sometimes hidden problems from a new perspective. For example, the authentic nondualistic experience of the *advaitin* represents a challenge to the Christian's doctrine or experience of the Trinity and may very well lead us to discover important new aspects of the same mystery.[3]

In this case I have chosen the opposite example, namely the challenge that the notion that God is Love, with all its implications, represents to an *advaitin* who claims to be beyond all dualisms and therefore—since love seems to presuppose dualism—also beyond love. This problem is primarily an internal matter for Hinduism, which in its main devotional trends is a religion of love (*bhakti*), and in its more contemplative and philosophical aspects a religion of knowledge (*jñāna*) (the latter claiming superiority over the former).

2. A LETTER FROM VRNDĀVAN

In a long conversation in Vrndāvan, the birth place of Krsna[4] and the town 'consecrated' to *bhakti*, I had a heart-to-heart dialogue with a fellow pilgrim in which we examined the question whether *bhakti* was justified in an *advaitin*. The following are some of the ideas suggested by our discussion.

a. Advaita

The common answer to the problem, which we quickly dealt with and dismissed, is that *bhakti* is only a first step to *jñāna*: Until the ultimate intuition dawns, one can do no better than follow the path of devotion. This is a typical *advaitic* answer; *bhakti* is no more than a preparation for *jñāna*, to be given up as soon as the latter is attained.

A second, equally traditional answer, is that the true *jñānin*[5] does not believe in *bhakti* for himself, but fulfills its requirements for others, as Śaṅkara is said to have performed the funeral rites for his mother, or as the priest functions at ceremonies that are for the people. But this is not quite satisfactory, particularly for that type of *advaita* that does not wish to ignore the radical claim of love. Is there a place then for love in a true *advaitin*'s heart?

Here my partner in the dialogue told me of a *sādhu*[6] who had come to Vṛndāvan because he had realized that the very structure of the only One is love, and that it is charged with a dynamic life; that love is indeed only another name for the experience of the Absolute. It is known that the *advaitic* experience is one of the void, but can it not also take the form of love? The same *sādhu* explained that he had given everything away, and told how over-whelmed he was with love and joy—so much so that once, when bathing in the Yamuna, he was even tempted to put an end to his life, letting it go, as it were, in the current of the river. Afterwards he did not know why he had not done so; he felt it was because he was not ready for it, not mature enough. The contrast was obvious: While the *advaitin* has by his very experience overcome time and also death, the *bhakta* wants to throw his life away as an act of complete surrender.

A third point suggested itself here. If love is not to be an empty word, it implies a certain tension between the lover and the beloved, or at least a certain distance between them. In fact, *bhakti* etymologically means either separation (from *bhañj*) or dependence (from *bhaj*). But there is yet more for us to consider.

The apperception of Being as crystallized love seems to lead to the experience of its structure as universal love, an outpouring of love without regard for the objects on which it is lavished: in other words, an all-embracing love for everything that has even a spark of Being in it. But is love only an inherent harmony, or is there not in it still another element? Can it exist without a certain affective dynamism? Does it not demand a special I-thou relation-ship in which the particular thou cannot be exchanged for any other? And is there really room for such particularized and per-sonal love in *advaita*?

It seems that the genuine experience of human love is not satisfied with involvement with the other as other in a general sense—in which the other is ultimately reduced to the self—but that it needs the other as a *particular* other, personal and unre-peatable. Every real love is unique: Where then is the place for universality? Can *advaita* admit the particular? Has the love of a mother for her child, for instance, or that of a Man for his beloved, an ultimate value? Can any *advaitin* feel such love? Will friendship find a place in heaven, that is, in God?

An *advaitin* can love everything: His affection, unconditioned by *nāma-rūpa* (name and form)[7] can embrace everything; for everything, insofar as it is, is the Self, and thus lovable. But is this love *real*? Can we apply the term 'love' to something that makes an abstraction of all that I have, and that in a way eliminates my person—so that my ego possesses nothing that can attract the lover, be given as a gift, or earn the devotion of the beloved? What lover or beloved would be satisfied with a love without eyes and face? Or are these merely anthropomorphic images with no ultimate significance?

The classic *advaitic* answer is well known: One does not love someone—say friend, wife or husband—for his or her own sake but for the sake of *ātman*.[8] Love is all there is; no lover or beloved—all distinction between them is blotted out. I feel that there is in this a deep truth—insofar as it answers the need to overcome dualism, but I am convinced that it is not the deepest truth of *advaita*, but rather a pitfall inherent in pure monism. I should think that *advaita* would oppose such pure monism as it opposes all dualism. In what follows I shall try to remain faithful to an intuition of *advaita* that transcends these extremes of monism and dualism.

My doubts, however, were not resolved by any of these traditional answers, and led me to attempt a solution that is perhaps not fully in accord with the atmosphere of Vrndāvan's holy gardens. And yet it is closer to genuine *bhakti* than the words of Yuddhisthira, who in the Mahābhārata is the very king of Dharma: "There can be no liberation for the Man who knows the bond of love (*snehena yukta*)."

And so we came to a fourth point, which alone, like the fourth quarter of *brahman*,[9] allows a full vision of the ultimate—and the ultimate mystery is what we are touching upon here.

If the structure of the ultimate is love, then it is loving Love, or love of love, self-love; in other words, it is like an 'eye' that sees itself, a 'will' that loves itself, a 'being' that pours itself out as 'Being', a 'source' that reproduces itself fully as an identical image, and that later emerges into Being as that which receives the source. The 'image' is the Being. The source of Being, because it is the source, is not Being—but precisely its source. Furthermore, if this dynamism and tension are not to jeopardize the Absolute's total Oneness, the 'mirrored' eye, the generated Being, the identical image does not stop the lavish flow of divine love but returns it again, loving with the same love, answering in the same measure, so that seen from the 'outside', it looks as if nothing had happened in the 'inner life' of the Absolute. Only one who shares in this dynamism can witness the unceasing flow of divine Life: a Love that gives itself up fully and is rescued, as it were, by the total answer of the beloved, returning the love of the Beloved by responding with love.

Now an *advaitin* is one who has realized the absolute nonduality of Being, Reality, the Ultimate, the Absolute—whatever the name we choose to indicate the Ineffable. There is no place for dualism, but there is none for monism either. Dualism cannot be ultimate, because where there are two, there is a relation between them that stands above and is more final than both. Monism cannot be ultimate either because it denies the problem's very assumption; in a pure monism there is no room even for factors like illusion, falsehood, time, a lower level of truth and speech.[10] Here I am not concerned with expounding *advaita* but only with finding out whether it has a place for love.

b. Advaita and Love

Let me put it in this way: An *advaitin* is established in the supreme and unique I (*aham-brahman*). Yet this I, by the very fact of being the I, implies, brings forth a Thou as its necessary counterpart (*alius, non aliud*, the partner—of the I—not another). In simpler terms, the I must somehow be reflected in a Thou, although this Thou is only the production of the I itself and not an external 'other'. In this Thou the I discovers itself, and really is (it, i.e., I). In other words: The Thou is the consciousness that the I not only has but is. In fact, this I knows Himself, but

His Knowledge is none other than the Knower. However, the Knowledge has come to be because the Knower has come out of Himself, as it were, has 'loved' that which by loving He knows to be His (own) knowledge, Himself as known by Himself. He could not know even Himself were He not driven out, or did He not 'despoil' Himself, only to recover Himself immediately in the 'subject' (person), in which He has fully invested Himself. This total gift of Himself is Love. Now we are better equipped to deepen our problematic.

The *advaitin* installed in that I—in the Absolute, who we may say knows and loves Himself—recognizes and loves the sparks of being (which float out of nothing) for what they 'are': 'parts' or 'objects' (though this is an improper use of the words) of that divine Knowledge and Love. He knows and loves 'things' (to use theistic terms) as God knows and loves them, in that unique act by which He knows and loves Himself and in which He associates all that we call beings on earth, whatever nature they may possess. The *advaitin* not only sees everything in the One, he has an intuition of everything as nondual, thus as not forming any kind of second vis-à-vis the only and unique One: *ekam eva advitīam*, 'one only without a second'[11] because no *dvanda*, no pair, no duality can be ultimate. He loves everything in the same way as the unique and universal Love. In extension and degree, the true *advaitin* loves as does the Absolute.

Now a thing, whatever it may be, is insofar as it is known and loved by the absolute Knowledge and Love. As already said, things are nothing if not crystallizations of divine Love. A thing is not only insofar as it is loved; it is that very love itself. In itself it is nothing. If a thing were not sheer nothingness it could not be the pure 'recipient' of that unique loving act of the Absolute I. Now because this divine act constitutes that very thing, the integral thing, i.e., the thing including its origin is the whole I, the total and indivisible Love. Seen with respect to itself alone, i.e., as the 'thing' in 'itself', it is a limited image of a boundless love, just as the whole sun is reflected, although not completely, in each piece of a broken mirror.

Now if this were to be expressed in theistic terms, it would be meaningless to say that God loves one thing more than another not only because the 'more' makes no sense with reference to God, but also because it is equally senseless with respect to the 'things' themselves. If God loved a thing a little *more* than He actually does, that 'thing'—as the crystallization of divine love—would cease to be what it is and instead be another 'thing'—the other thing with that plus.

Let us now consider the concrete question of the place of common human love in the heart of an *advaitin*. First of all, whimsical affection due to psychological or aesthetic causes must be eliminated; only that which has an ultimate ontological justification is admissible. In other words, we must either link human love with the very center of the Absolute or admit that *bhakti* is not on the same footing as *jñāna*.

I love my mother, friend, wife or son with a love that is not interchangeable. I do not love my beloved just because she is 'mother' or 'friend', but because it is *her*. No other mother would do, only *the* beloved can quench the thirst of the lover; there can be no substitute. Love does not admit indifference. Everything in the beloved is different and unique. Further, I do not love my 'mother' or 'friend' because it is *my* 'mother' or 'friend', but because of herself (in that she also is *brahman*). The Upaniṣad is right: It is for the sake of the *ātman*, the Self, but this *ātman* is neither her soul nor mine, nor different from us both.

Now the difficulty lies here. In the love of *advaitin* the problem does not even arise: He loves the other as other, the thou as that particular thou, experienced like an ultimate, with the consequent danger of idolatry. That is why in a dualistic context there is a certain antagonism between the love of God and the love of a creature, and dualistic religion stresses the necessity of loving the creature for God's sake. *Advaitic* love is incompatible with this dichotomy. If I love my beloved I cannot love him or her because of himself or herself, nor because of God. I must love her with the identical love with which I love the Ultimate; to be more precise, that same current of Love that sweeps me into the love of the Absolute makes me love my beloved as that spark of the Absolute which she truly is. Even more: Putting it in theistic terms, the love of the *advaitin* for his beloved is indeed the Love of God for both the beloved and the lover.

Person in the context of *advaita* is nothing but the concrete descent—or revelation—of (divine) love. The uniqueness of every person is based in this ever-different, and so unique, love-relation. *Advaitic* love does not love the individual, but the personal, not the 'property' of the beloved, but the divine gift bestowed upon her: that which the beloved does not possess, but is.

c. Advaitic Love

Let me try to describe this love. I love you, my beloved, without any 'why' beyond or any 'because' behind my love; I love you, simply, for in you I discover the Absolute—though not as an object, of course, but as the very subject loving in me. I love you with an inclusive and unique love, which is the current of universal love that passes through you, as it were, for in my love of you universal love is kindled and finds its expression. I love you as you *are*—i.e., insofar as you really are—the Absolute. I do not love you because of myself. This is important: Any egoistic love is incompatible with *advaita*; any kind of concupiscence, be it desire of pleasure, fulfillment, self-assurance, comfort or the like, is excluded. To love you for my own sake would amount to the worst kind of idolatry: egolatry. Any love that aims at enriching me, at complementing me, which, in a word, aims *at* me, may perhaps be a human and even a good love but it is in no sense *advaitic* love. The latter is neither for God's sake, as a foreign motivation for my love, nor—much less—for the *ego*'s sake.

The only love consistent with *advaita* is God's love—in both senses of the expression all in one: 'my' love for Him and 'His' love in me—passing through the creature I love. It is a passionate and true love that is sensitive to the finest, smallest details of true human love, yet it is passive because it is not ego-centered. From the outside it may even appear almost fatalistic. Every lover is taken up, wrapped in his love, overpowered by love. There is love in me and it happens to be directed to this particular person. It is a love that does not kindle in me my love for the Absolute, because it is that love itself which is not different from the Absolute. It is a personal and direct love that passes through me to the beloved, in a way, *making* the beloved to *be*. It is a creative love, because—in theistic terms—it is the very love of God towards a person which makes that person to be. An *advaitin* can love only if the Absolute loves; his love cannot be different.

This description may become a little more complete if we express this love in ontological terms. I love my beloved because my person is installed in the only I, and this I is Love and loves my beloved. In this sense, I 'share' in the love of God for that person. God loves that person personally, i.e., as she is, and so do I. She finds in my love the love of God, she 'feels' somehow that through this love of mine she is loved. And now we can perhaps solve the difficulty we mentioned at the beginning: If this is so, and God loves every being, that personal touch inherent in every human love is fully preserved, because though the lover is an 'associate' in God's universal love, he 'shares' the constitutive relation of God's love to his beloved; or, in other words, there is an ontological neighborhood between the lover and the beloved. They are like two moments, or two poles in the infinite love of God. I love my beloved because I am that love of God which makes my beloved to be. There cannot be a more personal love.

No doubt I have been employing terms that can easily be construed as dualistic. I have spoken of the lover and the beloved as two people here on earth and I have taken as example the love between a man and a woman. Yet I have also emphasized that these two subjects cannot be considered as if they were ultimate realities, two poles facing one another. The problem, then, is this: Can I as I am, a human person, love you as you are, another person, or shall I have to give up this notion of personal relationship and simply try to develop a universal and indiscriminate love because any kind of self-assertiveness is incompatible with *advaita*? Precisely here the purifying character of this highest type of love appears more clearly.

Advaitic love must be divine and cosmic, full of 'personality' but devoid of individuality, selfishness, caprice and concupiscence. It is the deepest and strongest love and also the most human because it reaches the core of the human being, its personality, its ontic relationship with God and with another being like itself. It is not a love of an individual's qualities, but of the heart of a person, love of the integral person: body, soul and spirit. It is loving you really as you, a love that both discovers and effects the identity of lover and beloved. Real human love does not consist in gazing at one another but in looking in the same direction, in worshiping together in a unitive adoration. It is not authentic and ultimate unless it is a sacrament—a real symbol of the divine identity discovered in two pilgrim sparks fusing themselves in order to reach the single divine Fire.

At this point, we cannot proceed farther without solving one of *advaita*'s main problems: the status of the person. It may well be that the concept of person needs revising and perhaps deepening, but we must resist attempting even an outline of this here. I wish to mention only one point relevant to our topic, viz., the implication of the Trinity. If God, the Father, is the ultimate I who calls—generates—the Son as His Thou, manifesting and reflecting Him, then the Spirit is not only the personified Love of the Father and the reciprocal self-gift of the Son, but the nonduality (*advaita*) of the Father and Son. In other words, *advaita* applied to the Trinity would mean that there are not three distinct beings (as if this would ever be possible ultimately!) but that the only I loves himself and discovers his nonduality (which is the Spirit) in the (him)self which is the Thou (the Son). The Trinity, on the other hand, applied to *advaita*, would show that nondualism can have room for Love—understood precisely as the inner movement of this 'One without a second' (*ekam eva advitīyam*).

The essence of the person is relationship; my person is nothing but a relation with the I. Properly speaking, the place of my personality is within the single Thou of the unique I. But my person is also related to others, it touches, so to speak, the shores of the reality of other people. My person is also related to my beloved whom I call thou, and this I-thou relationship makes us emerge from nothingness by the power of the life-giving Spirit who is Love. Thus we enter more and more into the Thou of ultimate I who is not different from God Himself. This is the ultimate level of human love and likewise the very condition of its possibility: when the Spirit responds through us to God. Here the personality reaches maturity, which is pure transparency.

Perhaps the last words of the book of *Revelation* may help express the same idea: "The Spirit and the Bride say, Come!",[12] the Bride assuming and symbolizing the Universal transformed into and transparent to Love, which is precisely the Spirit. 'Come' is the call to the Ultimate through Love, to *advaita* through *bhakti*. *Tat tvam asi*.[13] A *Thou* you are, Śvetaketu![14] We are in as far as we are the *Thou*, the *tvam* of the One.

NOTES

1. Advaita Vedānta, based mainly on Śaṅkarācārya's interpretation of the Upaniṣads and the Brahma Sūtras, is one of the Hindu philosophical schools that predominate in many spiritual circles today. It understands itself as the culmination of all religions and philosophies insofar as it leads to and interprets the 'ultimate experience' of nonduality, i.e., the essential non-separability of the Self (*ātman*) and 'God' (*brahman*). Among the three classical 'ways' of salvation in Hinduism, *karma* (works), *bhakti* (adoration and surrender) and *jñāna* (meditative knowledge), this school represents the last. In fact, 'realization' or 'liberation' is said to be reached only by an intuitive consciousness. *Advaita* (as differentiated from Advaita Vedānta) would be the fundamental principle of nondualism (*a-dvaita:* nonduality), devoid of its connections with the rest of the Vedāntic philosophical garb.

2. Cf. R. Panikkar, *The Intrareligious Dialogue* (New York: Paulist Press, 1978), chapter IV.

3. Cf. R. Panikkar, *The Trinity and the Religious Experience of Man* (London: Darton, Longman & Todd and Maryknoll, New York: Orbis Books, 1973).

4. Kṛṣṇa, the divine shepherd, is one of the main earthly manifestations of God (Viṣṇu). He is especially worshipped in Vrindaban (Vṛndāvan) where he is said to have performed his play of love with Men.

5. *Jñānin* is a follower of the path of knowledge (*jñāna*).

6. Hindu monk.

7. *Nāma-rūpa* stands for the limitation of the relative existence. For *advaita*, the Ultimate is beyond any name and form, but for *bhakti*, both are manifestations of the Divine (especially as the name of God and his image).

8. Cf. BU II, 4, 5.

9. According to MandU (esp. 3-7), there are four states in the Absolute, symbolized by the waking, dreaming and the deep sleep state (these three being conditioned), whereas the fourth (*turīya*) is beyond any conditioning.

10. Cf. the *pāramārthika* and the *vyāvahārika* of the school.

11. Cf. CU VI, 2, 1.

12. Rev. 22:17.

13. CU VI, 8, 7 sq.

14. Cf. R. Panikkar, *The Vedic Experience* (Berkeley and Los Angeles: University of California Press, 1977), pp. 747–753.

X.
The Supreme Experience:
The Ways of East and West

na saṁsārasya nirvāṇāt kiṁcid
asti viśeṣaṇam

There is no difference whatever between
temporality and eternity.
Nāgārjuna
Mādhyamika-kārikā XXV, 19 (+)

+ *Saṁsāra* is *nirvāṇa* and *nirvāṇa* *saṁsāra* because there can be no
place for any difference, which would appertain to either the one or
the other. Cf. the meditation on Being and beings and on the famous
relatio rationis of the Vedāntic and Christian Scholastics.

In order to expose with a certain order the core, and obviously only the core, of the question, we shall consider first the meaning of *experience*, second what *supreme* can possibly mean in this case and third, some of the different ways to express it. Were I to follow a more congenial way of putting the problem I would simply say: The *Myth*, the *Logos* and the *Spirit*.

1. THE PROBLEM OF EXPERIENCE

a. Prolegomena

The question about the nature and value of experience arises the very moment we begin to think about our experience. But then we no longer experience: We think. Or more generally expressed, the awareness *of* an experience is not the experience. Furthermore, an experience cannot be experienced again: It would be another experience. Experiencing, unlike thinking, does not allow for self-reflection. This is both its strength and its weakness. By experience we understand any immediate contact with reality. The perfect experience would mean no difference, no distinction whatsoever between the experiencing subject and the experienced object.

To situate the place of experience in human life, without claiming to state a full-fledged anthropological theory, we may assume that Man has three organs or groups of organs relating him with reality. *Sensory* consciousness relates us by means of our sense organs to what we could call the material part of reality. *Intellectual* consciousness opens us up to the intelligible world, to that web of relations which gives consistency to the material world and which we cannot equate with mere matter. *Mystical* consciousness identifies us in a special way with the very reality it opens up to us; it involves the total subject. Whatever name we may use to describe them, and no matter what interpretation we may give to the 'reality' opened up in each case, there seems little doubt about the existence of these three levels of consciousness. Further, there would not seem to be much disagreement in saying that these three orders of consciousness are ultimately not independent windows but three dimensions, different forms—the sensory, intellectual and mystical—of one and the same primordial consciousness.

The senses are not only 'knowing' instruments, acting tools, they are also part of the very reality they disclose. Neither is the intellect only a knowing mind; it is also an acting will. The intellectual web of reality is not just an individual's private property, but a commonality in which Men participate. Mystical consciousness is not mainly a source of knowledge but an aspect of reality itself, which discloses itself when it hits, as it were, a particular subject.

There is no need to interpret what has been said so far in an epistemic realistic sense. It also has meaning and validity within other epistemologies and within more than one metaphysical system. We do not affirm here what reality is or whether these human experiences are 'objectively' true or not. We only offer a general pattern that can be interpreted in many different ways. What has been stressed however is the unitary character of this trinity, i.e., the fact that any conscious human act has to a greater or lesser degree these three dimensions. When we call a human act a sensory activity or an intellectual action or a mystical awareness we are actually reducing, i.e., considering only one aspect of a more complex and unitary fact, which includes the sensual, intellectual and mystical all in one. Abstraction is needed, but we should not forget that we have been abstracting.

We could thus call consciousness that bridge, following the upaniṣadic metaphor (or that light, following the biblical one), that connects the two shores of reality or the two poles of the real: the subject and the object, the inside and the outside. The link established by the bridge (or made possible by the light), namely consciousness, is of three kinds: the sensory, the intellectual and the mystical—or as I call them elsewhere the cosmic, the human and the divine. In point of fact these three dimensions of consciousness are also the three dimensions of reality: The first dimension is the condition for acting, the second allows understanding and the third being. So much for consciousness.

Now if the concept of consciousness may be used to stress the overall character of this process and its supra-individual aspect, the concept of experience stands for the distinctive feature of the individual having or sharing in that consciousness. If consciousness is something in which we share, experience is something peculiar to each of us. We may almost say that by definition experience is the particular way one shares in a given state of consciousness. With these clarifications we may proceed to describe what can be understood by supreme experience.

b. The Empirical, the Experiment and the Experience

The entire history of human civilization could be envisioned as the playing of a single (musical) theme in three variations (the empirical, the experiment and the experience). The theme is personal realization, or playing on the common etymology of the variations themselves, the 'attempt' to integrate ourselves into reality by taking the 'risk' of 'undergoing' the 'trial' of 'passing through' whatever process is required.[1] It is obvious that this expertise, which is gained only in the 'crossing', the 'ferrying', of temporal reality, cannot be measured in chronological periods, either individually or societally. We call them *kairological* moments.

There is a first period in the history of mankind (one is tempted to say there is equally a first period in the development of human consciousness) in which (given) data are uncritically assumed and taken as bare facts. What is given, especially what is given to our senses, is taken as real. The empirical here does not only mean sense-knowledge. The philosophically uncritical mind also takes for granted what appears to it as given. And the spiritual vision is equally unreflective. This is the ecstatic vision, the overwhelming presence of the object in which the subject is utterly forgotten. It is the awareness of presence without the slightest cloud of self-awareness. In religion, philosophy and art we could substantiate this period by recalling the beginnings of almost any culture. This primacy of data is still visible in the last of human activities to handle the real. The natural sciences, in fact, are still almost in ecstasies under the spell of the data, here called scientific facts.

The second moment is represented by the predominance of the experiment. A certain doubt about the value of objectivity has crept in; Man has become more self-conscious and realizes that he cannot leave the acting subject untouched and unreflected upon. The doubt has to be checked by abandoning the passive attitude of the contemplator and taking a more active and aggressive approach: the experiment, the trial, the test, intervention in the object itself. This is the period of critical awareness, and it reverberates on all three levels of consciousness. The experimental sciences make their appearance. In order to know what a thing is, mere observation is not considered enough. The experiment is not limited to the object alone; it is also performed on the subject itself: Man begins to analyze the human mind and the whole spiritual organism. To the physical experiments in the natural sciences correspond the internal experiments of critical philosophy and the psychological introspection of the mystics. The European Renaissance offers a typical example: a flourishing of experimentation on all levels of consciousness. Not only are human and celestial bodies examined, but the human mind and spirit are also submitted to the scrutiny of experimentation. One and the same wind blows through Leonardo da Vinci, Luther, Servet, Saint Teresa, Galileo and Descartes, to mention only a few names from very different fields.

The third moment is the result of this continuing process. Man has lost confidence in empirical data; he asks for the criteria of truth and verification and is ready to accept only what he sees for himself. But the experiment is still too impersonal, too objective; it relies too much on the methods of the experimenter, it still requires a certain confidence in the skill, awareness and judgment of others. But by now Man is not satisfied with anything unless he experiences it himself. Only personal experience cannot err; only if he has the experience himself will he be convinced it is the case. The empirical is pure objectivity, the experiment blends the object with subjectivity, and the experience abolishes any kind of objectivity not assumed and integrated into subjectivity. Anyone today who seeks an experience of whatever kind—biological, psychological, scientific or religious—is saying he simply does not care for objectivity or for how others see, judge or sense things. He has to be personally involved, i.e., has to undergo the experience. And one cannot have an experience by proxy.

c. The Myth

Experience implies as a consequence not only an untransferable and personal contact with the experienced object, but it also excludes any intermediary, any third party that would render the experience impossible by turning it into an experiment through its instrumentation. This implies, further, that any authentic experience excludes any consciousness of distance between the object and the subject, so that the object is no longer seen as such, but is totally united with or plunged into the subject.

The difference between knowing about pain or God or love and experiencing pain, God or love is obvious. My ideas about any object can be corrected, checked, changed and eventually abandoned as inaccurate or wrong. There is a distance between the subject and the object that permits modifying the object without endangering the subject. Not so with experience, as long as it is my experience. When I experience pain there is no possible doubt that I am in pain, even if I am convinced that there is no organic or external or intellectual reason for it. I can doubt whether to make this or that choice as long as I am guided by anything short of experience. I may have to ponder and decide according to common sense, instinct, reason or the like as long as I do not have an experience that renders any further doubt or hesitation impossible. When experience dawns, it is incontrovertible.

What we must underscore here is not the analysis of the experience but its mythical character, which amounts to recognizing its primordial irreducibility. Any experience—sensory, intellectual or spiritual—in fact functions as a myth. To begin with, it performs the same role and presents the same structure. Myth, like experience, enables us to stop somewhere, to rest in our quest for the foundations of everything. Otherwise there would be a *regressus in infinitum*. You cannot go beyond a myth, just as you cannot go beyond experience. If you could, you would lose both the myth and the experience. Neither allows for further explanation. The moment you explain a myth it ceases to be myth; just as explaining an experience is no longer the experience. Neither allows for 'be-causes' and 'therefores'. They are ultimate. Any demythologization destroys the myth as any explanation destroys the experience. Both myth and experience are taken for granted when they are actually taken as myth and experience. They go without saying. If you feel the need for some justification they have ceased to be what they were. Neither mythical consciousness nor experiential consciousness allows room for critical self-awareness. It is their opposite pole. If metaphysics implies self-awareness and if philosophy is critical knowledge, then myth and experience are neither metaphysics nor philosophy. But perhaps the latter rely and are based on the former.

Both myth and experience present the same structure. In myth as in experience there is no distance between the subject and the object. You are in the myth as you are in the experience, you live in them, or rather you live them. You believe in the myth as you believe in the experience, without being aware that you do. Similarly, both present a kind of receding structure, i.e., they do not disappear altogether when challenged or endangered. When visited by the *logos* probing their validity or justification, they simply retrocede, they recede to a deeper level, to another region still untouched by the invading light of critical reason or the rational mind. The relations between science and religion offer constant examples of such strategic retreats.

Our main concern, however, is not to sketch their resemblances, but to point out that experience is a very peculiar form of myth. What we would like to do now is to tell the myth of the experience, i.e., the story of the human being believing that he has direct contact with reality, that he can participate not only in the ontic celebration of beings, but also in the ultimate worship of Being, that he has an immediacy that vouches for a direct contact with the real, so that once he has reached the experiential level he can stop and rest. The myth of the experience is another more subtle form of the myth of heaven and the celestial paradise. It is a sublimated form of the myth of the ultimate.

It should be stressed here that myths do not need to be overcome. When we overcome one myth, another creeps into its place, though perhaps on a deeper level. The process of demythologization so popular nowadays is really the dynamic of *trans*mythicization, a kind of mythical metamorphosis where obsolete and anachronistic myths yield to more modern and up-to-date myths.[2] Obviously, these new myths, like the old myths for those who believed in them, are not seen as myths by the new believers.

We may summarize this first section by saying that any experience is to be considered ultimate because experience means immediate contact with the real and, hence, that there is no possibility of going beyond it without destroying the experience.

2. THE QUEST FOR THE SUPREME EXPERIENCE

Human history, both collective and personal, proves that what was once considered to be ultimate or immediate is later discovered to be mediated and thus neither final nor ultimate. Innocence is lost the moment one is deceived. What then is the value of experience when you can no longer believe that the experience is going to be the last one, final and definitive? In other words, what happens to experience once it is demythologized? The process is worth analyzing. No genuine experience can have extrinsic criterion of its validity or authenticity. An experience is self-validating or it is no experience at all.

How then can an experience be the foundation of anything? What happens if I do not share your experience? Or again, what is the value of the experiences mankind has had that, so history shows, have triggered movements of all sorts, religious, philosophical, social, political? What about the experiences of the Buddha, Jesus, Muhammad? What is the value of our personal experiences when they are gone or have changed? How can we rely on experiences?

We cannot answer all these interrogations here; but keeping them in mind, we will concentrate on our concrete issue: the value of the ultimate experience.

Now we have two logical possibilities. Either we say that the experience remains the same, even when we see it changing, or appeal to the historical dimension of Man. In the first hypothesis the change is said to have taken place in the interpretation of the experience, not in the experience itself. In the second hypothesis we must renounce any possible objective criterion. In other words, either we say that the experience is atemporal (and thus everlasting), though our interpretation depends on the cultural level, the historical moment, etc., or we affirm that the experience is intrinsically temporal, which amounts to saying that Man, and eventually reality itself, is essentially temporal.

The first hypothesis, affirming that the experience remains the same, has the obvious difficulty of stating a fact for which there is no direct evidence whatsoever; it is an a priori derived from a certain world view. The second hypothesis, stating that all is inserted in a temporal flux, has the inconvenience of seeming to fall into total anarchy, for there seems to be no guarantee that human experience will offer any coherence and continuity along the temporal line. There is no reason why what is experienced today as positive, valuable and immediately evident will not appear tomorrow as utterly untenable.

Is there any way out of the dilemma? Must we choose either the timeless rigidity of everlasting values or the chaotic revolution of sheer relativism? The quest for the supreme experience seems to be relevant here; it could serve as an example of how the apparently most abstract and theoretical speculation can have practical and concrete relevance. Among other questions, are we not asking whether there is a middle way between the Maoist constant revolution and the liberal or capitalistic solution of unchanging abstract principles that take care of themselves if only allowed to develop unhindered? Are we not asking if this middle way exists without being either a betrayal (of one of them) or a compromise (between the two)? But before tackling problems of such moment, we should go back to our philosophical analysis of human experience.

a. The Experience, Its Expression and Interpretation

We should not too hastily assume that an experience is totally independent of its expression, or that its interpretation is irrelevant to the experience itself. Even if this were the case, it is not an evident case.

One of the most common affirmations regarding this sort of problem is to repeat time and again that the authentic experience is ineffable, that those who know do not speak and those who speak do not know. It may be that no words can communicate what it is, but not all communication needs be verbal. To affirm that some reality is unthinkable amounts to implicitly recognizing that thinking does not exhaust the realm of being. To assert that the ultimate experience leaves all beings behind amounts to confessing that beings are a relative reality, and that the spatial metaphor of the 'beyond' points toward something real, if the word real can still be used in this context.

Secondly, we have to become aware of the implications of the dichotomy between the experience and its expression. We understand by expression the manifestation of the experience, its first emanation *ad extra*, its first result as it were, so that the act of the experience cannot be said to be a solipsistic act with no repercussion or irradiation outside itself. Finally we must also distinguish the expression from its interpretation, this latter being the intellectual explanation of the experience as it is understood by our intellect.

If we accept the three levels of consciousness mentioned earlier, we can see an interesting correlation with these three facets of experience. On the one side there is a correlation between the interpretation and intellectual consciousness. The expression or manifestation of the experience would correspond to sensory consciousness. By this latter, we may understand not only the conventional sense organs but our whole body complex, so that the manifestation of the experience does not need to be a word or even a sound but may be its more primordial expression in our whole body, in our terrestrial and temporal life. The expe-

rience itself would correspond to what we called mystical consciousness. If this is the case, then we have also met the difficulty
of the so-called ineffability of the real experience. The experience
would be inexpressible in terms of our sensory and intellectual
consciousness, but would correspond to pure consciousness,
which evidently does not translate itself into another form or take
any other name, being itself the act that gives name and form to
everything.

Be this as it may, we ought to distinguish only so much as not
to break or disrupt the ultimate unity of reality. We should not
lose sight of the underlying unity of the three stages of consciousness and the three modes of realization: the experience, its manifestation and its interpretation. It is here that we should introduce what alone seems adequate to carry the full burden of the
three worlds: the symbol.

By way of summary, we may state that the symbol stands for
the whole of reality as it appears and manifests itself through its
own manifold structure. A symbol is precisely the thing; not the
'thing in itself', which is a mental abstraction, but the thing as it
appears, as it expresses and manifests itself. The symbol of a
thing is neither another thing nor the thing in itself but the very
thing as it manifests itself, as it is in the world of beings, in the
epiphany of the 'is'. Contemporary philosophy speaks of the on-
tologic or transcendental difference (that between beings and
their entity), of the theological or transcendent difference (that of
God and beings), including even the widely so-called ontological
or 'transcendentable' difference (that between beings along with
their entity and Being). We could, analogously, introduce here the
symbolic difference as the *sui generis* difference between the
symbol and its reality. The symbol is not another reality, it is not
another thing, nor the thing as we may imagine it in some nonexistent ideal realm. It is the thing as it really appears, as it really 'is',
in the realm of beings. The symbol is nothing but the symbol *of*
the thing, that is (subjective genitive), the peculiar mode of being
of that very thing which outside its symbolic form *is* not and
cannot *be*, because ultimately being is nothing but symbol. To be
able to discover the symbolic difference, i.e., to discover me as
symbol of myself or, in other words, to realize that my own being

is one of the real symbols of the I (certainly not of my little ego), could perhaps be called one of the ways to reach the supreme experience.

The symbolic difference, which overcomes the epistemic dichotomy between subject and object and the metaphysical one between thing and appearance, leads us to consider the relationship between the three levels of consciousness: the experience, its expression and its interpretation. The mystic runs the danger of clinging to the experience while neglecting the other two elements; the philosopher is tempted to identify the interpretation with the real 'thing', and the man of action risks the pitfall of mistaking the expression or manifestation for the whole of reality. Only a balanced and harmonic interplay of the three levels can help us to gain an integral awareness of the real. The symbolic difference stands for this attitude that does not reduce reality to only one of its many sides. It chooses neither the subject nor the object, but mediates via the symbol. But we must not now pursue this tangent farther, important as it is; we take up again the main thread of our story.

b. The Loss of the Subject

Let me ask a simple question: When do I begin to doubt the validity of my experience? If our description of experience is correct, there can only be one answer: I doubt the validity of my experience only when I cease to have that experience. As long as I have an experience I cannot doubt it. I begin to doubt when I begin to wonder whether what I am having is an experience or not. This occurs in the first place when I realize the experience as experience: When experience becomes aware of itself as experience, it ceases to be pure experience and becomes the reflexive consciousness of that experience. The experience of prayer, like the experience of pain, like the experience of love, is incompatible with the awareness that I am having that experience. In other words, when the *logos* enters into the experience, empowering that sort of self-awareness peculiar to the intellect, then the experience is no longer pure experience. Pure light dazzles, pure pain is numbing, pure prayer is mute, pure attention is unguarded, pure ecstasis is unconscious.

Let us imagine we are having an aesthetic experience contemplating the beauty of a landscape. The moment I become aware that I am having such an experience or that it is through the eye that I am seeing and having the experience, the real experience is lost to me. I have become aware of an intermediary that I did not consider before. Or, rather, there was no intermediary until I became conscious of one. The intermediary peephole through which I see at the same time separates what it unites. In a word, no critical awareness is capable of being an experience because it belongs to criticism to be conscious of itself.

We could prolong and deepen this analysis, but our thrust is already clear. The main question now is familiar to most cultures and religions: Is there any possible experience that excludes this destructive self-awareness? Might there be an experience in which the self that experiences is the same as the experience itself? We have already seen that in any real experience the object is lost. The ultimate experience would then be that experience in which the subject is equally lost. We should not, at this stage, commit the methodological mistake of trying to describe such an experience by relying on a particular interpretation of its contents, say in a theistic world view. We have to remain on purely formalistic grounds. Nevertheless we might describe it by leaning on a particular tradition for our terminology but without implying any allegiance to that particular way.

If I see the landscape or smell the flower or think the thought or will the action or understand the situation, I may have an experience of these objects when they merge into me so that there is no longer any distinction. But there is always the possibility of 'coming back', as a certain mysticism would say. This is so because although in the experience the object is lost in the subject, this latter is not lost, nor is the identification total in either direction (the object is not totally subsumed in the subject and vice versa). How can I see (understand, discover) that seeing (understanding, discovering) by which all the rest becomes seen (understood, discovered)?

By what would one know the knower? The difficulty is clear: You cannot see the seer of seeing, you cannot think the thinker of thinking. How could you know the knower? The knower you might eventually know would by this very fact no longer be the knower but what is 'known' by you. To be sure, there is one way the question might be answered. Not by knowing the knower or understanding the understander, but by being oneself the knower and understander. This is the only way in which the experience does not cancel itself; not merely by reaching identification with the object experienced but by becoming the experience itself, the knower, the understander.

In this sense, the supreme experience is neither supreme nor experience. It is not supreme because it is not superior or the first among many. It is not experience either because there is no subject experiencing an object.

c. The Ultimate Experience

If all that has been said so far makes some sense, the supreme experience will be synonymous with pure consciousness, and pure consciousness will stand for the core of reality inasmuch as only consciousness makes room for plurality of the sense-experience, the multiplicity of the intellectual-experience, and the ambiguity of the mystical-experience. Consciousness and consciousness alone allows the many and the one to blend harmoniously: The many states of consciousness and the fact of being conscious of the multiplicity does not make consciousness multiple; on the contrary, it reinforces its primordial oneness.

The supreme experience then, would be that experience that is so identified with reality itself that it is nothing but that reality. It is not the highest among the experiences; it does not experience anything. It recovers lost innocence in a way that is not even comparable to the original. The original innocence had no knowledge of good and evil, nor any experience of the manifold in its excruciating diversity, division and tension. It was a kind of blessed ignorance, what we still today call innocence. The recovery of innocence is, properly speaking, not a recovery, but a creation, a re-creation, a new state that is not 'brand new' because it is not a substitute for a former decrepitude. It is just reality.

The supreme experience is not an experience either, not in

the sense we may use the word in any other case. Not only is the object lost, the subject is also no longer there as substratum or basis for the experience. No one can *have* pure consciousness. It would no longer be pure if it had a foundation in any subject. Neither can it be self-conscious, if we understand by this any type of reflexive self-consciousness. We could rather call it un-self-consciousness precisely because it is mere consciousness: an awareness that it is not aware that it is aware, an infinite ignorance.

One way of describing the supreme experience with the minimum of philosophical assumptions could perhaps take the following form.

Let us begin with any experience, with perhaps the simplest of all: I am touching an object. I have the branch of a tree in my hand, I am pressing and caressing it, I may like to bite it and to smell and taste it eventually. My thinking is absent for the moment and my spiritual awareness as well. I am lost in contact with a bit of nature. This is a sensual experience, but it does not last forever. Perhaps an impertinent fly disturbs my 'distraction', or a fleeting thought crosses my mind or my body reminds me of the hour. I still want to remain in communion with that branch, but I have discovered, first, that neither the object nor the subject was pure, complete or exhaustive. The branch is not the whole tree and much less the whole of nature; my hands and all my senses are not the whole of my being and much less the whole of all other possible subjects. I would like to cling to my branch. I may begin to meditate on it, to concentrate not only my senses but also my mind and even my will on the branch. If I succeed, I may reach another type of experience in which the identification is at once much deeper and much wider. For a moment I may be identified with the branch and if I am lost deeply enough in the branch, my identification might not stop at the branch, but might go on to include the great part of nature, and eventually the whole of vegetal life. For a moment there may be identification between me and all nature. I do not touch a branch, I embrace the entire natural world.

But my experience need not stop here. It may grow in both

directions, losing the object until it reaches the totality and losing the subject until it in its turn reaches so to speak the other pole of the totality. Perhaps with the branch it may be a little difficult, but surely not impossible. I may leave the woods and throw the branch away. But I may equally go back to the branch, although it is no longer just a branch but the whole tree, the entire wood and the universe in its totality, something I cannot touch with my hands or feel with my sentiments, but a concrete mirror and reflection of the whole that I can somehow enter with all my being. I may lose myself in such an experience and perhaps more than one expert will tell me that I have had an experience of nature mysticism. But this is not all. One might assume that I believe in a personal God. This would allow for another type of experience, which some may call the vision of God. For a general description, however, I need not assume that I am a theist or an atheist. I am convinced that the experience may be the same even if the interpretations differ.

Now the contact with the branch may be so intense and profound that I am in contact, not with a bundle of electrons configured as a branch, but with that primordial matter in which all material things share. Entering into immediate contact with this primordial matter I am also in immediate contact with the very ground of being that gives consistency and existence to that primal matter. Some may call it God, some may not. In any case I am in direct contact with the ultimate reality of that branch which has to do ultimately with the same reality underlying everything. We may differ in the use of the word reality, we may disagree inasmuch as I may think that the crucial reality is the distinctive and not the uniting factor. But there is an experience here that as such, i.e., without any claim to metaphysical interpretations, reaches the very boundaries of reality.

This is not yet the supreme experience because it still has to grow into the total universalization of the subject having that experience. Until now I have been *carried away*, as it were; I am lost in the object or the object is lost for me. But I have not yet been *carried above* me so that there is no longer a 'me'. To concentrate on the branch (disregarding for now other possible requirements according to the different schools) and totally lose myself in the entire universe, I also need the action of the ultimate reality of that branch upon me. I need the opposite thrust in order to totally lose myself, my ego, and realize that the subject of the experience is no longer my senses or my mind or my mystical awareness, but something that overwhelms and overcomes me and about which I can only speak later on. It is something that does not leave any room for saying that the experience is in any way mine. In theistic terms I no longer 'see' the branch or the universe, but 'create' it, call it into existence, because it is no longer my *ego* doing this but the divine *I* in which my person is merged and with which my person is united, however we may prefer to express this process. This would be the beginning, the threshold, of the supreme experience. The explanations, the interpretations, may come afterwards. One thing might still be added: The manifestation of this experience can be detected; it totally transforms my life. The manifestation will not be my words or a recital of my experience; its real expression will be incarnated in my life, it will crystallize in my existence and be visible to any who may care to look.

We have called this the threshold of the supreme experience. In other words, it has been the supreme experience for the time being. Someone who has had such an experience will 'come back' to what mortals call ordinary life. But once it has taken hold of a Man, the supreme experience transforms that Man totally; he cannot be the same as before. It is a death and a resurrection. That person will perform the ordinary acts of human life like any other mortal; but he will not feel distracted by his ordinary life because there is no incompatibility of domains. The supreme experience is not psychological. Nevertheless it is understandable that most mystical schools dealing with these problems distinguish a double level even at this point: the supreme experience compatible with mortal life in the visible structures of space and time, and that other supreme experience in which time and space have been completely integrated into the experience itself. We cannot say much more (we have perhaps already said too much) about the supreme experience before proceeding to a certain typology of its manifestations.

If I were to describe the supreme experience in my own

personal, *advaitic* and trinitarian words, I would say nothing. Yet, if pressed to translate, I would say something like this: It is the experience of the *thou*, the realization of my-self as a thou: *tat tvam asi*, or again: *filius meus es tu*, or *ecce ego quia vocasti me*, or ἔσθε οὐ (to use the language of four traditions and to which one could add the experience underlying the *nairātmyavāda*).

It means to realize (myself as) the entire reality but capsized as it were, upside down, like the cosmic tree of the Upaniṣad, or the required *metanoia* (con-version, changing of *nous*, of mind) of the New Testament. That is, it means to discover me, image of the entire reality, at the meeting place of the real, at the cross-roads of Being, at the very center. But the center would be unreal if there were not the sphere (or what not) for which it is center. The image would be mere hallucination if the original were not real. The crossroads is where beings cross. And yet the one would not be without the other.

The supreme experience is pure consciousness, but this is not self-consciousness in the sense of experience of the self. Pure consciousness is thou-consciousness and it is in this thou-consciousness where we all meet, including the I that can be experienced only as in and through the thou. There is no I-consciousness. There is only consciousness, and this is pre-cisely the thou: the very consciousness *of* the I. The I has and is no consciousness, it is the source of it—if we won't stretch the metaphor too far.

One could venture also a purely philosophical formulation of the supreme experience (for lack of a better word) and affirm that the true and complete principle of identity, the metaphysical one and not merely logical, takes not the form of 'I am I' (which amounts to a barren tautology imprisoning the I in an inescapable solipsism), but the form of 'I am thou'. "Who are you?" says an extraordinary verse of one Upanishad, speaking about ultimate liberation. "I am you", says the answer and the text continues "then he releases him."[3]

3. THE WAYS OF WEST AND EAST

a. Eastern and Western Values

East and West have been separated for so long, misunderstanding each other and living worlds apart, that a certain inertia in our ways of looking at things may obscure the fact that East and West are no longer what were traditionally described under these two almost magical names. To being with, East and West cannot be considered purely or mainly geographical features. And this not only because we discovered long ago that the earth is round and that 'east' and 'west' are relative to one's perspective, but because today even these differences are minimal and to be found in any fair-sized nation state. Nor can East and West be called *historical* concepts. The history of the peoples of the world is no longer a patchwork of isolated fragments. The destiny of the West may well be settled by battles taking place in the East, while the future of the East may well depend on the policy of the West. Western and Eastern histories are no longer closed systems. For the first time human history is also the history of mankind.

Cultural distinctions also fade away or merely express oversimplifications and ignorances not yet totally overcome. Not only is the typically Western spirit to be found outside the West, but the traditional Eastern way of looking at things is also gaining ground in Western latitudes. Indeed, there is not a single cultural difference that could be called specifically Eastern or Western— surely neither logic nor mysticism, nor for that matter technology, science or metaphysics. Even *philosophical* idiosyncracies cannot be divided into exclusively Eastern or Western ways of thinking or philosophizing. Both the East and the West are too vast and variegated to allow overstating special features in their philosophical outlook on life. The times when a certain feature could be called peculiarly Eastern or Western are long gone.

Or again, *religious* divisions can no longer be credited to East and West. In spite of the continuing burden of the past, hardly any religion today fits into an East-West dichotomy. Most of the religions of the world were born in one place and flourished in another. To identify a religion with one particular continent seems almost fatuous today. It is hard to say whether Christianity is more Jewish than Greek or Roman, whether Buddhism is more Indian than Chinese, whether Judaism is more Palestinian than Babylonian, Eastern European, Spanish or whatever.

Is it then meaningless to speak of the ways of the East and those of the West? I don't think so. They still retain a deep significance, perhaps the deepest of all: Only if East and West are understood as *anthropological* categories will they find their place, justification and value in today's world.

In every human being there is an East and a West, just as any human being is in a certain way androgynous, but normally one of the two aspects of the human predominates. With the world on the way to becoming geographically and culturally one it would be monstrous if its people were still to remain isolated, unconcerned and at a loss for that symbiosis, which is the only hope for more than one world problem today. But this cross-fertilization is possible because the human being already has within himself the seeds of both values. In each of us there is a West and an East. Every human person has an orient, a horizon he never reaches, always beyond and behind, where the sun rises, a dimension of hope, a dim sense of transcendence, a matutinal knowledge (*cognitio matutina*). Every human being has likewise a dimension of West, of maturity, where the sun sets, where the values materialize and concreteness is valued, where faith is felt as a necessity, where the shapes and forms become relevant and the evening knowledge (*cognitio vespertina*), which discovers the immanence in the things themselves, is most prized.

We could go on indefinitely, but this may suffice for our problem. The burden of our tale is this: any interreligious and interhuman dialogue, any exchange among cultures, has to be preceded by an intrareligious and intrahuman dialogue, an internal conversion within the person. The gulf between so many abysses—between East and West in this case—can be bridged only if we realize the synthesis and the harmony within the microcosm of ourselves. We are the chasm and we are likewise the bridge.

b. Four Archetypes of the Ultimate

We cannot go on forever avoiding the problem of content and overlooking the different ways in which the supreme experience has been described by different schools and traditions. But then we must be aware of the limitations of any particular description. Here a study from the perspective of the History of Religions should prove fruitful and enlightening. Only very tentatively do I submit the following typology, based not so much on the textbook divisions between religions and cultures as along the lines of what has just been said of East and West as anthropological categories. If examples are drawn from the great religious traditions of mankind this should not contradict what we have been saying but simply bear witness to the fact that certain emphases are easier to find among certain peoples than others.

I repeat once and for all that I do not intend to describe any religious spirituality in particular or to deny that within a given religion there are not other trends of thought or even to affirm that this typology is a typology of religions. I speak of four archetypes of the human being, although they may be more visible in one place or time than in another. Moreover, it is distinctly characteristic of our times to begin to find all these four archetypes within the fold of one and the same religion.

It seems that the human spirit in its effort to understand and express the supreme experience has stressed either its transcendence or its immanence.

Within the first group we find two definite tendencies: the tendency to stress transcendence and the tendency to stress immanence. The former is typical of the Semitic religions: Judaism, Christianity and Islam. The latter could be said to form the Hindu type and is represented by the bundle of religious traditions that circulate under the name of Hinduism.

The group more inclined to emphasize immanence could equally be subdivided: one underscoring the transcendent character of the immanence, and we think here of Buddhism; the other accenting the immanent aspect of this immanence, and here we would see the Chinese religious tradition and curiously enough the modern secular spirit as well.

The following scheme sums up what we would like to sketch very briefly:

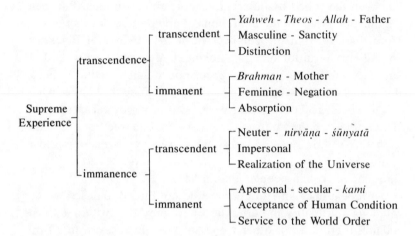

i. Transcendent Transcendence

Its attitude is markedly masculine. Force, Power, Glory, are some of its attributes. Be it Yahweh, the Christian Theos or Allah, this God is eminently Father and thus Creator and evidently outside the world. He is transcendent in such an absolute way that he mainly creates, looks after and judges the world. He does not mix with the world, as it were. The supreme experience is to see this glaring light face to face. Of course there is the softening effect of the Christian incarnation, like the more mellow tones of the Kabbala, of Hasidic spirituality and of Sufism (but we have already said that we are trying more to describe anthropological archetypes than to elaborate a typology of religions). God is preeminently the saint and holiness here means separateness, lofty segregation. God is utterly transcendent and it is this very transcendence that gives him the sovereign freedom to deal with Men. The supreme experience here is ultimately not possible for Men. It is reserved for the transcendent God. We can at most be united with him by love or by knowledge, according to the theological trends of different schools. The supreme experience cannot in any way represent an escape from the human condition. It has to be concrete, personal, and must preserve our peculiarities. At the same time it has to save us from our limitations. It has to throw us into the arms of the Absolute, but the distinction between the two is zealously guarded.

ii. Immanent Transcendence

The attitude here is visibly feminine. *Brahman* is equally transcendent, though not because it is distant, different and above, but precisely because it is below, common, the mere condition for being, the basis for any existence without being itself any particular existence. *Brahman* is transcendent because of its own and proper immanence; so immanent that it has so to speak no consistency of its own. It does not even know it is *brahman*. This would jeopardize its immanent transcendence, for it would then have the distance necessary for knowledge and could not be so radically immanent to the world. It is the *matrix*, the *yoni*, more like a mother nurturing from below than a command from above. It does not lead but sustains. The supreme experience would accordingly consist in being immersed in *brahman*, not perhaps to become *brahman*, which would posit a certain activity alien to the utter passivity necessary for its immanent transcendence, but to discover the *brahman* that is in me or that I am. The supreme experience is not so much to stay within one's own human condition, sticking to a name and form that are only passing and provisional, but to experience the totality, to be the totality from a 360-degree angle embracing all that is. This way is a negative path, it denies all individuality and all differences. One of the criteria for the authenticity of the genuine experience consists in checking whether the candidate has lost the fear of disappearing, of losing himself, or if he still clings to his little ego.

iii. Transcendent Immanence

Here the panorama changes radically. The attitude is no longer masculine or feminine but rather neuter (*ne utrum*), neither male nor female and yet somehow personal, although in a markedly nonanthropomorphic sense. Immanence here is so radical that only by transcending everything built up on it can one reach the ultimate. One has to reduce to ashes everything one can conceive of or think; every idea or imagination of being has to disappear in order that pure nothingness (*śūnyatā*) may emerge, obviously not as some-thing and much less as something else, but as the nonemergence of anything. *Nirvāṇa* is the supreme experience, the experience that is no experience at all, and that at once realizes that *saṁsāra* is *nirvāṇa*, i.e., that there is no transcendence other than immanence, and thus that only by transcending the immanence itself can Man somehow fulfill his life.

The supreme experience here is obviously not the experience of an Other and not even an experience different from any other human experience. It underlies all of them and can be reached only by quenching every desire to transcend the human condition. Yet precisely because this human condition is a negative experience, its negation—without wanting to transcend it—is the only way to salvation, to *nirvāṇa*. The supreme experience is reached neither by seeing God in all things (first way) nor by seeing all things in God (second way, though expressed in terms rather foreign to this way), but by refusing to divinize anything within the range of our experience. You are not having the supreme experience if you affirm or even doubt that you are. The supreme experience is that there is no such thing as supreme experience. Realizing this awakens us to real liberation.

iv. Immanent Immanence

The attitude here is radically terrestrial. Immanence is not to be transcended. If the other three attitudes still recognize, in a personal or impersonal way, that the sphere of immanence has to be somehow corrected, transcended, this fourth attitude does not recognize any escape from the factual human condition. There is no way out. There is no other world than this, and there is no use sublimating our longings and desires or projecting our dreams outside the realm of sober verification. *Kami* in Japanese means God for the Shinto, but also above, up, or anything for that matter superior to Man in any way, no matter how trivial. Traditional Chinese religiousness will not allow introducing any other factor into the human situation in order to handle it. Religion is ultimate unconcern. The supreme experience is that of the sage who fully knows the trickeries and depths of the human heart. The supreme experience is to renounce any extrapolation and to plunge into the real world situation without transcending it, not even negatively. Modern secular spirituality, by pragmatically refusing to speculate about any experience outside the range of the world, could also be adduced as an example of this attitude. In the concrete it finds the universal and the immanent; in the given, all that is needed.

c. **The Spirit**

Is there any way to find a certain equivalence for such variegated views and opinions? Are we to conclude that makind has no unanimity whatsoever? Is the unity of the human family only a biological trait or a utopian dream? Am I so right that the others must be wrong? Nations are at war one with another, religions consider themselves incompatible, philosophies contradict one another and now in human experience itself—in the very attempt to overcome all the pettiness of system and ideologies—divergencies appear cutting as deeply as into any other human reality. Was the thrust toward experience not mainly to overcome the discrepancies of sentiment and the divergencies of opinion? If there is no judge ulterior to our personal experience, must we give up all hope of peacefully understanding one another, and so prepare the way for new forms of imperialism and world domination (apparently the only other way to bring a certain coherence and harmony to mankind)? After two world wars and with several minor but no less horrible wars still ravaging humankind today, we cannot put much trust in pure reason and particular ideologies. Does human experience—supreme or not—offer any better starting point?

All these questions are far from rhetorical. They constitute a real challenge to any authentic theology and philosophy if these disciplines are to be more than barren and devitalized brain-juice for the dumbfounding of anyone still sensitive and sensible. We should not expect everything from philosophy or theology and we must beware of false messianisms, but the one extreme does not justify the other.

Is there any way of understanding and somehow accepting the manifold human experience, of integrating the variety of expressions of the supreme experience? If we can give a positive answer to this tantalizing query we shall not have solved the problems of the world, but shall have contributed in a very positive and efficacious way to their solution. At least we shall have removed one of the subtle obstacles: lack of mutual confidence due to lack of understanding. Misunderstanding the other we think him wrong, even in bad faith; we cannot trust him—and this is but one consequence. On the other hand, it would be a negative, even lethal, service to philosophy and a betrayal of mankind if led by a well-intentioned desire for mutual understanding we were to blur the issues and preach harmony and convergence when there is none.

To put it quite bluntly: If there is a God and if this is considered to be the only possible hypothesis for a fully human and meaningful life, even if we respect the right of others or acknowledge their good faith, we shall not be able to consider full citizens of academia, culture, religion or mankind all those who deny such a personal God. Or, the other way round: if we believe that there is no God and if the idea of God is still the 'hang-up' of an obscurantist epoch totally incompatible with an enlightened, nonsectarian and nonfanatical existence, all those who still cling to such superstitions are, to say the least, parasites on society and the greatest obstacles to a better world. We should not minimize or banalize the issue under the guise of academic etiquette. An investigation into ultimate experience cannot bypass this challenge.

Briefly but pointedly I would like to elaborate the direction of my answer. First of all, as the previous analyses may have already suggested, the shift in emphasis from objective values to the experiential truth can only be judged as a positive step toward a more mature conception of the whole and complex human situation. Orthodoxy cannot be the supreme value. Secondly, the distinction between agnostic or skeptical *relativism* and a realistic *relativity* seems important. The former is a dogmatic attitude emerging in reaction to another monolithic dogmatism. The latter is the recognition that nothing is absolute in this relative world of ours, that it all depends on the intrinsic and constitutive relationship of everything to everything else; isolation and solipsism are but the by-products of a particularly human hybris. The brotherhood of Man is not only an ethical imperative. Thirdly, and this is what we should draw from the foregoing analyses, human experience is not reducible to a single denominator. To be sure, the *logos* element in experience is important, it holds the veto (nothing contradicting reason can be accepted), but it is not Man's only power nor his highest endowment. Not only can everything not be words or concepts, but even here on earth not everything is *logos*.

The real philosophical and theological task today is to integrate not only the exigencies of the *logos*, but also the realities of the myth and, last but not least, the freedom of the spirit. This is the thrust of many of the chapters of this book.

NOTES

1. The Greek *peraō* and *peiran*, both at the base of our three words, come from the root *per* (in Sanskrit *par* [cf. *pi-parmi*]) meaning to conduct, to pass through, to test, trial, attempt (thus risk, danger). Cf. the Latin *porta, peritus, periculum, pirata*; the German *fahren* (whence *erfahren*); the English peril, fare, ferry; the French *périlleux*, etc. The empirical is the proven reality, because it has passed through our senses; the experiment is the same reality submitted to our testing (and trying) capacities; experience is the same reality that has already passed through—as the vedic *soma* through the pressing stones.

2. Cf. R. Panikkar, 'La demitologizzazione nell'incontro tra cristianesimo de induismo', *Il problema della demitizzazione*, edited by E. Castelli (Padova: Cedam, 1961).

3. KausU I, 2.

Part III

HERMENEUTICS

*is qui invenerit interpretationem
(ἑρμενεία) horum verborum non gustabit
mortem.*

He who discovers the interpretation
of these words will not taste death.
Evangelium Thomae 1

XI.
Metatheology
as Fundamental Theology

ἀλλὰ ὁ λόγος τοῦ θεοῦ
οὐ δέδεται

Sed verbum Dei non est alligatum.

Theo-logy is not in bondage.
2 Tim. 2:9 (+)

+ "But the word of God is not shut up" (NEB) or "but the word of God is not bound" (*AV* and *RV*) and the like are the contextually obvious correct translations.

1. A PARABLE

A teacher who was a Westerner or trained along Western lines was almost in despair: After a carefully built-up scientific explanation of malaria, its processes, causes, etc., the boys in a Ugandan primary school did not seem to have understood anything. 'Why does a Man catch malaria?' one boy asked timidly. 'Because a mosquito, the carrier of the parasite, bites him,' replied the teacher, who went on to give the whole explanation again. At this the class, still unconvinced and solidly behind the daring boy shouted, 'But who sent the mosquito to bite the Man?'

For those Ugandan boys, the schoolmaster had neither understood nor explained anything. They were not concerned with facts, scientific 'hows' or efficient causes, but with the living world (and perhaps the final cause), with the existentially relevant issue—for the real issue here (imagine you or one of your family with malaria) is why that particular individual has been bitten by that particular mosquito. Fundamental theology is like that teacher, and two-thirds or perhaps even three-fourths of our present generation resemble the schoolboys. Theoretical explanations about malaria or religion are all very well, but unless I can explain why the mosquito has bitten me . . .

2. THE TWO MEANINGS OF FUNDAMENTAL THEOLOGY

As commonly understood, fundamental theology is a pre-theological or philosophical reflection on the foundations of theology. Its reflections are directed either to justify the assertions of Christian doctrine—a discipline traditionally called apologetics—or to find out the sources and foundations of theology. The former purports to be a rational or at least reasonable justification of the elements elaborated by theology; the latter claims to disclose the very basis of theological self-understanding. I shall discuss only the second meaning.

3. ASSUMPTIONS AND PRESUPPOSITIONS

Two distinct groups, *assumptions* and *presuppositions*, underlie fundamental theology. Among the *assumptions*, we have first the notion that theology needs a foundation that is in some way outside it, and, second, that this basis can be known.

Both of these assumptions are to be found at the very start of fundamental theology; they were present even before the discipline received its current name. But as soon as the discipline acquired consistency, that is, as soon as Christian theologians felt the need for a foundation for theology *outside* theology, they by and large assumed that this was the right way to proceed. One of the most striking examples of this kind of thinking is the First Vatican Council, so many of whose pronouncements tend in the direction of just such a fundamental theology.

A dualistic conception of reality is proper to this type of thinking: God and the world, uncreated and created, Being and the beings, the ground and the structure built upon it. In this two-story construction of nature and supernature, grace is built on nature, faith on reason, theology on philosophy and so on. Their relation of dependence is neither an exigency from below nor a lack of freedom from above. Rather, the second level presupposes the first and the first is not *de facto* complete without the second. To be sure, the lower levels are called *preambula* not *fundamenta*, so as to maintain the freedom and 'gratuity' of the upper story. But it amounts to the same thing. If, for instance, you do not admit there is a God and a soul, how can Christian teaching make sense to you?

Among the *presuppositions*, one is that these foundations that sustain theology are universally valid. Since they allegedly serve all human beings without distinction, if somebody cannot grasp them this supposedly means that he has not yet reached the level of mental development that would enable him to understand these basic 'truths'. Consequently, a certain degree of 'civiliza- tion' was believed necessary before one could understand and then adhere to the message of the Church: Methods like the so- called precatechetical instruction or *évangelisation de base*—a certain philosophical indoctrination on the concepts of 'person', 'nature', 'substance', 'individual', 'private property'; the preach- ing of monogamy, or the effort to convince people to prefer other manners of eating and dress, etc.—were all considered tools of the Christian *kerygma*, necessary preconditions for proclaiming the Gospel.

4. THE CRISIS OF THE PRESUPPOSITIONS

The distinction between presuppositions and assumptions seems to me of capital importance. An *assumption* is something I may assume for many possible reasons: traditional, heuristic, axiomatic, pragmatic, hypothetical and so on. It is a principle I set at the base of my thinking process in a more or less explicit way. A *presupposition*, on the other hand, is something I uncriti- cally and unreflectively take for granted. It belongs to the myth in which I live and out of which I draw raw material to feed my thinking. The moment a presupposition is known as the basis of thought or the starting point of an intellectual process, it ceases to be a *pre*-supposition. Now only another person—or myself in a second reflexive moment—can make me aware of my pre- suppositions; when that happens I cannot just hold them as I had earlier. I either reject them or keep them as 'suppositions', as- sumptions. This is also why the moment theology becomes aware of its presuppositions—either by criticism from the outside or by a critical perspective from within—theologians begin to question the hitherto unquestioned basis of their science. The crisis thus produced is the sort that any living consciousness must pass through in order to grow.

Now both theology and fundamental theology were at home in one particular culture and world view; they took for granted the presuppositions of the Western world. The two sciences were grounded in the same myth and shared many presuppositions, some of which have recently been laid bare and now provoke theological confusion in an era of global encounter among religions.

Indeed, these uncovered presuppositions have even been questioned as assumptions. The current generation finds the traditional scheme insufficient. In fact, the ground on which theology rests has become more problematic than the Christian content itself.

5. THE CHALLENGE OF UNIVERSALITY

The real challenge of Christian faith today comes from within, i.e., from an inner dynamic toward universality, from its own claim to 'catholicity'. And now that the horizon of universality has outgrown the boundaries of Western civilization and its colonies, what was once considered 'catholic' becomes 'provincial'. Today any message directed to the whole of mankind that takes a part for the whole or ignores the variety of peoples, cultures and religions is bound to be suspicious from the outset. Christian faith has either to accept this challenge or declare its allegiance to a single culture and thereby renounce its claim to possess a universally acceptable message.

This problem facing fundamental theology cannot be solved by merely extrapolating, without previously justifying, a set of propositions that may be meaningful within a certain religious or cultural context, but irrelevant, meaningless or even unacceptable outside it. If fundamental theology is to have any relevance in our time of worldwide communication, it has to address itself to a radical cross-cultural problematic. It has to strive at formulating propositions intelligible to people outside Western culture (just as also for those in the West who no longer think, imagine or act according to the paradigms that still guide traditional fundamental theology). A simple glance at history will convince us that the differences between cultures are not minor. A principle we consider incontrovertible may be dubious in another culture. For the most part, people today are no longer prone to mistakenly imagine that everybody thinks and feels alike simply because they outwardly behave similarly. The encounter of peoples, cultures and religions is a major problem for fundamental theology, a challenge to its very anthropological and philosophical foundations. In this connection I would like to offer some general considerations.

6. FOUNDATIONS, A PRIORI AND A POSTERIORI

The basic need for more universal foundations for Christian theology cannot be ignored or explained away by assuming that the 'other' will sooner or later understand or be converted to 'our' point of view. Those days are gone. The problem is to seek foundations for Christian theology that at least make sense to peoples outside the fundamental theology's traditional milieu.

The only possible method for finding the foundations of theology must be a posteriori. That is, fundamental theology is not at the beginning of theological reflection but at its end. Christian faith is not based on certain foundations that fundamental theology lays bare (discloses). Rather the effort to understand the Christian fact leads us to discover some conditions of its intelligibility in given circumstances. Let us recall here that the primordial meaning of 'catholicity' is not geographical universality, but internal completion.

Here history is also a wise master, Not too long ago all sorts of ideas were considered fundamental to Christian theology, notions that today are dismissed as accidental or nonessential, because other interpretations—perhaps more plausible—have been found. These interpretations claim to save the real message precisely by purifying it of obsolete world views.

The real difficulty is to find the criterion for this operation. How am I to know whether something is essential to my faith or not? Where will the process end once I begin to demythicize?

7. THE UNITY BETWEEN THEOLOGY AND FUNDAMENTAL THEOLOGY

The thesis I am proposing tries to reestablish the unity—and so the harmony—between theology and fundamental theology. It asserts that fundamental theology is neither a necessary epistemological condition for nor the ontological basis of theology. Were theology to depend for its acceptability on an extra-theological base, it would lose not only its character of wisdom but also its intellectual cogency. Theology would be utterly at the mercy of whatever philosophy offered the better backing; it would depend wholly on an auction in the philosophical (or even the public) marketplace.

What I propose is the recovery of fundamental theology as a fundamentally theological endeavor, i.e., as being fundamentally theology. Reincorporating fundamental theology into theology as a whole will by this very process explode the only too narrow cage in which theology has sometimes been confined. It will liberate theology from the tutelage of philosophy so that theology will no longer depend on a foundation (one particular philosophy, world view or whatever) outside itself.

Accordingly, fundamental theology would be that theological activity (for which there is so often no room in certain theologies) which critically examines its assumptions and is always ready to question its presuppositions. But it does this not from a separate platform independent from faith and on which 'theology' would subsequently build up its 'own' system. Rather, fundamental theology is the effort to understand the actual theological situation in any given context. There is a difference, indeed, between the content of the Christian belief and the conditions of its intelligibility; but there is not a separation, since the content of faith is nothing but an intelligible crystallization of faith itself. Content means intelligible content, and it cannot be intelligible if it rests on premises that are explicitly not understood.

I am saying that the anthropological conditions necessary to understand and accept the Christian message cannot and so must not be severed from the interpretation of its content. Let me elaborate this point by means of an example.

8. ONE EXAMPLE: THE BUDDHIST, THE HINDU AND THE SECULARIST

The existence of God has traditionally been considered a philosophical truth independent of any theology; hence it was supposed to be one of the foundations of Christian doctrine. The Resurrection of Christ, on the other hand, belongs to the purely theological order. It is usually said that if you do not accept the existence of God you cannot understand what the Christian faith is about; it is also generally affirmed that if you do not accept the Resurrection of Christ you cannot be called a Christian. The difference between these statements is that while you do not need a specifically Christian belief to admit the existence of God, you do need it to accept the Resurrection of Christ. The affirmation 'Christ is risen', then, can be taken as one of the shortest and most accurate expressions of this Christian belief.

The situation today is more complex. Let us abruptly confront this example with a triple fact: a Buddhist who does not believe in any God whatsoever and yet has a highly developed and refined religion; a Hindu who does not object at all to the Resurrection of Christ; and a secularist theologian or a modern Westerner who calls himself a Christian and yet accepts neither God nor the Resurrection as traditionally understood.

The Buddhist would like to believe the message of Christ and sincerely thinks he could accept and even understand it better if it were purified from what he considers its theistic superstructure. The Hindu would wonder why he must join a physical and cultural community only because he is ready to believe in the divinity and Resurrection of Christ. The 'death of God' theologian, or whatever name we may choose for him, would say that precisely because Christ is the Savior, he can dispense with any conception of a transcendent God and the miracle of a physical resurrection.

Whether or not these three people can be called Christian will depend on the interpretation of what they say, i.e., on what they really *mean* to say. I shall not enter here into the merits of these arguments. But I will say that the three statements present the same pattern and it would be artificial and confusing to lodge the first in fundamental theology, the second in theology and the third in philosophy. Everything depends on what we understand by God and how we picture Christ's Resurrection; on our assumptions, our context and our understanding of how the Christian belief can be maintained within such religious, epistemologi-

cal and metaphysical patterns. Is it, for example, necessary to
have a theistic and substantivized conception of the divinity to be
loyal to Christian faith? Does one need a literal and fundamentalist
image of the Resurrection to be an orthodox believer? Is it essential to hold the Aristotelian-Thomistic philosophical scheme in
order to accept the Christian message? Must I really admit some
preambula fidei as part of faith itself, or does it depend on how I
interpret what my faith tells me, so that faith may have different
preambula?

The existential Catholic answer to the individual is very
clear: Your interpretation, your understanding of the Christian
fact, must be personally intelligible, but it must also harmonize
with tradition—hence with the *magisterium*—because dogma is
also a historical reality and has a communal character.

We are not, however, dealing with the problem of discipline
or with a specific case. My question would be whether, or on
what grounds, tradition and the *magisterium* have the right to
prevent the entry into the Church of people whose lives are
guided by different patterns of intelligibility. Or again, is the present historical crystallization of the Christian faith the only possible one? Theoretically the Church has never said this, but the
difficulty lies in discovering whether and which formulations are
equivalent. So the problem remains: Can several patterns sustain
and convey the Christian *kerygma*? To what extent can they do
so? Here only history will have the last word, for the Church itself
is inscribed in the historical process.

9. THE FUNCTION OF FUNDAMENTAL THEOLOGY

If we are aware of the problem we are already on the way to
overcoming it. The extraordinary fact is that this awareness is
only now dawning on the great majority of Christian theologians.
I mean this not as an accusation but as a statement of fact. Given
the historical development of Christian theology, it could not be
otherwise. To pour today's wine into old wineskins is reprehensible, but it was not when they were brand new.

The role of fundamental theology is therefore to make theological affirmations also intelligible outside the culture and even the religion where they had until then grown and prospered. I would say that if fundamental theology is to fulfill its role, it must not only clarify its own tradition, but paradoxically leave kith and kin to wander into *terra incognita* — although a promised land. And herein lies the immense difficulty. Fundamental theology is an Exodus theology. Thus it is not only a question of courage, but also of feasibility. Is it possible to take root in an alien, or even a nonexistent, soil? Can we jump over our own shadow? Can fundamental theology make theological statements intelligible outside their proper context?

We must take the differences between people, cultures and religions very seriously. Two-thirds of the world's population today does not live in the myth of history; half the people on this earth (believers and nonbelievers) do not share the Abrahamic conception of God; one-third of mankind is unconscious of separated individuality. These are only some of the many major differences we could name. Fundamental theology cannot ignore such questions and its function may well be to justify a theological as well as a religious pluralism. Fundamental theology is concerned with finding a common language through which to express theological insights, while being well aware that language is more than just a tool, that it is, rather, the first expression of these very insights.

10. METATHEOLOGY

Fundamental theology then becomes a kind of *diacritical theology* in the sense that *diacrisis* was understood in Plato's *Sophist* or *viveka* in Śaṅkara's *Vedānta*. I feel, however, that the simple term *metatheology* is more apposite, for it suggests a total human attitude that, on the one hand, transcends merely intellectual elaborations of the message of different religions (theologies) and, on the other, goes beyond the *theos* as the subject matter of these theologies and the *logos* as the instrument for dealing with it. I am not arguing against this conception of the *theos* or this use of the *logos*. I am only pleading that the *theos* not be taken for granted nor the *logos* divinized. Metatheology could also be described as the religious endeavor to understand that primordial human relatedness we perceive in dealing with ultimate problems. This is not derived from a particular concept of human nature, but is the fruit of pluri-theological investigation. I am not assuming a kind of objectifiable common ground or certain universally formulable statements held in common. I am only asking for truly open dialogue. The meeting ground itself may have to be created, but a brighter stream of light, service and understanding will emerge in the intermingling of religious currents, ideas and beliefs. I only foresee (and in a way prophesy) an earnest religious struggle, an authentic human commerce and intercourse at the deepest level of humanity, the fruit of love, not lust or ambition, pregnant with the good news of a new creature. Surely the Christian should not fear to be born again, nor for that matter should the adherent of any other religion. Nor should any faith shun the genuine search for truth. Confidence in truth is already a fundamental religious category.

11. UNDERSTANDING THE CHRISTIAN KERYGMA

Two important ideas follow from what has been said so far. The first is the need for a radical change in the orientation of fundamental theology itself; in other words, its conversion, its *metanoia*. From within a Christian perspective I would put it in a way practically opposite to the customary one, although in this divergent formulation I am most traditional, for tradition is often paradoxical and has even taken this turn several times before today. I would say, then, that the role of fundamental theology is not to find some extra-theological principles on which to base theological speculation, but to search for the intelligibility of the Christian fact in any authentic human attitude and genuine philosophical position; to examine how far is the Christian kerygma tied to a particular religious tradition. It would explain, for instance, not that accepting the existence of God is a necessary prerequisite for understanding and accepting the Christian belief, but that the Christian proclamation could perhaps find justification and meaning also under the hypothesis that there is no God. These last two words mean to suggest the possibility that if there is (or were) a truly atheistic society, the Christian *kerygma* should not first need to clear the ground by proving the existence of God and only then proceed further, but that it could find a meaningful *kerygma* by transmythicizing the God-talk. I am not saying that this effort should always succeed, but that it should always be tried—for its very failure may bear fruit.

Metatheology is not just another system of theology any more than metaphysics is simply a more refined physical science. A theological system may be theistic; metatheology need not be. Metatheology may, for instance, be at the origin of a nontheistic 'theological' reflection; it does not encroach upon the different systems or jeopardize the theological schools of the most disparate systems and religions. And yet it belongs to all theological investigation. In fact, as a result of its activity, metatheology modifies both the underlying system and the Christian self-understanding (albeit not according to any preconceived pattern).

I may clarify this idea from a double perspective. From the speculative angle I could say that fundamental theology tries to understand the fundamental theological issue (for the Christian: Christ) in a *given* philosophical, religious and cultural situation. From a pastoral and Christian angle I would add that it tries to do and say in another context what Christ did and said in the place and time in which he lived.

12. THE ECCLESIAL AND DIALOGICAL CHARACTER OF FUNDAMENTAL THEOLOGY

The second idea has already announced itself. It is the communitarian or ecclesial character of this enterprise. This cannot be the work of Christians alone or of 'religious' people exclusively, but must result from the common effort of all those interested enough (or 'condemned', as Fichte would have put it, although I prefer 'called upon') to perform this major work of dialogue, communication and communion, in spite of and even through the conflicts that may arise.

Here is where theology and religion meet, where life and speculation encounter each other, where the wiser the scholar, the simpler he is as a Man. Neither side or party can unilaterally lay down the rules of the game, or fix the conditions or the outcome of the experience. Fundamental theology becomes lived religion, a mystical faith prior to or beyond any formulation. It is the religious quest for a ground of understanding, for a common concern still to be lived, delimited, verbalized.

What I am aiming at is this: Dialogue is not simply a device for discussing or clarifying different opinions, but is itself a religious category. Dialogue becomes a religious act, an act of faith (which comes from hearing), a mutual recognition of our human condition and its constitutive relativity.

If the aim of fundamental theology is to elaborate the assumptions on which a theology may be based, it requires dialogue on an equal footing, the collaboration and positive contribution of the 'others'. Only they can help me discover my presuppositions and the underlying principles of my science. In brief, *das Ungedachte*, the unthought, can be disclosed only by one who does not 'think' like me and who helps me discover the unthought magma out of which my thinking crystallizes. For my part, I can do him the same service.

This procedure throws us all into the arms of one another. The amount of risk and good faith required is patent. It is truly a religious act, full of faith, hope and love. But it also fulfills a methodological need. If I must dig out a foundation on which the other can also stand, I need his help so that he may at least be able to tell me if the ground I find is also a ground for him.

I need his interpretation of myself and my theology in order to understand myself and my theology; he needs the same from me. Fundamental theology is not an esoteric science or a discipline *ad usum delphini*; it is the forum of a worldwide *ecclesia*, of all people for whom care for the other is as sacred as a concern for one's own household. I shall never be able to love my neighbor as myself if I do not know him as my *self*. This sentence obviously goes both ways. The place *in between*, where we meet, is the basis for fundamental theology and also the ground for human encounter. The kingdom of God is *between* us.

XII.
The Philosophical Tradition

ὀρθῶς δ᾽ἔχει καὶ τὸ
καλεῖσθαι τὴν φιλοσοφίαν
ἐπιστήμην τῆς ἀληθείας

It is certainly also proper that
philosophy is called the science
of truth.
Aristotle
Metaphysics II, 1
(993 b 19-20) (+)

+   Cf. Thomas Aquinas's commentary: "Nam ille videtur sapientiae
amator qui sapientiam non propter aliud sed propter seipsam
quaerit. Qui enim aliquid propter alterum quaerit, magis hoc amat
propter quod quaerit, quam quod quaerit." *In Metaphys*. lect. 3, n.
56.

1. INTRODUCTION

The modern world presents among other features two antithetical characters. On the one hand there is the apogee of science and technology. The prestige of these two cultural products has been enhanced by their success in technically 'unifying' a great part of the world. On the other hand this very success has brought into closer contact the different 'philosophies' of the peoples of the earth. And it is this very contact that makes it almost necessary to call into question the very foundations of the technological civilization. This fact, among others, makes imperative for our times a fundamental reflection on the nature and function of philosophy throughout human history[1]. Just to give some examples: Seen from a cross-cultural perspective, the Cartesian conception of philosophy is likely to appear one-sided, the Marxist corrective biased and the Vedântic idea insufficient.

The following pages do not intend a phenomenological diagnosis on the state of philosophy today. They attempt a rather philosophical prognosis based on the analysis of the different conceptions of philosophy throughout the long history of that human activity which is generally covered by this name.

2. THE FOUR KAIROLOGICAL MOMENTS OF PHILOSOPHY

First of all, I would like to consider dividing philosophy (and not just the history of philosophy) into four periods. These four periods are not meant strictly as chronological ages, since they are not unequivocally fixed in linear time; they mutually permeate one another, and yet each is borne by its predecessor. We are speaking rather of *kairological* moments in the self-understanding of philosophy itself.

a. The Religious

We may call the first philosophical period the *religious* epoch: in both East and West philosophy began as the intellectual dimension of religion. Philosophy was not the servant of religion, but neither was it a thing apart. Philosophy was religion 'philosophically' seen, i.e., intellectually presented and eventually evaluated. In this context, philosophy is sacred: It brings peace and joy; it is wisdom and preparation for death, the recognition of a gracious divinity, the blessed life. Philosophy is not the handmaiden of religion, but she belongs, as it were, to the household of religion. Philosophy is part of religion; it is religion insofar as it perceives itself and attempts to express itself intellectually. At the beginning of every tradition, philosophy stood in this intimacy with religion. Philosophy in this first era understands itself as working out the right model people should have; it sees itself as the principle, the linguistic expression of religion. Philosophy is religion as it finds expression in propositions, for it is born the moment religious Man begins to reflect on his experiences and tries to formulate them.

b. The Metaphysical

From this first period in philosophy a second era followed, which could be called the metaphysical. Man becomes the spectator of reality, he wants to gaze upon the whole. For this however he needs an objective distance, he must take a step backwards in order to distance the thing from religion. He wants to see reality, regard it: vision, contemplation, Greek clarity, objectivity—all these ideas characterize the attitude of this period. Philosophy is metaphysics; it does not want to be the model, but the mirror of reality. It 'speculates', its task is not to bring salvation directly, but to see and show objective reality.

Since Plato and Aristotle we are accustomed to repeat in the West that the beginning of philosophy lies in astonishment:

thaumazein. It is significant that in Indian philosophy, disillusion and not astonishment is said to be the beginning of the philosophical activity. Man is disillusioned by reality as it appears to him; sorrow and death, two fundamental phenomena of human experience, do not let him deceive himself about ultimate reality. But in the final analysis, the fundamental attitude—the spectator's objectivity—is the same in both traditions whether one is disappointed or astonished that things are not what we think they are. Our thinking had led us to different expectations. The tension and the rupture between thinking and being appears. Objectivity is philosophy's focal concern, and this presupposes a tension, a rupture. The tension arises precisely because one expected something other than what is, to one's astonishment or one's disillusion. This rupture, this original dissension, on the one hand is caused by philosophy and, on the other, philosophy also claims to mend it. It is philosophy's fate to alienate Man from his environment—for it makes him aware of his distance from it—and at the same time philosophy offers Man the possibility of overcoming this alienation. Philosophical awareness makes us conscious of reality at the price of differentiating us from it, and simultaneously it offers to reunite us with the real.

Philosophy here is not the principle or the expression of religion, but its surrogate—good or bad according to different views. Religion is for the common folk; philosophy true religiousness. The metaphysicians who know the causes no longer need religion because they have 'sublimed' it in their knowledge. Philosophy *qua* philosophy has saving or liberating power. The mirror reveals the real.

c. The Epistemological

The third era of philosophy, which in the modern West certainly attained its first unequivocal expression with Descartes, but whose beginnings we find already with Socrates in Greece and Yājñavalkya in India, represents the epistemological phase of philosophy. It is certainly necessary to know the objective world; further, as the second period illustrates, intuition and contemplation are doubtless essential to intellectual life. Yet, the metaphysical view contained an assumption that it did not consider: Man's knowledge of his knowledge. In this period Man discovers himself as knower, he becomes aware of both the strength and weakness of his ability to know. Here only such a critical philosophy is considered genuine; everything else is dogmatic slumber. Philosophy no longer mirrors reality, but discovers itself as the inner soul of reality. In the preceding period either being or reality is the chief category; here truth stands at the center. This era discovers hitherto unexpected dimensions of subjectivity: The individual is born. One feels constrained to analyze everything, to penetrate everything with reflection. Consciousness becomes self-consciousness, philosophy becomes aware of its assumptions, it wants more than merely to know the objective thing, it wants to catch the knowing subject in the act of reflection.

If during the second era philosophy is the mirror of reality and a surrogate for religion, in this third era it opposes itself to religion, and claims that it is itself the inner soul of reality. It discovers truth as at once the bridge to reality and a part of that same reality.

d. The Pragmatic or Historical

The fourth era, or dimension—I repeat, they all constantly interpenetrate and each period bears within itself the preceding one—is what we can call the pragmatic or perhaps the historical period. Here the matter at hand is not so much to know the world but to control it, to rule over it, remodel and transform it, to re-create it or, at least, to make it better. The ideal is action, mankind is understood as a historical collective. Philosophy is not only a discovery but a creation and a formation in which the historical factor plays an important role. Reality must be reshaped as philosophy dictates: it is reality that imitates philosophy, so to speak. This era claims totally to overcome religion as a guiding principle.

*   *   *

Summing up, the four fundamental attitudes of philosophy:
1. the ecstatic dimension: the ideal is the holy Man, reality is itself sacred, the religious dimension prevails;
2. the gnostic dimension: reality must be looked at, discovered

and contemplated, the philosopher is the Man who takes a step backward and is aware of the thing;

3. philosophy as subjectivity: Man as individual, knowledge as self-knowledge, pure philosophy as the self-grounding of philosophy;
4. action stands at the center; reality, even being, is historical, unfolds itself, is changeable, dynamic.

A glance at any contemporary philosophical congress shows clearly that all four attitudes are represented and even clash.[2]

To summarize this first part I would like to tell a little story: A young man holds a letter in his hand, lamenting, tears in his eyes: 'For two years I have written faithfully every day to my fiancé. Now, she writes that she is going to marry the postman!'

Just this has often befallen philosophy in the course of its history. When it found itself no longer in immediate contact with reality, it delivered itself constantly to the intermediary (the postman), and finally married the *logos*. Philosophy, which began with such sublime claims—seeking to bring salvation and to save humanity—has directed its attention so exclusively to the intermediary that it is no wonder that after millenia of daily trafficking in letters, it has finally married the bearer of the news about reality, the *logos*. Today philosophy is concerned almost exclusively with the *logos* (which to be sure includes not only reason but intellect as well).

In other words, we have deified the *logos*, and have forgotten the cult, the game, the dance, the myth and the rite. Apparently all these have nothing to do with philosophy. Theologians have spoken of the *verbum dei* and regarded this *verbum dei* as God (although they add in parentheses that this *verbum* is the Son of God). Metaphysicians have constructed the *verbum entis* and this *verbum entis* is understood as being (which was not infrequently also deified). The epistemologists were concerned with the *verbum mentis*; this *verbum mentis* is philosophy's final criterion for determining truth. Later philosophers made the *verbum mundi* the starting point and the philosophers of science, along with the modern language philosophers, avow the *verbum hominis* as the ultimate. But we have not only forgotten being, we have ignored myths as well, and this carelessness has also affected the *pneuma*. Needless to say, we are summarizing all this in a very concentrated way.

The content of this first part of this chapter may be schematized in the square below:

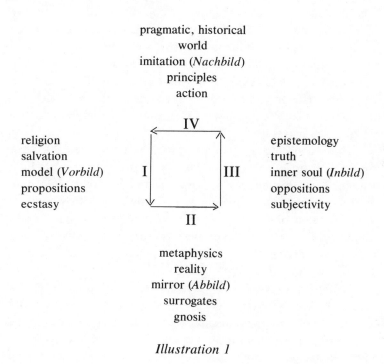

Illustration 1

If this schema does nothing but focus the anguishing contemporary rupture between philosophy and religion, it is sufficient. It shows that we presently lack a global philosophy and impels us to leap directly into the heart of the question by asking what relationship between philosophy and religion is possible today. This relation can neither be uncritically assumed as self-evident, nor adopted as a compromise. It can only follow from an analysis of religion and philosophy as they understand themselves. Here the concept of *ontonomy* may prove useful.[3]

We could perhaps see the relation between philosophy and religion in three ways. *Heteronomy* refers to domination; one is assumed superior to the other. The higher, superior one establishes the laws the lower one must obey. The history of religions and philosophy provide numerous examples: philosophy as the handmaiden of religion, religion as pop philosophy for the unenlightened masses. Clearly we cannot accept this position. Subjecting philosophy to religion destroys philosophy or degrades it to an ideology, making of it the mercenary of some nonphilosophical power (even if we call it God). On the other hand, subjecting religion to philosophy spells death for religion by reducing it to a poor translation of philosophical speculation, to the belief of the masses.

The second attitude is *autonomy*, the understandable reaction to any sort of external imposition. It affirms complete independence and disconnection, ignoring the fact that philosophy and religion have the same concern. Ultimately both would collapse: Without philosophy, religion is blind fanaticism; without religion, philosophy examines merely a corpse, not a living being. Their relation cannot be to maintain peaceful 'frontiers' because there is only one 'territory'.

Ontonomy expresses this peculiar relationship, neither dominance nor sullen independence. The disciplines are intrinsically connected and this relationship is constitutive: They are interrelated in such a way that the laws of one have repercussions for the other. Philosophy is not a substitute for religion, nor is religion an excuse to dispense with philosophy. Philosophy is itself a religious problem, and religion is also philosophical inquiry. Is an authentic Philosophy of Religion possible today? I think it suffices in this context to pose the question and outline some of its ramifications for philosophy.

3. THE THREEFOLD GIFT AND TASK OF PHILOSOPHY

The sign for what follows is a triangle, the threefold gift and so also the threefold task of philosophy in the intellectual situation of our times:

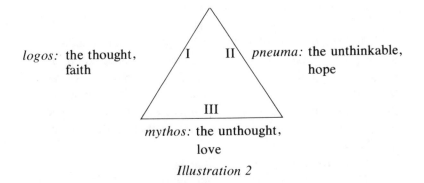

Illustration 2

Nowadays there are indeed indications (temptations?) of a global philosophy: philosophy is not only the love of wisdom but also the wisdom of love (which perhaps does etymological justice to the word): philosophy as the integration of the body, of society, of the cosmos with the infinite or with the human spirit. But perhaps even this has not been radical enough and perhaps the discomfort of today's philosophy arises precisely from this: that these three tasks, these three gifts of philosophy, have not been sufficiently considered. The main emphasis has been one-sided. I would like to offer a suggestion, not for a global philosophy, but for a common philosophical task.

a. Acceptance of the Logos

The *acceptance of the logos* is the first business of philosophy. Certainly the *logos* has primacy and privilege in philosophy. The *logos* must not be abolished, superseded or given up in favor of irrationalism, emotionalism, fideism or some other rebellions, all one-sided. In philosophy the *logos* plays an irreplaceable double role: that of illuminating, clarifying, and that of critiquing, testing, controlling. If anything contradicts the *logos*, it cannot be accepted: The *logos* has the veto power in philosophy. The *logos*, however, must recognize its lower and upper limits and remain aware of them. It dare not suppress either *mythos* or *pneuma*, the other constituents of philosophy. To cite the Kāṭha Upaniṣad:

> Neither by the word nor by the spirit
> nor by sight can he ever be reached.

How, then, can he be realized
except by exclaiming: 'He is!'?[4]

The perspective of other philosophical traditions perhaps
permits us to grasp in words what is properly unspeakable. Is the
word the only medium of philosophy? Furthermore, have we not
reduced the word to only a single facet of its many dimensions? Is
the word not this realm between objective being and subjective
thought that is richer than mere intelligibility, than what has
merely been thought?

As the Ṛg Veda says:

The Word is measured in four quarters,
The Wise who possess insight know these four divisions.
Three quarters, concealed in secret, cause no movement.
The fourth is the quarter which is spoken by Men.[5]

Perhaps then every speaking is already a hermeneutic, an
expression; but is there no other way to communicate than spoken expression? *Logos* is *vāc*, *śabda*, *brahman*, sound, contents;
but it is also icon, *eidos*, gesture, expression, form.

b. Taking up the Mythos

There is however a second side to philosophy, which has a
right not only to be philosophy, to participate in philosophy, but
also to coexist with it: Not only does the *acceptance of the logos*
belong to philosophy, but *taking up the mythos* as well.
Philosophy is not only entry into the thought, but also into the
unthought. Man knows through the *logos* that he unearths from
myth and that he still remains in myth. *Mythos* is the second
dimension of speech itself, the silence between the words, the
matrix that bears the words. The mythical always runs its course
above time and space. It is not quite enough to say it is always
present, nor that to live myth is to live in the past. Only from the
perspective of the *logos* does the myth occur in the past; myth itself
does not know these temporal coordinates of past, present and
future. If I try to explain myth with the *logos*, I can only represent
it *in illo tempore* which is interpreted as past. No living myth—and
we all live in myths—can be interpreted through the strainer of
mythology. The light of the *logos* dispels the darkness of myth and

myth measured by the standard of the *logos* cannot withstand it. *Logos* finds *mythos* ridiculous, just as myth is not disconcerted by mythology. Nobody living mythically would acknowledge as valid the interpretation of mythology given by rational philosophers. To assume, for instance, that a sun-worshipper appeals to a heavenly body defined by Newtonian categories would be to deceive oneself utterly. The sun-worshipper will feel not only misunderstood but astonished at the naiveté of the interpreter—as if Newton were not also drawing from another myth.

We cannot possibly understand myth by logical illumination—an effort that contradicts itself—but mythology can also be *mythos-legein*. *Legein* means telling, and in this telling sense we can bring mythology into harmony with *logo-myth*. For *logos* has also a mythical connection, otherwise it could not exist. *Mythos* is also an organ of philosophy, but neither as reflexive consciousness, nor as a second-class organ somehow subordinate to the *logos*. *Mythos* is not ancillary to *logos*. The mythical dimension does not mean that I think the unthought—for then it would obviously cease to be unthought. It is an important task of philosophy to admit *mythos* as an organ *sui stante*, a contact with reality.

Now we cannot perceive our own myths *qua* myths; we can only recognize the myths of others or those of our own past. Myths are ultimate because they do not have any other background over against which they could be recognized as such. We can only take up living myths and allow them to unfold. Our prejudices (prejudgments), our presuppositions, our unreflective convictions, these all have a mythical character. Demythicization is necessary once one is unhappy with his 'myth' because the *logos* has already replaced it; but each demythicization brings with it a remythicizing. We destroy one myth—and rightly so if that myth no longer fulfills its purpose—but somehow a new myth always arises simultaneously. Man cannot live without myths. You know you have a stomach, but if it is functioning healthily, you do not think about it. This attitude of confidence is absolutely necessary for a healthy development of philosophy.

The meaning of dialogue comes into the picture here. The

necessity for dialogue in philosophy is grounded in the fact that no one is aware of his own myths, his mute presuppositions, and that we must reciprocally disclose and make these myths conscious. A presupposition I recognize as presupposition is no longer presupposed; it is a supposition, an assumption, a rule agreed upon, a principle. I can, however, discover the other's presuppositions, and vice versa; a mutual critique and fertilization then becomes possible. Solipsism is not only methodologically barren, it is also unphilosophical. Dialogue is necessary, not as something we welcome in our vast tolerance, but precisely because only the other is able to recognize and criticize my myths, my silent presuppositions. But we should not want to stick willingly to one particular myth, for then it would be no longer myth but 'bad faith'. Although myth ceases to be myth each time it is discovered, detached, made *logos*, it still remains the inexhaustible source of renewal. The procession from *mythos* to *logos* is inexhaustible.

This process is not an isolated event, not a monologue; it demands dialogue for two reasons. Dialogue first of all is *duologue*, i.e., two *logoi* meet and mutually unearth their mythical presuppositions. Dialogue presupposes that neither partner is self-sufficient, perfected, complete. But secondly, dialogue means *dia-logos*, i.e., it is not just a pair of speeches, but a transcending of the *logos*, a going-through the *logos* by means of the *logos*. The way leads from myth through *logos* to the *pneuma*.

In sum, the task of philosophy is to let the unthought be, but also to allow thought to emerge from it, and in this operation the unthought is never exhausted.

c. **Reception of the Pneuma**

The third task with which philosophy is gifted I would call the *reception of the pneuma*. I use *pneuma* because neither *Spirit* nor *Geist* really expresses what is meant. Not only does the unthought (*mythos*) together with the thought (*logos*) belong to philosophy, but also the unthinkable (*pneuma*). This I can neither think nor leave intact as unthought, but I must receive it as the never quite thinkable. The unthinkable does not exist in itself as a fixed dimension; at any given moment it is the provisional, the historical that accomplishes itself in the future, in hope. As the Alpha is always more original, so the Omega is always more ultimate. Receiving the *pneuma* is a permanent passage, a *pascha*, a pilgrimage; the procession from *mythos* through *logos* to *pneuma* is endless. Precisely this pneumatic dimension guarantees the constant openness into which we may take a step forward. This philosophy-on-the-way cannot allow itself to stop. If it stops it risks making the *pneuma* into an object, and thereby falls into idolatry, or again, by reflecting on the *pneuma* it thereby tumbles backward onto the plane of the *logos*. We can only say: We should not trouble the *pneuma*.[6]

To summarize: *logos*, *mythos* and *pneuma* correspond to the thought, the unthought and the unthinkable. These three interpenetrate, there is a *perichoresis*, they dwell within one another.

4. THE ONE MYSTERY

The following tetrahedron can symbolize this presentation:

mysterion

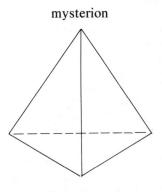

Illustration 3

The four faces contain the four dimensions of philosophy of which I spoke at first. That they are triangles represents the threefold gift and task of philosophy as integral integrity. The point in which all converge, and from which the whole tetrahedron issues, I would call the *mysterion*. I have said nothing about this because there is nothing to say.

*   *   *

Nowhere better than here can we detect the precariousness of our words. This is almost always the case when we try to speak in a cross-cultural perspective. To have written, for instance, *māyā* or *brahman* for *mysterion, vāc* or *buddhi* for *logos, cit* or *manas* for *pneuma* (and worst *kathā* or *dharma* for *mythos*) would not have helped our analysis because the entire problematic should have then taken a basically different turn. Yet, to have climbed by one particular way up to the heights of reality does not prove that there is only one peak, but from one summit we may have a better view.

NOTES

1. Cf. the chapter 'Necesidad de una nueva orientación de la filosofía india' in R. Panikkar, *Misterio y Revelación* (Madrid: Marova, 1971), pp. 51-82.

2. A few citations from the various resolutions distributed during the XIV International Congress held in Vienna in 1968 might illustrate this collision. For instance: "Philosophy cannot liberate itself by ignoring its weakness," and philosophy must understand itself "as part of the process of society's life." Philosophy "should bring about the destruction of global antagonisms," but "philosophy proclaims its weakness and thereby renounces praxis." "This Congress must eschew all political overtones," and yet must affirm the principle that "philosophies can change the world."

3. Cf. R. Panikkar, 'Le concept d'ontonomie', *Actes du XIè Congrès International de Philosophie, Bruxelles 2-26/Aug. 1953*. (Louvain: Nauwelaerts, 1953), vol. III, 182-88.

4. KathU VI, 12.

5. RV I, 164, 45.

6. Cf. Eph. 4:30.

XIII.
The God of Being and the 'Being' of God. Religion and Atheism

kasmai devāya haviṣā vidhema

What God shall we adore with
our oblation?
RV X, 121, 1

1. INTRODUCTION

The modern Western world has been astonished by the unexpected fulfillment of a peculiar prophecy: the coming of atheism. Atheism had generally been considered an aberration, a revolt against the true order of things. Yet today it has been defended not only by Men of both intellectual and moral integrity who confess no 'religious' beliefs, but also by Christians who claim the real Christian message in a world 'come of age' is fundamentally connected to this new godless outlook on life and to an atheistic insight into Christ.

The purpose of these reflections is to help focus the place of atheism in Western thought from the double perspective of Eastern and Western religious traditions.[1]

Taking a broad view of human history, we discover, as we have already indicated, a threefold thread running throughout. One thread is mythical: Man cannot live without myths. God is here present in all the Gods. On the other hand, neither can Man subsist on myth alone: The passage from *mythos* to *logos* — the distinctive feature of the last five or six thousand years of civilization — is the second thread. The result has been the absolutization of the *logos* in one of its many forms: trinitarian, ontological, epistemological, cosmic; *verbum dei*, *entis*, *mentis*, *mundi*, *hominum*.[2] Here God is synonymous with the Absolute. Today Man tries to overcome this stage, an attempt befitting our present stage of anthropological mutation. Yet killing the *logos* in Man is tantamount to suicide. *Mythos* and *logos* always and only coexist in the spirit, the third thread. Now the spirit is freedom—even from Being. Here God is not so much the free Being as the very freedom of Being itself. In this we are neither telling a myth nor just playing with words—*logoi*—because the statement makes sense only coming from myth and transcending the *logos* in the spirit. We cannot regain a lost innocence. *Mythos*, *Logos* and *Pneuma* or, if we prefer, *māyā*, *cit* and *ānanda*, or Tradition, Intellect and Love, form the triple braid that may become a rope of salvation or a noose with which to hang ourselves. Willy-nilly, human destiny is in our hands.

Here I shall deal with only one question among the many arising from a serious study of modern atheism.

The identification of God with Being cannot be considered a universally recognized axiom. Not only does a certain contemporary atheism deny God, because it does not recognize his monopoly on Being, but from an opposite point of view a large number of religions have existed and still flourish that accept God without argument and yet do not identify him with Being. The problem appears from either angle:

1. the divinization of Being (the God of Being);
2. the de-ontologization of God (the 'being' of God).

A great part of the destiny of philosophy and the future of religion depend on working out the relationship between these two perspectives. Christianity, for example, has so deeply committed itself to identifying God and Being that denying the equation seems to question the very essence of Christianity.

Indeed, Being can be understood as a noun (substance), an adjective (quality), a verb (relation); in other words, as an existence, an essence or a relationship (Being, being, be-ing). These distinctions call for important qualifications we cannot expound here. Nevertheless all three assume God *is*.

The history of many a human culture seems to show that Man must either divinize Being or ontologize the Divinity. At this level there cannot be two: Both God and Being claim superiority in the same sphere. There seems to be no other solution than a fight to the bitter end: Either God and Being are identified or the one kills the other. In the latter case, we are left with only Being-without-God or God-without-Being. How Being can survive without (being) God is indeed a serious question, but the naked existence of God without (being) Being is still more so.

Simply stated: If 'philosophically' we start with beings and Being, very soon we shall come across Gods and God, and shall have to assign them a place in metaphysics. Now God does not resign himself to playing second fiddle; he is not one among others in the scale of beings. So he must break through to reach Being. The beginnings of Greek philosophy offer a paradigm for this problem. God may come later and from outside philosophy, but inevitably he tends to conquer the summit of the ladder of beings or die in the escalade.

Similarly, if 'theologically' we start with God, the problem of Being appears as soon as God has to be concerned with the world and must clarify his connection with it. Identification between God and Being is here not dialectically necessary, as in the first case, but somehow God must rule over beings and will not admit any higher court of appeal. A private God may avoid having it out with Being, but when the divine hierarchy and the scale of beings is established, the connections between them will perforce be so close that they soon become one and the same.

This seems to be the destiny of human thought, including the Western trends, up to our times. Ontology and theology, carried to extremes, cannot but concur. Today our age doubts precisely this concurrence, the result of centuries of speculation and 'progress'.

Our problem is this: What happens to God and Being if we disentangle them? Can we return to the 'primitivism' of a God who wants nothing to do with thought (for thought is what discloses Being to us), a God who does not suffer philosophical scrutiny? Or must we plunge forward and peremptorily abandon a God who has usurped the throne of Being for centuries? Here we need a multicultural and pluri-religious outlook to find a solution. First we must ask whether it is possible to de-divinize Being without doing damage to God and, second, whether it is possible to de-ontologize God without harming Being. If this is not feasible, the only alternative is to identify God and Being or accept nihilistic atheism.

The problem is far from theoretical. Isn't the strong reaction of many young people in the West a new form of anti-ontological and aphilosophical religiousness? Isn't the equally sincere and spontaneous reaction of many Eastern young people a new form of antiritualistic, 'areligious' humanism?

2. THE GOD OF BEING (DIVINIZATION OF BEING)

Not only do the primordial religions not envisage God as Being, but in almost every religion it is considered far from necessary to make them identical. The exciting history of the divinization of Being has still to be written. I would suggest three attitudes: anthropomorphism, ontomorphism and personalism.

Needless to say, these attitudes should be considered neither consecutive periods in a linear sequence of time and history, nor necessary moments in a dialectical process. Rather they should be seen as the triple dimension of a single problem, which we can solve only if we do not throw overboard any of its positive components. We need to find a fusion temperature high enough to allow their combination without either contradiction or syncretism. A history of humanity would perhaps speak of *kairological moments*.

I am well aware that, given the spiritual situation of our times, we are still far from a solution. The tensions and differences among these three points of view are strong, but they seem recently to have lessened. What follows is the framework for these attitudes.

a. Anthropomorphism

God may indeed have created Man in his image and likeness, but undoubtedly Man has conceived God according to his own picture and resemblance. It could hardly be otherwise: If God is to make sense to Men, he has to be, in one way or another, homologous to Man. Anthropomorphism is necessary for Men to think of God and for God to reveal himself to Men. If we 'refine' and 'purify' God too much from the human, he fades away. In fact, ever since Man's religious beginnings, God or the Gods have always had anthropomorphic features. Without them, there is no prayer, no cult, no possibility of human relationship with the divine. The *karma-mārga* (the way of action), the sacrifice, the rite and the like are fundamental elements of any religion. God is the Lord, the Other, the Superbeing, but above all he is like Man. The very superiority of God needs Man as a point of reference, and is consequently an anthropomorphic feature.

b. Ontomorphism

Yet regardless of this anthropomorphism, Man is a thinking being with the power to abstract from himself and he cannot help desiring to know more and more. Philosophy and theology are the ways open to him for relating the divine to the exigencies of the thinking mind. Indeed, the believer says that the intellect itself is the effect, or grace, or creation of the Lord. Nevertheless the human effort to understand demands that God no longer be an unpredictable Will or a whimsical Power beyond any possible apprehension (awe and fear are perhaps the earliest religious categories); but that he be Truth, Goodness—in a word, Being. In this way he conforms to the rules of the ontic play, allowing Men to discover God's will and his nature not only by asking him directly but by scrutinizing the mystery of reality and human existence. Truth is the will of God and Goodness his nature. This being the case, to call God Being means there need no longer be an irreconcilable conflict between faith and reason, theology and philosophy, the world and religion. *Jñāna-mārga* (the path of knowledge) is the way to salvation. Real tragedy in the classical sense is no longer possible because there is no destiny outside or above the realm of God.

c. Personalism

But Man is a religious person, he cannot help but desire an authentic personal life. This amounts to aspiring to an integrating relationship with the divine, which too philosophical a notion of God only blurs. Man is a living being, and his awareness of suffering and evil puts the concept of God in unavoidable crisis. If God is Being, he is also responsible for the dark side of the world. If he is not, he must give up his claim to be supreme and almighty.

Further, if God is *absolute* Being, he is incapable of love and Man can scarcely enter a relation of prayer, entreaty, joy or thanksgiving with such a God. Man needs *bhakti-mārga* (the way of love) as much as he needs action and knowledge. This is why the third attitude tries to synthesize both not by saying that God is anthropomorphic, or that he is just immutable and static Being, but by asserting that Being itself is personal, that the Absolute itself has a personal nature.

Now a personal supreme being cannot be alone, for person implies society. Christians may welcome this idea by pointing out that this is precisely what the Trinity means. But the relationship should neither be substantialized (there would then be either three supreme Beings or none at all), nor considered exclusively *ad intra* (this God is not only person for himself). Further, God's relation to the nonpersonal world should also be rethought.

None of these fundamental attitudes satisfies the great part of humanity today, yet they cannot be dismissed altogether. God has climbed onto the throne of Being and now begins to feel uncomfortable there. The dominion of the God of Being over the people seems to have ceased. Either he abdicates or he is overthrown.

No need now to voice all the criticisms against these views; they are in the air almost everywhere. Nor need we elaborate further that an eclectic 'solution'—drawing now from one attitude, now from another, according to the doubts or queries of the so wrongly called 'unbelievers'—will not satisfy anybody. Moreover, the weakness of a pastoral approach is that it keeps the pastor from being approachable—it assumes he knows the answers, whereas here the question itself is put in question.

The insufficiency of these attitudes raises the second major problem: What happens to God if he is disentangled from Being. Can he survive?

3. THE 'BEING' OF GOD (DE-ONTOLOGIZATION OF GOD)

Following Aristotle in Europe and the Upaniṣads in India, Being is primarily substance. Being is what subsists and supports the rest of reality. As the basis of everything, it is hidden; but hidden does not mean unreal. Being is the subject, the *ousia*, the *ātman*.

Accordingly, if God exists he cannot but identify himself with Being: He is the ultimate Subject, the Substance—the basis of everything—the *brahman* identical to the *ātman*, hence the primary Cause, the unmoved mover, the ultimate Creator, infinite Goodness, the perfect Idea, the utmost Justice, the supreme Being. Nowadays such an identification collapses from both sides, that of Being and that of God.

On the part of Being, it breaks down because substantialistic thinking is no longer dominant and decisive; consequently substance has lost its privileged ontic position. Calling God a 'super-being' or a 'super-substance'(!) may solve the problem of pantheism or monism but it avoids the more fundamental issue, because the 'super' always remains a qualification of the 'being'—and thus, if it is to be real, already belongs to the realm of 'being'. The so-called 'ontological difference', as well as the classical distinction between essence and existence, and many currents in modern philosophical thought arise from premises other than those upholding the primacy of substance. But if Being is simply a function, can God be reduced to being the play without a player of such a role? We could formulate the question negatively or positively.

The *negative* way would read: How does God escape from ontology? That is, how does he escape the nets of ontology so that we may justify both? The peaceful symbiosis between God and Being that since Aristotle has constituted the spine of Western culture is no longer possible. In fact, whenever ontology ran up a blind alley, it appealed to God for backing. Descartes, for example, needed divine truthfulness to maintain his system. On the other hand, when the concept of God is confronted with insurmountable difficulties, Men turn to ontology with a concept of Being with which to overcome the apologetic obstacles. For example, the problem of evil: The divine Father who as a good person cannot condone evil can permit it because he is the Being that includes everything.

Can we disentangle God and Being so that there can be a place for God near or below the Being of ontology? Here the problem refers to God more than Being; he would have to emancipate himself from the tutelage and refuge metaphysics has so far provided him. How can God get rid of the rank of Being?

The *positive* formulation of the same problem will simply refer to God's connection with Being, for it could hardly consent to refer to what kind of 'being' God is, or what God's place is in the universality of Being.

Can a religious attitude escape the exigencies of thought, avoid the spiderweb spun by thought? We could discuss the exact connection between Being and thought running from Parmenides and the Upaniṣads until today, but one thing seems evident: If being is, thought will discover it for us, at least partially. This is the minimum in common between thinking and being, although the connection may be much more intimate. Thinking is not being as such but the organ of being; it discloses being to us.

Now, is a post-critical attitude possible, an attitude that is reflective, not merely instinctive, vital or preconscious, one that gives rise to a real connection with God without encroaching on the field of thought, i.e., without touching the sphere of being? There can be a thinking that does not refer to God, but can there be a God that does not refer to our thought? Can thought hide and keep itself respectfully outside the ambit of God? The unsolved problem is to decide who limits thought. If the limits are self-imposed, they are not real limits. If on the other hand they are forced, nothing can prevent thought from disregarding the prohibition and approaching the tree of knowledge of good and evil in its own attempt to become like God. Can God be or become apparent, meaningful or even real to us if we leave our faculty of thought aside?

We can not reply now to such questions. If the history of the God of Being is still to be written, the history of the 'being' of God is still to be lived and experienced. This history would represent the *kairos* of our present world. For the most part, the contemporary post-critical attitude has been trying to de-ontologize God, an understandable if not always well-balanced reaction. As a result we have hurriedly *denied* God, instead of *reforming* the concept. The denial of God belongs to the process of remythicizing 'him'.

Just as the three attitudes described earlier represent constitutive dimensions of human religiousness, so the factors I am going to sketch constitute three acts in the drama of Man trying to de-ontologize God.

a. Atheism

The serious challenge of atheism lies not in its anti-theism, which negates the personal character of God, but in its denial of God's existence or essence; in other words, in its refusal to consider God as Being or as any kind of absolute. Atheism criticizes whatever idea of God we may put forward. From this point of view, it seems irrefutable. It is weak, on the other hand, when it tries to offer a positive substitute for the theistic vision. Atheism is necessary as a constant corrective to any belief in God, but it always betrays its mission when it becomes a substitute for God, religion or whatever. Atheism is a constant reminder that Man cannot transfer the burden and joy of his own existence onto Another, that there is no Presence somewhere, ready to excuse Man for being just Man. For atheism, God is the great absence, just the echo of Man's voice, which should not frighten its author.

b. Apophatism

More than one religious tradition would say that God is not only Being but corresponds to Non-Being as well. If atheism negates God as Being, apophatism denies God as Non-Being. It is as inappropriate to say he exists as to affirm he does not exist. Human silence may indeed be the epistemic category that reaches God and ontic silence his own first attribute. The *Logos*, the Speech, the Word is not God, but his Son, Image, Manifestation. So that Being is not God but God's epiphany. The only way to guarantee divine transcendence is simply not to play with or manipulate that concept, not even by sham analogy. This attitude will say that the only way to make room for God is to not try to squeeze him into the frame of our thinking. Faith in God demands such total confidence that we do not bother about his being or existence. God utterly transcends our being and our thinking powers. It is not that his ontic density, as it were, dazzles and overwhelms us; it is rather that he has no ontic density at all because he *is* not. Modern and ancient descriptions of God as love or pardon and the like have sometimes tried to verbalize what others have preferred to keep silent.

While atheism is inclined to declare itself incompatible with any theistic affirmation (contradicting itself in the process, for then atheism becomes a substitute for theism), this second attitude declares itself compatible with any type of theistic formulation. If atheism is cataphatic, this second moment is purely apophatic; it sinks into an utter silence, and raises its voice only to quieten our impulse to ask self-contradictory questions. How can I question the unquestionable?

c. Radical Relativity

If the two preceding acts are correctives to the corresponding affirming attitudes, this third act of our drama is pure affirmation and does not claim to rise above its own limits. It says not that everything on earth is prey to an all-destructive 'relativism', but, on the contrary, that without transcendent, immanent or skeptical escapism, we can envision God as the one 'pole' of the totality never exhausted in itself. Because Reality is the *radical relativity* of all things, it shows the divine neither as one aspect of things, nor as a pure totality or otherness, but as the pure and really infinite mutual relatedness of all things. Reality is nothing else. The whole is but an inexhaustible bundle of relations. In other words: The genuine experience of contingency leads Man to discover, not that he leans on 'another' being in order to subsist, but that his own being is nothing but an *in*, a *from*, a *part*, a *tension*, a *pole*, an *element* of the whole, and that this whole is the sum of the existing infinite factors as the relationship of everything. Here God is neither being nor non-being; he neither exists nor does not exist; he is neither one with the World or Man, nor different and other; he is the very relationship, the radical relativity, the non-dualistic dimension, ground, or summit or whatever name we might choose.

In summary, we have tried to explore only one issue and do not claim to have reached any conclusion, except perhaps to say that the aspects of human religiousness we mentioned are constitutive and yet insufficient dimensions of Man's inexhaustible quest for Reality. We could perhaps remember the answer of the Buddha when asked about the purpose of *nirvāṇa*: "This question, O Rādha! cannot catch its limit." It is really not a question. Any attempt to answer it will only entangle us more and more in unnecessary complications. Perhaps the query about God has an answer only when it quiets the very question. But then it is not a quiet question, nor is silence an answer to it. Rather, the question does not arise because the question is quieted: 'Blessed are the poor in spirit!'

NOTES

1. This essay presents in a condensed way some of the ideas developed in the author's book *El Silencio del Dios* (Madrid: Guadiana, 1970).

2. Cf. chapter XII.

XIV.
The Law of Karma and
The Historical Dimension of
Man

iyam karmagatir vicitrā
durvijñānā ca.

This course of *karman* is mysterious
and difficult to discern.
YSB II, 13 (+)

+ *Vicitra* may also mean variegated, manifold, strange, wonderful,
   etc., *durvijñāna*, understanding with difficulty.

1. THE PROBLEM

Contemporary Man reflects critically on his historical situation and asks himself whether historicity is not a constitutive dimension of his being. Westerners tend to consider historicity a characteristic almost peculiar to Semitic-Christian culture and are somewhat proud of this monopoly. Starting with the assumption that nowadays any problem that is not stated in universal terms contains a methodological flaw from the very outset, the aim of this study is to offer some considerations on the historical nature of Man, taking into account the concept of *karma*.[1] It should be said from the very beginning that the purpose of this paper is not to compare the Indian concept of *karma* with the Western concept of historicity, because in neither camp do these concepts appear clear-cut. There is a multitude of opinions on the matter both in India and the West. Further, I wish not to compare the two concepts in any strict sense, but to understand and deepen a philosophical (or religious) problem with the aid of more than one philosophical (or religious) tradition. What I would like to attempt is a clarification of an authentic philosophical problem with all the tools at my disposal, that is, with the insights and ideas I may have learned from both traditions. By tools I do not mean only external instruments for expressing an idea but also internal means for grasping the particular problem. A real culture does not only provide tools; it also offers the very field in which these tools are effective.

Formulating the rules for a meeting of cultures is an urgent need of our times.[2] No particular culture has the right to set the pattern, and no pattern can be set without a certain preunderstanding of the other culture. A pattern can be established only if some people succeed in undergoing a genuine internal experience of both cultures. Extrapolation will not do here. Only living 'rosettas' will help the mutual decipherment.

The ideal is to discover the growing points in one culture that are sensitive to the problems of another culture. In this way a natural growth becomes possible, through a cultural metabolism that combines endogenous and exogenous elements in assimilable portions.

I stress that this is relevant not only theoretically but also at the most practical and concrete political level. Today the world is impelled toward a common destiny. Oriental ways of life are emigrating West, Marxist ideologies of many types are taking root in Asian fields. Social or rather socialistic consciousness is emerging violently in this—Eastern—part of the world. Allergies, schizophrenias, repressions and obsessions are maladies that afflict not only individuals but also societies. I consider the topic of this study vitally important and plead for insight and collaboration; repentance and true revolution go together. Otherwise we have only chaos, repression and counterrepression.

2. SOME INDOLOGICAL NOTES

Karman is a noun meaning action and comes from the root *kṛ*, 'doing, acting, performing, etc.' The concept and even the Sanskrit word are found in most Asian religious traditions from ancient *brahmanism* to modern Japanese Buddhism. Beginning about three millenia ago, it has a long history, from Iran to Japan, from Mongolia to Borneo. There is hardly a more widespread concept. In general one could say that a trait common to almost all Asian religions is the acceptance of the central intuition underlying *karma*.

Little wonder, then, that the meaning of *karma* varies from one extreme to the other on the scale of possible interpretations, and yet it seems that one fundamental intuition underlies all the meanings. This basic concept I would like to examine in one of its aspects *only*, namely, what in modern Western languages could be rendered by 'historicity', understood as an anthropocosmic dimension.

From among the many Asian traditions, I have chosen the Sanskritic Indian one for reasons of expediency. I could equally have chosen the Buddhist line which is also of Indian origin and, in fact, the acme and the most penetrating analysis of *karman* is to be found there. Buddhism affirms pure *karma* because there is no *ātman* to offer any resistance to it or to condense or condition *karma*. There are only the acts themselves (*karman*) and their fruits (which again produce new acts), without any actor or agent (*kartṛ*). As a matter of fact the Buddhist intuition may be nearer to the ideas developed here, but it is more challenging to take up the *ātmavādic* line of Indian thought to make this interpretation more convincing. Similar studies of other sources may qualify some of my statements, but I would venture to say that on the whole they would substantiate from another angle what I am propounding.[3]

a. Vedas and Brāhmaṇas

In the Ṛg Veda, *karman* in its many forms appears a number of times with the meaning of action, especially sacred action, sacrifice.[4] Scholars discuss whether or not the idea of rebirth is present in the Ṛg Veda.[5] The texts are not clear and certainly do not use *karman* to express what could be interpreted as reaping in another life the fruits of a previous one.[6] The only text traditionally given in support of the rebirth theory says:

> Your eye will have to go to the Sun;
> your spirit (*ātmā*) will have to go to the Wind;
> Go to heaven or earth according to your merit (*dharmaṇā*),
> or go to the waters if this is your lot;
> settle down among the plants with all your bones.[7]

This text could be read against the background of many others.[8] The meaning is that the life of the individual has neither an absolute beginning nor an absolute end and that the many constituents of life continue their existence in other realms of the world. Significantly, the word *karman* does not appear. *Dharma* is used instead.

What is stressed again and again in the Ṛg Veda is the fact that human fullness and cosmic salvation are reached only through the sacred action, the sacrifice that completes the creative action by which the world came into being and continues to exist.[9]

The Atharva Veda has some passages stressing the importance of *karman*,[10] and in one text it seems to correct or complement the Ṛg-Vedic vision of a famous hymn that says that ardor or energy was the origin of cosmic order and of truth,[11] affirming that this energy or ardor (*tapas*) was born from *karman*.[12] This universe is the fruit of a divine action and through another set of integral or theandric actions it is conserved and saved.[13]

This is the main idea the Brāhmaṇas will develop, that the sacrifice or sacred action is the ultimate cause and dynamic of this world.[14] Now if sacred action has such power, the human being is responsible for using it properly. Moreover, the world itself depends on the performance of such acts. And here we have in a nutshell all the future motifs of *karma*. In the Śatapatha Brāhmaṇa we find that 'a Man is born into the world he has made',[15] and that the idea of judgment according to one's deeds is already common.[16]

b. The Upaniṣads

Perhaps the earliest text concerning what is called transmigration is found in the Bṛhadāraṇyaka Upaniṣad,[17] which sums up a long development of thought. Later in that Upaniṣad we find:

> Now this Self (*ātman*) is brahman indeed. It consists of understanding (*vijñāna*), mind (*manas*), life-breath (*prāṇa*), sight (*cakṣuh*) and hearing (*śrotra*) of earth (*pṛthivī*), water (*āpaḥ*), wind (*vāyu*) and space (ether, *ākāśa*), light (*tejas*) and darkness (*atejas*),[18] loving desire (*kāma*) and indifference (*akāma*), anger (*krodha*) and non-anger (*akrodha*), righteousness (*dharma*) and the absence of it (*adharma*); it consists of all things. This is the meaning of the saying: it consists of this, it consists of that.

As one acts (*karman*), as one behaves, so does one become (*yathākārī yathācārī tathā bhavati*). Acting well something becomes good, acting ill it becomes evil. By meritorious acts one becomes meritorious (*puṇyaḥ puṇyena karmaṇā bhavati*), by sinful acts, sinful (*pāpaḥ*).

Some have said: this person (*puruṣa*) consists of loving desire (*kāma*) alone. As his loving desire, so his will (*kratu*), as his will, so will he act (*karman*); as he acts so will he attain.[19]

The operant ideas are clearly visible if we take into account the whole context. Man is an aggregate or a principle of activities that have a wider repercussion than he imagines; his actions as well as his constitutive elements are not his private monopoly, they belong to the wide world and to the wide world they return; Man has an ontological and not merely an ethical stewardship. Man's actions receive not only reward and punishment, they also carry an ontological weight that does not depend only on the private endowment of their actual performer.

The passage from the Bṛhadāraṇyaka Upaniṣad that answers the one just quoted is worthwhile summarizing, for it opens up the actual meaning of the text. Jāratkārava Ārthabhāga is questioning the great Yājñavalkya regarding several problems; they come to discuss the meaning of life and its connection with death. What happens at death?

'When a person dies, what is it that does not depart from him?'[20]

After having answered that it is the name that is infinite and immortal, Yājñavalkya goes on to disclose the cosmic law of the conservation of all the elements in the universe:

'. . . the voice enters into the fire, the life-breath into the air (or, goes with the wind), the eye into the sun, the mind into the moon, the ear into the regions, the body into the earth, the self into the space . . .'

What then happens to this person?

'Ārthabhāga, my friend,' said he, 'take my hand. We two alone

shall know about this. It is not for us to unfold this in public.'
Away they went together and together they spoke with one
another. What they were discussing was *karman* and what they
were praising was *karman*. Indeed one becomes meritorious
by meritorious action and sinful by sinful action. Then Jārat-
kắrava Ārthabhắga kept his peace in silence.[21]

Here *karman* no longer appears as the sacrificial act or, as in
the Gītā, the truly moral and thus ontologically real action, but as
that core which remains of the person and yet transcends all
individuality.

There are many other places in the Upaniṣads stressing the
peculiar nature of *karma*,[22] the cosmic destiny of Man's actions,[23]
the importance of a Man's last acts,[24] the continuation of Man's
attributes[25] and the inherent justice of this procedure,[26] the details of the transmission,[27] the end of the deeds retaining one on
earth,[28] the nature of release[29] and its release to the sacrifice,[30]
etc.[31]

We may sum it all up with a short sentence from a relatively
late Upanisad: "The doer of the acts . . . he is the enjoyer."[32]

c. Tradition

It may suffice to adduce some recognized texts. The
Bhagavad Gītā could be said to be the consecration of the way of
karma to such an extent that for the Gītā, *karma* is the constitutive element of our creatureliness.[33] A substantial part of it is
dedicated to this theme; chapters II and III deal thematically with
the question of action and inaction, works and not works.[34] The
law of *karma* is fully recognized.

The Brahmasūtra contributes two important passages that
also supply a leading thread to the development of the idea in the
traditional commentaries throughout the centuries.[35]

The Yogasūtras also offer some basic references to the understanding of *karma*. Īśvara, the Lord, is a special kind of Self
precisely because he is untouched by *karma*.[36] Release amounts
to the cessation of all *karma*,[37] obtained by eliminating all latent
deposits of *karma*,[38] a process that entails alternate advance and
recession in the development of *karma*,[39] neither of which need
be conscious.[40] Only he who witnesses to his own self (*ātmasāk-*

ṣātkāra) over against the individualistic 'I-am-ness' (*asmitā*) reaches salvation.[41]

The discussion of the relation between the theology of works and that of knowledge, or between the way of sacred or secular action and the way of traditional or modern scientific knowledge, may be said to be one of the pivots of all Indian culture from its beginning until our own days.[42] There is a striking continuity discernible only to a sociologist: Today's temples may be new constructions, but the rites are ancient.[43]

As a representative example of the traditional Indian thinking I would like to quote one passage from the Prince of the Advaitins:

> But, to raise a new objection, there exists no transmigrating soul different from the Lord and obstructed by impediments of knowledge; for Sruti expressly declares that 'there is no other seer but he; there is no other knower but he' (BU III.7.23). How then can it be said that the origination of knowledge in the transmigrating soul depends on a body, while it does not so in the case of the Lord?—True, we reply. *There is in reality no transmigrating soul different from the Lord*.[44]
>
> Still the connection (of the Lord) with limiting adjuncts, consisting of bodies and so on, is assumed, just as we assume the ether to enter into connection with diverse limiting adjuncts such as jars, pots, caves, and the like. And just as in consequence of connections of the latter kind such conceptions and terms as 'the hollow (space) of the jar', etc. are generally current, although the space inside a jar is not really different from universal space, and just as in consequence thereof there generally prevails the false notion that there are different spaces such as the space of a jar and so on; so there prevails likewise the false notion that the Lord and the transmigrating soul are different; a notion due to the non-discrimination of the (unreal) connection of the soul with the limiting conditions, consisting of the body and so on. That the Self, although in reality the only existence, imparts the quality of Selfhood to bodies and the like which are Not-Self is a matter of observation, and is due to mere wrong conception, which depends in its turn upon an antecedent wrong conception. And the consequence of the soul thus involving itself in the transmigratory state is that its thought depends on a body and the like.[45]

No need to comment; the texts show that the locus of the *karma* theory is not merely the ethical realm, but that it is intrinsic to a whole conception of reality.

As for the rest of Indian tradition, we are here assuming that it, together with its Western counterpart, is sufficiently known.[46]

d. Summary

In attempting to bring together the many threads of Indian tradition we can detect three operant ideas:

i. Karma as the saving sacrificial action; sacrifice understood as the truly theandric action by which the human and the divine collaborate to maintain the universe and cause it to reach its goal. This aspect, which is the original idea, is expressed in the Vedas and the Brāhmaṇas.

ii. Karma as *karmamārga*, that is, the path of action, of good works, as the way to human salvation and fulfillment. Action is inevitable and so not entangling if performed in the right way, with the right spirit. Not detachment from action is required, but non-attachment in action from its expected fruits. The Bhagavad Gītā still remains the highest example of this attitude.

iii. Karma as the subtle structure of temporal reality that remains once the prima facie elements have faded away or been transformed, as that which all existing beings have in common. Here the concept of historicity, in the human and cosmic sense, finds its place. The lasting message of the Upaniṣads accentuates this aspect, which also underlies all the philosophical schools. Yoga, for instance, has developed many physical and spiritual implications of this experience.

3. THE KARMIC CONCEPTION OF THE UNIVERSE

To explain the karmic conception of the world I will now break up this unitary vision into a few particular rays, each of which may give us in prismatic refraction one of the colors of the spectrum. There are three fundamental options regarding the nature of the human person, all of them well represented throughout the history of thought.

First, the core of the human being has never been born, therefore neither does it die. Birth and death are only 'epiphenomena', superficial appearances. Only the body is born and dies, not the real person. The Self that has to be realized was always there and remains untouched by the temporal flow of external events. Real human freedom is a direct consequence of this vision: Man is above the superficial events of history. This is the option Indian culture has stressed.

Second, the core of the human being is certainly born, but it does not die; it is immortal. Man has a soul that has originated either in this world or in another stage of existence, but that will never cease to exist. Each person is sacred and an end in itself because of the immortal soul it embodies. Human dignity is linked with this idea. This is the option Greek and post-Hellenic culture has emphasized.

Third, the core of the human being is both born and mortal. It comes into existence as a really new and fresh beginning. Man is real, but he also has a real end, a human annihilation: Man is mortal. The direct consequence of this attitude is an urge to better the human condition and to work for this world as long as there is still time. This is the option modern secularism underscores.

My contention is that the insight of *karma*, like many other fundamental human intuitions, has a cross-cultural value because, though wrapped in a certain cultural garb, it is intended to explain a basic human attitude. Thus, although traditionally linked with the first option, it can serve equally well as a fruitful hypothesis for the other two. The nature of *karma* will of course be interpreted differently, but its quintessence, so to speak, will be the same in all three cases.

In the first option, *karma* stands for what has to be burned away, the obstacle to realization. It is the coefficient of *illusion* and unreality.

In the second, *karma* represents the raw material, as it were, that the immortal soul must elaborate (or assimilate) in order to disentangle itself (or grow to the point of liberation) from the temporal and mortal world. *Karma* here is the coefficient of *creatureliness*.

In the third, *karma* is identified with Man himself. The *humanum* consists of the karmic contents of the universe that bridge the gulf between the individual and the world. *Karma* is the anthropological coefficient of reality, of *humanness*.

In all three conceptions, however, there remains an underlying unity that may be brought to light by simple semantics. *Karma* has been translated as *work*, but in modern languages this word does not convey all the aspects of *karma*. It should rather be rendered as action in the scholastic sense of *actio*, taken both actively and passively (*active et passive sumpta*), i.e., it is at once the metamorphic power that turns the wheel of existence and the passive material to be metamorphosed, burnt, annihilated. It is that action by which the world comes into being and perdures, the action whose echoes ring in every nook and cranny of being, the action that every deed and activity only mirrors, gives back, individualizes, channels, expresses and lays bare. It is the act and the acted (thing), the action and the effect of the act. *Karma* stands for the undivided, nondualistic view of reality where the act is not severed from its effect. The act is act precisely because it has its own effect, because it acts. The karmic view of reality is thus the integrated insight that links all things together, allowing for differentiation and discrimination, but not for separation or ontological dichotomies.

a. The Mythical and the Mythological

Popular belief, East and West, usually holds that the theory of *karma* means what the names 'transmigration' and 'rebirth' encompass. According to this belief, you, individual E, are going to be born in an individual F according to your *karma*, i.e., according to your deeds, good or bad, so that as a reward or punishment you are reborn in a higher or lower being. When E was born he inherited the past *karma* of individual D and so the karmic line has neither beginning nor end, except for the released person, the saint, who has burnt all his *karma* and leaves behind no remnant with which to be born again. This interpretation, first of all, gives every individual a chance to win eternal life, if not at one stroke, then after a number of births. Secondly, it gives a *prima facie* account of two scandalous human facts: the inequalities of nature and society on the one hand, and the problem of evil and suffering on the other. As to how these past *karma* came into existence, different schools propound different theories, including human free will.

I submit that this picture is a simple caricature of something that gets fundamentally distorted in passing from the mythical to the mythological. A parallel example in Christian thought would be to consider heaven a big air-conditioned hall where for all eternity the Christian God amuses and entertains his worshipers who behaved bravely on earth, or as a paradise where all the desires repressed in earthly existence find their fulfillment.

I do not mean to suggest that popular beliefs are wrong. I am only insisting that the passage from the mythical to the mythological represents a *metábasis eis állo génos*, a passage to another genre, which disfigures the original image. Those who live in a particular myth express their beliefs in terms and images that lose their message and truth the moment they are uprooted from their original soil. The words may be the same, but their meaning has completely shifted. Our problem is the more aggravated in that it involves not only the passage from one particular kind of understanding to another, but also from one particular culture and world view to a completely foreign one. To begin with, even the terms we use—'metempsychosis', 'transmigration', 'rebirth', *et al.*—are either misnomers or mistranslations. [46a]

Here *mythical* refers to all those symbols and contents we take for granted, the horizon over against which our conceptions of reality are intelligible. *Mythological* is intended to express that conscious awareness which results when the *logos* enters into the myth and partially transposes mythical contents into a logical context. Mythological reduction more or less conserves the 'letter' or formal aspects of the myths without conserving belief in them. By this very fact mythology changes the object of mythical consciousness; that is, mythical intentionality points to something altogether different from its mythological contents. The God of my belief—Śiva, Zeus, Yahweh or any other—is my myth; the concept of God you may make of it without believing in him is the mythology you draw from my myth. Similarly, Democracy, Justice, Patriotism or whatever ideal I may believe in, without knowing in *what* I believe, and which directs my course of action constitutes my myth; while your concepts of my values, in which you yourself do not believe, constitute the mythology you discover in my beliefs. We all live in myths and at times we all discover the mythological contents of some of them and so discard and replace them by means of the *logos*, that is, by the self-aware and critical faculty of human knowledge. The passage from myth to *logos* makes for human culture and civilization, but the recession from forgotten *logoi* into the magma of new and emerging myths is what accounts for the inexhaustibility of human progress—without ever reaching the heavens as at Babel.

My task here is to discover whether it is possible to explain the mythical without mythological distortion. The key to the procedure is a belief in truth, which must accompany us throughout our enquiry.

Our quest is the more important because the theory of *karma* is probably the result of a historical process of secularization from the Vedic and *brāhmaṇic* conception of sacrifice to the general understanding of life itself as a kind of sacrifice. The idea could perhaps be summarized in this way: Sacrifice is the sacred action par excellence which brings salvation and various kinds of well-being (according to the type of sacrifice offered). It is not difficult to see that the danger of magic and priestly exploitation is all too near. So salvation and well-being needed to be rescued from the danger of dependence on the priestly class or on external ritual observances. The idea of *karma* offers the desired solution. The whole of life resembles a rite conducive to salvation and happiness; sacred actions are not a few acts performable only by experts or through them, but comprise the whole of human activities. The sacred has shifted from the altar to the sphere of life. In this way the theory of *karma* was experienced as a liberating process from a certain conception of the sacred. 'As a Man sows so will he reap' might be a simple formulation of it; or 'as the acts, so the results'. We should be very prudent and careful with words, but a certain wind of secularization could be detected in this process.

b. Karma and Cosmos

The first general idea of *karma* is that it expresses cosmic solidarity and ontological relationship.

It has been said time and again that the idea of *karma* denotes universality, that it is the causal link at work in the universe. Everything has a cause and produces an effect because the universe is a *kosmos*, an order, and not a chaos.[47] The idea of *karma* gives expression, first of all, to this inter-relatedness of everything in the world: Nothing gets lost, nothing is isolated or disconnected, any action reverberates to the very limits of universe; there are no hidden or secret actions on the karmic level.

Whatever its ontological constitution, the law of *karma* is universal. It pervades the whole universe and is coextensive with it almost by definition, so that if anything escaped the law of *karma* it would also escape the realm of world-reality. Not only are all transformations in some way the fruit of *karma*, but the underlying structure that makes the transformation possible and intelligible is also related to *karma*.

The Greek intuition 'the world is *kosmos* and not *chaos*' finds its counterpart in the Asian insight 'the world is *karman* and not *brahman*', meaning: this world or (as many texts of the Scriptures say) 'all this' (*idaṁ sarvam*), i.e., all that falls or can fall within the range of experience (of any kind) is *karman*. This is to say, it is all ordered and causally connected; it all builds a net of relationships between actions and reactions in which some convergences have the power to direct the threads in one or another direction, thus building up or reducing the karmic structure of the universe.

At this point one can determine that the two main areas of study for defining the nature of *karma* are: (1) its relation with the Absolute, and (2) its relation with the individual.

c. Karma and the Absolute

Karma is this cosmos. It is the peculiar causal structure of this universe and phenomenologically it shows itself as a pattern of pure relationship. In other words, *karma* is not the Absolute but rather the very symbol of the nonabsolute. It stands for that factor, that aspect (real or unreal, according to one's school), which distinguishes earthly existence from Absolute Being. Just as it is redundant to speak of an ordered cosmos, it is redundant to speak of a karmic world. The whole universe is *karma*; indeed, it is nothing but a concentration of *karma*, a crystallizing of karmic lines crossing one another to give the impression (again, true or false according to various schools) of this earthly reality.

The law of *karma* governs the entire 'contingent' world, the whole 'created' universe, all 'nonreal' Being, all 'provisional' existence, the whole of 'temporal' reality. Whatever *karman* may be it is not *brahman*, not *nirvāṇa*, not *mokṣa*, not *sat* (when considered as absolute being), etc. On the contrary, *karman* has to do with *saṃsāra* (the world), *kāla* (time), *duḥkha* (suffering), and the whole human and cosmic pilgrimage toward realization. *Karma* is the symbol of the relative, the changing, the provisional and temporal. The locus of *karma* is the temporal existence of reality, the temporal existence of this world and, above all, of Man.

Karma means the nonabsolute in a logical, epistemological and ontological sense.

Logically, *karma* is essentially relationship, mutual relatedness and so mutual dependence; it is the relative par excellence and not the absolute, the unrelated.

From an epistemological slant, karmic knowledge is knowledge about the 'working' of the universe, 'know-how' about the mutual relationship among things. It is phenomenal knowledge or scientific knowledge. The knowledge of *karma* will not tell us what things are, but how they 'work', behave, act and react. It will tell us nothing about the ultimate nature of things, only about their pragmatic interactions.

From the ontological point of view, *karma* is what claims to be nonabsolute, passing, provisional, not ultimate and definitive. Practically every ontology that deals with the notion of *karma* will distinguish a double level: the real, absolute, metaphysical and eternal level (called *pāramārthika*, *nitya*, *sat*, *ātman*, etc.); and the unreal, relative, phenomenonal and temporal one (called *vyāvahārika, anitya, asat, anātman,* etc.). One of the thorniest problems of Indian philosophies is how to relate these two levels.

So *karma* is the earthly realm of intraworldly causality. It represents the mutual cause-effect relation between all beings of the universe and their mutual repercussions. *Karma* is thus the nonmetaphysical structure of reality. To know what is beyond *karma* or how to transcend it constitutes the goal of most Indian philosophical systems.

d. Karma and the Individual

The karmic world view is a phenomenal and nonabsolute world view. Further, it is a nonindividualistic conception of the factual structure of the universe that in fact cannot be individualized. When everything is seen as a net of causal gross and subtle relationship, there is no possible criterion for an ontologically dividing line between individuals. The individual can only be a pragmatic device for naming things or for manipulating phenomena. The net of relationships constituting the karmic structure of reality (real or unreal according to the several systems) has no loose threads, no limits, no points of privilege that might indicate the beginning or end of any one individual.[48]

Moreover, we lack a criterion for individualization: If there were such a thing as a *pure* individual, i.e., sheer unrelatedness, it would for this very reason be outside the karmic realm. It would not be karmically detectable, it would exist outside the realm of mutual causality. It would be unconditioned and this can only be God, the Absolute, the *puruṣa* of Sāṃkhya, or an *avatāra*, a descent of the divine, a mutation or rather a discontinuity in the karmic structure of the world. In Buddhism it can only be *nirvāṇa*. If there is something outside time and causality, outside the reach of mutual relations and influences, it can by definition only be the realm of the Absolute. With this in mind many a system of Indian philosophy becomes understandable. If we postulate the existence of a *jīva, puruṣa, ātman,* a soul above the karmic realm, it can only be uncreated and so divine, belonging to another world.

We could put the same idea the other way round. There are no privileged individuals because each thing is unique. Each point, each karmic crossing, as it were, is unique. This is the well-known theory of momentariness so thoroughly developed in Buddhist philosophy. All that exists is only a succession of moments of existence (or of consciousness, according to how one stresses the relation between existence and consciousness).

It needs to be added that this conception makes sense only if accompanied by a spiritual quest for perfection, that is, for salvation. The fact that you discover the karmic nature of the universe indicates that there is 'something' that belongs to another realm or, more accurately, that there is nothing within the karmic structure that can appease the existential urge for 'salvation'. A fundamental distinction seems relevant here if we are to understand the deep intuition underlying *karma*: the distinction between individual and person.

Without embarking on specific philosophical considerations, we may readily agree that the notion of individuality is based on a numerical distinction and so that it needs some material basis for its expression. An individual is a singularity somehow complete in itself and separable from others; it is an indivisible ontic unit (in its own field) different from others precisely because of its singularity. The traditional image of atoms is perhaps the best example. A person, in contrast, is a center of relationships based in the qualitative distinction of uniqueness. A person is unique and incomparable, and so in some way a mystery, for uniqueness is the phenomenological expression of any ontological mystery: It cannot be com-pared, there is no point of reference, it remains a mystery.

In the karmic view of reality, the human being can in no way be considered a single individual—there is nothing in him that could be isolated or considered separable from the rest. All the elements of which the human being is said to consist are constitutively related to others and depend on such relations: physical elements, body, mind, will, the psychic reality of ego-consciousness, etc.; it is all nothing but a bundle of relations.

In such a view, can the human being be considered a person? In other words, is there any place for the ontological uniqueness of the human being as person?[49]

To be sure, the answer depends on the meaning we give

'person'. If we say 'person' but mean 'individual', then it defi-
nitely has no place here. If *ego* means individual consciousness
and the conviction that I myself am a kind of monad or spiritual
atom (that is, something with unique ontological reality in this
world), then we shall have to say there is no place for the *ego* in
the karmic conception of the world. More accurately, we shall
have to say that the whole karmic dynamism tends to treat this
illusion of ego-ness as the main evil, both ontological and moral,
and tries to eliminate it.

If by 'person' we understand the incidence of a nonkarmic
factor upon the karmic structure of reality that makes a particular
crossing of *karma* a center of freedom and decision, then we can
say there is place for the person as an incidence of a superior
order, which cannot be confused with the karmic one. The only
condition a karmic vision of reality would make is that the person
should respect the rules of the karmic game, which are the rules
of the entire cosmic order.[50]

From this perspective I would offer the following definition
of person: The person is that point of convergence of *karma*
which has the power (*puruṣakāra*) to burn *karma*. The person is
the one reality that has power over the whole karmic structure of
the universe, that is capable of directing the karmic threads in one
direction or another. To use a more congenial metaphor, the person is that power which has the capacity to destroy *karma* or to
engross it. The person is the great *māyin*, the cosmic artist or
magician able to create or annihilate *karma*. In a word, the person
is the center of freedom. How could he modify and steer *karma* if
there were not a superkarmic agent?

Anybody versed in Indian philosophy will recognize here the
echoes and the quintessence of one of the underlying motives of
most Indian systems: the play between *prakṛti* and *puruṣa*, the
intercourse between *brahman* and *Īśvara* in and through *māyā*.
And here also the last and most important of all the *mahāvākyāni*
acquires its liberating meaning: *tat tvam asi*. 'That thou art', i.e.,
this (you) are: *thou*, a thou of *brahman* and thus above *karma*
because *thou* canst handle *karma*.[51]

From this point of view, a nonegocentric understanding of

karmic human existence would stress, among others, the following points.

'My' *ego* is not the owner of 'my' life. This life does not begin with me, but was given to 'me'. I found it; I met it at a certain point endowed with positive and negative values. Or, rather, it found me. It is up to me to pass it on increased and embellished, or diminished and damaged. A series of elements, of karmic lines, have crossed and are constantly crossing within me, and I have to manage this truly human condition to the best of my abilities for my personal enjoyment and that of the whole world, without a sense of tragedy, however, for nothing on this level is ultimate and absolute. This allows non-tachment and perspective, love and play, gives a sense of relativity to all joys and softens the cruel face of all sorrows. My *ego* does not take itself too seriously or too tragically, as if it were the center of the universe or an absolute value. At the same time, I feel a cosmic responsibility because the entire universe depends on the positive handling of the *karma* at my disposal. I am the connecting link between the past and future, between myself and others, and this on a cosmic and universal level from which not a single being is excluded. It is obvious that the motivation for doing, for work, and for good actions will have to be something more than a crude or even reformed and refined eudaemonism for enjoying myself on any level. I shall act ethically only when the motives for my actions have reached an egoless motivation that is rooted in maintaining the whole universe: *lokasaṁgraha*.[52]

As for 'me', I shall find my enjoyment in having been called to play my role in the drama of this cosmos. As for 'me', I shall be given the opportunity to discover the vertical meaning of existence, to transcend the spatio-temporal structure of reality and overcome *karma* altogether. There is no frustration for the realized person, for his or her success is not measured by an objective yardstick that gauges objective achievement, but rather by living in such a way that, while giving life away, living it out, he or she reaches the other shore, the shore of fullness—or nothingness.

At this point I shall endeavor to clarify a widely held and

harmful misunderstanding and also to explain why it became so popular. I am referring to the incorrect identification of the theory of *karma* with so-called 'reincarnation'.

If there is something the law of *karma* does not say and that in fact contradicts all that it stands for, it is this popular misinterpretation. The law of *karma* insists that all a Man is—his energies, thoughts, merits and vices, his corporal elements, all that he had or was able to handle during his life—that all the *karma*, in a word, are not lost; rather they enter into the cosmic net of causality and solidarity. The exception is the psychological *ego*, which is either an illusion with no consistency whatsoever or a mere pragmatic label or a totally mortal thing, for it is the conglomerate of those qualities that fall asunder at the death of a particular human being. What transmigrates is all but the individual—if transmigration is to have any meaning at all.

The popular belief springs from an inability to get rid of what the whole karmic conception of the world intends to eradicate: selfish egocentricity. It may also be said to originate when individual consciousness emerges without a corresponding change in the cosmological world view; then the mythical becomes mythological, at least in the eyes of those who try to interpret the beliefs of others.

May I be allowed to be anecdotal for one paragraph? I have witnessed more than once a simple Indian peasant, believing in the law of *karma*, being driven to say what he does not, in fact, believe because of the exigencies of dialogue and the limitations of his own vocabulary when faced with an 'enlightened' questioner. Certainly he feels that he bears a treasure greater than himself, he is convinced that what he has in his hands, his life, is something over which he has no property rights. He senses that his existence did not begin with him nor will it end with him. But he is not saying, much less meaning, that *he* will be reborn, that *his* personality comes from someplace else and goes to another. He does not have the impression that what a modern would call the 'individual' goes on transmigrating. He is much closer to the already quoted saying of Śaṅkara that the Lord is the only transmigrator, that Life is what goes on, and that all the qualities he has cultivated will not be lost, nor will the vices he has accumulated. It is only when confronted with the idea that it might be he himself who will survive that his eyes may kindle at the temptation and he may yield, saying it may be so.

I might offer yet another hypothesis for what it is worth. Individual consciousness has for the last few centuries been so deeply rooted in the occidental mentality that Western Man can hardly imagine another type of thinking. We are now perhaps witnessing in the West a sharp reaction to this, but whatever the present trend, the fact is that the encounter between Western and Asian minds these last centuries was so entangled in the myth of the reality of the individual that no dialogue was possible without presupposing this view, indeed, taking it for granted. In this way, words like the transmigration of souls, reincarnation, etc., came into existence and with them a deformation of the original meaning of the Asian doctrines.

All this said, it must be added that this process of individualization is not only a Western phenomenon but seems inherent to the development of human consciousness.

4. KARMA AND HISTORICITY

All that follows should be understood within the limits of a *formal* philosophical investigation, not a *material* one. I am attempting to speak a language that will make sense for the follower of more than one philosophical tradition—a risky task perhaps, but necessary if one is to do justice to a cross-cultural investigation.

a. Karma and Time

The karmic conception of reality relativizes time and turns it into the very expression of the law of *karma*. This is the law of the temporal flux. The degree of reality time has corresponds to the degree of reality *karma* has. For those who consider *karma* real, time is real; for those for whom *karma* is unreal or partly so, time suffers the same fate. In fact, time is nothing but the flow of *karma*. *Karma* is a kind of condensation of time. Time past means past *karma*, and future time means *karma* to come.

The so-called 'circular' time is nothing but a transference of the beginninglessness of the karmic world to the sphere of time. Time is supposed to be circular simply because *karma* is considered to be inexhaustible without being absolute. To transcend *karma*, to burn it, to extinguish all *karma,* means to escape time, to go beyond it and enter the timeless. Now the beginninglessness of *karma* has quite often been misunderstood and construed as an ontological theory, when the original intuition was only phenomenological. *Karma* has no beginning and no end because it is not an entity in itself nor has it an end in itself. The only beginning of *karma* is the beginning that is taking place every moment; the only end (aim, goal) of *karma* is the end (extinction) of it. But to affirm that all *karma* will one day disappear is a sentence that has no meaning within the karmic context in which alone it can be formulated.[53]

Both time and *karma* allow for formal treatment, that is, for a consideration of their nature independent of temporal things or the things themselves. Yet this is only a thinking abstraction because in the last analysis there cannot be time without things temporal, just as there can be no *karma* without the actions and the results of different agents. Both *karma* and time are indissolubly tied to the things themselves.

b. Karma and History

The law of *karma* expresses what modern Western language might call the historical dynamism of beings. It is clear that if the center of gravity resides in and the attention of history is directed towards events easily datable externally, the law of *karma* does not pay them much attention. What the law of *karma* describes and registers are the inner modifications, the happenings internal to the beings themselves; karmic law centers its attention not on what beings did, but on what happened to them as they did it.

We may define historicity as the capacity to accumulate the past, as it were, and assume it into the present, or as that quality of human existence by which the past emerges into the present and configures it. This is not by a simple process of remembrance or by a gathering up of physical or spiritual bits and pieces of the past, but by assimilating or integrating them into the present in a special way. Again, if we define this same concept as that peculiar character by which the future too, somewhat similarly, becomes active and present in hope and reality in the here and now, so that one cannot define a person without including his past and future, then we may say that all those human peculiarities that today we sum up under the name of 'historicity' are practically all present and effective in the conception of *karma*.

Karma is the crystallization of actions past, as well as of the results of acts that are no longer in the past, but that emerge and are present in the contemporary situation of whoever bears that particular *karma*. In a way I am as much what I 'was' and equally what I 'shall be' as what at present I 'am'. Both past and future are already present in my present real situation.

We could use the familiar distinction between having and being. Properly speaking, *karma* is not what I *am*, but what I have. What I *am* belongs to the mystery of the person, and ultimately one can only say 'I am' (*aham asmi*). What I have is my *karma*, and with it I have to deal with my earthly existence. But if we overlook that 'I' for which the 'am' is ultimately meaningful, then all actions of the human being, including psychological consciousness, 'are' its *karma*: a condensation of acts past, a dynamism of tendencies to be realized in the future: all that composes the present.

In this sense a great part of Indian philosophy could be considered a philosophy of history; not a philosophical reflection on external events, but a philosophical meditation on the historicity of being, on the peculiar temporal character of the human being and all cosmos, which is so configured that nothing is lost. Everything accumulates and emerges in a present that condenses all past actions and realities. And this to such an extent that to consider a being as only what it is now, neglecting what it was and ignoring what it shall be, could be called a philosophical sin.

This awareness of historicity in the karmic sense is built into the Asian mentality. It is almost taken for granted that I am a condensed result of the past, that all I *have* is simply *karma* (historicity), that there is no original newness, no genuine beginning, that revolutions are childish, politically speaking, if it is supposed that they can begin with a *tabula rasa*.

The traditional concept of *avatāra* or descent of the divine is intimately connected with the theory of *karma*. And this gives to the *avatāra* what Christian theology would term its docetic character. The *avatāra* is justified precisely because cosmic history shows experientially a kind of negative inertia: By itself, the world tends to go downhill and requires again and again the intervention of the divine, of the nonkarmic order, to reverse the trend. So we have an option between two fundamental views of historicity: history as a declining process or as an uphill path. Indian thought tends to accept the idea of a redeeming power that saves the karmic world from getting more and more involved in such a density of relations that it would bring about a kind of ontic asphyxia.

c. Karma and Man

I am reading from, rather than into, Indian scripture and tradition when I assert that the theory of *karma* does two things: It elevates the entire world to the human sphere and abolishes human privileges, putting Man on a level with the rest of the universe. In other words, there is a universal law that governs both Man and the World without distinction. The karmic structure is common to all beings. Some see this as degrading Man to the level of a mere thing. Others may prefer to say it entails enhancing the whole contingent world up to the level of human dignity.

One thing is certain—the entire realm of being is under one and the same law, and this law is temporal or rather historical. It is this law of *karma* that says that the structure of reality is such that it allows mutual interactions in space and, especially, in time, though differently from that described by Newton's physical laws of action and reaction. This law, by contrast, is built on the pattern of reality itself. Being is karmic; being is temporal and historical. Being has a dimension to which the separation in space (which makes individuals) or in time (which makes things and multiplicity) is no longer sufficient or valid. An isolated being is an abstraction, an artificial and anti-natural separation from the existing and given reality. All is stitched together in the warp and woof of *karma*.

The law of *karma* gives expression to the fundamental human condition, yet at the same time allows us to overcome it, not by postulating a 'better' idealized human condition, but by transcending it altogether. Man is more than 'Man', but as long as he is 'Man', not only must he play the human game, but there is no escaping his human condition. He will cease to be 'Man' and this just may be his hope: not to prolong his human conditionings indefinitely, but to abandon them totally and without regret. Even in Man's earthly life he has glimpsed that other shore which allows him to pierce through space and time and, abandoning all human values, reach that Life which is neither separable nor distinguishable from his everyday karmic existence. Only an irresistible joy bubbles up. The end of 'Man' is Man, but when that end is reached, Man ceases to be 'Man', and this is salvation: neither a jump outside history nor its negation, but the realization that 'Man' is history and that history, like 'Man', is only for the time being.

NOTES

1. The proper form for this neuter noun is *karman*. English literature often uses *karma* and in this form it has passed into common usage. Although the latter is, strictly speaking, the less correct form, we shall use it since it is more familiar to the Western reader. We shall also use the adjectival form 'karmic', an acceptable and almost unavoidable neologism.

2. Cf. R. Panikkar, *The Intrareligious Dialogue* (New York: Paulist Press, 1978), chapter III.

3. Cf. a single and typical example of the Sikh Scriptures (fifteenth century): "*Karma* determines how you are born, but it is through grace (*nadar*) that the door of salvation is found" (*Japji*, 4).

4. For example: I, 22, 19; I, 31, 8; I, 55, 3; I, 61, 13; I, 62, 6; I, 101, 4; I, 102, 6; I, 112, 12; I, 121, 11; II, 21, 1; II, 24, 14; III, 33, 7; VI, 37, 2; VIII, 21, 2; VIII, 36, 7; VIII, 37, 7; VIII, 38, 1; IX, 46, 3; IX, 88, 4; IX, 96, 11; X, 28, 7; X, 66, 9; X, 55, 8; etc.

5. Cf. R. Panikkar, 'Algunos aspectos de la espiritualidad hindú', *Historia de la Espiritualidad,* edited by L. Sala Balust and B. Jiménez Duque (Barcelona: Flors, 1969), especially pp. 466–474, for further development of this idea.

6. Cf. RV IX, 59, 2 where the word *dhiṣaṇā* is used to denote the

priestly work, the sacred work, the action of the Gods. From the root *dhā*, put. See also I, 22, 1; I, 102, 1; I, 96, 1; I, 109, 4; III, 2, 1; IV, 34, 1; X, 17, 12; X, 30, 6; etc.

7. RV X, 16, 3. Cf. Muir, *op. cit.* V, 298.

8. Cf. RV X, 90, 13; AV V, 9, 7; V, 10, 8; VIII, 2, 3; XI, 8, 31; XXIV, 9; SB I, 5, 3, 4; VI, 2, 2, 27; X, 3, 3, 7; XI, 8, 4, 6; TB III, 10, 8, 5; BU III, 2, 13.

9. Cf. R. Panikkar, *Le mystère du culte dans l'hindousime et le christianisme* (Paris: Cerf, 1970), pp. 53-58, and also the pertinent Vedic texts in my book *The Vedic Experience* (Berkeley and Los Angeles: University of California Press, 1977) *passim.*

10. AV VIII, 2, 15; XVIII, 3, 13; XVIII, 4, 62; etc.

11. RV X, 190, 1.

12. AV XI, 8, 6.

13. We could adduce here that half verse of the YV III, 47: *akram karma karmakṛtaḥ* ("having worked their work the workers of work"), having performed their work; a text that, though the context may be different, has also been utilized for the theory of *karma.*

14. Cf. SB X, 5, 9-10.

15. SB VI, 2, 2, 27.

16. Cf. SB X, 3, 1; XI, 2, 7, 33.

17. Cf. BU III, 2, 12-13.

18. *Tejas-atejas* could also be translated as heat and cold, energy and inertia.

19. BU IV, 4, 5.

20. BU III, 2, 12.

21. BU III, 2, 13.

22. Cf. MaitU III, 2, 1-3.

23. Cf. CU V, 10, 7.

24. Cf. MaitU VI, 34, 2-3.

25. Cf. KausU I, 2; SU VI, 7, 11.

26. Cf. BU IV, 4, 23; IV, 3, 8-9; KathU V, 7; MundU I, 2, 7.

27. Cf. KausU II, 15.

28. MundU II, 2, 8; IsU 2.

29. MundU III, 2, 7.

30. Cf. KausU II, 6.

31. Cf. besides MaitU II, 6-7; CU V, 3; BU I, 3, 10; KathU I, 1, 5-6.

32. SU V, 7.

33. BG VIII, 3.

34. Cf.some fundamental references: BG II, 42-43; II, 47-57; III, 4-9; III, 14-15, III, 19-20; III, 22-25; IV, 14-24; IV, 32-33; V, 1-14; XVIII, 2-25.

35. BS III, 1, 17; IV, 1, 15 and the *bhāsyas* on them.

36. YS I, 24.

37. YS IV, 30.
38. YS II, 12.
39. YS III, 22.
40. YS IV, 7.
41. YS II, 6.
42. India stresses the threefold ways of works (*karma*), knowledge (*jñāna*) and loving faith (*bhakti*) just as the theologies of James, John and Paul, respectively, emphasized these three *kāṇḍas*.
43. Cf., as an example, the passionate plea for modernity by A.D. Moddie, *The Brahmanical Culture and Modernity* (London: Asia Publishing House, 1968).
44. Italics mine. The text says literally: *satyaṁ neśvarād anyaḥ saṁsārī*, "In truth no other than the Lord wanders through." As a noun, *saṁsāra* means a going or wandering through, and is a compound of *sam* and the root *sṛ* which, like the root *sru*, means flow. *Sam-sṛ* is thus the verbal form meaning flow together with, go about, wander or walk or roam through. Cf. its usages in Monier-Williams' *Sanskrit-English Dictionary*. One could equally have translated: "In truth no other (or no different) than the Lord transmigrates."
45. Śaṅkara, *Brahmasūtrabhāṣya* I, 1, 5, according to the English translation of G. Thibaut, *The Vedānta-Sūtras with the Commentary by Śaṅkarācārya, The Sacred Books of the East*, edited by F. Max Müller, vol. 34 (Delhi: Motilal Banarsidass, 1962), pp. 51-52.
46. The following literature may be useful, in addition to general works on Indian philosophy: E. Benz (ed.), 'Reinkarnation. Die Lehre von der Seelenwanderung in der philosophischen und religiösen Diskussion heute', *Zeitschrift für Religions- und Geistesgeschichte*, IX, 2 (Köln: Brill); E.S. Deutsch, 'Karma as "Convenient Fiction" in the Advaita Vedānta', *Philosophy East and West*, XV, 1 (January 1965), 3-12; R. De Smet, 'The Law of Karma', *Indian Phil. Annal*, II (1966), 328-355; M. Falk, 'Nairātmya and Karman', *Indian Historical Quarterly*, 16 (1940), 429-464, 647-682; J.N. Farquhar, 'Karma: its Value as a Doctrine of Life', *Hibbert Journal*, 20 (1921-22), 2-34; H. von Glasenapp, *Doctrine of Karman in Jaina Philosophy* (Bombay, 1942); E.W. Hopkins, 'Modifications of the Karma Doctrine', JRAS (1906), pp. 581-592; (1907), pp. 665-672; C. Humphreys, *Karma and Rebirth* (London, 1943); C.G. Jung, 'Die verschiedenen Aspeckte der Wiedergeburt', *Eranos Jahrbuch* (Zürich: Rhein, 1939), pp. 399-447; Umesh Mishra, 'The Annihilation of Karman', *Proceedings of the All India Oriental Conference*, 7 (1935), 467-480; K.H. Potter, 'Naturalism and Karma: A Reply (D. Walhout, A Critical Note on Potter's Interpretation of Karma),' *Philosophy East and West*, XVIII (1968), 82-84; R. De Smet, 'A Copernican reversal: The Gītākāra's reformulation of karma,' *Philosophy East and West* XXVIII, 1 (January 1977), 53-63.

46a. Cf. as recent examples J. Head and S.L. Cranston (editors and compilers), *Reincarnation* (New York: Julian Press/Crown, 1977), with its six hundred pages of text, and Q. Howe, Jr., *Reincarnation for the Christian* (Philadelphia: Westminster, 1974).

47. The Greek word *kosmos* originally meant order and good order, both in the material and moral sense. Then it came to mean ornament, organization, constitution, glory, etc., and then the world, the inhabited world, etc. It is probably connected with the Latin *censeō* and the Sanskrit *samsati*. Cf. the root *śās* (*śis*), order. Cf. P. Chantraine, *Dictionnaire étymologique de la langue grecque* (Paris: Klincksieck, 1970), *i. h. l.*, though he does not give the Sanskrit root.

48. YSB II, 13, where individuals are said to be like knots in a fisher's net.

49. Cf. R. Panikkar, 'Singularity and Individuality: The Double Principle of Individuation' *Revue internationale de philosophie* XXIX nr. 111-112 (1975) 141-166.

50. Cf. the behavior of a *jīvanmukta*, a realized soul, who has transcended time and space and yet still lives among mortals.

51. Cf. CU VI, 8, 7.

52. Cf. BG III, 20; etc.

53. Cf. R. Panikkar, 'Temps et histoire dans la tradition de l'Inde' in the UNESCO book, *Les cultures et le temps*, (Paris: Payot/Unesco 1975), pp. 73-101, and 'El presente tempiterno' in A. Vargas-Machuca (ed). *Teología y mundo contemporaneo*, (Madrid: Cristiandad, 1975) pp. 100-178, which relieves us here from being more explicit.

XV.
The Subject of Infallibility.
Solipsism and Verification

καὶ ὁ λόγος . . . ἐσκήνωσεν ἐν ἡμῖν

Et Verbum . . . habitavit in nobis

And the Word . . . dwelt among us
Jn. 1:14

1. THESIS

The thesis of this chapter is the following: *The notion of infallibility is coherent only within a closed system*; in other words: *The rational affirmation of infallibility leads to solipsism*; or simply: *Infallibility is incommunicable*. This amounts to saying that *infallibility is unverifiable*, that *infallibility has no other basis than its own self-affirmation*. Or, again: *Infallibility belongs to the order of myth*. The moment it enters the realm of the *logos* and is formulated in a logical statement it cannot have any verification that does not already assume an equal degree of infallibility. The reason why somebody is infallible has to be equally infallible if his infallibility is to have any meaning. The upshot of our thesis is plain: In the sublunary world, *humanity is the ultimate subject of infallibility*. Once the *logos* has come to 'dwell among us', there is no higher instance than our incarnated, earthly *logos*.

2. THE NOTION OF INFALLIBILITY[1]

The notion of infallibility, unlike those of truth and error, implies an element of volition. An infallible statement cannot be reduced to the simple formula '*A* is *B*'; it always implies a third element: 'when *p* affirms that *A* is *B*, so it is'. If we let *m* = '*A* is *B*', we can express infallibility by the formula: '*p* posits *m*'. So public judgments, not private truths, are infallible. *P* is not infallible when thinking but when proclaiming, declaring. Infallibility does not mean inerrancy, i.e., the absence of error; it means the impossibility of erring, of committing a mistake when making a particular declaration. For this reason infallibility applies first of all to God, who is by definition infallible.[2]

The very etymology of the word[3] suggests this moral character of not erring, deceiving, betraying or failing.[4] Strictly speaking, a proposition can be infallible only in relation to a subject who affirms or receives it. Infallibility expresses a relation between the one who affirms some judgment as infallible and the one who receives it as such. Thus even as a charism, in the most traditional sense, infallibility is not bestowed for the private profit of the beneficiary, but is for 'edification', for the benefit of others. A proposition can be said to be infallible only if it has been endowed with the property of infallibility by the peculiar act of the infallible declaration of the proposition declaring it such. Furthermore, infallibility does not belong only to the pure intellect or to reason alone. Infallibility implies that a person does not err in the *act* that is considered infallible. Infallibility then is a character proper to action, and is not only a logical feature of a proposition. Whence the remark, or rather the hermeneutical advice, that in order to understand the affirmations of Vatican I on infallibility we must bear in mind that the Council's perspective was that of a court of law issuing specific decrees, not an academy spinning theories.[5] Infallibility does not belong to the realm of mere speculation; it is practical, it belongs to the realm of *orthopraxis*, as we shall see.

In other words, we cannot separate the subject who pronounces the infallible judgment from the concept of infallibility itself. When someone says that the 'canons' defined as dogmas by the Church are infallible, this means that the authority that has defined them as infallible has not erred, and that anyone who adheres to them is not mistaken.[6] Otherwise, i.e., if the infallible pronouncement were only a statement of fact and not a judgment, then it would suffice to say that the dogmas are true. In this case, reason or common sense—not the defining authority—would compel the listener's adherence to those pronouncements.

An infallible judgment can be an active or a passive act, but it must at least be passive. For instance, the statement *p* affirms *m* expresses the act whereby I take *p* to be infallible when it affirms *m* so that I accept *m* because *p* affirms it. Without this trust in *p* there would be no infallibility. Those who have personally experienced or have studied certain types of charismatic movements will readily substantiate this with innumerable cases in which the saint, the leader, the guru or the like is taken to be infallible without his having made this claim at all. The others make him infallible. *Magister dixit.*

Passive infallibility is the ultimate one, for even when *p* claims infallibility, it does not mean that it is *p* that makes *m* to be the case, but that *p* sees and discovers *m*—that is, '*A* is *B*'—where others perhaps can or could not see it. Infallibility does not make truth, but proclaims it. When Pius XII proclaimed the dogma of the Assumption, for example, he claimed infallibility not because he thought he individually could not be mistaken, but because he believed he was interpreting the faith of the Church infallibly, i.e., without the possibility of erring. In the final analysis, papal infallibility is also passive, for the Pope is considered to be only the vessel of that infallibility which Christ promised his Church. So, too, when a Christian affirms that Mary was assumed into heaven body and soul, he is convinced that he cannot err, because he is simply confirming this very infallibility given by Christ. When a believer affirms that Man is composed of body and soul, however, he admits that he could be mistaken. The first affirmation would be infallible, the second would not. The first rests on an external infallible authority (the Pope or the Church), while the second rests on a personal judgment that could perhaps change since it cannot refer to such an external court of appeal.

3. THE SOCIOLOGICAL AND THE PSYCHOLOGICAL CONTEXT

We shall take as an example the dogma of the Assumption of Mary. To affirm infallibility in this case implies that the Pope's *act* is infallible, i.e., that the Pope did not err in making his solemn declaration.[7] That he did not err means he proclaimed an objective, i.e., public, truth, not just a subjective or private truth. He did not necessarily express his intimate conviction, but he proclaimed that something has to be believed as truly belonging to the deposit of Revelation. Proceeding with scholastic casuistry we could very well assume that the Pope does not personally believe in what he proclaims, and nevertheless he would remain infallible as Vatican I understood him to be.

The distinctive character of any infallible declaration lies in its claim to add an *extrinsic criterion* of truth to the affirmation '*A* is *B*'. In the case of the Roman Church, infallibility does not even purport to state new 'truths', but only declares that a certain 'truth' is (or was) contained in the deposit of Revelation.

This extrinsic criterion—something not inherent in the proposition itself—must be understood first of all in function of its particular sociological and psychological contexts within a historical period. Let us explain. To explicitly declare a judgment infallible represents a first step in the process of demythicization. Prior to this pronouncement, the surrounding myth vouched for the truth of that judgment. It is only when the myth begins to break down that you feel the need to be reassured by some external authority. You demand this reinforcement of your belief because you have seen *in obliquo* the necessity of grounding it in something other than the proposition itself. You feel the need to declare infallible only those formulas or judgments that you fear could be 'fallible'. We are here clearly dealing with convictions, and so we are on sociological and psychological terrain. Reason was proclaimed infallible in the European 18th century by virtue of the same process by which the Pope was declared infallible a century later.

A sociological law could be formulated here: The importance of and the need for an infallible pronouncement increases in inverse proportion to the conviction that supports that pronouncement, or, the other way round, in inverse proportion to the belief in the truth of the proposition. If I can depend on a *p* that affirms infallibly that Man has landed on the moon (and so, for example, be rid of the doubt that it might all have been a trick concocted by the mass media to enable the United States to dominate world politics), this reassures me more than if p infallibly affirms that $2 + 2 = 4$, a proposition that does not stand in need of being reinforced by an infallible authority. And if someone tells me infallibly that there is a possible hell for Man, this disturbs me much more than the infallible affirmation that there is also death lurking on my horizon. For the person who has doubts about the moral value of liberalism (or communism), an infallible declaration that reaffirms its morality is more desirable than, for instance, an infallible statement condemning slavery, which is seen today without any doubt as a condemnable institution.

If the proposition 'A is B' is considered self-evident, an infallible declaration of its truth would be superfluous since infallibility adds nothing to the proposition as such. The proposition is not *made* true by the infallible declaration, but only recognized as true and thus (infallibly) proclaimed as such. At the other extreme, if the proposition 'A is B' is considered contradictory, an infallible declaration of its truth would not be able to change my conviction either, since infallibility does not add anything to the truth of the proposition. These two extreme cases do not contradict our sociological law, for in both cases evidence 1 or evidence 0 would satisfy our formulation. The need for and importance of the infallible declaration in one case equals my conviction (*1*) and in the other becomes meaningless (*0*) when my conviction is nil. Between these extremes lies the whole gamut of real situations. It might be interesting for a sociology of religion to note that the tendency to desire the certitude of infallibility stems from a crisis of conviction (or of belief, a theologian might say). As long as you do not feel the need for epistemological *certainty*, you do not ask for infallible declarations. There is an obvious link between the post-Cartesian attitude that requires the security of rational knowledge and the felt need for infallibility—a need that culminated in the First Vatican Council.[8] In a pre-Cartesian world, the infallibility proclaimed by the Council would scarcely make sense. Thus the Orthodox Church, which has not suffered the Cartesian impact, does not feel the need to declare its dogmas infallible because the need for an additional certainty is not felt.

Now in order for the infallible affirmation to reinforce my

conviction, I must obviously accept it as infallible. It is all the more desired if the affirmation helps to convince.[9] A psychology of religion will say here that I will all the more readily accept the infallibility of 'A is B' if I am already inclined to accept that A is B. In this case, the relation is a direct proportion: The more I believe A is B, the more easily I will accept 'A is B' as an infallible statement. This is just the opposite of the sociological relation proposed above: the more a social consciousness is convinced that A is B, the less it feels the need for an infallible statement to that effect, whereas the less I am convinced that A is B, the more I need the certitude of infallibility.

Combining the sociological and the psychological aspects, we could say that the need for infallible pronouncements increases the stronger the desire to believe (in 'A is B') and the weaker the internal coherence of that in which one believes (in the 'B' which is 'A'). From the perspective of the history of religions, it would be worthwhile to examine how different forms of infallibility have emerged the very moment a crisis existed in those structures which had until then expressed a reliable order of truth.

All this explains why infallibility presents a particular ambivalence, which makes this theme extremely delicate to handle, even today. On the one hand, infallibility seems to save the beliefs of the majority from collapse; this leads many to emphasize the value of authority, of definitions, of precise and concrete directives, etc. More than one historian would tell us that, without the rock of infallibility, much of Christianity would have long since been engulfed by superficial innovations and extremist reactions. On the other hand, infallibility seems to impede and even prohibit any effort at understanding positions that are not majoritarian; it seems to cripple the impetus of progress and evolution, freezing the gamut of interpretations and also undermining the foundations of true spirituality, since the religious edifice does not rest on arguments that affirm authority, but on free conviction and personal experience. So we can well understand the anguished appeals of conscientious people when faced with the danger of stagnation that every form of infallibility carries with it, and the fear of sheer anarchy when we are left without limits of interpretation. For this reason, it seems that some philosophical clarification will be useful and even important.

It is in this context that we should recall what has been said in previous chapters concerning myth and transmythicization. When, perhaps because formulated in obsolete concepts, the belief in particular dogmas seems to cease being mythical and thus it asks for reasons, then a new myth of infallibility dawns, which will give the requisite additional security to these particular dogmas. Now when infallibility itself is questioned, i.e., ceases to be a mythical belief, then we must jump into another order altogether. And precisely here the vital circle of myth is most conspicuous: the Christian community or the Church is infallible because it continues the life of an infallible Christ on earth and it continues the life of Christ—i.e., it remains loyal to Christ's spirit—because it is infallible. Infallibility is the very expression of the Christian myth; but to spell it out weakens the myth. The myth of infallibility is undermined by the *logos* of infallibility. This is what we are going to examine.

4. CAN THERE BE A HERMENEUTIC OF INFALLIBILITY?

'*P* posits *m*' is an infallible act when *p* cannot err in affirming *m*. If *p* does not err in affirming *m*, this means that *m* is a true proposition. Now as we have said, infallibility adds nothing to the truth inherent to the proposition '*A* is *B*', but only gives the security, to those who believe in infallibility, that *A* is certainly *B*.

The problem appears as soon as we analyze this *something more* (security, certainty, belief) that belongs to an infallible declaration. I may believe that *p* cannot err when it affirms '*A* is *B*', but what guarantees that I will adhere to *p*'s '*A* is *B*' and not instead to '*A* is B_1' (which I cannot distinguish from '*A* is *B*')? The Pope has declared that Mary was taken up body and soul into heavenly glory, and I can affirm this as an infallible judgment. But am I sure my understanding of body and soul is the same as the Pope's? Which body? what we call the glorious body? or rather what the biologist or biochemist studies? Which soul? Or again:

Do I have an adequate understanding of heavenly glory? do I even have the same understanding as the Pope?

What can we do? We cannot wait for yet another infallible pronouncement to give the precise meaning of each word, because the process would be interminable. In order to clarify these concepts we would have to use others, *et sic in infinitum*.

In order for this affirmation '*p* posits *m*' to be infallible for me, I must recognize it as infallible. It follows, then, that the act by which I accept the affirmation as infallible must also be infallible. Otherwise, if I could be mistaken when I say that *p* is infallible, its infallibility would be meaningless as far as I am concerned.

We may answer this difficulty by saying that the believer adheres to the infallible proposition as it is defined by the authority proposing it. This is the classical solution. Ecclesiology has long since admitted that (active) infallibility *in docendo*, in teaching, would make no sense were there not (passive) infallibility *in discendo* to receive, to understand, and to effect it.[10] An infallible authority could affirm and proclaim any number of infallible propositions, but they would remain ineffective and dead letter if those who ought to receive and benefit from them did not possess a reciprocal passive infallibility. This notion of passive infallibility is indeed much older and more widespread than the idea of active infallibility.[11] We know, for instance, that the Orthodox Church follows the ancient tradition whereby the *ecclesia discens* must ratify all synodal decisions or declarations. And, while the concept of a single infallible authority is only rarely found in history, the notion of passive infallibility frequently appears. We can think not only of religious examples drawn from a religion, a community, etc., but also of the contemporary examples of the infallibility of reason, of human conscience, of nature and even of basic social structures. Even in Christianity, the notions of *sensus ecclesiae*, of *lex orandi lex credendi*, of council, of mystical body and of Church itself are closely related to the gift of the Spirit whose continuing presence is necessary in order to discern and then follow the right path, and this points to a passive infallibility.[12]

This leads us to say that no hermeneutic of infallibility is possible, because in order to understand infallibility as it asks to be understood, we must participate in the infallible act itself. Without doubt we can analyze the *concept* of infallibility, but we cannot interpret the infallible act outside the hermeneutic it gives to itself. Contemporary theology has glimpsed this and generally maintains that the subject of infallibility in the Church must be a single one.[13] A dual subject of infallibility would be contradictory and, from every point of view, superfluous.[14]

But the problem is even more subtle. Certainly the Pope and the Council are not two independent infallible authorities, but two organs of one and the same authority. We can also say that reason and faith cannot contradict each other because their source of infallibility is the same. This is quite true, and yet the problem remains, not only regarding the de facto conflicts that do arise (between reason and faith or Pope and Council, for example), but also regarding their day-to-day coordination or subordination.

To pursue the example of the infallibility *in docendo* of the Church's hierarchy and that *in discendo* of the ecclesial people, let us imagine that the entire Church *magisterium* is unanimous in proclaiming the dogma of the Assumption. In order for this declaration to have its full meaning, the 'learning' Church, i.e., the ecclesial people, must understand the dogma in the same way as the teaching authority that propounds it. Now if we must postulate a special assistance for the infallible *teaching*, we must do the same for those *taught*. We may agree that understanding is by means of concepts, but then we will also have to recognize that the ecclesial people live on diverse cultural levels and that each context bears a different understanding. The assistance required, then, would have to be more than extraordinary. It would have to be almost personal, a thesis no theologian has ever defended. Moreover, such assistance represents a kind of supernaturalism that would render ecclesiastical infallibility superfluous, since it amounts to affirming that individual conscience is infallible.

It seems we must look for an explanation on a different level. Here Christian theology could profit from the knowledge and experience of other cultures and religions.[15] In terms of the history of religions, we might say that the passive subject of infallibility adheres to the proposition '*A* is *B*' mythically, i.e., not analytically or conceptually, not as a proposition intelligible in or by itself, but as part of a mythic whole. You adhere to '*A* is *B*' by participating in the infallibility of *p*, and without analyzing the content of '*A* is *B*'. This is the case when there is no critical distance between the proclaiming authority and the listening people. It amounts to saying that the two 'infallibilities' coalesce when the people really believe that the 'authority' speaks for them, is their speaker, their true representative, so that the current of communication, in a way, does not descend from the 'heights' but ascends from the people upward to its hierarchical symbol. This is obviously not to denigrate the existence of the notion of an infallible authority as myth. History, past and present, shows us the reality and even the vitality of such adherence to myths.[16]

Now myth as myth is incommunicable because it is the very foundation of all communication; it is the horizon you accept without question and that makes possible a certain communion, the condition for any subsequent communication. Myth is never the object of thought (i.e., of the *logos*), nor is it objectifiable; rather myth is what allows thought to conceptualize itself, and faith to express itself. Myth is what enters every thought, every idea and even every formulation of faith without being identified with any of them, and yet it does not exist separately from them (this *sui generis* relationship of *mythos* and *logos* is occasionally glimpsed in the process of demythicization—the *logos* is 'disengaged' from one myth only to be remythicized, embedded in another myth[17]).

Ultimately this is what traditional theology says when it affirms that the infallible authority only explicates and formulates the faith of the Church in a clear and distinct way. The notion of infallibility thus presents an uncomfortable ambiguity. On the one hand it still upholds the myth. It expresses the fact that the authority articulates and formulates in terms of the *logos* what the people believe. It is not a dictatorial act, not the imposition of a new decree. It is the articulate organ of expression (*logos*) of what the Church believes. On the other hand, it also begins to abolish the myth by making it so explicit that in explaining it, it explains it away. Infallibility wants to make a certain and secure crystallization (in the form of *logos*) of the undifferentiated magma of myth. It wants to 'speak' the unspoken. It is important to note that the dynamism here goes from the people to the authority, not vice versa. It is not an individual charisma, but *ex officio*—and for the public function of that office. This is why infallibility is not inspiration or revelation, but a special assistance bestowed according to a hierarchical order to guide the people of God on their way to the heavenly city. It is not an automatic dynamism, nor is it bestowed 'democratically', but it is a work of the divine *Logos*.[18] But does such reasoning not empty infallibility of whatever rational sense it might contain on its own? Is infallibility at all necessary on the level of conceptual explanation? Does infallibility represent just an effort to demythicize what cannot be demythicized, namely belief?[19] By wanting to affirm infallibility with reason, don't we end up contradicting it? In short, any hermeneutic of infallibility seems to destroy it. Without a hermeneutic, however, we cannot talk about it, we cannot communicate it. You accept infallibility when you accept it *in toto* along with your faith, without analyzing or interpreting it. Divorced from this holistic attitude of the believer, it makes no sense. The proper functioning of democracy needs the belief in the people's infallibility.

5. THE INTERNAL LOGIC OF INFALLIBILITY

In trying to understand infallibility we have until now assumed that we accept it without examining the concept as such. We must now test the value of our hypothesis by analyzing the subject of infallibility in its most elementary philosophical sense.

We have already seen that a proposition per se cannot claim to be infallible; there must always be someone who declares it infallible: either one who affirms '*A* is *B*' or one who accepts this proposition. But who can say '*p* is infallible'?

Here it seems evident that only an affirmation in the first

person can have any meaning. If someone says 'you are infallible', this infallibility equally implies the infallibility of the one
who affirms it. Likewise for the third person. If someone says '*p*
is infallible', it means two things: recognizing *p*'s infallibility (if
not indeed conferring it), and acknowledging the authority of the
speaker who affirms (or confers) that infallibility. For example, if
a Council defines the infallibility of the Pope, it seems obvious
that papal infallibility would then depend on the infallibility of the
Council that conferred or acknowledged it.

'You are infallible' or 'he is infallible' are not final propositions since they rest on the infallibility of another, namely the
speaker who affirms that 'you are infallible' or 'he is infallible'.

We cannot escape this logical exigency by saying that the
first person does not confer but only recognizes the infallibility of
the second or third person. In our example, the Council would
then say that it is not infallible, that it only recognizes a papal
infallibility that exists in and of itself, and not by the power or
delegation of the Council. So the Council would only explicate
what already existed. Another example might be that of a group
that recognizes, through whatever external criteria, that the little
shepherd is really the king and proclaims him as such. This group
has not appointed him king, just as the Council has not given
infallibility to the Pope; both have merely recognized preroga-
tives, kingship or infallibility.

To this we must reply that recognition by another is essential.
The shepherd-king will reign only if he is acknowledged by the
people. The Pope will be effectively infallible only if recognized
as such. Subtle casuistry cannot weaken this argument. If we say
the process is irreversible, and that once the Council has recognized pontifical infallibility, it opens up a new awareness that
cannot then be closed, we must also suppose either that the
Council no longer recognizes papal infallibility or that it continues
to acknowledge it. In the latter case, the whole force of papal
infallibility still comes from its recognition by the Council. In the
former instance, infallibility cannot be maintained unless the
Pope himself maintains it or a third party affirms it. Then this
third party becomes the final criterion, since infallibility recog-

nized by no one is meaningless. Where the Pope sees himself (and proclaims himself) as infallible, we are no longer within the limits of our hypothesis and have come to the only intelligible form the concept has: first-person infallibility.

In sum: to say 'p is infallible' without adding 'and I, when I affirm this, am also infallible', amounts to making infallibility totally irrelevant.

'I am infallible' would thus be the only proposition that holds. But this proposition is incommunicable. The only communication possible would be to convince another to accept my statement 'I am infallible' without his becoming aware that he too must be infallible in order to accept my infallible proposition. If he perceives his own infallibility—in the first person: 'when I affirm this, I too am infallible'—he becomes the conscious criterion and judge of infallibility.

In order to be communicable, the proposition 'I am infallible' must be able to elicit the assent of another: 'Yes, you are infallible', which also implies, 'and my recognizing your infallibility is also infallible'. Both expressions must be equally infallible; otherwise they are meaningless. If I can err when I affirm 'You are infallible', in response to *your* declaration 'I am infallible', *your* affirmation of infallibility is no longer infallible for me.

Or again, this infallibility cannot be proven by arguments stronger than those that are rooted upon an infallibility held in common by the one who affirms his own infallibility and by whoever confirms it. To say 'I am infallible because God, who is infallible, has promised it to me', implies, if it is to be communicated to others (even over and above any other presuppositions), that whoever accepts my statement cannot be mistaken. So my infallibility depends on the infallibility of his understanding and agreement, and not on my 'divine credentials'. I can appeal to natural reason and its evidence to make the other understand my argument, and then this rational evidence becomes the touchstone of my infallibility as far as he is concerned. But I cannot give him *more* infallibility than he already has. If I depend on the infallibility of his reason, then that guarantees my own infallibility. My 'higher' infallibility, if in fact it exists, is incommunicable.

This means that infallibility is unverifiable because it is its own principle of verification. If it were to seek another, this principle would have to be infallible as well. To say 'this act is infallible' amounts to saying 'this act has in itself its own principle of verification'.

Obviously there is still a way out of this solipsistic impasse and, indeed, history shows us that infallibility takes the form of a collectivity that claims the privilege of infallibility. In the first person to be sure; but in the first person plural: *'we are infallible'*.

Without doubt, we can go much further with the plural: the Church, the Council and the Pope, all three of us, *we* are infallible since Christ promised the assistance of the Spirit until the end of time (even if the form in which this infallibility expresses itself differs in every case). But we are still at a dead end and out of communication with—may I say even excommunicated from?—the outside world. We lack communication not only with an external world, but also with that part of *ourselves* which collectively or personally remains outside our group and which questions the reason, or the function, or the justification or even the suitability of our infallibility. If someone in the bosom of the Church—i.e., if one within the *us*—asks for 'proof' or reasons for his own infallibility, we cannot answer him, since he cannot jump over his own shadow. You cannot be infallible and demand reasons for this infallibility at the same time. In other words: Papal infallibility is the same as my own (i.e., the Council's, the bishop's, the simple Christian's, the person's), even though it manifests itself differently. Still, *we* are infallible, although the others or another (a Council, the Pope) may explain my own faith in an explicit fashion, using words and concepts I would not normally use. Infallibility has meaning as long as it constitutes *us*, a unified and homogeneous whole. But as soon as any sense of separation, alienation or estrangement comes between *us*, our common infallibility breaks down. Infallibility becomes *their* infallibility and is no longer my own. The moment I stop believing that the others (or another) are expressing my own faith, they no longer express it, and their infallibility is only their own, in which I cannot participate. Infallibility is only *ad usum nostrorum*, and thus a true sign of discrimination.

But isn't this what tradition has always said when it insists that infallibility has no sense except within the faith? Of what use is it to want to prove it or submit it to philosophical analysis? It would simply become a tautology if we did. Infallibility is quite tenable as a truism, but becomes meaningless when we try to separate it from the circle of faith and defend it as a truth in itself or as a separate dogma.

What is relevant here is not so much this internal crisis of infallibility that currently troubles so many Christians as the philosophical solipsism inherent in any infallibility. Whatever entity believes itself infallible, individual, collective or moral, ex-communicates itself from everything else. Moreover, even on the very level where a person believes himself infallible he cannot establish communion with others. And there is no human or natural remedy for this; my infallibility is without appeal.

Modern Man believes himself infallible by virtue of his humanity and so has excommunicated himself from other animals at this level.[20] When philosophers appeal to a reason they uncritically consider infallible, they alienate themselves both from one another and from that part of mankind which does not share this pattern of intelligibility. Insofar as they believe themselves infallible, Christians remain united among themselves to be sure, but they distance themselves from the rest of humanity, and no amount of dialogue can reestablish communication; insofar as bishops, priests and the Pope believe that they possess the personal privilege of infallibility (albeit in different degrees), they separate themselves from and remain 'incommunicado' for those who do not have the same privilege.[21] The snare of solipsism is at hand! We could multiply these examples within the realm of religion (the saint is always one 'set apart') as well as in the secular sphere. All privilege confers some power, but at the same time it isolates, makes different.

Here a philosopher would speak of solipsism, a historian of religions of spiritual totemism,[22] a sociologist of esotericism, etc. Whatever the name, it follows from the same principle: realizing identity through differentiation and affirming difference by separation.[23]

I, the Pope, the Party, the State, the Nation—we, the

bishops, the Christians, the democrats, the socialists—we cannot err. To be sure, we can be mistaken about a good many specific things and ideas, but in the general thrust of our life, our orientation, our ideals, etc., we are infallible. Such affirmations make no sense for those outside my group, outside the *us* that speaks in each instance, because my infallibility is meaningful only for me and for those who participate in it with me. For you it would have only the sense that *you* give it by (fallibly) interpreting me.

We could express it thus: In each case, infallibility bears its own hermeneutic and is only as infallible as that hermeneutic. The 'weight' of infallibility, then, lies on the hermeneutic and not on the infallibility affirmed. So the infallibility depends completely on the validity of its hermeneutic. On the other hand, infallibility without a hermeneutic is closed in on itself and shirks its genuine duty, to communicate the truth. History simply confirms this point.

But, at bottom, doesn't an infallible declaration serve as a concrete hermeneutic of the intellectual content of the act of faith? Doesn't declaring a proposition infallible, or more precisely declaring a judgment infallible, really amount to declaring how the proposition or judgment in question ought to be interpreted?

All this is not to say that the concept of infallibility ought to be completely rejected. The notion of infallibility opens up a hope of going beyond the rationalist and even intellectualist framework of much of contemporary culture, provided it is rethought, reformed and, I daresay, converted.

A more rigorous examination of the statement 'we are infallible' leads us to the conclusion of our thesis. Indeed, if it is to be intelligible, the phrase cannot be verified except by a principle of verification that 'we' all recognize. Now if I am not within this group, this *us* that is infallible, I cannot verify this affirmation. The Roman Church's doctrine of infallibility, recognizing that there is only one single subject of infallibility (the Church, despite the many voices), implicitly takes the stand that the Church is the representative of the entire humankind, that the Church is the *sacramentum mundi*, the *humanitas perfecta*, a leaven on behalf of the whole. If the underlying ecclesiology is disputed, the doctrine of a vicarious infallibility loses its ground.

6. HUMAN INFALLIBILITY

If infallibility sets its own limits and the only given human limits are those of humankind itself, does not affirming that humanity taken as a whole is infallible amount to a tautology? and not only in a godless universe, but also in a theistic world? Yet what is wisdom if not the discovery of tautologies? What is evidence if not a qualified tautology? But let us return to our immediate concern.

There is nonetheless a fundamental difference between a purely epistemological infallibility that admits no 'point' (center, being, principle—whatever one may call it) outside or above itself, and a more ontological infallibility on the order of grace, which acknowledges a transcendent reference point usually called God. In the first hypothesis, infallibility without an alpha or omega point would be a truism, since there would be nothing outside humanity to judge the fallibility or infallibility of anything; whereas in the second case infallibility becomes the expression of a hope, since it is quite conceivable that humanity could 'fall', 'fail' and not accomplish its destiny, not fulfill itself.

But is there a criterion outside humanity that determines if we have erred? Even if we admit some revelation of the truth, we must be able to perceive and understand it. If, suddenly, mankind saw clearly that $2 + 2 = 5$, we could no longer call this proposition false. We would say that historical documents prove that once Men believed $2 + 2 = 4$, and the most learned would say that *what* was once called 4 is today called 5, so that it is all a question of semantics; but no one could now say that 5 is the wrong answer. But this amounts to saying that we all agree in denying the meaningful possibility of $2 + 2 = 4$. And this confirms our thesis, namely that we believe, and we cannot *not* but believe, in human infallibility. But in what areas?

Theology smiles a bit here and reminds us that infallibility does not deal with speculative propositions, but with the existential facts of faith and morals. So the problem is not to brood over whether 2 and 2 shall ever be 4, but whether torture, for instance, could some time be justified. According to a certain theistic hypothesis, it is possible that practically all mankind could go astray, and that only a prophet or a very small 'remnant' would be left as a reminder that it has erred, that its ways are not the ways of truth, justice or love. Any deep reflection on infallibility deals with questions that far surpass the limited problematic of infallible judgments and specific propositions.

Yet we cannot play games with history: For centuries hardly anyone found slavery immoral, or punishment according to the *lex talonis* unjust. Nor is there the slightest doubt that human self-understanding has sensibly changed in its long millennia of history.

We are not, however, concerned with mere doctrinal speculation on the nature of change. Infallibility need not be challenged because doctrines have changed with the times. The realm of infallibility, as we have said before, is not that of general ideas or abstract formulations. Infallibility belongs to the existential domain of my personal decision, the realm of orthopraxis. To return to our example of the Assumption: What is infallible would be the decision to believe in the dogma, i.e., the human act that commits itself to a particular belief following a particular guidance.

These considerations place us in a proper perspective for a final philosophical reflection. Within the hypothesis of a complete negation of transcendence (admitting that this were possible), infallibility would amount to a truism, even if we make mankind its subject. Here, if everyone is infallible, no one is, because there is no criterion except personal perspective. If, however, we follow the other hypothesis, i.e., if we admit transcendence, infallibility could be an external and gratuitous promise of that very transcendence (this is its mythical aspect) or it could become a fertile tautology that helps us to better grasp the nature of transcendence and at the same time responds with hope to the deepest human faith. We can consider infallibility (starting at the bottom) as the epistemological condition for human reason. We can also view it (starting at the top) as a grace bestowed upon a particular group. The first and purely 'philosophical' notion of a universal infallibility is insufficient; the second and exclusively 'theological' notion of an elitist infallibility is not satisfying. We are looking for a certain synthesis in our analysis of infallibility, perhaps as a conquest, as an omega point if we prefer, which becomes real to the extent that we recognize it. Grace is not excluded, but neither is nature. This is our final point.

7. INFALLIBILITY AND ORTHOPRAXIS

The aim of any religion is to save or to free Man. No matter how we interpret this salvation or liberation, religion is always the means by which Man arrives at his destination, reaches the other shore. Now in order to save or free myself, I must *do* something, even if this act is only an interior act of faith or a mere ritual affair. This leads us to say that what constitutes the core of religion is not a doctrine but an act, even if this act is considered to be adherence to a doctrine. In other words, *orthopraxis*, not orthodoxy, is the constitutive element of religion. Thus, as a religious phenomenon, infallibility is grounded in orthopraxis. Having considered it to stem exclusively from the sphere of orthodoxy has been the cause of more than one misunderstanding and many an insurmountable difficulty.[24]

As we have said, strictly speaking there are no infallible truths or propositions, only infallible 'definitions', i.e., affirmations, infallible acts. In certain 'educated' milieus, laughter greeted those who naively thought the Catholic dogma of infallibility was a sort of insurance against sinning. Nevertheless these 'ignorant' people, who doubtless misunderstood the dogma, at least perceived that infallibility concerns action not speculation, orthopraxis not orthodoxy; they saw that infallibility belongs not to theory but to life as it is lived.

This is not to say that orthodoxy does not have its rights, and a *raison d'être* in its proper domain. But, within its limits, there is scarcely room for pluralism, except for a very restricted pluralism that accepts different formulations only provided they say the same thing or diverse concepts provided they are equivalent. On the contrary, pluralism is connatural to orthopraxis because every act is unique. Orthopraxis is characterized by a transconceptual intentionality of the action itself, rather than by an (orthodox) identity of content. We could say that 'all roads lead to Rome' indeed, provided they are genuine roads and not dead ends, that is, provided we don't stop—even at Rome![25]

In this light, infallibility appears as good news. It is tantamount to that confidence in Life, or in Providence if we wish, or in the presence of the Holy Spirit if we prefer, which sustains a realistic optimism about the meaning of human existence and about the sense of the universe. It also leads to the profound conviction that our life is not a meaningless passion, that it is not a mistake, that to have lived and suffered are values that cannot be effaced, that remain even if forgotten. But let us proceed step by step.

I cannot meaningfully say that I am infallible if you do not accept my statement; we cannot declare ourselves infallible if we exclude the very people to whom we declare this, because the affirmation would make no sense to them. A real proclamation of infallibility must embrace the entire world and include in 'us' all who do not excommunicate themselves from it.

A pioneering and particularizing effort was needed to achieve this reflective awareness that humanity is infallible; the Roman Church provides one striking example. But now an osmosis is also necessary in order to spread this awareness, this awakening of consciousness, from some 'high places' of the world religions to all humanity, in order to promote throughout the world what some would call a process of 'consciencialization', and what others, perhaps, a step toward authentic 'evangelization'. We are unraveling here a universal dynamism active in almost every sphere: What was once the privilege of a minority has passed to an ever-increasing majority, if not yet in fact then at least by right. We need not think only of technology, which has placed in the hands of the many—for good or ill—what had once been the privilege of the few. We can and must also consider the change in the notion of God, that classic archetype that has dominated the material and spiritual economy for over four thousand years. Ever since polytheism was swallowed by monotheism, the positive value of any object has been seen as a function of its scarcity.

God is the greatest value, so there can be only one, and he must have only one name. Religion is the depository of ultimate values, hence it must be one. Gold is the most beautiful and the rarest metal, so it must also be the dearest—most costly as well as most precious (a link that confirms what we have been saying). Love between a man and a woman is the greatest love, it must not therefore be portioned out. We could go on like this and give examples from the most diverse fields. Heaven or salvation is what everyone wants most, therefore it must be rare, i.e., the destiny of very few. We find this *sensus* and *consensus fidelium*—the belief that the number of the elect is always very small—in practically all religions up to and including those of recent times.[26] It is still widespread among the traditional 'faithful' of nearly every religion and is found even in modern secular religions. In spite of all modern democratization, we still think in modified oligarchic categories. Today it is no longer blood, race or religion, but money, power, knowledge, education and even the passport that make the difference.

Given this context we can understand why infallibility was considered a privilege and we might add that now the privilege of the 'privileged' is to share what had before been 'concentrated' in one segment of humanity. Could not the salvation histories of Israel and of the Church lend themselves to just this interpretation? what about the parables of the salt, the leaven and the light?[27]

But this cannot be proclaimed by saying: 'I am infallible, and you will be too if you believe me.' We have already seen that it is impossible to communicate infallibility. Nor can we say: 'We Christians are infallible, but you non-Christians are not', since this declaration—assuming it is not blasphemous—is incomprehensible as well as incommunicable. Communication is possible only within a preexisting communion. Communication only makes explicit or reveals this underlying communion. The Christian does not just transmit the news: 'Christ is risen'; he adds immediately, 'and we—you also—are risen with him'.

This does not mean that salvation is automatic or that infallibility guarantees an insipid or facile optimism that mankind cannot go wrong. It is not a question of eliminating the mystery of existence or of preaching a happy ending, come what may. On the contrary, the awareness of infallibility means assuming a new responsibility.

In the language of modern philosophy, we could say that what is involved is discovering the passage from infallibility as an *existentielle*, as a character peculiar to a group or even to a person, to infallibility as an *existenzial*, as a category of human existence. But this is not just a mechanical shift of gears, it is a *pascha* marked by strife, rupture, death, resurrection—and certainly it is not an individual privilege but something bestowed upon mankind *ex officio*.

8. INFALLIBILITY: COSMIC HOPE AND ESCHATOLOGICAL VISION

We can and even should ask ourselves what infallibility may mean, given this universal perspective. Does it not become self-defeating? What does it mean to say that humanity as a whole cannot err if the individual can, or that there is no criterion to distinguish the fallible from the infallible? If everyone is infallible, then no one is.

We can look for an answer on two levels, the personal and the cosmic.

At the level of the person, we could say that we are infallible in what we believe and to the extent we believe in it. For this reason, our faith will save us. Good faith does not save because it is 'subjectively' true even if it is 'objectively' false; good faith saves because it is infallible (and here the word 'infallible' has its proper orthopractical character). Bad faith condemns not because it is false, but because it is bad, because it wants to err. Nevertheless, nothing prevents us at this level from believing that this saving faith is expressed through the Church or any other agency. I am merely situating these beliefs in a context that is more universal and, it seems to me, more true.

At the cosmic level, infallibility is of *kairological* and capital importance, precisely today when we run the risk of panic and collective hysteria on a worldwide scale. To be sure, Mankind can commit suicide, Man has the power to annihilate the human race and eliminate all planetary life. Modern pessimism cannot be construed as a fruit of the somber humors of a few people; it results from a profound analysis of the current situation. Human infallibility does not present itself as a sort of intellectual utopia or as an automatic destiny so universal that it lacks content. It presents itself by contrast as a challenge, as a message that is like a real 'sign raised among the nations' (as the First Vatican Council had quoted[28]), as a hope that saves. The important thing is this good news that the peoples of good will must proclaim to the four corners of the earth.[29] Humanity is infallible. And this amounts to an authentic *kerygma* of salvation. In fact, one of the most urgent tasks for our times is to proclaim that humanity is on the road to a new heaven and a new earth (be they called alpha, omega, or nothing). That someone sees a personal power directing this human tumult from on high, where another envisions a cosmic dynamism (theories that differ on the doctrinal level) does not touch the heart of what we have been saying. Christians should not claim a monopoly here; quite the contrary, they proclaim from the rooftops a message that belongs to and affects all creation.[30]

This human infallibility is not *actu*, in actuality, but *potentia*, in potency we might say, reviving old categories; it is not automatic or fated, but becomes real only thanks to a principle, a divine seed—a Church one could add—that sustains the hope of mankind towards this infallible end, despite numerous failings. Human infallibility has an eschatological character—not that of a 'happy end' according to our dreams.

Just as belief in the redemption convinced Christians that the creation was good, so now accepting the Church's infallibility can make them confident that humanity as such is bearer of infallible values.[31] The theological virtues are also cosmological.[32] The belief in this cosmic infallibility restores confidence in ourselves. It is already eschatological, it belongs to the Spirit, to the divine immanence permeating the universe.[33] Infallibility is an expression of a truly secular spirituality: Man is infallible! But he must accept the risk this entails. It is not that he cannot fail, but that he does not need to; that he can survive (also in the Teilhardian sense of *survie*).

'In theological language, does infallibility mean eliminating risk?' we are asked.[34] I would answer plainly: Authentic infallibility entails the most complete assumption of risk, for the greatest risk is to accept the infallibility of each moment of our life, fully aware that the next moment may well bring another insight because a new reality dawns upon us and not because, pleading fallibility, we refrained from exhausting the present. As long as we leave loopholes in our affirmations, as long as we do not commit ourselves totally to what we say and believe, with all the risk that this implies; as long as we are not identified with ourselves, that is, as long as we do not truly express who we are; in short, as long as we do not take infallibility seriously, we have not attained that human maturity which also entails belief in and respect for the infallibility of others. This means at the same time recognizing our own insufficiency, acknowledging that I do not exhaust the totality of human experience. It impels us toward dialogue. And like a mediaeval tourney or the Roman games, authentic dialogue is an experience of death—but also of resurrection.

I see in the phenomenon of infallibility existing in so many human traditions a memorable gesture in the awakening of human awareness. This should not be interpreted as in any way wanting to rescue a dogma, or as a strategic shifting of perspective. It entails what I still consider a Christian belief, namely a catholic concern for the entire cosmos, humankind in particular, and a vision that sees the act of Christ in a universal perspective.

Infallibility may thus be seen as an unhappy formulation of a grand awareness, not that a little group has a divine privilege, but that Man now has the burden of this dignity. The danger now lies in not daring to announce it to the entire universe, not daring to share this privilege, not daring to assume responsibility for it. We are all thrown together in this adventure that propels us closer and closer to the perfect Man—ϵἰς ἄνδρα τέλειον—[35] or, if we prefer, to the free reception of the Spirit: to be a Man, a fallible being who must believe himself infallible in order to survive. The experience of the *We* amounts to the realization of the *ātman (brahman).*

NOTES

1. In spite of the theological furor over this problem, I have not found a philosophical analysis of the question as suggested in this chapter.

2. Cf. the concise expression of the First Vatican Council, which speaks of faith *propter auctoritatem ipsius Dei revelantis, qui nec falli nec fallere potest* (Denz. Schön. 3008).

3. *Fallo (fallere)* means to err, also in the sense of deceiving someone, breaking a promise, betraying one's word, etc. Cf. σφάλλω which, in addition, means falling (and this also in the figurative sense of falling into disgrace, having difficulties, having an accident).

4. For this reason Hans Küng suggests the word be rendered by *Untrüglichkeit* (indefectibility) rather than by *Unfehlbarkeit* (infallibility) (*Die Kirche*, Freiburg: Herder, 1967, p. 406; English translation: *The Church*, New York: Sheed and Ward, 1967, pp. 342-343). Cf. the more detailed discussion in the same author's *Unfehlbar? Eine Anfrage* (Zürich: Benziger, 1970), pp. 147 sq. (English: *Infallible? An Enquiry,* London: Collins, 1971, pp. 149 sq.). Cf. as a curiosum Pascal writing in a letter of November 5, 1656, to Mlle de Roannez: "Je ne puis m'empêcher de vous dire que je voudrais être infaillible dans mes jugements. . . ." *Oeuvres complétes,* ed. I. Chevalier (Paris: Gallimard, Pléiade, 1954, p. 511).

5. "It was no accident that in the Vatican Council of 1870 and in the Roman Catholic Church outside that imposing assembly the conflict resolves itself into a bitter opposition between the scholarly and the administrative genius of the Church, the former as hostile to the definition of papal infallibility as the latter was urgent in its favour. The Curia is a court, not an academy. Its utterances are decrees, not theories. Its language is not theological so much as legal, and is to be interpreted and judged as such." W.A. Curtis, 'Infallibility', ERE, VII, 257.

6. Cf. M. Schmaus, *Katholische Dogmatik*, Vol. III: *Die Lehre von der Kirche* (München: Hueber, 1958) and in particular pp. 177 and 793 sq.

7. To situate our example, we quote the Apostolic Constitution *Munificentissimus Deus* (1 November 1950): "Quapropter . . . ad Omnipotentis Dei gloriam . . . auctoritate Domini Nostri Iesu Christi, Beatorum Apostolorum Petri et Pauli ac Nostra pronuntiamus, decla-

ramus et definimus divinitus revelatum dogma esse: Immaculatam Deiparam semper Virginem Mariam, expleto terrestris vitae cursu, fuisse corpore et anima ad caelestem gloriam assumptam" (Denz. Schön 3903).

8. "It is clear that not infallibility but ordinary certainty is the basis of our faith, at least as far as the necessary knowledge of the fact of revelation and most of all its essential parts is concerned. We have mistaken the need for certainty for the need of infallibility. Actually we are certain without it, and infallibility itself is less certain than the fact and major components of the revelation." Thus affirms the Catholic bishop F. Simons in explaining the post-Cartesian mentality in his book *Infallibility and the Evidence* (Springfield, Illinois: Templegate, 1968), p. 65. He seeks to go beyond the dogma of the Roman Church, not by enlarging the interpretation of infallibility but by humbly and sincerely recognizing that there is no such dogma, and consequently true Catholic orthodoxy has nothing to do with it. Given the Indian context from which he writes and the unspoiled or naïve faith of the bishop, our sociological law is reinforced: He does not need 'infallibility' for his Christians of Indore (it sounds superfluous and redundant), but Rome does.

9. The formula of Augustinian origin (cf. P.L., 38, 734): *Roma locuta causa finita* could give rise to a most interesting psychological analysis. Cf. on the other hand, *Pythia locuta, causa finita* in K. Kerényi's 'Problème sur la Pythia', in the volume edited by E. Castelli *L'infaillibilité, op. cit.*, pp. 323-327.

10. The expression is attributed to Franzelin. Cf. Chapter III in Y. Congar's *Jalons pour une théologie de laïcat*, Part II (Paris: Cerf, 1953; English translation: *Lay People in the Church* [Westminster, Md.: Newman Press, 1965], ch. VI, pp. 271-323, esp. 289-294) where infallibility is considered as a prophetic function of the Church. Cf. also G. Thils, 'L'infaillibilité de l'Eglise "in credendo" et "in docendo" ', in *Le premier symposium internationale de théologie dogmatique fondamentale* (Torino, 1962), pp. 83-122.

11. Cf. Y. Congar, 'Konzil als Versammlung und grundsätzliche Konziliarität der Kirche', in the Karl Rahner Festgabe, *Gott in Welt* (Freiburg: Herder, 1964), vol. II, 135-165.

12. Cf. H. Rahner, *Symbole der Kirche, Die Ekklesiologie der Väter* (Salzburg: Müller, 1964), *passim*, but esp. pp. 473 sq.

13. Cf. vgr. K. Rahner in K. Rahner and J. Ratzinger, *Episkopat und Primat* (Freiburg: Herder, 1961), pp. 86 sq. (English translation: *The Episcopate and the Primacy*, New York: Herder & Herder, 1962, pp. 64 sq.); H. Küng, *Strukturen der Kirche* (Freiburg: Herder, 1962), pp. 335 sq. (English translation: *Structures of the Church*, London: Burns & Oates, 1964, pp. 305 sq.); M. Löhrer in J. Feiner & M. Löhrer, *Mysterium Salutis* (Einsiedeln: Benziger, 1965), vol. I, 577 sq.

14. The theological discussion would center more on the question of

whether the subject *primo et per se* were the Pope, the Council or the Church.

15. Personally I know of no such comparative study devoted to this problematic. I am thinking for example of a cross-cultural theological encounter between this Christian doctrine and the Hindu mīmāṁsā. Cf. vgr. R. Panikkar, 'La demitologizzazione nell'incontro tra Cristianesimo e Induismo', in *Il problema della demitizzazione*, edited by E. Castelli (Padova: Cedam, 1961).

16. Cf. G. Lanczkowski, 'Neuere Forschungen zur Mythologie', *Saeculum*, XIX, 2/3 (1968), 282-309, for the current state of the question.

17. Cf. my chapter 'La transmythisation', in *Le mystère du culte dans l'hindouisme et le christianisme* (Paris: Cerf, 1970), pp. 171 sq.

18. In this sense one could understand the decree *Lamentabili* (3 July 1907) in condemning the proposition: "In definiendis veritatibus ita collaborant discens et docens Ecclesia, ut docenti Ecclesiae nihil supersit, nisi communes discentis opinãtiones sancire" (Denz. Schön. 3406). And yet the authority does not proclaim new beliefs.

19. Cf. the entire volume *Mythe et Foi* (Paris: Aubier, 1966), and especially the Introduction by the editor, E. Castelli, pp. 11 sq.

20. This prompts me to note that precisely this modern excommunication is the reason so-called civilized Man finds it difficult to understand the seemingly bizarre attitude of the so-called primitive in his relations with animals, taboos, totems, regulations, etc. The problem of sacrifice is also intimately connected to this problematic. Cf., to cite a classic work: W. Robertson Smith, *Lectures on the Religion of the Semites* (New York: Appleton, 1889), pp. 251 sq.: "The life of his clansman was sacred to him [early man], not because he was a man, but because he was a kinsman; and, in like manner, the life of an animal of his totem kind is sacred to the savage, not because it is animate, but because he and it are sprung from the same stock and are cousins to one another" (p. 267).

21. Need I quote the remark of a friend who said: "Heaven for the temperature, but hell for the company!" The community of sinners would seem much more animated, intense and human than the communion of the 'perfect'.

22. Cf. a statement that is valid outside its immediate context: "Among primitive peoples there are no binding precepts of conduct except those that rest on the principles of kinship" (W. Robertsom Smith, *op. cit.*, p. 269).

23. Elsewhere I have tried to show that the primacy of the principle of noncontradiction broadly characterizes Western (Semitic) culture and that the primacy of the principle of identity can explain the character of Oriental (Indian) thought. Cf. my *Mystère du culte*, *op. cit.*, pp. 37 sq.

24. Cf. Ch. Journet, *L'Eglise du Verbe Incarné* (Paris: Desclée,

1955, 2nd edition), vol. I, ch. VIII, where the author has generally succeeded in salvaging papal infallibility once one accepts its context.

25. Roman Catholic positions, for example, could more easily find agreement with the Protestant intuitions if the discussions would shift from the realm of *orthodoxy* to *orthopraxis*.

26. Membership in the Communist Party is a privilege to which all are not called. Who then is the good humanist? the good atheist? Where do we find the real Christian? the perfect Buddhist? Here scarcity is the criterion of authenticity.

27. This idea should prove fruitful in the important contemporary problem of the encounter of religions. It is not a question of universalizing at the price of a superficiality that neglects the concrete. On the contrary, it is a matter of sharing, participating, growing together.

28. Cf. Is. 11:12. In the context cited, cf. Denz. Schön. 3014.

29. Cf. Mk. 16:15; etc. Moreover, this is the only valid exegesis from the pastoral point of view.

30. "To some extent, all culture is a gigantic effort to mask this [death, want, destruction, . . .], to give the future the simulacrum of safety by making activity repetitive, expective—'to make the future predictable by making it conform to the past' [Burke]" (C. Kluckhohn, 'Myths and Rituals', in W.A. Lessa and E.Z. Vogt, *Reader in Comparative Religion. An Anthropological Approach* [New York: Harper and Row, 1965, 2nd edition], p. 152).

31. We ought not to underestimate the importance of the ecclesial *hapax* that the Constitution on the Church in the Modern World, *Gaudium et Spes*, represents.

32. Cf. R. Panikkar, 'The Relation of Christians to their Non-Christian Surroundings', in J. Neuner (ed.), *Christian Revelation and World Religions* (London: Burns & Oates, 1967), pp. 148 sq., reprinted in *Cross Currents*: 'Christians and So-called "Non-Christians" ', XXI, 3 (Summer-Fall, 1972), 281-308.

33. Cf. the words of Teilhard de Chardin in 1948: "Pour un chrétien . . . le succès biologique final de l'Homme sur Terre est, non seulement une probabilité, mais une certitude: puisque le Christ (et en Lui virtuellement le Monde) est déjà ressucité" (*L'Avenir de l'Homme, Oeuvres* [Paris: Seuil, 1959], vol. V, 304-305).

34. Cf. E. Castelli in his Introduction to *Débats sur le langage théologique* (Paris: Aubier, 1969), p. 13, and his opening remarks to the volume *L'Infaillibilité, op. cit.*, pp. 17-26.

35. Cf. Eph. 4:13; Col. 1:28; 2 Tim. 3:17; Jas. 3:2.

XVI.
Hermeneutic of Religious Freedom:
Religion as Freedom

'Υμεῖς γὰρ ἐπ' ἐλευθερία
ἐκλήθητε

In libertatem vocati estis.

Freedom claimed you when you
were called.(+)
Gal. 5:13

+ Knox translation, trying to bring together the *ecclesia* with the call,
precisely, to freedom.

1. FREEDOM OF RELIGION

καὶ ἡ ἀλήθεια ἐλευθερώσει ὑμᾶς

et veritas liberabit vos. [1]

It is undeniable that our epoch is presently undergoing an important, even disruptive, change in the notion and above all the experience of human freedom. We may ascertain this more clearly by studying the different ways of dealing with the age-old problem of the relations between freedom and religion.

First I shall try to depict this change, one of the most striking turnabouts of our day. Since the sociological phenomena of freedom and liberation are well known, I shall confine myself to underscoring the philosophical problematic regarding religious freedom.

Second, I shall attempt to show that this change runs much deeper than might appear at first glance. It implies a new awareness of human religiousnous—I wonder if it could be called transmythicization? It is in fact Man's religious dimension that today undergoes this profound, and I hope purifying transformation.

In short, the *hermeneutic of the freedom of religion* brings me to consider *religion as freedom*. To recognize the 'freedom of religion' amounts to disclosing the *religiousness of freedom* and consequently *religion as freedom*. This is the thesis I shall develop.

* * *

a. Freedom As a Duty

Traditional Western thinking has repeatedly proclaimed the freedom of *religion* and thus even of the religious *act*, but has somehow neglected the concrete *Man* himself, the ultimate subject of this free act. The reasoning went somewhat like this: Man has a duty to follow the true religion because he is made for truth, the true religion incarnates the truth, and truth is the good. To 'help' the individual to perform that duty is a supremely moral act. If Man finds himself faced with the choice between good and evil, this comes from a weakness of his freedom. God is perfectly free and yet he is not confronted with the choice between good and evil. Certainly, the free act, by definition, has to allow for its own negation. But strictly speaking, Man is not free to choose evil, he merely has the possibility of doing so by being carried away by the attraction of evil, and if he takes this road, he sins. If, then, a higher authority, in spite of the individual's will, steers him clear of evil by constraining him to follow the good and the true path, his freedom is not violated. Evil is here considered error, and goodness truth. Hence if the Church or the Emperor, for instance, does someone violence by wresting the individual from error, the latter is only being helped to become free. In all these traditional considerations freedom has from the start an ambivalent character, but its negative taint is stressed: It is the abuse of the freedom to sin, to refuse God's gift, to choose evil. Significantly enough, the first act of freedom of which the Bible tells us is Adam's sin, and the first creaturely act it describes is another abuse of freedom, the sin of the angels: in both instances, a misuse of freedom to disobey. In order to avoid making God responsible for the world's ills, evil was imputed to freedom. Evil is then the result of freedom. No wonder that freedom has not had a very good reputation. "Libertas perditionis"[2] and "libertas erroris"[3] are two quotations from Saint Augustine that the popes of the past century were fond of quoting.

Following this mood, freedom has been allied with contingency, with human limitations and imperfections. Man is free because he can say no, even—mainly?—to God. Faced with a free choice it is Man's *duty* to choose the good and thus the truth. Freedom is the price Man must pay to become like God, and for this, freedom is ambivalent, at once a good and an imperfection. Perfect freedom would make Man God. The fissure between the objective and the subjective order of things is the gauge of Man's creatureliness. Every Man, precisely because he is free, chooses 'his' good. Further, since Aristotle it is recognized that this good can only be defined as that to which the will is directed. Freedom always makes a choice *sub specie boni*, but the fissure appears when this subjective good to which the will is directed is not at the same time an objective truth. Objective truth is obscured by passions and selfishness. Error and evil are possible in the human sphere precisely because the objective and the subjective do not coincide. Freedom is the guarantor, so to speak, of Man's responsibility, his merit and his dignity, but it is also answerable for error and evil. The vision of Man 'condemned to be free' is but a recent expression of a traditional Western notion.

In the social life of Church and State, the argument was pursued in the most logical fashion. The heretic is he who voluntarily chooses error; hence he sins against human nature, for Man is a rational animal and the heretic refuses to accept truth. One is not humanly, i.e., rationally, free to opt for truth or error, since true freedom is to choose the truth. It alone will set us free. Man is only potentially free; he acquires more and more freedom in the extent to which he chooses, and lives in, the truth. But the Church being the 'depository' of truth, there is no question of a free choice between belonging or not belonging to it (only ignorance in good faith can save the infidel). You are not morally free when facing the truth; even ignorance can be culpable. So it is not a matter of a free choice, but rather of a free—spontaneous and reasonable—adherence to truth, since you have acknowledged the right of truth and Man's duty to adhere to it. Truth is liberating, but you must first acknowledge the duty to embrace it; only then does liberation ensue. You cannot even recognize truth if you are not rooted in it. Only if we 'believe in it', if we are its 'disciples', if we 'know' the truth, will it free us. Morality in the broadest sense is a sine qua non for adherence to truth. Even to devote oneself to philosophy, and thus to searching out the truth, one was obliged in several cultures to evince a practical and moral engagement. If our works are not good we will not even be able to recognize truth, and if we do not recognize truth wherever it is, wherever it shows itself, we may very well doubt we are on the way to the good.

The same was traditional in the socio-political sphere for thousands of years: If you escape your tribe you shall be killed, you have to realize your being within your caste, guild, class, nation. The slave, the outcast, the rebel will have to pay with his life for his excommunication. In many countries the passport is still a privilege and not a right. If the count, the duke, the king, the emperor, but equally so if the president, the parliament, the party or the country calls you, you have to obey and cannot object. From the days of Arjuna, the first conscientious objector who was convinced or at least defeated by Lord Krishna, until our recent times, you could not even argue against the idea not only that the common good has the primacy, but that it is the hierarchical status quo that determines the common good.

It is noteworthy that the very word 'religion', whether in its etymology or its numerous classical usages, always indicates a bond, a decision, an obligation, a reversal (when it is not a scruple, a superstition, etc.). In other words, religion usually indicates a duty, a dependence, an obedience, an acknowledgment of our contingency, and it is this same set of ideas concerning dependence and obligation that seems so opposed to any notion centering on autonomy and freedom.

The famous pontifical condemnations, in the last century and the beginning of our own, of so-called freedom of conscience, freedom of thought, freethinkers, liberalism, etc., show just how far the conviction was kept alive that freedom is a duty (and equally a danger) and how the connotation of the word was always rather pejorative. To recognize the dangers of freedom, and the ravages of libertinism, to accept our ties and our limits, to be on guard against a spirit of independence, and our own judgments; Christian spirituality vigorously emphasized these many negative characteristics of its day in order to foster obedience and humility, and to bolster the unflagging effort towards perfection. Freedom was considered the stronghold of Man's self-assertive will standing against the rights of God or against the objective rights of truth. *Plato amicus, sed magis amica veritas; pereat mundus, sed iustitia adimpleatur; oboedentia tutior*; etc.[4] were so many maxims with the only possible alternative of either stubborn self-assertion, by an abuse of our freedom, or of submission to God (*cui servire regnare est*, we were told[5]) through one's superiors. From Plato and the Stoics up to and including the majority of Christian writers, freedom was found pejoratively associated with autarchy, independence, self-mastery, and so with pride, self-sufficiency, the rejection of the bonds that bind us and that 'make' Man: ἐλεύθερον τὸ ἄρχον ἑαυτοῦ.[6] But Man, so they said, is neither his own ἀρχή nor his own ἄρχον.

Certainly, it was said, there is a natural law, all authority comes from God, who is a God of freedom; one must resist an unjust law, etc. But all these arguments could not be used against the authority that, they said, comes from God. Individual conscience is doubtless the final arbiter—here one knowingly quotes Saint Thomas—but the individual cannot constantly be questioning everything; he lacks the necessary training or data. Once you have so to speak examined the Church's credentials as the vehicle of Revelation, once you have critically acknowledged that she possesses the authority of God and the promise of the Holy Spirit's assistance, you regard yourself as justified in signing a blank affidavit and believing everything she teaches with no further need to question or take other steps. It would be interesting in this regard to study what tradition has said on the famous problem of regicide. Mariana was condemned by Church and State.

We should ponder the fact that Giordano Bruno could escape the jurisdiction of the Church as little as a citizen of a modern nation can escape the power of the State by renouncing his nationality. A certificate of birth may today bind an individual more than a certificate of baptism.

Historically speaking one could put forward the hypothesis

that the communist ideology seems to be the successor of this mentality, which now many of the traditional religions want to overcome. I am not saying that there are no differences between the 'people of Israel', the 'church of God' and the 'Party', or that 'corporate destiny' is the same as 'collective mission'. I am signaling a common horizon.

Whatever this may be, objectivity here carries the day over subjectivity, essential truth over existential authenticity, the community over the person, and, by an interesting transference from the epistemological to the ontological sphere, a certain supernaturalism prevails over the natural. And it is to this 'inferior' realm of the natural that the so-called rights of Man specifically belong. That there be no misunderstanding here: It would be premature, even false, to reject utterly this hierarchical and objective conception of the universe. We have only tried to describe it as briefly as possible. *Intelligenti pauca.*[7]

b. Freedom As a Right

Today's situation begins to be different. The same words previously charged with negative connotations now convey positive values. The climate is changing, not only in some parts of the so-called secular world, but in the religious world as well. The ecumenical Council of Churches speaks of tolerance and understanding, the Second Vatican Council of religious freedom, Hinduism of a new interpretation of caste, Eurocommunism strikes a humanistic and democratic note, etc.[7a]

The great modern myths—suspect not long ago in ecclesiastical circles—such as tolerance, dialogue, pluralism, democracy, justice, progress, etc., have as their common denominator the more or less explicit idea that freedom is a supreme and inalienable right of the human person and so that freedom excels any other value whatsoever. We begin these days to speak of the *rights* of Man, we even proclaim them in a 'charter'. Although many of us remember the criticisms voiced against the Declaration of San Francisco in 1945: 'The duties of Man should rather have been proclaimed...!' Let us not forget that when victorious Japan in the Versailles treaty, in 1919, proposed, when drafting the Covenant of the League of Nations, that race or nationality should not be discriminating factors, in law or in fact, it was defeated, mainly because of the opposition of Britain and the United States of America.

The change cuts deep. We only now begin to take account of it. In fact we are still submerged, so to speak, in the transition and most of these words still retain a disquieting ambivalence. This is easily verified by reading Kierkegaard or modern existentialism or the Christian literary output since the Second World War on the tension between the Church and the Modern World, etc. Dictatorship was not a bad word only a couple of generations ago. Dictatorship of the proletariat could be a very positive slogan. Today, everywhere we have 'peoples' democracies'. It all may be a tactic, but this is irrelevant for our thesis. The important change is that this is the general language employed by those of the right and those of the left. We are entering a new myth.

To be sure, for perhaps thousands of years there have been aristocrats of the spirit who would not be tied up by racial, social, religious and other differences, but such ideals had to remain esoteric. There were some who said we Men are all brethren, even the enemies should be loved, no degrading distinction should be made between male and female, Greek and Jew, rich and poor. Yet all this was taken not only *cum grano salis*, but also embedded in a larger horizon of a structured, hierarchical and immutable objective order: 'slaves, obey your masters!'

But we may leave aside the study of historical facts to indicate certain philosophical features that seem to belong to the *mythemes* of our contemporary myth.

i. In the first place, there is clearly a shift in emphasis from the objective to the subjective, from objective truth to subjective truth, from the category of essences to that of existences. What seems above all important today is the human person and his subjectivity, not the objective order of ideas or the exigencies of a theoretical objectivity deemed independent of Man and superior to him.

It is not only, nor basically, a moral consideration that leads us to recognize that we should not impose upon others something they do not readily accept. This would bring us to suppose that the first hypothesis is itself immoral, and we do not believe this is so. We should not commit the *katachronism* of judging a past era with ideas current today. Although the first world view may lend itself to an abuse of authority, appropriate distinctions were in fact drawn to avoid, at least theoretically, the abuse of power and the constraint of conscience. In spite of all possible manipulations there was always a transcendent and supreme God. On the other hand, a certain liberal or liberalist notion might also lead to a disregard for the individual—rendered incapable of shouldering his own responsibilities, overwhelmed as he is by the spiritual, intellectual or material powers that surround him. With *habeas corpus* and 'constitutional rights' there may be as much human exploitation as without them. We are speaking of a change in consciousness and not endorsing an idea of human linear progress—although this change is obviously not without practical consequences. Indifference toward the weak and noninterference in our neighbor's calamities may be sheer cowardice and callousness cloaked in 'respect' for their 'freedom'. The moral questions stem from another order altogether and they are extant in both modes of thought we are presently studying.

Our problem is equally independent of any psychological consideration of the subjective convictions of individuals. It goes without saying that we must respect the awareness of others, that there are different psychological types, that what carries conviction for some may not for others, that we can approach reality by several paths and that there can be a healthy perspectivism. All this was well known before today. The rights of subjectivity are not purely a psychological affair.

The moral and psychological issues are two very important questions in which the modern era has taken a particular interest, but I believe that the transmythicization we are now studying oversteps these two spheres utterly. We should look for the roots at an ontological level and an anthropological stratum. This new awareness was not totally absent in the past but it was the privilege of the few, whereas now it begins to enter the universal human consciousness.

We are becoming more sensitive to the fact and open to the

experience that any objectivity demands a subjectivity, or rather
that we should never cut the umbilical cord uniting the two.
Hardly anybody, of course, has defended sheer objectivity;
nevertheless it was considered to be the decisive element. The
tension between the two was not so great precisely because objectivity was based in the subjectivity of God, and God's existence was by and large unquestioned. The modern epoch shows
itself more reserved, more respectful and skeptical, when it
comes to ascribing ideas and concepts to God. The very objectivity of Revelation, for instance, cannot be severed from the subjectivity of the one to whom it is revealed.

At bottom we find a relational awareness recovering importance not only in the realm of science but in other spheres of
human life as well. We might mention here the fundamental distinction between an agnostic *relativism*, indifferent to truth, and a
relativity, aware that truth is a relationship, that beings themselves are relational, quite as much as thoughts and the other
products of human culture.

ii. Related to the preceding consideration, we may add the primacy of the dignity of the person as a theoretical characteristic of
our times. To be sure, people have talked about personal dignity
before now, but they had situated Man's dignity in exterior
objectivities—insofar as he embodies transcendental values, participates in the divine nature, belongs to a particular religion,
nation, class, race, civilization, etc. The dignity of the person, in
the final analysis, was located outside the person. Even today the
sole justification for capital punishment (other than atavisms) relies on the dichotomy enforced between the person of the 'criminal' and the human dignity he has lost. Civil justice claims to kill
the criminal in order to preserve *his* human dignity. The same
anthropological justification goes for traditional forms of suicide:
'I commit hara-kiri in order to save my personal dignity—which
is outside me—by eliminating 'me''.' Modern suicide would be
almost the opposite: 'I kill myself because I am the last instance'.

Our age begins dimly to glimpse that the concrete person
embodies the highest possible value, over and above any social or

objective category whatsoever. This amounts to discovering that the freedom of the person is an ontological freedom, superior to 'objective truth', even to objective religion; and that the person, in its ontological nudity and with all its constitutive ambivalence—for it is ever in relation—always presents a core irreducible to 'categories' of abstract truth or goodness. In other words, the particular existence takes precedence over essence or ideas, and so (personal) authenticity proves superior to (objective) truth.

The often violent and impassioned discussions throughout the 19th century on freedom in its most varied facets—philosophical, theological, social, political, etc.—cannot be explained away as a simple speculative disagreement or a difference in perspectives, but as a true crisis of growth in Man himself, appearing in and through a new awareness, although not always expressing itself with sufficient clarity or precision. We may be in the presence of a genuine transmythicization and it will not help to attempt to shield today's positions—with apologetic intent— by saying they were already maintained in the traditional notion of Man and theology. To say, for instance, that we learn nonviolence from the Bible is a beautiful confession of one's beliefs, but an exegetical capriole.

Further, the Christian 'fact' conceived as static, complete and potentially accomplished, needing only to expand and be actualized, is rather an Aristotelian category than a Christian exigency. Moreover, to recognize this transmythicization furnishes a proof of the vitality of the Christian faith, which has no need to continually justify itself by an exclusive 'fidelity' to the past, but which can also present itself as a 'hope' for the One destined to come yet again. The Christian fact need not be understood exclusively as a seed in the process of growing, but it also asks to be seen as a creation ever new, ever approaching the creative act and leaving behind the creaturely state: Man being as much a hope to be as a potency of being. Of course a mystical vision and a deep intuition leap far beyond these conceptual skeletons, and one has the impression that the great masters of antiquity have even anticipated us. But whatever the outcome, we must also take into account the scandal this language and these theories represent for a traditional mentality, when they are upheld today by thinkers seriously concerned about orthodoxy and fidelity to tradition.

'How can religion be sustained with a thesis like this? Will the whole edifice, not only of Christianity but of all religious life and even all order, not collapse?' Briefly, then, it may appear that we uphold the right to error, not as such, i.e., error in the abstract, but error as far as it is incarnated in a person who follows his or her own conscience, however twisted or erroneous. No need to discuss now this latter possibility; suffice to affirm that *in concreto* there is no higher court of appeal than the conscience and consciousness of the person. Men all have the same rights and at this level we have renounced any merely objective criterion of truth, since although objective truth need not be denied, it scarcely has any meaning if the concrete subject, the person, does not make it his own. The person in the concretion of his living relationship with his world is a supreme value, permitting no possible recourse to anything that might transcend him. Is this not precisely what is understood by atheism? But did Vatican II Council not defend just that? *Dignitatis humanae personae* is the title (and first words) of the *Declaratio* on Religious Freedom (which quotes at the very outset John XXIII's *Pacem in terris*).

The experience of pluralism, in the air almost everywhere today, was not foreign to the atmosphere of the Council. Pluralism has, so to speak, undermined the hitherto unshakable confidence in the absolute character of one's own convictions. It is not agnosticism to discover the relativity of our ideas, our formulations, even our beliefs. So we come to put confidence in the other, not only regarding his good faith but also regarding the truth—partial, limited, unilateral or what you will, but truth after all—of his viewpoint. The other thus becomes a source of knowledge—and not merely an object of knowledge—which consequently cannot be reduced to my judgment.

With reference to our particular point, the philosophical structure underpinning the Council's reasoning comes down to

the following: 'The human person has a right to religious freedom.' Now Man is not infallible, he can make mistakes: Consequently religious freedom must also consider the fact that the
person may objectively be in error. All the same, he has a right to
religious freedom, for this freedom has its foundation in the dignity of the human person. (*Jus ad libertatem religiosam esse
fundatum in ipsa dignitate personae humanae* — 'the right to religious freedom is grounded in the very dignity of the human person'.) This is to say that human freedom has a certain *ontonomy*
vis-à-vis the adherence or nonadherence to objective truth. We
have no right to encroach upon freedom, for it is this freedom in
which the dignity of the person is grounded. What has supreme
value, what constitutes the dignity of Man, is his freedom, i.e.,
the fact that he is capable of acting freely. If we rob Man of this
we degrade him to a subhuman condition. Now, the essential
claim of all religions is to help Man acquire (or recover) his full
dignity, which is another term for salvation, liberation, fullness,
final goal and the like. In other words, any religious act tends
ultimately to let Man acquire his dignity, his salvation or liberation. Hence if an act is not free it cannot be religious. Here we
come back to our thesis: To recognize the fact of religious freedom leads to the affirmation that the fundamental act of religion is
the free act, and that the free act is the religious act par excellence. Thus the freedom of religion leads us to religion as freedom.

To sum up the transmythicization that has taken place regarding freedom and human dignity, we could quote the well-known
Pauline saying: "Where the Spirit of the Lord is, there is freedom", but instead of reading it as only saying that the Church,
being where the Spirit dwells, is the place of freedom, we read it
as also saying: 'Where there is freedom, there is the Spirit of the
Lord.' The kingdom of freedom is built by the Spirit of the Lord.
The Church, by definition, is the place of freedom. Freedom *is*
the Spirit of the Lord. The ecclesiastical calling, the vocation, the
congregatio that constitutes the Church, is a call to freedom: ἐπ'
ἐλευθερίᾳ ἐκλήθητε.

2. RELIGION AS FREEDOM[8]

οὗ δὲ τὸ πνεῦμα κυρίου, ἐλευθερία
Ubi autem Spiritus Domini, ibi libertas.[9]

It seems that the antinomy between religion and freedom appears the moment we begin to reflect on the problem. In a sense freedom stands in antinomy with everything else, since liberty, once put on the level of the norm, is the anti-*nomos* par excellence. Dialectically speaking freedom and law are certainly 'antinomic'; but what we are looking for is a nondialectical relation between freedom and *nomos*, *ṛta*, *ordo*.

Whatever this may be, from the traditional point of view it is necessary to uphold the exclusively functional value of freedom; everything depends on how we use it; we cannot 'substantialize' freedom and convert it into a good 'thing'. To canonize freedom above everything else would amount to libertinism, anarchy, the fiercest individualism and, in the final analysis, to the most radical solipsism—each Man his own king, a law unto himself. So we compromise, we limit exterior personal freedom by respect for the freedom of others, we trim the individual's freedom to the needs of society, etc. Now, to institutionalize freedom spells its destruction, independently of possible abuses on the part of authority (which still has a brake when it 'comes from God', but turns into tyranny when it becomes autonomous). To want to instrumentalize freedom is a contradiction in terms. The impasse is real: You cannot leave freedom 'free' if you want to safeguard order and religion. Man can live only in a state of conditioned freedom. Freedom is at the most free will, and that is all. Man's life on earth is on parole. We cannot elaborate here an analysis of the assumptions on which such a vision is based, or suggest the principles for a new vision of Man and reality. Suffice it to say that the traditional view is coherent: If Man is regarded as a substance, and substance as static being with no possible dynamism other than accidental change, and if being is considered as a given at its beginning and not at its end; if, further, time is an accident and ideas have a so-called divine immutability, etc., then freedom is a mere psychological feature of the human being—which will sooner or later open the door to an extreme Skinnerian interpretation.[10] I am not suggesting that the traditional notion is radically false. I am simply saying that as it presents itself to the contemporary spiritual situation it appears unsatisfactory. Rightly or wrongly a new myth seems to emerge and our intention has been one of trying to understand this transmythicization as far as possible.

Let us confine ourselves to this particular but central aspect of the relation between freedom and religion. If religion is fundamentally the link, the string or rather the rein that somewhat bridles the wild animal that is Man, leading him to a goal, which he somehow seems to want and to shun, then freedom can only be the result of acknowledging that the prescribed way is the right path and that within it he may run 'freely'. The way is somewhat fixed and determined.

Now, perhaps religion is not only this. A very traditional Christian concept may help us here.

Metanoia is the constant challenge of faith to every epoch, in every culture and religion, and so also to contemporary Christianity. Now this constant change of mind, this ongoing or rather 'in-going' conversion, seems to indicate that the transformation faith requires of us is not to make freedom a religion (at which tradition would be justifiably outraged) but to discover the very nature of religion in real freedom. We shall try to explicate this.

It is certainly necessary to deepen the notion of freedom, but we must also rethink the concept of religion. This is not a matter of making freedom into a new form of religion, with its laws, duties, rites, etc., but of recognizing that *what* was formerly represented by Law, Worship, Duty, etc., and to which the name religion has been given, has freedom at its core or as its soul. I am not proposing a change of name; I propose simply a radical *metanoia* of religion itself, or rather, a *metanoia* of human religiousness, a metamorphosis of Man's deepest dimension, which until now has been called the religious dimension.

We can only give a few insights into the problem. I shall try to describe first what *religion* represents, then what *freedom* means for contemporary Man, and finally a *Christian* hermeneutic about this question.

a. Religion, Way to Salvation, Means of Liberation

While the substantive definitions of religion stress the dependence, obligation, creatureliness, duty, contingency, etc., of a being insufficient unto itself, it seems to me that the following existential definition of religion may be able to assume the numerous descriptions already given and also include the new problematic: *Religion means way to salvation*, or indeed *religion claims to be a way of liberation*. I call this definition existential because it refers to religion as an existential reality— *orthopraxis*—without seeking to fix an essential boundary for the contents of the concepts employed.

I must stress once and for all that this is an attempt to use a language that should be valid, as far as possible, for a wide range of religious and philosophic persuasions. We are consequently not concerned with settling the question whether a certain notion of the way or ways is in fact a 'means' effectively conducive to salvation or not. Nor is there any question here of deciding whether salvation, as Man's perfection, can be reached by one way rather than another. By *way* I understand whatever means—action, mind, love, will and so on—Man must employ, discover, believe, initiate, put into practice, etc., in order to attain his salvation, destiny, end, goal. We can as well interpret this salvation from the most varied perspectives: from perfect union with God to mere survival in society, in an otherworldly heaven, individual annihilation, death, the absurd, or whatever. Intercultural, interphilosophical, and above all interreligious dialogue must know how to handle words and reach that which probably does not exist without concepts, but is not exhausted by them either.

We must say that the same goes for the word religion. This word is a particular expression of a much larger and deeper reality; the word religion stems from a rather circumscribed order of thinking, valid only in a certain civilization. We know very well it is not found with its current sense in either the Bible or classical

Latinity, nor can we find a strict translation for it in the other religious traditions of mankind. For this reason, to avoid terminological argument, I shall consider as religion not only what circulates under this label, but everything that claims to perform the function that religion *strictu sensu* is said to perform. In this broader meaning, any ensemble of means that claim to convey Man to his life's goal, however this goal might be conceived, can be considered religion.

For the last few centuries it has become habit to accord the word religion a very specialized meaning. Some have even wanted to exclude Buddhism from this definition since it does not recognize a supreme and personal God. On the other hand, religion had almost been identified with its conceptual expression, which was called orthodox doctrine. The word also came to mean a particular virtue alongside other more or less important virtues. It was not easy, nor is it today, to recognize the fundamentally religious character of Communism, Humanism and even Secularism, since these movements do not fit the artificially restricted definition of religion. This would also explain the repugnance these same ideologies, or whatever you call them, feel toward considering themselves religions—so thoroughly has religion been reduced to certain notions of the way to salvation. For this very reason the proposal has lately been made to abandon the use of the word religion altogether; nevertheless, I believe that for want of a better word and also to underscore the basic continuity between what was once called religion and today's new forms of religiousness, we may still employ the same word, having broadened and deepened it along the lines just indicated.

It is not for us now in this context to judge the degree of truth or the moral value of any human attitude toward Man's ultimate problematic. We may question the value or the truth of contemporary modes of religiousness, call them aberrations, substitutes or even false religions, but our task does not consist now in judging these religions or so-called ideologies but in disengaging from them their functional claim to lead their *believers* to their goal.

It should be clear by now that the intention of this chapter is neither to defend nor to attack religion, but to understand that peculiar human dimension expressed by this word. Moreover the religious act does not necessarily need to be good. By the same token that the religious act claims to lead to salvation, its contrary act—equally religious—will lead to failure, damnation. A really free act has this power: It may lead us to our fulfillment, but equally to our bankruptcy. Religion is a double-edged sword.

We should like only to say one thing and from it to suggest another: to say that Man's religious dimension is not indispensably bound to a predetermined concept of religion; and to suggest that the religious crisis of mankind today is not due to the disappearance of religion as a human dimension, but to the new reclamation of a sphere of the secular that in the last centuries of Western history seemed to have been removed from religion. Whether this should take place at the price of burying the sacred, or of discovering the sacredness of the secular, is again quite another question. But certainly separation of Church and State should not be confused with divorce between religion and life.

This said, we can pursue our path by stating that Man's religious dimension is on the way to finding its most authentic expression in, precisely, freedom.

One may have a more, or less, well-defined notion of freedom, but in one way or another freedom is always deemed Man's goal. Religion is that which makes the fundamental claim to liberate Man. That to which one adheres in order to acquire what one considers Man's fundamental freedom is a religion. In the cultural constellation of today's world, freedom remains the most deepseated characteristic of salvation, however one envisions human perfection.

If religion has always promised to save Man, then what mankind today eagerly awaits is precisely freedom, liberation from the sufferings, fears, doubts, anxieties and insecurities of life. Humanity today, especially in the West, feels imprisoned by its own inventions, enslaved by its own means of power. Technology frees Man from so many of his traditional and endemic nightmares that for the first time he can truly forge his own destiny in a spectrum of possibilities unsuspected just a century ago. But he finds himself trapped in his own snare. The freedom to which he aspires is a political freedom as well as an economic and social freedom, but it is above all a personal, even individual, freedom. When you attend vast human gatherings—religious in the broadest sense of the word—you feel a sort of wind, a liberating breath, pass through the head and heart of the crowd, but you also realize that these salutary effects are only transient, because after the liturgical catharsis we relapse into everyday life, which clamps us like a vice and seems to let slip away that cup of liberation for which we ever thirst, and which modern Man seldom finds in the mere repetition of the past.

Man today thirsts for deliverance, that he would be free from everything, from every limitation, and for this reason from all religion as well, in the sense that the 'bond' of 'religion' seems to him incompatible with the freedom to which he aspires. The religious act par excellence is seen and lived in the act of liberation—from everything, even from religion and from oneself—and we may recall Meister Eckhart's injunction to get rid of God for God's sake. All prophetic activity is basically the effort—always a failure—to rid oneself of religion in the name of religion. 'If you see the Buddha, kill him', as the great Mahāyāna sages and mystics would say—with no need to quote Zen.

This then would be the first part of our thesis: The goal of Man is liberation, this being nothing other than deliverance from every constraint, from all limitation, for any limit stands like a wall, blocking us, preventing our flowering. If religion claims to save Man, it can do so only by putting him on the path to realizing his destiny. We may recall the myth of Śunaḥśepa as the story of deconditioning Man.

To sum up: The act of ontically exercising freedom is the religious act by which Man is saved (or doomed). The religious act is the act of freedom. The fact of becoming alive to the freedom of religion, that is to say, the fact of having recognized that the freedom of the religious act is this act's primordial element (in such a way that if an act were not free we could not call it religious), this fact leads us to define religion as freedom, and freedom as the fundamental religious category. Only thus do we circumvent the objections raised by those who even lately oppose religious freedom in the name of religion.

b. Religion As the Free Act of Liberation

Man wants to be free. Religion wants to free Man. Present-day thought is deeply convinced that the way leading to freedom must itself be a free way, i.e., a way freely chosen or accepted. It is a road that opens out before the traveler, but that at the same time springs up from its own depths; a road that creates itself in the traveling. In traditional terms we could say that religion must be a free act so that Man may come into the entirety of his freedom.

An act that is not itself free cannot liberate. But what is a free act? When does a person act freely? We can answer from a double perspective: he is free who *does* what he wills, or else *wills* what he does. In the first case the will is given, in the second the action, but in both cases there is a certain harmony, even adequation, between the intimate depths of being and its expressions and manifestations. In this sense, freedom is truth. Only a free being can be true, for only then will it express what it is. For this reason, there is in any desire for freedom always an impetus to truth.

All the same, there is a vital and characteristic circle in freedom: If I *do* what I will I am free, but my willingness could always be predetermined, unfree; if, on the other hand, I really *will* what I do, my psychological freedom is guaranteed, since I express what I believe in my action. But what assures me that my actions are not imposed on me, more or less unconsciously, by external circumstance? Do we not make virtue of necessity?

How can we jump out of this circle? (If I do what I will is it not because I will what I do? and vice versa.) If freedom is only internal (wanting to do what I do), it can very easily turn into passive acceptance of what is imposed from outside. If it is but to carry out external action (to do what I will), then apart from possible conflicts with the freedom of others (which will oblige me to limit my own), it can from this side turn into individualistic, anarchical caprice, which is at bottom only a new form of the slavery imposed by action. Only a synergy of these two modes of freedom can bring about authentic human freedom.

The well-known distinction between *freedom-from* and

freedom-to (which could moreover express the characteristic modes of Eastern and Western spirituality, respectively) may serve as well to express the two faces of freedom we have just mentioned. *Freedom-to do* what I will (West) would thus be counterbalanced by *freedom-from willing* what I do (East).

Now, is Man not *free to free* himself *from* everything that opposes his salvation, his liberation? This is the crux. Most religions would qualify this freedom. They claim precisely to lead Man to his freedom. Grace could be what gives Man this *freedom-to* so that by it he may *free* himself *from* every obstacle to realizing his salvation; however, very often grace—by definition absolutely gratuitous—is in fact dependent upon regulations and institutions that seem to interpose themselves between personal freedom and the liberation of Man. We touch here on a complex of well-known and delicate problems—on human nature, sin, grace and free will—that we do not wish to pursue.

I repeat: It is not a matter of considering freedom a superior form of religion, or as religion and nothing more, but exactly the contrary; that is, to see that the essence of the religious act consists precisely in the realization of freedom.

The first attitude, the opinion that freedom is the true religion, represents a traditional idea in most religions. But here we cannot escape one of two difficulties: Either we institutionalize freedom in order to make it a religion in the traditional sense, or we fall into libertinism. One could write a whole history of religions centered on the constant tension, creative or destructive, between these two tendencies: On one side we find a 'subjugated' freedom in the bosom of an institution accepted as 'mother', refuge, liberator or what have you, freedom as a recompense for the docile and obedient; and on the other side, unbridled anarchy, since a religion that seeks to be pure freedom should abjure not only every constraint but every norm and directive as well. The tension becomes tragic when the structures do not allow themselves to be overstepped, when rebellion and revolt lead to the same impasses as docility and submission. What makes the lives of certain saints so exciting is not their way of surmounting the conflict—which indeed they do not resolve—but their manner of sustaining defeat by projecting onto a true eschatology, which is not an evasion, the solution that will be possible precisely after their failure. Sanctity is in fact the harmony between impossibles. If by night all cats are grey, in the future every aporia will have a loophole. Tragedy only rears its head when you kill time, when you can neither wait nor hope.

What we are now analyzing is precisely the possibility of a new alternative; this constitutes the novelty of our era and what I have called a change of myth. I have already formulated our principle: The essence of the religious act, that which we find in the heart of what we call religion, is precisely freedom.

We shall now pursue a certain sequence in the ascent of our thinking.

i. First, an act that is not free cannot be called a religious act. A forced act would have no religious value. The more freely an act is performed, the more human and religious value it has.

ii. Secondly, the religious act is a free act. Free in the one who performs it, and free in its effects. Religion is distinguished from its counterfeit, magic, by the fact that freedom is essential to the religious act. Worship is distinguished from ritualism by the fact that the former may fall short, for it always runs a risk: It is ever a new act, a (re)creation.

We could try to clarify all this with a little help from the history of classical religions. A very brief resume would draw, it seems to me, the following picture. Religion is the set of means used by Man to reach, or make, his salvation (whether the means are given by the divine or not). Now what saves is by definition *sacrifice*, that is, participation in the cosmic and primordial act through which the world is 're-made', comes to its final destination, remakes in inverse the act that gave birth to the universe, etc. Participation in this sacrifice may take innumerable forms, ranging from rites valid in themselves, which consequently save almost physically or automatically, to an interiorization of these rites by thought or intention; there is as well a spectrum of interpretations from individual morality to the realm of social or even political action. Every religion demands an *orthopraxis* by which Man collaborates in this process. In every case we find a human act freely performed. Now participation in the saving act, performance of the sacrifice, assimilation of the sacramental structure, worship or rite that Man believes he must accomplish to reach or approach salvation, has until today been dominated, in general, by the authority of the objective order, by the power of the divine factor, by the efficacy of the rites, the knowledge of the Party, the might of nature, the resources of science, etc. In other words, the essence of the religious act was seen as submission and obedience, even adoration, the acknowledgment of human dependence and divine power, the acceptance of creatureliness and of the human condition and similar attitudes, which could perhaps be summed up in the word fidelity. Religion furnished the 'objective' means of salvation and the person's duty was to lay hold of them, assimilate them, make them his own. Of course with all this nobody claimed to encroach upon freedom. This freedom was said to be the acceptance, recognition and discovery of the real and existential situation. It was the necessary condition for attaining, in a way befitting the human being and yet meritorious, the salvation that grace presented to us.

This procedure can be expressed in the most divergent ways, following one or another spirituality or religion, but with very few exceptions we would finally come to what we are in the midst of setting forth, that is, the concept of salvation as a 'favor' from God, a 'gift' of the Party, a 'gratuitous' discovery, an unmerited intuition, a predestination freely accepted, a 'package deal', and so forth. Even traditions like the Buddhist, which strongly stresses Man's self-redemptive character, do not fail to insist not only that it is the Buddha who has brought us the message of deliverance, but also that we must in some way or other undergo the experience of the Enlightened One in order to be saved. In short, one *ought*, even though freely, to accept, adhere, follow, obey, recognize. . . .

In one way or another, although people have held very different notions of freedom, the religious act has always been considered a free act, free because fully human.

iii. Our third point is simply that the contemporary myth is differ-

ent. It is not only that people profess themselves no longer satisfied with Latin, literary Arabic, Pali or Sanskrit, because they
want to understand; nor is it merely a question of a somewhat
pressured adaptation to procure more meaningful, and so truer,
rituals. It is not enough to discover that we want to be aware of,
and consciously collaborate in, the religious act. To be sure this is
most traditional, but the difference lies in the fact that this saving
free act is no longer seen either in or necessarily connected with
the rites, doctrines or actions of established religious norms. A
Catholic may not feel he is betraying his faith by not going to
Sunday Mass; a Protestant may find no betrayal of his Christian
commitment by indulging in extramarital sexual life; a Muslim
may not feel any longer guilty if he does not follow the quranic
eating and drinking regulations, a Hindu may drop all observations and still consider himself a good Hindu, etc., etc. Still, in
traditional terminology, it is the new sacrifice (identified with the
primordial sacrifice), which Man himself freely makes because he
feels it surge up from inside his very being. That gives him the
requisite awareness of collaborating and participating in the act
by which he comes to the fulfillment of his being.

Summarizing humanity's present situation in a single phrase,
I would call it a *crisis of the intermediary*. Whether this intermediary is named king, concept, priest, sacrament, institution,
even prayer or interpretation, there is nonetheless in every case a
desire for immediacy, for direct experience. People have lost confidence in the intermediary. People are tired of anything interpos-
ing itself between the free, spontaneous act of the person and the
end of that act. They have lost confidence not only in the faith of
others (theologians, doctors, parents, saints, sages, scientists or
Church), but in the knowledge of elites, in the 'gifts' of authority
exercised in whatever domain, in anything they do not personally
see or experience. They want the thing, the reality, the experience, the intuition; yesterday's hierarchical order has collapsed.
Supermarkets where the shopper can choose directly, universal
suffrage by which you believe you have a direct participation, the
royal priesthood of all believers, etc., are so many examples of
this new situation, but its roots should be sought in the subsoil of

Man himself, who more or less suddenly and deeply finds himself the maker of his own destiny, his own architect; in a word, free—with the terrifying awareness that freedom is no longer a sort of refuge or protection, but a freedom that leaves us totally exposed, a freedom that is itself free, so to speak, not tied to an established or preestablished order. Perhaps this will also explain why many people today, foreseeing or even tasting this freedom, have preferred the comfortable captivity of Egypt, offered these days by technology, anonymity, etc., to the perils of an authentic freedom.

This crisis of the intermediary should not be confused with the need for a *mediator*. A mediator is not a foreign or external agent. A mediator shares in both of the natures it mediates, and so is involved in what we may still experience as a schism. A mediator is the medium, which is not just betwixt and between but the center that encompasses all sides without dominating any of them. A seed can be the mediator of roots and stems, a kernel of core and husk, a child of father and mother, a Christ of Man and God. An intermediary is a broker, a go-between, an independent agency, a 'disinterested party'. At most the intermediary is an impartial instrument or a catalyst, a leverage, but is not an involved participant.

It is this intermediary, on all levels, that is today in crisis. This is most visible in the rupture of the rapport between means and ends that any sociological analysis of the state of contemporary Western society would bring to light. The younger generation revolts at considering itself a means—a transitional period—to the end of adulthood; education as a means to subsequent ends has long been untenable; and asceticism as a means to an end is also disappearing. People want the now and have no patience to wait for a future in which they no longer hope. Equally, for our generation, either a vertical paradise in an 'other' world, or a horizontal 'utopian' future, seems almost laughable in the face of our double disappointment—by a promised heaven that does not prevent Man's inhumanity to Man, and by a perfect or classless society that never comes.

I have just sketched in sociological terms what happens in

the depths of personal awareness to most people once they awaken to the contemporary problematic. The crisis is profound and acute: Religion, formerly the bond of human solidarity, of individual and collective security, religion, once indissolubly linked with tradition, has become personal in a sense that far outgrows, say, 19th-century individualism in Europe. It is not now a question of withdrawing into the individual (in understandable reaction to a certain prior alienation), but of taking upon oneself the totality of responses and responsibilities normally expected from religion.

Passing now from the anecdotal to the categorical, we may reverse the classical proposition that says that the religious act must be a free act, by emphasizing that *the free act is the religious act par excellence*. So it is not enough to say that an act that is not free cannot be a religious act, because the religious act is basically free; but we must add that the religiousness of the act, so to speak, comes from its freedom. Only a free act can be a religious act, precisely because what constitutes the essence of the religious act is the freedom of that act. The religious act is that which puts Man on the road to his salvation; it is the saving act. And by the same token, we repeat, it is the religious act that also entails the possibility of failure. Now Man cannot consider himself saved while he is still subject to limitations, while he is bound by entanglements that come to him from outside or from inside. If Man is able to perform a free act, an act by which he expresses, shows and makes himself, he is saved, or at least he has performed an act that carries him toward his liberation, his salvation or fulfillment. And this is the essence of the free act.

Let us now try to proceed a little further, open to the novelty of the new myth, without totally breaking continuity with the old: a real study in transmythicization.

c. Religion As Creative Freedom

We may approach this question from a double perspective, that of the past or that of the future, or to take it further, from a perspective static on the one hand and dynamic on the other. These two points of view do not coincide completely but here we may consider them together.

From one side, then, we may envision Man's liberation as the simple recovery of a threatened freedom, the reconquest of a lost paradise, the rediscovery of a vanished reality. In this case everything is reduced to rediscovering Man's true nature, reverting to the point of departure, regaining the primitive, even primordial state, returning to God as the source of all there is. God is immutable for this notion: It is not for God to return to the past, nor is it really for Man either; but as psychological orientation Man must return to the past to 're-source' himself, to reach back to his origin, which from God's viewpoint is atemporal. Man's task is to recover the undistorted image, to polish the immaculate mirror, to reflect the true image, and so on.

Hinduism, Buddhism, Christianity and many other religions can furnish us several examples of spiritualities founded on this presupposition. To recognize reality amounts to a true birth into that reality, to dispel ignorance means salvation, for Man's true being is always there, has always been there, even if unnoticed. All gnosis, and a certain contemplation, is founded on this principle that reality is already there. Only knowledge, in this case, can truly save. Every discovery presupposes that reality is merely covered, every revelation that the Savior is only veiled, every epiphany or salvific theophany that God is but hidden (unless by a twist characteristic of our time you assert the fact of discovering, revealing, etc., to be what *makes* reality). At bottom this is the religion of *homo sapiens*. He is free who can think, the Stoics said.

The other perspective situates salvation ontologically in the future. We say ontologically in order to make it clear that this is a future that no discovery can attain because it has yet to be traversed, arrived at, created. There is little room here for the priest who unveils mystery or keeps the treasure of the faith. There is place here for the prophet who foresees the future and guides into it. Liberation here is not simply discovering a latent situation already extant and real, or recovering a lost (paradisiacal) condition; on the contrary, it is the creation of a new reality, the invention of a situation that did not before exist. This is the religion of *homo faber*. He is free who knows how to act, we might say here.

It is clear, then, that this liberation that so to speak unleashes the unsuspected potentialities of the person is more than a simple purification, and much more than cleaning the dirty lenses that keep us from seeing Man's true nature. From this perspective, Man would not yet possess his true nature, whatever we call it, and it would be precisely through his freedom that he creates it. So a *freedom-to* create his destiny is needed besides a *freedom-from* all the obstacles existing on the way.

Let us now try to describe that dimension of religion which is central in the experience of contemporary Man. In brief: the experience of freedom and the experience of creativity; or, better said: the belief that Man can make himself and fashion the world. Could this not be called a λειτουργία? And significantly enough the Indo-European root for freedom (ἐλευθερία) means also belonging to the people (*leudh-ero-s* [ἐλεu]; cf. Latin *liber-tas* and German *Leute*).

i. From an Anthropological Viewpoint

Our century has had massive experience of the vital need for tolerance. Without tolerance in every domain, human individuals and groups are irremediably doomed to disappear. In the religious sphere the phenomenon is parallel: We feel driven to concede a freedom of religion in order to coexist. In one way or another this leads us to become more sensitive to the fact that not only has freedom an important role in human relations, but that it is essential to every religion, since without freedom these religions cannot exist. Even more, we are led to recognize that freedom is fundamental to religion *per se*, since the exercise of freedom is preeminently a religious act.

This freedom, to which Man has forever aspired, but which in our day has become, under a thousand headings, the explicit ideal of almost every movement, means far more than instinctive spontaneity, far more than political, black, women's, sexual, educational, younger generations' or younger peoples' liberation and the like. It means rather a freedom of the whole being, an ontological spontaneity we might say. Man is free not when he does what he wills or wills what he does, but when his whole being is free, liberated, indeed when it *is* freedom.

But when is being free? What is it to be freedom? To answer and even to formulate this pivotal question we must choose some philosophy or other, if only as a frame of reference. What follows must be understood in this sense. Being is truly free as being when all its being is freedom. The free being is not someone who has one part, one limb free so to speak (the will, for example), but one who has the totality of his being free, who is freedom.

Now being freedom, being free, the freedom of being as being (three expressions we treat here as synonyms), can come about only if being is not determined by anything exterior or foreign to it. In this sense only a totally independent being could be fully free, but the conscious affirmation of independence implies an affirmation of self-identity, and this, in a second moment, would already mean the weakening of this total freedom, for that being would no longer be fully self-determinate but dependent upon a prior moment. The identical image is not free to be different from its source. Strictly speaking, only an eternal being, above and outside time, can be free in the fullest sense. Man's historical character, his temporality, is a burden that renders complete freedom impossible. Man's present state is already conditioned by his own past. The historical being Man is can attain freedom only when his past, as it emerges in his present, is, so to speak, forgiven, destroyed, transformed, burnt, to give way to a new future, not conditioned by any prior circumstance. Man is free insofar as he destroys his *karma*, we might say, insofar as he launches himself into his future without the millstone of his past. Under this light one may perhaps understand the Vedic conception of human existence as the absolving of all *ṛṇas* or 'debts' Man has with reality, the insistence of the Buddha for the *anātmavāda*, i.e., the ever-momentary nature of our existence because there is no *ātman* that we have to drag along in our temporal existence, and the Christian emphasis on forgiveness, i.e., of being liberated from the negative factor of creatureliness in order to lead an authentic or divinized life.

The free act par excellence is the unconditioned action, which is to say that only the creative act is perfectly free. Every act, to the extent it is free, is creative; if it does not create it is not free but merely reshuffles given conditions. An action is free insofar as it is performed without constraint of any kind, without extrinsic determination. Now Man as artist or technician has all the initiative that his intelligence or his mastery over nature gives him, but he is always conditioned by the limits to his knowledge, and by conditions imposed by the materials he uses.

There is a domain where Man has a very special autonomy: himself. Man is more than an artisan who constructs himself as he fashions nature: He is his own artist, and this precisely when he acts freely, when he forges his own destiny. Human creativity is to produce the future, not from mere previous conditions, but with a spontaneity that neither follows a path mapped out in advance nor simply discovers a hidden but already existing road. This production of the future is a true creation inasmuch as it is not conditioned by the past or influenced by anything prior. Non-free beings have no future, they have only a fate. Man, as a free being, is a being with a future: His being shall be; he has a 'future tense', he can attain being.

Human freedom is not only, or basically, the capacity to make decisions about things, events or people. Real freedom takes root in the core of Man, which possesses this power to become himself, in religious terms, to save himself. The prerogative of human freedom is not limited to the choice between given possibilities; it is not the power, either, to do or to make just anything, but to make oneself, to make oneself *oneself*. In theological terms we may say: The salvation to which Man aspires is not an extrinsic gift, something supererogatory, but a personal conquest—to realize oneself, to achieve one's being. To put it in Christian terms: Christ does not save by a heteronomic act, offering an alien salvation foreign to Man, but by becoming flesh and blood so that he may be eaten, assimilated, and by this divine metabolism transform Man also into Son of God. In the Christian conception salvation comes neither by hetero-redemption (through an other) [monotheism] nor through auto-redemption (by oneself) [Pelagianism], Christ being at once truly Man and truly God, an authentic Mediator. Christian salvation comes neither as from an outside rope, nor as from an inside power, but as from an in-spiration (of—and in—the entire Trinity), which links these two extremes together.

Or in Buddhist terms: Buddha does not confer direct illumination to anyone, offering an objective method to overcome *duḥkha*, but he simply points out the way, leaving to the concrete person the effort and diligence to work out his/her salvation. *Nirvāṇa* does not come from 'above' or as a result of an innerworldly causality. *Nirvāṇa* is so free and unconditioned that the very desire for 'the other shore' destroys it. The purity of being that is required cleanses us from all creatureliness.

The free human act is the one by which Man wills what he does and does what he wills. Now this identification can be actualized only in ourselves; this constitutes the vital circle to which we have alluded. It is when Man makes himself that he is free, and at the same time he frees himself (from all that is not him, from all inauthenticity).

To make oneself means to mold one's future, to create what did not exist before; otherwise it would not be a real future. The paradigm of artistic creation does not apply here, and consequently the categories of substance and accident and the theory of the four causes are also inappropriate. It is not a question of rearranging givens from my past into a more or less satisfying future; rather it is to live an authentically human life, and so to grow in my being human. Now human growth, different from any other growth, is much more than developing the power latent in the seed, and goes well beyond any progressive linear continuation of preliminary data. Human growth is free. Not only can it direct or develop itself in one or another direction, choosing among several possibilities, but it can flower in forms not given in advance, unsuspected: a true creation toward a state that does not exist, a growth in being, which is more than simply conservation or evolution—this is what a new creation means. We may note in passing that the notion of pre-given possibilities presupposes a static vision of the universe, where reality is at least potentially already there. From the perspective we are indicating the future is future precisely because it *is* not. The potentiality of being is in this case a sheer mental abstraction. The true future of being does not stem from a final cause that contrives it.

All this does not block the possibility of interpreting liberation via the grace of God, because this grace, precisely because it is divine, cannot be considered merely an external boost of some sort, but a divine—transcendent as well as immanent—force that transforms human nature without doing it violence, and so makes it possible for Man to attain the fullness of his being. Our analysis makes sense given either hypothesis, that of self-liberation and that of salvation through divine grace. In other words, that for this free act one needs the grace of Christ, or the preaching of the Buddha, the teaching of Scripture, the task entrusted by the Party, the inspiration of Truth or Science, the mandate of History or of whatever Prophet, does not contradict what we have just said. As long as one has not personally appropriated the message, gift, grace or task that conveys salvation, as long as Man does not realize by himself the preeminently free act, he will gain none of the benefits religion might furnish him.

The moral, theological and ecumenical consequences of this vision seem to me important; I shall not develop them here, but simply mention one anthropological consequence. Freedom, in the sense we have just described, means thus Man's creativity. The human being is that being which creates its own future. The human future does not exist; the models we entertain of it belong at most to epistemology, never to ontology. Human life on earth, inasmuch as it pursues its goal and does not relapse into tellurism, is a true creation, an expansion that has no other law but the freedom of Man, who as he gradually advances creates his own future, his own situation, his being. Freedom is human creativity. Man is free insofar as he creates, or better, to the extent that he creates himself.

It is not for me here to show how God is not necessarily denied in all we have said, although the conception of God emerges modified, and purified as well it seems to me.

Not only is the kingdom of God the kingdom of freedom, but God himself is absolute Freedom. At heart, the least imperfect way Man can conceive the infinite is through his experience of freedom. By freedom we realize what it means to have no limits, no barriers, no constraints; we experience the non-finite, the infinite. The rupture of every bond, that is freedom. But the limitation of being finite is the bond that preeminently constitutes creatureliness. God is the absence of every limit and Man is called to rejoin him by conquering his freedom, by stepping up from his creatureliness. Man arrived, achieved, perfect, *will have been* a creature (and this fact remains); he no longer *will be* one: he simply *is*.

It seems superfluous to me, but it may help to dispel a possible misunderstanding, to underscore that the freedom we are speaking of here has nothing to do with its caricature or its abuse. Liberty is not libertinism; the breaking of all *bonds* does not mean the smashing of our constitutive structures. Overcoming limits does not mean giving free rein to passions, ambitions and ego-centered whims. Freedom does not mean a denial of our itinerant condition or contingent being, blurring all frontiers and overflooding all boundaries. All this does not set us free, but enslaves us to ever-greater powers—τὰ στοιχεῖα τοῦ κόσμου, Saint Paul called them.

ii. From a Cosmological Viewpoint

To further describe this transmythicization we could perhaps say that the function exercised by the transcendent God of so many religions is now fulfilled in the world's heart by the immanent divinity in secular religiousness. All too often the general concept of divine immanence was a sort of inverse transcendence and not a true immanence in things. The secular religiousness of our day, however, is in the midst of realizing the genuine experience of divine immanence. People devote themselves to the service of the earth, humankind, culture, society, science and even technology with the same *pathos*, the same seriousness, with which they formerly consecrated themselves to the service of God. The secular, which was for some time relegated to the profane, has again become sacred. Man, having eliminated other-worldly attitudes as outmoded religiousness, has projected into the secular most all of the religious values of the sacred. The Absolute, which for a time took refuge outside the universe, has reentered the world—even the Gods are coming back (if they ever deserted the world).

In a certain traditional notion Man took refuge in the transcendent God to attain salvation, and in a certain sense abandoned the world. The spirituality of the immanent divinity makes modern Man fling himself into the arms of the World as into an absolute, as the immanent God he has discovered. Human salvation is seen as a liberation not of Man alone, but of the whole cosmos, as a liberation of the forces of nature, as freedom for the World as well. The World is no longer an enemy to vanquish, exploit or crush, neither is it any longer an 'other' to love; it is part of the whole to be freed from physical necessity by the sacerdotal act of its human liberator. We hasten to add that a purely transcendent God is as nonexistent as an exclusively immanent God, or, if we prefer, that an absolute, an ideal (whatever name we give it) located either outside the World or inside it cannot have the reality of this cosmotheandric mystery that many of the traditional religions still readily call God. But all this goes beyond the limits of these pages.[10a]

The experience of contemporary Man finding himself, and moreover believing himself, not master of the universe, but in a certain sense its builder, its responsible partner, is a fundamental religious experience. Man has suddenly felt himself bound to the earth, joined with it in a communal destiny, playing his part in a cosmic whole of which he is the awareness. Human religiousness cannot henceforward dissociate itself from the earth, this earth of Men, and every effort towards salvation now calls for a genuine integration with all universe.

Doubtless an optimistic vision of reality, this, but not idealized to the point of eliminating sin, error, fall, failure. Man makes himself when he acts freely, but he can run aground in this act, he can choose, he can take fright at his responsibility, fall back on the past, take refuge in security, instead of hurling himself into the risk of living, the adventure of faith, the realization of freedom, into what religions of all times—but often outside time—have wanted to bring him: liberation, joy, the infinite, or in the language of most religions: God.

All this leads us to see religion as the dimension of Man in which his freedom dwells, or as the synergy of the ways leading Man to realize his own creative freedom. The religion of freedom, in this hermeneutic, is precisely that human act by which Man conquers his being, his freedom. This does not make established traditional religions obsolete. On the contrary, the call to freedom is a refreshing and purifying injunction. To be sure, it kills legalisms and servile attitudes and it makes the believing communities sharers in a new liberating myth, but it does not deny the need of religious structure.

d. A Christian Hermeneutic

The mutation in human consciousness alluded to in the beginning of this chapter finds a striking example in the unprecedented move of the Second Vatican Council. The already quoted document has recognized in the most explicit fashion the primacy of the freedom of the person over any other value whatsoever. Now if the human being has the right, and also the duty, to follow his own conscience, to act always in accord with his personal freedom, this means that the Roman Church recognizes that the free human act bears the greatest possible human dignity, to which everything else must be subordinated.

In this, the Council both acknowledges that mutation and establishes continuity with the most Christian tradition. Few themes, in fact, have been more emphasized by Paul, and particularly by John, than the freedom Christ came to bring Man: liberating him from the Law, from sin, from himself, etc.; explicitly calling him to freedom. It is the Son who sets us free, John will repeat, putting these words on the very lips of Jesus.

In a time of ecumenism and encounter of religions as if by historical imperative, this new stage of awareness acquires a considerable importance. It is not Christianity as a religion but Christ as symbol that becomes central.

The message of Christ is a message of freedom; it carries the freedom requisite to perform the free act that saves. It is clear, moreover, that only an interior Christ (which does not deny a historical Christ identified with him) can make possible the realization of an act that is truly free, spontaneous and fully human; otherwise it would just be a new imposition from outside. For this reason, the free act as such, and not the act adapted on the surface to Christian doctrine, is the real, religious and Christian act. To carry out this free and saving act, there is no strict need of any 'religion', let alone Christianity. Only the faith of the human person is required. We have here the foundation of true pluralism. What matters is freedom.

"Why do you not judge for yourselves what is right?" (τὶ δὲ καὶ ἀφ' ἑαυτῶν οὐ κρίνετε το δίκαιον)[11] Christ once said. Christian freedom is human freedom and Christ the Liberator. Christ is the principle of freedom illumining every Man coming into this world; he came to tell us we must judge for ourselves, shoulder our responsibilities, bring our given talents to fruition, and learn to forgive. What is at stake in freedom is not a galactic circulation of dead stars, but a perpetual creation and recreation; by our participation in the creative act of forgiving, we give life to ourselves and to others.

"All that does not proceed from faith is sin," Saint Paul says. In this the Gospel is a good and joyful news, that it announces freedom, not an objective, dehumanized—not to say inhuman— freedom, but a concrete, real, existential freedom, to each Man's personal measure. A hermeneutic of the freedom of religion brings us to religious freedom and a hermeneutic of this, to religion as freedom.[12]

* * *

By way of conclusion we may sum up our thesis in several statements:

The religious act has to be a free act—ultimately because it is a human act and Man is a free being (in the many senses freedom may be interpreted).

This implies that any routinely 'religious' act is not truly religious if not freely performed—although there are several degrees of freedom.

The relation between religion and freedom is so intimate that it permits the inversion of the statement: Every truly free act is a religious act—that relates us with the Ultimate (in whatever sense we may interpret 'it').

This implies that religion is more than an objective set of

doctrines, rituals and customs claiming to deal with the ultimate goals of human life; it is also and mainly a set of freely accepted and recognized symbols in which one freely believes: It is the realm of the myth.

It amounts to closing the vital circle: The human right of 'freedom of religion' appears as a tautology, for without such freedom there is no religion, no religious act.

But it is a qualified tautology, as all ultimate statements are bound to be, for they cannot have any instance beyond by the very fact that they are ultimate; they have to show from within themselves that such is the case. In this sense the self-revelatory character of religion appears once more as belonging to its proper nature.

3. APPENDIX

The following references situate us in the perspective we have tried to follow. Our thesis fits into tradition by continuing it.

1. "Religionem imperare non possumus, quia nemo cogitur, ut credat invitus." Cassiodorus (*Variae*, II, 27 [*apud* Mommsen's *Monumenta Germaniae Historica: Auctores ant.* XII, 62] reporting the words of (his) king Theodoric the Ostrogoth (493-526) to the Jews of Genova: "We cannot command 'religion', because nobody can be forced to believe against his will."

2. "Conscientia obligat non virtute propria sed virtute praecepti divini: non enim conscientia dictat aliquid esse faciendum hac ratione quod sibi videtur sed hac ratione quia a Deo praeceptum est." ("Conscience binds not by its own power, but by power of the divine precept; for conscience tells us what is to be done, not because it sees it so, but because it is prescribed by God.") D. Thom., *In II Sent.*, d. 39, q. 3, a. 3 ad 3.

3. "Quicumque autem ex amore aliquid facit, quasi ex seipso operatur, quia ex propria inclinatione movetur ad operandum." ("Now whoever does a thing through love, does it of himself so to speak, because it is by his own inclination that he is moved to act. . . .") D. Thom., *Sum. Theol.* II-II, q. 19, a. 4, c.

4. "Unde quod liberum arbitrium diversa eligere possit, ser-

vato ordine finis, hoc pertinet ad perfectionem libertatis eius: sed quod eligat aliquid, divertendo ab ordine finis, quod est peccare, hoc pertinet ad defectum libertatis. Unde maior libertas arbitrii est in angelis qui peccare non possunt, quam in nobis qui peccare possumus." ("Hence it pertains to the perfection of its liberty, for free choice to be able to choose between different things, keeping the order of the end in view. But it pertains to the defect of liberty, for it to choose anything by turning away from the order of the end. And this is to sin. Hence there is a greater liberty of choice in the angels, who are not able to sin, than there is in ourselves, who are able to sin.") D. Thom., *Sum. Theol.*, I, q. 62, a. 8 ad 3. (Cf. *etiam* II-II, q. 88, a. 4 ad 1.)

5. "Utrum voluntas discordans a ratione errante sit mala." ("Whether the will is evil when it is at variance with erring reason.") Answer: yes. "Utrum voluntas concordans rationi erranti, sit bona." ("Whether the will is good when it abides by erring reason.") Answer: no, it may be evil. D. Thom., *Sum. Theol.*, I-II, q. 19, aa. 5 and 6.

6. E 'l duca a lui: Caron, non ti crucciare:
vuolsi cocsì colà dove si puote
ciò che si vuole, e più non dimandare. Dante, *Inferno,* III, 94-96. ("Then said my guide: 'Charon, why wilt thou roar/ And chafe in vain? *Thus it is willed where power/And will are one*; enough; ask thou no more." Tr. D.L. Sayers.) Cf. also *Inferno* V, 23-24.

7. "La liberté consiste à faire tout ce qui ne nuit pas à autrui: ainsi l'exercice des droits naturels de chaque homme n'a de bornes que celles qui assurent aux membres de la société la jouissance de ces mêmes droits." *Declaration des droits de l'homme de 1789*, art. 4.

8. ". . . si la liberté de pensée ou de conscience était absolue ou illimitée, il s'ensuivrait que la raison humaine serait indépendante dans sa pensée et dans ses jugements et, conséquemment, dans son existence aussi bien que dans son essence. Or cela répugne absolument, car la raison humaine est la faculté d'un esprit créé qui, préciseément parce qu'il est créé, ne peut pas être sa propre loi." A. Vacant, E. Mangenot and E. Amann, 'Liberté',

Dictionnaire de Théologie Catholique (Paris: Librairie Letouzey et Ané, 1926), p. 691.

9. "La liberté est une catégorie spirituelle et religieuse et non pas naturaliste et métaphysique." ("Liberty is a spiritual and religious category, not a naturalistic or metaphysical one.") N. Berdiaev, *Esprit et Liberté* (Paris: 'Je sers' 1933), p. 137.

10. "Dieu ne peut vouloir que la liberté, parce qu'elle constitue son Idée, son dessein du monde. Il ne peut désirer que l'on accomplisse sa volonté formellement en s'y soumettant aveuglement, parce qu'il ne peut y avoir une volonté separée de l'idée de Dieu. . . ." ("God can only will freedom because it is his idea and his plan for the world. He cannot desire that Man should carry out his will in a formal way with blind submission, because there cannot be a will separated from the idea of God. . . .") *Id.*, p. 167.

11. ". . . la liberté est toujours un acte créateur. . . ." L. Lavelle, *De l'acte* (Paris: Aubier, 1946), p. 184.

12. "Tout le problème de l'amour est de savoir comment une liberté peut devenir un objet pour une autre liberté. . . . Alors, nous découvrons l'identité réelle de la liberté et de l'amour . . . L'amour est donc l'actualité de la liberté." *Id.*, pp. 352-533.

13. "Nous somme seuls, sans excuses. C'est ce que j'exprimerai en disant que l'homme est condamné à être libre." ("We are alone, without excuse. That is what I would express saying that Man is condemned to be free.") J.P. Sartre, *L'existentialisme est un humanisme* (Paris: Nagel, 1946), p. 37.

14. "Objektiv besteht die Freiheit darin, dass den Christusgläubigen nicht eine Summe von Vorschriften bindet, sondern, dass die Liebe zu jenem Du, dem er von Wesen her zugeordnet ist, ihn zu seinem Tun führt. Subjektiv empfindet er die Freiheit darin, dass er tun darf, wonach sein von Gott verwandeltes Herz begehrt, nämlich lieben. . . ." M. Schmaus, *Katholische Dogmatik* (München: Hueber, 1938), p. 791.

15. ". . . dann is die menschliche Freiheit ursprünglicher gegeben in der Übereinstimmung des wirklichen Selbstvollzugs eines Seienden mit seinem konkreten Wesen, so, dass es durch diesen Selbstvollzug wirklich bei sich selbst und so in seiner Wahrheit is." K. Rahner, 'Vorbemerkungen zum Problem der re-

ligiösen Freiheit', *Theologische Fragen heute* (München: Hueber, 1966), p. 9.

16. "Die religiöse Wahrheit als solche ist grundsätzlich nur im Akt der Freiheit als solcher gegeben." *Id.*, p. 11.

17. "Immer dann wenn ein Mensch in Freiheit handelt, tut die Welt ihren letzten Schrift." R. Guardini, 'Freiheit und Unabänderlichkeit', *Unterscheidung des Christlichen* (Mainz: Grünewald, 1963), p. 120.

18. "Das Wesen der Wahrheit enthüllt sich als Freiheit." M. Heidegger, *Vom Wesen der Wahrheit* (Frankfurt: Klostermann, 1954), p. 18.

19. "Everyone has the right to freedom of thought, conscience and religion; this right includes freedom to change his religion or belief, and freedom, either alone or in community with others and in public or private, to manifest his religion or belief in teaching, practice, worship and observance." United Nations *Universal Declaration of Human Rights*, *Art. 18* (Part A of Res. 217 [III], approved by the General Assembly Dec. 10, 1948).

20. "1. A sense of the dignity of the human person has been impressing itself more and more deeply on the consciousness of contemporary man. And the demand is increasingly made that men should act on their own judgment, enjoying and making use of a responsible freedom, not driven by coercion but motivated by a sense of duty. . . .

"This sacred Synod likewise professes its belief that it is upon the human conscience that these obligations fall and exert their binding force. The truth cannot impose itself except by virtue of its own truth. . . .

"2. This Vatican Synod declares that the human person has a right to religious freedom. This freedom means that all men are to be immune from coercion on the part of individuals or of social groups and of any human power, in such wise that in matters religious no one is to be forced to act in a manner contrary to his own beliefs. . . .

"The Synod further declares that the right to religious freedom has its foundation in the very dignity of the human person, as this dignity is known through the revealed Word of God and by reason itself." ("*Jus ad libertatem religiosam esse fundatum in ipsa dignitate personae humanae, qualis et verbo Dei revelato et ipsa ratione cognoscitur.*" Nr. 1045 of the original.) Vatican Council II, *Declaratio Dignitatis Humanae Personae*, *The Documents of Vatican II* (ed. W.M. Abbot, New York: Guild Press, 1966), pp. 675 sq.

21. For those who would like to check the mutation in the Roman Catholic Church they may compare the words of the previous document with the following statements of the last century popes as in the Denzinger Nrs. 2730, 2731, 2858, 2979, 3250, 3251, etc. Significantly enough the new edition of the Denzinger has eliminated the old paragraphs: 1617, 1618, 1642, 1666, 1690, which dealt with the same problem and probably in the eyes of the new editors were not only obsolete, but almost offensive to present-day mentality.

We may simply quote from Leo XIII encyclical of 1888, *Libertas humana*: "Itaque ex dictis consequitur, nequaquam licere petere, defendere, largiri cogitandi, scribendi, docendi, itemque promiscuam religionum libertatem, veluti iura totidem, quae homini natura dederit. Nam si vere natura dedisset, imperium Dei detrectari ius esset, nec ulla temperari lege libertas humana posset" (Denz. Schön. 3252). ("And so from what has been said it follows that it is by no means lawful to demand, to defend and to grant indiscriminate freedom of thought, writing, teaching and likewise of belief, as if so many rights which nature has given to Man. For if nature had truly given these, it would be right to reject God's power, and human liberty could be restrained by no law.")

NOTES

1. Jn. 8:32. "And truth shall set you free."
2. Denz.-Schön. 3178.
3. Denz.-Schön. 2731.
4. "I am a good friend of Plato, but still more a friend with truth; may the world perish, but let justice be fulfilled; obedience is the surest thing."
5. "Serving him means to reign."

6. *Pseud.* Plat., *Def.*, 415 s.

7. Cf. 'Libertad de pensamiento', in my book *Humanismo y Cruz* (Madrid: Rialp, 1963), pp. 77-89, for the various pertinent references that I excuse myself from giving here, and for an understanding and defense of the traditional attitude.

7a. Cf., as a single and impossible example a few decades ago, the Fall 1977 issue (XIV, 4) of the *Journal of Ecumenical Studies* dedicated to *Religious Liberty in the Crossfire of Creeds*.

8. Cf. R. Panikkar, 'Freiheit und Gewissen', *Neues Abendland* (München, 1955), I:25-32 for the theological basis of the second part of this study.

9. 2 Cor. 3:17. "Where the Spirit of the Lord is, there is freedom."

10. "Almost all living things act to free themselves from harmful contact", B.F. Skinner begins his chapter on Freedom in his book *Beyond Freedom and Dignity* (New York: Knopf, 1972) and ends the chapter writing that "Man's struggle for freedom is not due to a will to be free, but to certain behavioral processes characteristic of the human organism, the chief effect of which is the avoidance of or escape from so-called 'aversive' features of the environment".

10a. Cf. R. Panikkar, '*Colligite Fragmenta:* For an Integration of Reality,' in *From Alienation to At-one-ness* (Proceedings of the Theology Institute of Villanova University), edited by F.A. Eigo and S.E. Fittipaldi (Villanova, Pa.: The Villanova University Press, 1977), pp. 19-132.

11. Lk. 12:57

12. Cf. bibliographical appendix on religious freedom and tolerance.

XVII.
Bibliographies

1. ON INFALLIBILITY

Antón, A., 1972, 'Infalibilidad: problema ecuménico,' *Gregorianum*, 53(4):759-70.

Aubert, R., 1960, 'L'ecclésiologie au concile du Vatican,' *Le concile et les conciles*. Paris: Cerf et de Chevetogne, pp. 245-284.

Baum, G., 1971, 'Truth in the Church—Küng, Rahner and Beyond,' *The Ecumenist*, 9:33-44.

Baum, G., Lindbeck, G., McBrien, R., and McSorley, H.J., 1971, *The Infallibility Debate*. New York: Paulist Press.

Betti, U., 1972, *La constituzione dommatica 'Pastor aeternus' del Concilio Vaticano I*. Roma: Antonianum.

Bouyer, L., 1971, 'L'infaillibilité. Expression de la vie de la verité dans l'Église.' Notes sur une conférence du Pere L. Bouyer, *Pax* (abbaye de Landevannec) (January), 19-26.

Butler, B.C., 1954, *The Church and Infallibility*. New York: Sheed & Ward.

Castelli, E. (ed.), 1970, *L'infaillibilité, son aspect philosophique et théologique*. Paris: Aubier.

Caudron, W., 1960, 'Magistère ordinaire et infaillibilité pontificale d'après la constitution "Dei Filius",' *Ephemerides Theologicae Lovanienses*, 36:393-431.

Chavasse, A., 1960, 'L'ecclésiologie au concile du Vatican. L'infaillibilité de l'Église,' *L'Ecclésiologie au XIXè siècle*. Paris: Cerf.

Congar, Y., 1970, 'Infaillibilité et indéfectibilite,' *Revue des sciences philosophiques et théologiques*, 54:601-08.

———, 1974, 'Après *Infallible?* de Hans Küng: bilans et perspectives,' *Revue des Sciences Philosophiques et Théologiques*, 58(2):243-52.

———, 1974, 'Saint Thomas Aquinas and the Infallibility of the Papal Magisterium *(Summa Theol.* II-II, q. 1, a.10),' *Thomist*, 38:81-105.

Dejaifve, G., 1961, *Pape et évêques au premier concile du Vatican*. Paris: Desclée De Brouwer (esp. 93-137).

Dessain, C. S., 1968, 'What Newman Taught in Manning's Church' In *Infallibility in the Church. An Anglican-Catholic Dialogue*. London: Darton, Longman & Todd, pp. 59–80.

Dickinson, J. C., 1968, 'Papal Authority.' In *Infallibility in the Church. An Anglican-Catholic Dialogue*. London: Darton, Longman & Todd, pp. 47–58.

Dirks, W., 1970, 'Das Dogma von den fehlbaren Päpsten. Die Wandlung der. katholischen Kirche seit 1870,' *Deutsches Allgemeines Sonntagsblatt* (January 11).

Doyle, J. P., 1971, 'The Infallibility of the Roman Pontiff: Problems in Understanding.' In G. Devine (ed.), *New Dimensions in Religious Experience*. New York: Alba House, 187–205.

FitzPatrick, P., 1974, 'Infallibility—a Secular Assessment,' *Irish Theological Quarterly, 41:*3–21.

Ford, J. T., 1971, 'Infallibility—from Vatican I to the Present,' *Journal of Ecumenical Studies, 8:*768–91.

Fries, H., 1969, 'Das Lehramt als Dienst am Glauben,' *Catholica, 23:*154–72.

Fuhrmann, H., 1969, 'Päpstlicher Primat und pseudo-isodorische Dekretalen,' *Quellen und Forschungen aus italienischen Archiven und Bibliotheken, 49:*313–39.

Ganoczy, A., 1968, *Ecclesia ministrans. Dienende Kirche und kirchlicher Dienst*. Freiburg-Basel-Wien: Herder.

Houtepen, A., 1973, *Onfeilbaarheid en hermeneutiek. De betekenis van het infallibilitas—concept op Vaticanum I*. Brugge: Emmaüs.

Hughes, G. J., 1973, 'Infallibility in Morals,' *Theological Studies, 34:*415–28.

Jaspert, B., 1973, 'Die Ursprünge der päpstlichen Unfehlbarkeitslehre,' *Zeitschrift für Religions-und Geistesgeschichte, 25*(2):126–34.

Jedin, H., 1964, *Bischöfliches Konzil oder Kirchenparlament. Ein Beitrag zur Ekklesiologie der Konzilien von Konstanz und Basel*. Stuttgart: Heibing und Lichtenhaln.

Jüngel, E., 1971, 'Irren ist menschlich. Zur Kontroverse von Hane Küngs Buch, "Unfehlbar?—Eine Anfrage",' *Evangelische Kommentare, 4:*75–80.

Karrer, O., 1961, 'Das ökumenische Konzil in der römisch-katholischen Kirche der Gegenwart.' In H. J. Margull (ed.), *Die ökumenischen Konzile der Christenheit*. Stuttgart: Evang. Verlag Werk, pp. 237–84, esp. 241–64.

Kasper, W., 1962, 'Primat und Episkopat nach dem Vatikanum I,' *Tübingen Theologische Quartalschrift, 142:*68–77.

Kéramé, O., 1971, 'The Basis for Reunion of Christians: The Papacy Reconsidered,' *Journal of Ecumenical Studies, 8:*792–814.

Kottukapally, J., 1973, 'Infallible? Fallible?,' *Indian Journal of Theology, 22:*92–112.

464   BIBLIOGRAPHIES

Küng, H., 1970, *Unfehlbar?—Eine Anfrage*. Zürich-Einsiedeln-Köln: Benziger (English translation: *Infallible? An Enquiry*. London: Collins, 1971).

———, 1971, 'L'Église selon l'Evangile, Response à Yves Congar,' *Revue des Sciences Philosophiques et Théologiques, 55:*193–230.

———, 1971, 'Im Interesse der Sache,' *Stimmen der Zeit, 187:*43–64.

———, 1973, 'Papal Fallibility, O felix error!,' *Journal of Ecumenical Studies, 10:*361–62.

———, 1973, 'Versöhnliches Schlusswort unter eine Debatte,' *Publik-Forum 2*(11):12–15.

———, 1973, 'Mysterium Ecclesiae' (Interview by *Herder Korrespondenz), Tablet, 227:*835–39.

———, (ed.), 1973, *Fehlbar? Eine Bilanz.* Einsiedeln-Zürich: Benziger.

Küng, H., & Rahner, K., 1970–71, Correspondence, *Stimmen der Zeit, 186–87, passim.*

———, 1973, 'Authority in the Church: an exchange of letters,' *Tablet, 227:*597–99. Also appeared as: 'Working Agreement to Disagree; exchange of letters,' *America, 128:*9–12.

Langren, J., 1871–76, *Das Vatikanische Dogma von dem Universal-Episcopat und der Unfehlbarkeit des Papstes in seinem Verhältnis zum Neuen Testament und der exegetischen Ueberlieferung.* Bonn.

Lirà, J. B., 1973, *A infalibilidade pontifícia (à luz de Bíblia, da história, da razão, do bom-senso e em face da filosofia maçônico-cristá).* Rio de Janeiro: Ed. Espiritualista.

Löhrer, M., 1971, 'Towards a discussion of infallibility,' *Worship, 45:*273–89.

Miller, J. 1971, 'Understanding Papal Infallibility: 1870 to 1970.' In G. Devine (ed.), *New Dimensions in Religious Experience.* New York: Alba House, pp. 207–218.

Mordek, H., 1974, '"Dictatus papae" e "proprie auctoritates apostolice sedis". Intorno all'idea del primato pontificio di Gregorio VII,' *Revista di Storia della Chiesa in Italia, 28*(1):1–22.

Murray, R., 1968, 'Who or What is Infallible?' In *Infallibility in the Church. An Anglican-Catholic Dialogue.* London: Darton, Longman & Todd, pp. 24–46.

Rahner, K., 1970, 'Kritik an Hans Küng. Zur Frage der Unfehlbarkeit theologischer Sätze,' *Stimmen der Zeit, 186:*361–77.

———, 1971, 'Replik: Bemerkungen zu Hans Küng. Im Interesse der Sache,' *Stimmen der Zeit, 187:*145–60.

———, 1973, 'Mysterium Ecclesiae,' *Cross Currents, 23:*183–198.

———, 1973, 'Reply [to H. Küng],' *Tablet, 227:*956–958; 981–983; 1005–1027.

———, (ed.), 1972, *Zum Problem Unfehlbarkeit, Antworten auf die Anfrage von Hans Küng.* Freiburg-Basel-Wien: Herder.

Reyners, B., *et al.* (eds.), 1964, *L'infallibilité de l'Église, Journées oecuméniques de Chevetogne 25–29 Septembre 1961.* Chevetogne: Ed. de Chevetogne.

Schenk, M., 1965, *Die Unfehlbarkeit des Papstes in der Heiligsprechung.* Freiburg: Paulus Verlag.

Sewrey, C. L., 1973, 'Infallibility, the American Way and Catholic Apologetics,' *Journal of Church and State, 15*:293–302.

Steck, K. G., 1970, 'Die Autorität der Offenbarung. Das Erste Vatikanum im urteil evangelischer Theologie,' *Publik* (January 16).

Sterns, J., 1973, 'L'infaillibilité de l'église dans la pensée de J. H. Newman,' *Recherches de Science Religieuse, 61*:161–85.

Stevens, C., 1973, 'Infallibility and History,' *Journal of Ecumenical Studies, 10*:384–87.

Swidler, L., 1971, 'The Ecumenical Problem Today: Papal Infallibility,' *Journal of Ecumenical Studies, 8*(4):751–67.

———— , (ed.), 1974, 'Unity Priorities: Primacy, Episcopacy Structures,' Special Issue of *Journal of Ecumenical Studies, 11*(2).

Thils, G., 1961, 'Parlera-t-on des évêques au concile?,' *Nouvelle Revue Théologique, 93*:785–804.

———— , 1969, *L'infaillibilité pontificale. Source—conditions—limites.* Gembloux: J. Duclot.

Tierney, B., 1972, *Origins of Papal Infallibility, 1150–1350. A Study on the Concepts of Infallibility, Sovereignty and Tradition in the Middle Ages.* Leiden: Brill.

Torrel, J. P., 1961, 'L'infaillibilité pontificale est-elle un privilège "personnel"?,' *Revue des Sciences Philosophiques et Théologiques, 35*:229–45.

Vischer, L., 1972, 'The Infallibility Debate. Some Recent Publications,' *The Ecumenical Review, 24*(2):225–34.

Vooght, P. de, 1970, 'Les controverses sur les pouvoirs du concile et l'autorité du pape au concile de Constance,' *Revue Théologique de Louvain, 1*:45–75.

Winckelmans, C., 1973, 'Catholicity and the Petrine Office,' *Indian Journal of Theology, 22*:113–26.

Collections: 1973, *Église infaillible ou intemporelle?* (Le centre des intellectuels français—Mai, 1972, Colloquium). Paris: Desclée (Recherches et Débats, 79).

2. ON RELIGIOUS FREEDOM AND TOLERANCE

Adeney, W. F., 1934, 'Toleration.' In *ERE, 12*:360–65. New York: Scribner's Sons.

Adorno, T., et al., 1950, *The Authoritarian Personality*. New York: Harper.

Alcorta, J. I., 1968, 'El espíritu, raiz de la libertad,' *Verdad y Vida* (Madrid), *26:*469–74.

Amariú, C., 1960, *L'Église au service de la liberté*. Paris: Ed. France Empire (English translation: *The Church in the Service of Liberty*. P. A. Barrett (tr.), St. Louis: Herder, 1963).

Amato, D., 1969, *Il problema della libertà*. Palermo: Tip. Valguarnera.

Amphoux, H., 1969, *Michel de l'Hôpital et la liberté de conscience au XVIè. siècle*. Genève: Slatkine (rep. of Paris, 1900 edition).

Arasa, F., 1966, 'Consideraciones sociólogicas, científicas y religiosas en torno a la libertad,' *Folia Humanística, 4:*901–16.

Arnold, T. W., 1934, '(Muhammedan) Toleration,' in *ERE, 12:*365–69. New York: Scribner's Sons.

Aron, R., 1970, *An Essay on Freedom*. H. Weaver (tr.), Cleveland: World Publishing Company.

Aubert, R., Bouyer, L., Cerfaux, L., et al., 1955, *Tolérance et communauté humaine*. Paris-Tournai: Casterman (English translation: *Tolerance and the Catholic*. New York: Sheed & Ward, 1955).

————, 1965, *Essais sur la liberté religieuse. Recherches et Debats*. Paris: Fayard.

Audi, R., 1974, 'Moral Responsibility, Freedom and Compulsion,' *American Philosophical Quarterly, 11*(1):1–14.

Augustin, P., 1966, *Religious Freedom in Church and State, a Study in Doctrinal Development*. Baltimore: Helicon.

Bainton, R. H., 1951, *The Travail of Religious Liberty*. Philadelphia: Westminster (new edition: New York: Harper Torchbooks, 1958).

Barion, J., 1971, *Was ist Ideologie? Studie zu Begriff und Problematik*. (2nd rev. ed.) Bonn: Bouvier.

Barrett, P., 1963, *Religious Liberty and the American Presidency*. New York: Herder and Herder.

Bartsch, H.-W., 1968, 'L'idée de tolérance chez Paul.' In E. Castelli (ed., *L'herméneutique de la liberté religieuse*. Paris: Aubier, pp. 197–205.

————, 1974, 'Die Ideologiekritik des Evangeliums dargestellt an der Leidensgeschichte,' *Evangelische Theologie, 2:*176–95.

Bates, M. S., 1945, *Religious Liberty, An Inquiry*. New York and London: Intern. miss. council.

Bea, A., 1966, 'L'Église et la liberté religieuse,' *La Documentation Catholique:* 1183–1194. Also appeared as: 'The Church and Religious Freedom,' *Month 35* (1966): 267–273.

Beauchesne, G., et al., 1965, La Libertad. *Perspectivas científica y teológica*. Buenos Aires: Troquel (Biblioteca El tema del hombre).

Benz, E., 1934, 'Der Toleranz-Gedanke in der Religionswissenschaft,' *Deutsche Vierteljahresschrift für Literaturwissenschaft und Geistegeschichte, 12:*540–71.

Berofsky, B., 1970, 'Conceptions of Freedom,' *The Journal of Philosophy*, 67:208–20.

Betz, H. D., 1974, 'Geist, Freiheit und Gesetz. Die Botschaft des Paulus an die Gemeinden in Galatien,' *Zeitschrift für Theologie und Kirche*, 71(1):78–93.

Boillat, F., 1964, *La liberté religieuse*. St.-Maurice, Suisse: Ed. St.-Augustin.

Bonet-Maury, G., 1885, 'Akbar, un initiateur de l'étude comparée des religions et un précurseur de la tolérance dans l'Inde,' *Revue de l'Histoire des Religions*, 11:133 sq.

_____, 1900, *Histoire de la liberté de conscience depuis l'Edit de Nantes*. Paris: F. Alcan.

_____, 1969, *Les précurseurs de la réforme et de la liberté de conscience dans les pays latins de XIIè. au XVè. siècle*. Genève: Slatkine (rep. of Paris, 1904 edition).

Bornkamm, H., 1962, 'Toleranz in der Geschichte des Christentums,' *RGG*, 6:933–46.

Bortolaso, G. (S.I.), 1966, 'Ideologia e filosofia,' *La Civiltà Cattolica*, 117(4):231–40.

_____, 1968, 'Ideologia e filosofia e confronto,' *La Civiltà Cattolica*, 119(1):548–56.

Botero Salazar, J., 1967, *La libertad religiosa (cartas pastorales)*. Madellín: Universidad Pontificia Bolivariana.

Boche-Leclerq, A., 1911, *L'intolérance religieuse et la politique*. Paris: Flammarion.

Broglie, G. de, 1964, *Le droit naturel à la liberté religieuse*. Paris: Beauchesne.

_____, 1965, *Problèmes chrétiens sur la liberté religieuse*. Paris: Beauchesne.

Brown, R. McA., 1974, 'Reflections on "Liberation Theology".' *Religion in Life*, 43(3):269–82.

Bucolo, P., 1968, *Libertà e società*. Cantania: Tip. La Nuovagrafica.

Bugan, A., 1965, *La comunità internazionale e la libertà religiosa*. Roma: Desclée.

Burt, D., 1960, *The State and Religious Toleration*. Washington: Catholic University of America Press.

Cadier, J., Chevrot, G., and Couturier, P., 1950, *Unité chrétienne et tolérance religieuse*. Paris: Éditions du Temps présent.

Campos, P. N., 1966, *Liberdade Religiosa*. São Paulo: Ediçôes Paulinas.

Carrillo de Albornoz, A.-F., 1961, *Le catholocisme et la liberté religieuse*. Paris: Ed. Universitaires.

_____, 1963, *The Basis of Religious Liberty*. New York: Association Press.

_____, 1964, 'Religious Liberty and the Second Vatican Council,' *The Ecumenical Review* XVI: 395–405.

—— , 1967, *La libertad religiosa y el Concilio Vaticano*. Madrid: Ed. Cuadernos Para El Diálogo. English trans.: *Religious Liberty*. J. Drury (tr.), New York: Sheed and Ward, 1967.

Castelli, E. (ed.), 1968, *L'herméneutique de la liberté religieuse*. Paris: Aubier.

Chapey, F., 1966, 'Le chrétien est-il libre?,' *Études*, *325*:519–28.

Chauchard, P., 1957, 'Les conditions cérébrales de la liberté,' *Cahiers d'études biologiques* (Paris), *4*:36–40.

Chomsky, N., 1970, 'Language and Freedom,' *Abraxas*, *1*:9–24.

Cleve, F. M., 1969, 'Freedom: A New Approach,' *New Scholasticism*, *43*:491–508.

Colombo, C., 1965, *La liberté religieuse*. La Documentation Catholique: 1195–1208.

Condorelli, M., 1960, *I fundamenti giuridici della toleranza religiosa nell'elaborazione canonista dei secoli XII-XIV*. Milano: Eiuffre.

Congar, Y., 1950, *Vraie et fausse réforme dans l'Église*. Paris: Cerf.

Coste, R., 1969, *Théologie de la liberté religieuse (Liberté de conscience—liberté de la religion)*. Gembloux: Duculot.

Creighton, M., 1895, *Persecution and Tolerance*. London and New York: Longman, Green & Co.

Crippa A., 1970, 'O têrmo ideologia,' *Convivium* (Sao Paulo), *9*:42–6.

Dalmasso, G., 1971, 'Discussioni sulla secularizzazione come ideologia,' *Revista di Filosofia Neo-Scolastica*, *63*:354–67.

Daniélou, J., 1956, *Les saints 'paiens' de l'ancien Testament*. Paris: Editions du Seuil (English: F. Faber [tr.], *Holy Pagans of the Old Testament*. New York: Longmans, Green, 1957).

D'Arcy, E., 1961, *Conscience and Its Drive to Freedom*. New York: Sheed & Ward.

Davidovitch, M., 1968–69, 'Das Reich der Freiheit,' *Hegel-Jahrbuch*, 229–32.

Dawydow, J., 1969, *Freiheit und Entfremdung*. W. Hoepp (tr.), Frankfurt a. Main: Verl. de Marxischen Blätter (Marxistische Taschenbücher, Marxismus aktuell).

Day, J. P., 1970, 'On Liberty and the Real Will,' *Philosophy* (London), *45*:177–92.

Delhaye, Ph., 1965, 'Le problème de la liberté religieuse,' *L'ami du clergé* (22 juillet et 23 septembre).

Delmonte, C., de Santa Ana, J., Semino, M. A., and Carrillo de Albornoz, A.-F., 1967, *Problemas de la Libertad Religiosa*. Montevideo: Ediciones Tauro.

Denghien, S., 1928, 'Tolerance.' In A. d'Alès (ed.), *Dictionnaire apologétique de la foi catholique*. Paris: Beauchesne, *4*:1714–26.

Derisi, O. N., 1970, 'Materia y necesidad, espíritu y libertad,' *Sapietia*, *25*:5–10.

De Vries, J., 1958, 'Fremde. Religionsgeschichtlich,' *RGG*, 2:1125–6.

De Waelhens, A., 1968, 'Sur les fondements possibles de la tolérance.' In E. Castelli (ed.), *L'herméneutique de la liberté religieuse*. Paris: Aubier, pp. 387–98.

Dietzelbinger, H., 1956, 'Toleranz und Intoleranz zwischen den Konfessionen,' *Evangelischer Presseverband für Bayern*.

Díez-Alegría, J., 1965, *La libertad religiosa*. Barcelona: Instituto Católico de Estudios Sociales, Editorial Balmes.

Dondeyne, A., 1957, 'L'idée de tolérance,' *Les études philosophiques* (Actes du IXè Congrès des Sociétés de philosophes de langue française), *12*.

Duméry, H., 1968, 'Freedom and Religious Intolerance.' In *Faith and Reflection*. New York: Herder and Herder, 28–69.

Dworkin, G., 1970, 'Acting Freely,' *Noûs, 4:*367–83.

Ebbinhaus, J., 1950, 'Ueber die Idee der Toleranz,' *Archiv für Philosophie, 4*(2):1–34.

Eccles, J., 1972, 'Science and Freedom,' *Humanist, 32:*15–18.

Edelby, N., et al., 1966, *Religious Freedom*. New York: Paulist Press *(Concilium*, Vol. 18).

Egenter, R., 1966, 'La libertad cristiana en concreto y desde sus fundamentos,' *Folia Humanística, 4:*939–51.

Ehman, R., 1968, 'Freedom,' *The Journal of Value Inquiry, 2:*108–24.

Emerson, A.E., and Burhoe, R.W., 1974, 'Evolutionary Aspects of Freedom, Death and Dignity,' *Zygon, 9*(2):156–82.

Fabro, C., 1971, 'Orizzontalità e verticalità della libertà,' *Angelicum, 48:*302–54.

Farré, L., 1972, *Hombre y libertad. Problemática de ser y comprenderse libre*. Buenos Aires: Ed. Columba (Col. Esquemas, 116).

Faurey, J., 1929, *L'édit de Nantes et la question de la tolérance*. Paris: Éditions de Bocard.

Flam, L., 1967, *Idéologie en filosofie*. Brussel: Universitaire Publicaties.

Fraisse, J.-C., 1974, 'Les categories de la liberté selon Kant,' *Revue Philosophique de la France et de l'Étranger, 164*(2):161–66.

Freund, M., 1927, *Die Idee der Toleranz im Englander grossen Revolution*. Halle: M. Neimeyer.

Fridell, W. M., 1972, 'Notes on Japanese Tolerance,' *Monumenta Nipponica, 27*(3):253–71.

García-Gómez, J., 1970–71, 'A meditation on liberty. On the possibility of total involvement and the existence of philosophic reason,' *Abraxas, 1:*47–60.

García Martínez, F., 1964, 'Libertad religiosa o libertad de las conciencias,' *Razón y Fé, 169:*453–474.

Geiger, L. B., 1960, 'On Freedom,' *Philosophy Today, 4:*184–95.

Giannini, H., 1965, 'Sobre la tolerancia,' *Reflexiones acerca de la con-*

vivencia humana. Santiago de Chile: Facultad de Filosofía y Educación.

Girardi, G., 1970, 'Il problema della libertà nel dialogo tra credenti e non credenti,' *L'ateismo contemporaneo* (Vol. IV: Il cristianesimo di fronte all'ateismo). Torino: Società editrice internazionale, 541–577.

Golubović, Z., 1973, 'Self-fulfilment, Equality and Freedom,' *Praxis, 9*(2–3):153–60.

Goumaz, L., 1950, 'Calvinisme et liberté. Contribution à l'étude de la liberté de conscience,' *Conscience et liberté, 3.*

Goyau, G., 1925, 'L'Église catholique et les droits des gens,' *RCADI, I.*

Grabska, S., 1974, 'La liberté chrétienne d'après les écrits de Karl Rahner,' *Ephemerides theologicae Lovanienses, 50*(1):75–91.

Granero, J.-M., 1964, 'La libertad religiosa,' *Razón y Fé, 196:*603–616.

Guterman, S. L., 1951, *Religious Toleration and Persecution in Ancient Rome.* London: Eiglon Press.

Gutiérrez, G., 1971, *Teología de la liberación. Perspectivas.* Lima: CEP. English translation: *A Theology of Liberation, History, Politics and Salvation.* Sr. C. Inda and J. Eagleson (trs. & eds.), Maryknoll, New York: Orbis Books, 1973.

Hacker, P., 1957, 'Religiöse Toleranz und Intoleranz in Hinduismus,' *Saeculum, 8*(2–3):167–79.

Hadley, H., 1963, *A Free Order: National Goal and World Goal.* New York: Dodd, Mead.

Halkin, L. E., 1939, *De l'Inquisition à la tolérance.* Bruxelles: La Cité Chrétienne.

——— , 1950, *Intolérance et inquisition.* Paris.

Hartmann, A., 1955, *Toleranz und christlischer Glaube.* Frankfurt: Knecht.

——— , 1958, *Vraie et fausse tolérance.* Paris: Cerf.

Hauer, J. W., 1961, *Toleranz und Intoleranz in den nichtchristlichen Religionen.* Stuttgart: Kohlhammer.

Heer, F., 1959, *Die dritte Kraft. Der europäische Humanismus zwischen der Fronten des Konfessionellen Zeitalters.* Frankfurt: Fischer.

Heitiger, M., 1968, 'Freiheit: Verantwortung und Entscheidung. Einige Ueberlegungen zum Problem einer jenen Begriffen verpflichteten wissenschaftlichen, Pädagogik,' *Akten XIV. Int. Kong. Phil., I.* Wien: Herder, 218–225.

Herzstein, R., 1967, 'The Phenomenology of Freedom in the German Philosophical Tradition: Kantian Origins,' *The Journal of Value Inquiry, 1:*47–63.

Hevás, J., 1966, *La libertad religiosa.* Madrid: Edicion Palabra.

Hook, S., 1962, *The Paradoxes of Freedom.* Berkeley: University of California Press.

——— , (ed.), 1958, *Determinism and Freedom in the Age of Modern Science.* New York: New York University Press.

Horst, F., 1958, 'Fremde im Alten Testament,' *RGG, 2:*1126.

Huart, G., 1956, 'Hindouisme et tolérance religieuse,' *Nouvelle Revue théologique, 9–10:*834–52.

Ingle, D. J., 1971, 'The Nature of Personal Freedom,' *Zygon,* 6(1):39–47.

Jack, H. A., 1972, 'Elimination of All Forms of Religious Intolerance' (UN Committee on Human Rights' Subcommittee), *Christian Century, 89:*856–7.

James, M., 1964, *The Tolerant Personality.* Detroit: Wayne State University Press.

Janssens, L., 1964, *Liberté de conscience et liberté religieuse.* Paris: Desclée. English trans.: *Freedom of Conscience and Religious Freedom.* New York: Alba House, 1966.

Jiménez-Blanco, J. (tr.), 1968, *La libertad y el hombre del siglo XX* (Groupe Lyonnais d'Études Medicales). Madrid: Ed. Razón y Fé.

Johns, V.-J., 1940, *Forty Centuries of Law and Liberty.* Portland, Ore.: Pacific Press Pub. Assoc.

Jordan, W. K., 1965, *The Development of Religious Toleration in England.* Gloucester, Massachusetts: Peter Smith.

Journet, C. 1951, 'Droits de la vraie religion et tolérance civile des cultes,' *Nova et vetera, 1.*

Jurji, E. J. (ed.), 1969, *Religious pluralism and world community. Interfaith and intercultural communication* (Studies in the history of religion. Supplement to *Numen, 15*). Leiden: Brill.

Kada, L., 1959, *Libertá di religione, di stampa e d'associazione.* Roma.

Kamen, H., 1967, *The Right of Toleration.* London: Weidenfeld & Nicolson; New York: McGraw Hill.

Kangrga, M., 1970, 'Ethik und Freiheit,' *Praxis, VII,* 471–557.

――――, 1970, 'Ideologie als Form des menschlichen Daseins,' *Philosophische Perspektiven, 2:*158–67.

Kelle, W. Sch., 1969, 'Erkenntnis- und Ideologiefunktionen der Soziologie,' *Sowjetwissenschaft. Gesellschaftswissenschaftliche Beiträge, 8:*768–75.

Kelsen, H., 1945, *General Theory of Law and State.* A. Wedberg (tr.), New York: Russell and Russell.

Kruse, C., et al., 1957, *Tolerance: Its Foundations and Limits in Theory and Practice.* Stockton, California.

Kühn, H., 1966, 'La libertad como donación y como logro,' *Folia Humanística, 4:*887–99.

Küng, H., 1966, *Freedom Today.* C. Hastings (tr.), New York: Sheed and Ward.

Kuvačić, I., 1973, 'Middle Class Ideology,' *Praxis, 9*(4):335–56.

――――, 1973, 'Post-industrial Society and Freedom,' *Praxis, 9*(2–3):187–90.

La Calle, F. de, 1974, 'Teología de la Liberación y segundo Evangelio,' *Estudios, 30*(105):169–220.

472   BIBLIOGRAPHIES

La Chapelle, Ph. de, 1967, *La déclaration universelle des droits de l'homme et catholicisme*. Paris: Librairie Générale de Droit et Jurisprudence.

Lanarès, P., 1964, *La liberté religieuse dans les conventions internationales et dans le droit public general*. Paris: Ed. Horvath.

Lecler, J., 1955, *Histoire de la tolérance au siècle de la Reforme*. Paris: Aubier (Coll. Théologie).

———, 1966, 'La Déclaration conciliare sur la liberté religieuse,' *Études, 324:516–530*.

———, 1966, 'Liberté de conscience. Origine et sens divers de l'espression,' *Récherches de science religieuse, LIV: 370–406*.

Lecler, L., and Volkhoff, M.-F., 1970, *Les premiers défenseurs de la liberté religieuse*. Paris: Cerf.

Leclerq, J., 1963, *La liberté d'opinion et les catholiques*. Paris: Cerf (Coll. Rencontres).

Le Guillou, M.-J., 1964, 'Tolérance et liberté religieuse,' *Bulletin du Cercle Saint Jean Baptiste*, No. 51:15–30.

Lehrer, K. (ed.), 1966, *Freedom and Determinism*. New York: Random House.

Lerch, D., 1962, 'Toleranz. Sozialethisch,' *RGG, 6:946–47*.

Lichtheim, G., 1972, *Concepto d'ideologia*. F. Mira i Casterá (tr.), Barcelona: Ed. Lavinia (Coll. Quaderno 3 i 4, núm. 4).

Lind, Th., 1969, 'Réflexions sur la liberté de l'homme,' *Revue Philosophique de la France et de l'Étranger, 94:319-26*.

Lobo, Alonso, J. A., 1968, 'Interpretación de la libertad religiosa,' *Estudios Filosóficos* (Santander), *17:551–68*.

Locke, J., 1968, *Epistola de tolerantia*. (A Letter on Toleration.) Ed., R. Klibansky, trans., T. W. Gough, Oxford: Clarendon Press.

López Jordan, R. (ed.), 1964, *Problematica della libertà religiosa*. Milano: Ed. Ancora.

Lortz, J., 1958, 'Sind wir Christen tolerant?,' *Hochland, 50(5):430–45*.

Luca, P. de, 1969, *Il Diritto di Libertá Religiosa nel pensiero constituzionalistico ed ecclesiastico contemporaneo*. Padova: CEDAM.

Lutz, Heinrich (ed.), 1977, *Zur Geschichte der Toleranz und Religionsfreiheit (Wege der Forschung*, 246). Darmstadt: Wissenschaftliche Buchgesellschaft.

Lyon, T., 1937, *The Theory of Religious Liberty in England (1603–1639)*. Cambridge: Cambridge University Press.

MacKay, D., 1967, *Freedom of Action in a Mechanistic Universe*. Cambridge: Cambridge University Press.

Madariaga, S. de, 1970, *On Freedom*. Bern: Swiss Eastern Institute Press.

Malet, A., 1970, 'Structuralisme et liberté,' *Revue d'Histoire et de Philosophie Religieuses* (Strasbourg), *50:209:20*.

Mandelbaum, S. 1964, *Social Setting of Intolerance.* Chicago: Scott, Foresman.

Marcel, G., 1940, 'Phénoménologie et dialectique de la tolérance,' *Du refus à l'invocation.* Paris: Gallimard. Republished in *Essai de philosophie concrète.* Paris: Gallimard, 1967, pp. 309–326.

Marcuse, H., 1969, *An Essay on Liberation.* Boston: Beacon Press.

———, 1970, 'Freedom and Freud's Theory of Instincts.' *In Five Lectures: Psychoanalysis, Politics and Utopia.* J. J. Shapiro and S. M. Weber (trs.), Boston: Beacon Press, pp. 1–27.

———, 1972, 'Freedom and the Historical Imperative.' In *Studies in Critical Philosophy.* J. de Bres (tr.), London: NLB, pp. 209–223.

Maritain, J., 1957, 'Tolérance et verité,' *Nova et Vetera, 32:*161–69.

———, 1957, *Truth and Human Fellowship.* Princeton University Press.

Marković, M., 1973, 'Gleichheit und Freiheit,' *Praxis, 9*(2–3):135–52.

Martelet, G., 1964, 'La liberté religieuse,' *Revue de l'action Populaire, 180:*780–806.

Massuh, V., 1969, *La libertad y la violencia.* 2nd ed. Buenos Aires: Ed. Sudamérica (Col. Perspectivas).

Matagne, J.-M., 1970, 'Contribução a determinação conceitual do têrmo ideologia,' *Convivium, 9:*46–54.

Matagrin, A., 1905, *Histoire de la tolérance religieuse.* Paris: Fischbacher.

McNicholl, A., 1969, 'La libertá cristiana,' *Incontri culturali, 2:*112–18.

Meinhold, P., 1973, 'Freiheit als Norm christlichen Glaubens und Handelns,' *Stimmen der Zeit, 191:*516–28.

Mensching, G., 1953, 'Toleranz, eine Form der Auseinandersetzung der Religionen,' *Theologische Literaturzeitung, 78.*

———, 1955, *Toleranz und Wahrheit in der Religion.* Heidelberg: Quelle und Meyer. (English translation: *Tolerance and Truth in Religion.* H. J. Klimkeit (tr.), 1971, The University of Alabama Press.)

———, 1962, 'Toleranz. Religionsgeschichtlich,' *RGG, 6:*931–33.

Mesnard, P., 1956, 'Une nouvelle perspective sur les débuts de l'esprit de tolérance,' *Revue Thomiste, 56*(2):300–21.

Metz, J.-B., 1971, *Freiheit in Gesellschaft.* Freiburg: Herder.

Metzger, A., 1955, *Freiheit und Tod.* Freiburg i. Br.: Rombach (rep. 1972).

Meunier, J.-G., 1974, 'Langage et idéologie,' *Dialogue, 13*(2):283–98.

Miano, V., 1971, 'Discussione della filosofia della libertà di G. Girardi,' *Aquinas, 14:*629–44.

Michel, A., 1946, 'Tolérance,' *Dictionnaire de théologie catholique, 15*(1):1208–23.

Miegge, G., 1957, *Religious Liberty.* London: United Society for Christian Literature.

Miller, D. L., 1969, *Modern Science and Human Freedom*. New York: Greenwood Press.

Moltmann, J., 1974, 'The Gospel of Liberation,' W. Pipkin (tr.), *Word, 136*.

Montero Moliner, F., 1971, 'La interpretación dialéctica de la libertad,' *Teorema, 1(1):75–89*.

Monzel, N., 1956, 'Das Problem der Toleranz,' *Münchener theologische Zeitschrift, 7*(2):8–88.

Moore, K. (ed.), 1964, *The Spirit of Tolerance*. London: Gollancz.

Morra, G., 1969, 'La libertá del cristiano,' *Incontri culturali, 2:*101–11.

Mossé-Bastide, R.-M., 1969, *La Liberté*. 2é edition. Paris: P.U.F. (Initation philosophique, 73).

Motta, G., 1968, 'Christianismo e ideología,' *Ethica, 7:*215–30.

Murray, J. C., 1945, 'Freedom of Religion I. The Ethical Problem,' *Theological Studies, 6:*229–86.

———, 1954, 'The Problem of Pluralism in America. An Analysis of Political Unity and Religious Diversity,' *Thought, 29:*165–208.

———, 1963, 'On Religious Liberty,' *America, 109:*704–706.

———, 1964, 'The Problem of Religious Freedom,' *Theological Studies, 25:*502–573.

———, (ed.), 1965, *Freedom and Man*. New York: P. J. Kenedy.

———, (ed.), 1966, *Religious Liberty: An End and a Beginning. The Declaration on Religious Freedom. An Ecumenical Discussion*. New York: Macmillan.

Murray, J. C., Schillebeeckx, E., and Carrillo de Alborncz, A.-F., 1965, *La Liberté religieuse. Exigence spirituelle et problème politique*. Paris: Ed. du Centurion.

Murtas, G., 1970, *La libertá religiosa nella Pacem in Terris*. Cagliari: Editrice sarda Fossatro.

Musulin, J. (ed.), 1959, *Proklamationen der Freiheit. Dokumente von der Magna Charta bis zum ungarischen Volksaufstand*. Frankfurt: Fischer.

Neely, W., 1974, 'Freedom and Desire,' *The Philosophical Review, 83*(1):32–54.

Nestle, Dieter, 1967, *Eleutheria. Studien zum Wesen der Freiheit bei den Griechen und im Neuen Testament*. Teil 1 - Die Griechen. Tübingen: Mohr, Siebeck.

Netzky, R., 1974, 'Playful Freedom: Sartre's Ontology Re-appraised,' *Philosophy Today*, 18(2–4):125–36.

Neuner, J., 1957, 'Christian Tolerance,' *Clergy Monthly, 21*(1):3–13.

———, 1957, 'Tolerance within the Church,' *Clergy Monthly, 21*(5):132–43.

Noack, H., 1966, 'La conciencia de la libertad posible en el "Occidente libre",' *Folia Humanística, 4:*803–16.

Nobile Ventura, A., 1968, 'L'Ermeneutica della libertà religiosa' [Atti del VIII Convegno Intern. di Roma, 7–12 gen., 1968], *Ekklesia*, 2(4):127–75.

Northcott, C., 1949, *Religious Liberty*. New York: Macmillan.

Oertel, H., 1970, 'Zur Genesis des Ideologiebegriffs,' *Deutsche Zeitschrift für Philosophie*, 18:206–11.

O'Farrell, F., 1974, 'Kant's Concept of Freedom,' *Gregorianum*, 55(3):425–69.

Oldfield, J. J., 1973, *The Problem of Tolerance and Social Existence in the Writings of Félicité Lamennais*, Leiden: Brill.

Onimus, J. (ed.), 1971, *Les idéologies dans le monde actuel*. Paris: Desclée (Centre d'Études de la Civilisation Contemporaine).

Panikkar, R., 1961, 'Pluralismus, Toleranz und Christenheit,' *Pluralismus, Toleranz und Christenheit*. Nürnberg: Abendländlische Akademie, pp. 117–42.

Pavan, P., 1965, *Libertà religiosa e pubblici poteri*. Milano: Ancora.

Peperzak, A. Th., 1971, 'Freedom,' G. d'Lima (tr.), *International Philosophical Quarterly*, 11:341–61.

Perelman, C., 1969, 'Autorité, idéologie et violence,' *Annales de l'Institut de Philosophie*, Bruxelles, 9–19.

Petruzzellis, N., 1969, 'La libertà e la conscienza del limite.' *Rassegna di Scienze filosofishe* (Napoli), 22:139–43.

Post, W., 1969, 'Tolerance.' In *Sacramentum Mundi*. Basel: Herder, 4:934–43.

Pribilla, M., 1937, 'Erziehung zur Toleranz,' *Bildung und Erziehung*, 4:353–65.

——— , 1949, 'Dogmatische Intoleranz und bürgerliche Toleranz,' *Stimmen der Zeit*, 4:27–40.

Quéguiner, M., 1956, 'Intolérance hindoue, tolérance indienne,' *Études*, 290:161–76.

Rahner, K., 1964, *The Dynamic Element in the Church*. W. J. O'Hara (tr.), New York: Herder and Herder.

——— , 1965, 'Der Dialog in der pluralistischen Gesellschaft.' In J.-B. Metz and J. Splett (eds.), *Weltverständnis im Glauben*. Mainz: Matthias Grünewald, pp. 287–97.

Rahner, K., Maier, H., Mann, U., and Schmaus, M., 1966, *Religionsfreiheit*. München: Hueber.

Ratzinger, J., 1960, *Die christiche Brüderlichkeit*. München: Kösel.

Reitmeister, L. A., 1970, *A Philosophy of Freedom. An Attempt to Explain the Natural Basis of Freedom*. New York: Poseidon Books.

Ricoeur, P., 1974, 'Science et Idéologie,' *Revue Philosophique de Louvain*, 72(14):328–56.

Ridder, J. de, 1905, 'La liberté de conscience en droit international,' *Revue de droit international et de législation comparée*, pp. 283 ff.

Riedmatten, H. de, 1964, 'La liberté religieuse au forum international,' *Études, 320:*293–307.

Riggs, T. L., 1973, 'Religious Tolerance,' *Commonweal, 99:*153 (reprint of November 26, 1924).

Rivier, W., 1972, *Une philosophie de la liberté*. Neuchâtel: Editions du Griffon.

Roberts, L. D., 1973, 'Indeterminism in Duns Scotus' Doctrine of Human Freedom,' *The Modern Schoolman, 51*(1):1–16.

Roche, J., 1966, *Église et liberté religieuse*. Paris-Tournai: Desclée.

Roig Gironella, J., 1968, 'Las antinomias de la libertad y medio para resolverlas,' *Espíritu, 17:*189–93.

———, 1968, 'Filosofia e ideología,' *Espíritu, 17:*72–8.

Röttges, H., 1974, 'Kants Auflösung der Freiheitsantimonie,' *Kant-Studien, 65*(1):33–49.

Ruether, R. R., 1972, *Liberation Theology: Human Hope Confronts Christian History and American Power*. New York: Paulist Press.

Ruffini, F., 1967, *La libertà religiosa. Storia dell'idea*. Milano: Feltrinelli.

Rüsch, E. G., 1955, *Toleranz. Eine theologische Untersuchung und eine aktuelle Auseinandersetzung*. Zürich: Evang. Verlag.

Rusche, H., 1958, *Gastfreundschaft in der Verkündigung des Neuen Testaments und ihr Verhältnis zur Mission*. Münster: Aschendorff.

Schaaf, J. J. 1970, 'Interesse, Institution und Ideologie,' *Philosophische Perspektiven, 2:*225–39.

Schaull, R., 1968, 'A Theological Perspective on Human Liberation,' *New Blackfriars, 49*(578):509–17.

Schlette, H. R., 1963, 'Toleranz.' In H. Fries (ed.), *Handbuch theologischer Grundbegriffe, 2:*679–86. München: Kösel.

Sciacca, M. E., 1965, *La libertà e il tempo*. Milano: Marzorati.

———, 1966, 'La libertad como peso y su "descarga" en la elección "corriente". La libertad "idiota",' *Folia Humanística, 4:*789–802.

Silva, J. R. da, 1966, 'A liberdade religiosa,' *Revista Portuguesa de Filosofia, 22:*376–92.

Simon, J., 1857, *La liberté de conscience*. Paris: Hatchette.

Six, J. F., 1970, *Du Syllabus au dialogue*. Paris: Seuil.

Smet, De, R., 1967, *Pour un climat de liberté*. Paris-Bruges.

Sokolović, D., 1973, 'Propriété et non-liberté,' *Praxis, 9*(2–3):195–215.

Splett, J., 1965, 'Idéologie und Toleranz. Die Wahrheitsfrage in der pluralistischen Gesellschaft,' *Wort und Wahrheit, 20*(1):37–49.

———, 1974, 'Flucht vor dem Risiko der Freiheit,' *Stimmen der Zeit, 192:*128–34.

Staal, J. F., 1959, 'Ueber die Idee der Toleranz in Hinduismus,' *Kairos, 1:*215–218.

Stadter, E., 1971, *Evolution zur Freiheit*. Stuttgart: Kohlhammer (Urbantaschenbücher, Bd. 810; Reihe 80).

Steiner, H., 1974, 'The Natural Right to Equal Freedom,' *Mind*, 83(330):194–210.

Stern, L., 1973, 'Freedom, Blame and Moral Community,' *The Journal of Philosophy*, 71(3):72–84.

Sternberger, D., 1947, 'Toleranz als Leidenschaft für die Wahrheit,' *Die Wandlung*, 231–50.

Stransky, T. F. (ed.), *Declaration on Religious Freedom of Vatican Council II*. New York: Paulist Press.

Strasser, S., 1968, 'Endliche Freiheit,' *Akten XIV. Int. Kong. Phil., I.* Wien: Herder, VI:166–174.

Suchý, J., 1968–69, 'Freiheit als Notwendigkeit des geschichtlichen Geschehens,' *Hegel-Jahrbuch*, 223–28.

Szczesny, G., 1971, *Das sogenannte Gute. Vom Unvermögen des Ideologen*. Reinbeck B. Hamburg: Rowolht.

Tadić, L., 1973, 'The Limits Set to Human Freedom by Private Property,' *Praxis*, 9(1):5–20.

Thelin, G., 1917, *La liberté de conscience*. Genève: Kundig.

Thiry, A., 1967, *Liberté religieuse et liberté chrétienne*. Paris-Bruges: Desclee de Brouwer.

Toinet, P., 1973, *Dieu et la liberté de l'homme; essai de théologie d'un laic*. Paris: Beauchesne.

Toth, J., 1968, 'Dignité de l'homme et dignité de conscience,' *Justice dans le monde* (décembre).

Trías Sagnier, E., 1970, *Teoría de la ideologías*. Barcelona: Ed. Península (Col. Nueva colleción ibérica, 4).

Uscatescu, G., 1970, *Antinomia della libertà*. Firenze: Città di vita.

Vacandard, E., 1907, *De la tolérance religieuse*. 2nd ed. Paris.

Van Loon, H., 1925, *Tolerance*. New York: Boni and Liveright.

Vermeersch, A., 1922, *La tolérance*. 2nd ed. Paris. 1st ed., 1912, Paris: Beauchesne.

Völker, K., 1912, *Toleranz und Intoleranz im Zeitalter der Reformation*. Leipzig: J. C. Heinrichs.

Von Raumer, K., 1953, *Ewiger Friede, Friedensrufe und Friedenspläne seit der Renaissance*. Freiburg-München: K. Alber.

Vuillemin, J., 1971, 'Sur la tolérance,' *Revue Internationale de Philosophie*, 25:198–212.

Weischedel, W., 1966, 'Anotaciones en torno a la polémica sobre la libertad,' *Folia Humanística*, 4:817–22.

Wieland, W., 1974, 'Praxis und Urteilskraft,' *Zeitschrift für Philosophische Forschung*, 28(1):17–42.

Wilcox, W., 1974, 'The Theology of Freedom,' *Religion in Life*, 43(1):52–9.

Wismar, A., 1927, *A Study in Tolerance as Practiced by Muhammad and His Immediate Successors*. New York: Columbia University Press.

Wogaman, P., 1967, *Protestant Faith and Religious Liberty*. Nashville: Abingdon Press.

Wolff, R.-P., Moore, B., and Marcuse, H., 1965, *A Critique of Pure Tolerance*. Boston: Beacon Press.

Wood, H. G., 1974, *Religious Liberty To-day*. New York: Octagon (rep. Cambridge University Press, 1949 edition).

Wood, J. E., 1973, 'Theological and Historical Foundations of Religious Liberty,' *Journal of Church and State, 15:*241–58.

Zabkar, J., 1973, 'Le Saint-Siège et la liberté religieuse,' *La Documentation Catholique, 70:*385–87.

Zavalloni, R., 1968, *A liberdade pessoal*. Rio de Janeiro and Petrópolis: Ed. Vozes.

Zeltner, H., 1974, 'Ideologie und Idee,' *Zeitschrift für Philosophische Forschung, 28*(1):3–16.

Zundel, M., 1960, *La liberté de la foi*. Paris: Plon.

Collections: 1952, *L'Eglise et la liberté*. Paris: Centre catholique des itellectuel francais.

1962, *Témoignage chrétien, proselytisme et liberté religieuse* (Rapport aux soins du Conseil oecuménique des Églises). Neuchâtel: Delachaux et Niestlé.

1971, *Cristianesimo e liberazione oggi* [Lezioni, dibattiti, communicazione del IV Convegno di Motta per insignanti di religione delle Scuole Secondarie Superiori, 1970]. Milano: Ufficio catechistico diocesano.

1974, 'Liberation des hommes et salut en Jésus-Christ; propositions d'ateliers retenues par le Conseil permanent de l'Episcopat français,' *La Documentation Catholique, 71:*161–63.

1977, *Religious Liberty in the Crossfire of Creeds, Journal of Ecumenical Studies*. Entire issue: vol. XII.

XVIII.
Indexes

1. Index of Subjects

2. Index of Names

3. Index of Scriptures and Spiritual Texts

Scriptural references are in brackets. Some non-canonical texts have also been included, especially when the authors are traditionally not given or unknown.

Sit finis libra non quaerendi

Brahmaṇe namaḥ